SYRIA

LAND OF CIVILIZATIONS

Canadian Cataloguing in Publication Data

Fortin, Michel

   Syria, land of civilizations

   Translation of: Syrie, terre de civilisations.

   Co-published by: Musée de la civilisation de Québec.

     1. Syria — Antiquities — Exhibitions.   2. Syria — History — Exhibitions.

3. Syria — Civilization — Exhibitions. I. Musée de la civilisation (Québec).

II. Title.

DS94.5.F6713   1999   939'.43'0074714471   C99-940989-1

The publisher gratefully acknowledges the support of the Société de développement des entreprises culturelles du Québec for its publishing program.

We gratefully acknowledge the support of the Canada Council for the Arts for its publishing program.

We acknowledge the financial support of the Government of Canada through the Book Publishing Industry Development Program (BPIDP) for our publishing activities.

Legal deposit: fourth quarter 1999
Bibliothèque nationale du Québec

ISBN 2-7619-1521-6

This book was produced by Les Éditions de l'Homme using a laser imaging system comprised of:

A Scitex Smart TM 720 digitizer and
Kodak products;
An RIP 50 PL2 image processor combined with the new Lino Dot® and Lino Pipeline® technology by Linotype-Hell®.
Printed in Canada
02/2000

EXCLUSIVE DISTRIBUTORS:

- For Canada and the USA:
MESSAGERIES ADP*
955 Amherst
Montréal, Québec
H2L 3K4
Tel.: (514) 523-1182
Fax: (514) 939-0406
*A subsidiary of Sogides Ltée

- For France and other countries:
INTER FORUM
Immeuble Paryseine, 3 Allée de la Seine
94854 Ivry Cedex
Tel.: 01 49 59 11 89/91
Fax: 01 49 59 11 96
Orders: Tel.: 02 38 32 71 00
           Fax: 02 38 32 71 28

- For Switzerland:
DIFFUSION: HAVAS SERVICES SUISSE
Case postale 69 - 1701 Fribourg, Switzerland
Tel.: (41-26) 460-80-68
Internet: www.havas.ch
E-mail: office@havas.ch
DISTRIBUTION: OLF SA
Z.1. 3 Corminboeuf
Case postale 1061
CH-1710 FRIBOURG
Orders: Tel.: (41-26) 467-53-33
          Fax: (41-26) 467-54-66

- For Belgium and Luxembourg:
PRESSES DE BELGIQUE S.A.
Boulevard de l'Europe 117
B-1301 Wavre
Tel.: (010) 42-03-20
Fax: (010) 41-20-24

For more information about our publications, please visit our website: **www.edhomme.com**
Other sites of interest: www.edjour.com • www.edtypo.com • www.edvlb.com www.edhexagone.com • www.edutilis.com

SYRIA

LAND OF CIVILIZATIONS

MICHEL FORTIN

English translation by Jane Macaulay

MUSÉE DE LA
CIVILISATION
Québec

LES ÉDITIONS DE
L'HOMME

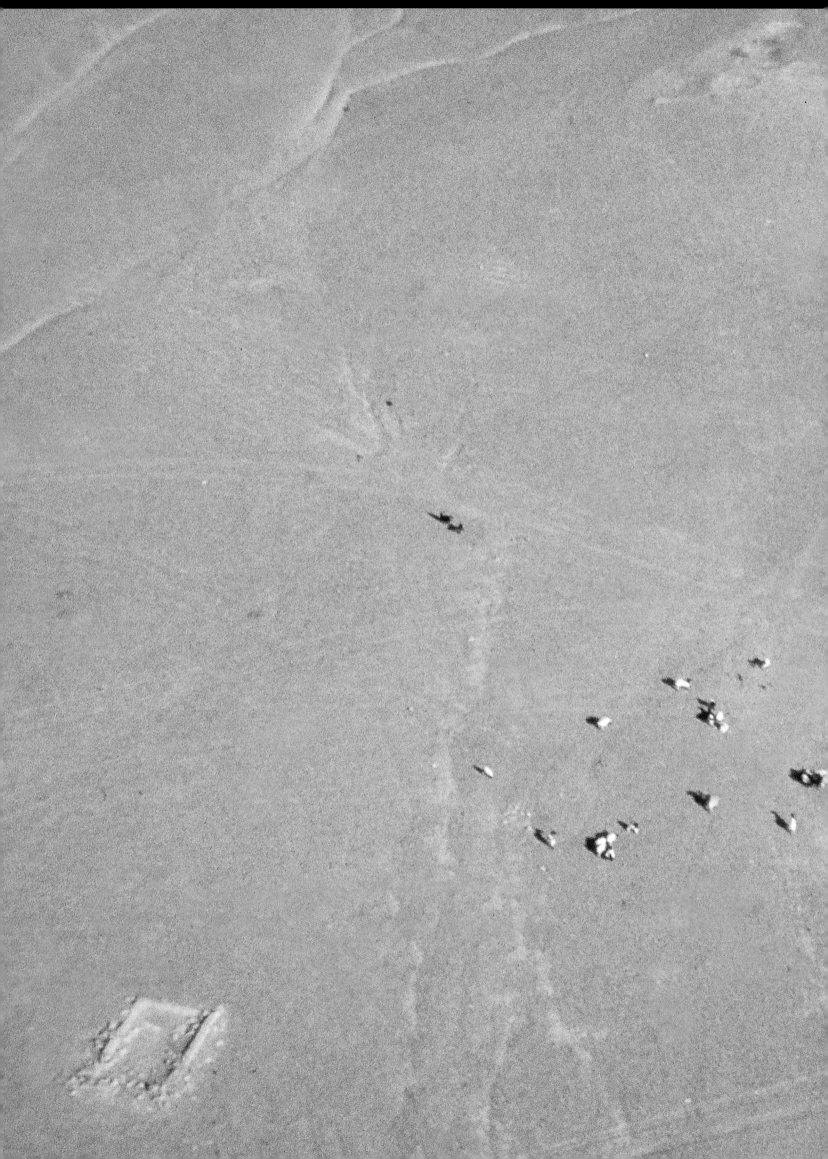

Syria, Land of Civilizations

An exhibition under the patronage of

Hafez al-Assad
PRESIDENT OF THE SYRIAN ARAB REPUBLIC

Jean Chrétien   **Lucien Bouchard**
PRIME MINISTER OF CANADA   PRIME MINISTER OF QUÉBEC

A traveling exhibition organized by the

Musée de la civilisation de Québec

in collaboration with

the Ministry of Culture, Directorate General of Antiquities
and Museums of the Syrian Arab Republic

Honorary Board

Organization Committee

Prof. Dr. Sultan Muhesen
DIRECTOR-GENERAL OF ANTIQUITIES AND MUSEUMS, SYRIAN ARAB REPUBLIC

Dr. Khassan al Laham
DIRECTOR, HAFEZ AL-ASSAD NATIONAL LIBRARY, SYRIAN ARAB REPUBLIC

Managing Committee

Roland Arpin
DIRECTOR-GENERAL, MUSÉE DE LA CIVILISATION, QUÉBEC, CANADA

André Juneau
DIRECTOR, DIRECTORATE OF EXHIBITIONS AND INTERNATIONAL RELATIONS,
MUSÉE DE LA CIVILISATION, QUÉBEC, CANADA

Dr. Peter Blome
DIRECTOR, ANTIKENMUSEUM BASEL UND SAMMLUNG LUDWIG, SWITZERLAND

François Tremblay
DIRECTOR, INTERNATIONAL EXHIBITIONS SERVICE,
MUSÉE DE LA CIVILISATION, QUÉBEC, CANADA

Dr. Philip H.R. Stepney
DIRECTOR, PROVINCIAL MUSEUM OF ALBERTA, CANADA

Muhamed Kadour
DIRECTOR OF MUSEUM AFFAIRS, SYRIAN ARAB REPUBLIC

Jill Freeman
DIRECTOR, ROSICRUCIAN EGYPTIAN MUSEUM AND PLANETARIUM, U.S.A.

Bashir Zouhdi
CHIEF CURATOR, NATIONAL MUSEUM, DAMASCUS, SYRIAN ARAB REPUBLIC

Dr. Craig Morris
SENIOR VICE PRESIDENT AND DEAN OF SCIENCE,
AMERICAN MUSEUM OF NATURAL HISTORY, U.S.A.

Whalid Khayyata
DIRECTOR OF ANTIQUITIES AND MUSEUMS,
ALEPPO REGION, SYRIAN ARAB REPUBLIC

Susan E. Neugent
PRESIDENT AND C.E.O.,
FERNBANK MUSEUM OF NATIONAL HISTORY, U.S.A

Prof. Dr. Rolf A. Stucky
PROFESSOR OF CLASSICAL ARCHAEOLOGY,
UNIVERSITY OF BASEL, SWITZERLAND

Prof. Dr. Jean-Marie Le Tensorer
PROFESSOR OF PREHISTORY,
UNIVERSITY OF BASEL, SWITZERLAND

David Harvey
VICE PRESIDENT FOR EXHIBITIONS, AMERICAN
MUSEUM OF NATURAL HISTORY, U.S.A.

Exhibition Directors

François Tremblay
DIRECTOR, INTERNATIONAL EXHIBITIONS SERVICE,
MUSÉE DE LA CIVILISATION, QUÉBEC

Prof. Dr. Michel Fortin
SCIENTIFIC ADVISOR, UNIVERSITÉ LAVAL,
QUÉBEC

Exhibition contributors

Dr. Yossra al-Koujok
CURATOR, PREHISTORY SECTION, NATIONAL MUSEUM, DAMASCUS

Jamal Haidar
DIRECTOR, DEPARTMENT OF ANTIQUITIES AND THE MUSEUM, LATTAKIA

Muyasser Fattal-Yabroudi
CURATOR, EASTERN ANTIQUITIES, NATIONAL MUSEUM, DAMASCUS

Farid Jabour
DIRECTOR, DEPARTMENT OF ANTIQUITIES, HOMS

Dr. Jaoudat Shaa'dé
CURATOR, CLASSICAL ANTIQUITIES, NATIONAL MUSEUM, DAMASCUS

Nidaa Dandashi
CURATOR, HOMS MUSEUM

Mouna al-Mou'azen
CURATOR, ISLAMIC ANTIQUITIES, NATIONAL MUSEUM, DAMASCUS

Abdellazar Zarzouq
DIRECTOR, DEPARTMENT OF ANTIQUITIES AND THE MUSEUM, HAMA

Dr. Antoine Souleiman
CURATOR, PREHISTORIC SECTION, NATIONAL MUSEUM, ALEPPO

Kamel Chehade
CURATOR, AL'MAARAT MUSEUM

Naser Sharaf
CURATOR, EASTERN ANTIQUITIES, NATIONAL MUSEUM, ALEPPO

Abdoh Asfari
DIRECTOR, DEPARTMENT OF ANTIQUITIES AND THE MUSEUM, IDLIB

Radwan Sharaf
CURATOR, CLASSICAL ANTIQUITIES, NATIONAL MUSEUM, ALEPPO

Murhaf Al-Khalaf
DIRECTOR, DEPARTMENT OF ANTIQUITIES AND THE MUSEUM, RAQQA

Fddwa Oubeid
CURATOR, ISLAMIC ANTIQUITIES, NATIONAL MUSEUM, ALEPPO

Assad Mahmoud
DIRECTOR, DEPARTMENT OF ANTIQUITIES AND THE MUSEUM, DEIR EZ-ZOR

Rachid Issa
DIRECTOR, DEPARTMENT OF ANTIQUITIES, TARTUS

Khaled al-Assad
DIRECTOR, DEPARTMENT OF ANTIQUITIES AND MUSEUMS, PALMYRA

Ramez Hawash
CURATOR, TARTUS MUSEUM

Dr. Hassan Hatoum
DIRECTOR, DEPARTMENT OF ANTIQUITIES AND THE MUSEUM, SUWEIDA

Traveling Exhibition Collaborators

Rabab Al Shaar
CURATOR, DEPARTMENT OF EASTERN ANTIQUITIES, NATIONAL MUSEUM, DAMASCUS

Maria Yakimov
MUSEUM REGISTRAR, AMERICAN MUSEUM OF NATURAL HISTORY, NEW YORK

Samer Abdel Ghafour
CURATOR, DEPARTMENT OF EASTERN ANTIQUITIES,
NATIONAL MUSEUM, ALEPPO

Dr. Charles S. Spencer
CURATOR, DEPARTMENT OF ANTHROPOLOGY,
AMERICAN MUSEUM OF NATURAL HISTORY, NEW YORK

Dr. Ella van der Meijden Zanoni
CURATOR, ANTIKENMUSEUM BASEL UND SUMMLUNG LUDWIG, BASEL

Shirley Howarth
PRESIDENT, HUMANITIES EXCHANGE, MIAMI

Andrea Bignasca
VICE DIRECTOR, ANTIKENMUSEUM BASEL UND SUMMLUNG LUDWIG, BASEL

Christian Denis
CURATOR, MUSÉE DE LA CIVILISATION, QUÉBEC

Anita Kern
DIRECTOR OF EXTERNAL PROGRAMS, FERNBANK MUSEUM OF NATURAL HISTORY, ATLANTA

Marie Beaudoin
DESIGNER, MUSÉE DE LA CIVILISATION, QUÉBEC

Maxwell Miller
ARCHEOLOGIST, FERNBANK MUSEUM OF NATURAL HISTORY, ATLANTA

Monique Lippé
PROJECT MANAGER, MUSÉE DE LA CIVILISATION, QUÉBEC

Catalogue

MAIN TEXT

Prof. Dr. Michel Fortin
UNIVERSITÉ LAVAL, QUÉBEC

COORDINATION

François Tremblay
MUSÉE DE LA CIVILISATION, QUÉBEC

CONTRIBUTORS

Prof. Dr. Sultan Muhesen

Khaled al-Assad

Prof. Dr. Giorgio Buccellati

Dr. Klaus Freyberger

Hassan Hatoum

Whalid Khayyata

Prof. Dr. Kay Kohlmeyer

Prof. Dr. Jean-Marie Le Tensorer

Assad Mahmoud

Prof. Dr. Jean-Claude Margueron

Prof. Dr. Paolo Matthiae

Prof. Dr. Miguel Molist

Mouna al-Mou'Azen

Prof. Dr. David Oates

Prof. Dr. Joan Oates

Dr. Danielle Stordeur

Dr. Georges Tate

Abdellazar Zarzouq

Bashir Zouhdi

PHOTOGRAPHS

Jacques Lessard, Musée de la civilisation, Québec

Dr. Georg Gerster, Zurich, Switzerland

Mohamad Al-Roumi, Damascus, Syrian Arab Republic

Alain Saint-Hilaire, Montréal, Québec

EDITORIAL COLLABORATION

Nicole Blain, Rachel Fontaine,
Martine Lavoie and Linda Nantel,
Les Éditions de l'Homme, Montréal, Québec

Pauline Hamel, Musée de la civilisation, Québec

GRAPHIC DESIGNER

Josée Amyotte

LAYOUT AND WORD PROCESSING

Johanne Lemay

TRANSLATION AND REVISION

Odette Lord

Jane Macaulay

Cynthia Taylor

Acknowledgements

We are grateful to the following people who helped us at various stages in the preparation of the exhibition and the catalogue:

Michel Côté and Hélène Bernier, respectively Director of the exhibition and international relations division and Director of the international exhibition service throughout the period of the project's preparation.

We also want to thank Marc Simard and Raymond Montpetit, who collaborated during the initial stages of preparation of this catalogue.

Patricia Anderson, Dominique Beyer, Pierre-Marie Blanc, Pierre Bordreuil, Monique Cardinal, Annie Caubet, Jean-Marie Dentzer, Michael Fuller, Massoud Hussein, Marie Le Mière, Michael C.A MacDonald, Robert Mason, Andrew Moore, Eva Strommenger et Dietrich Sürenhagen.

Symbols and Abbreviations Used

[125] = The number in brackets refers to the number of the item in the catalogue.

The abbreviations found in the "Catalogue sections" are listed at the end of the book under the headings "Abbreviations used in the catalogue."

Traveling Exhibition

ANTIKENMUSEUM BASEL UND SAMMLUNG LUDWIG, BASEL, SWITZERLAND

November 3, 1999 to March 31, 2000

MUSÉE DE LA CIVILISATION, QUÉBEC, CANADA

May 30, 2000 to January 7, 2001

THE PROVINCIAL MUSEUM OF ALBERTA, EDMONTON, ALBERTA, CANADA

February 10 to May 13, 2001

ROSICRUCIAN EGYPTIAN MUSEUM AND PLANETARIUM, SAN JOSE, CALIFORNIA, U.S.A.

June 13 to September 2, 2001

THE AMERICAN MUSEUM OF NATURAL HISTORY, NEW YORK, U.S.A.

October 10, 2001 to January 6, 2002

FERNBANK MUSEUM OF NATURAL HISTORY, ATLANTA, U.S.A.

February 15 to May 20, 2002

SYRIA, LAND OF CIVILIZATIONS...
Now and always

T he sun in all its splendor and the stars in the vaults of heaven mean more to our world than simply warmth and light. Since the dawn of time, the movement of celestial bodies through infinite space has provided us with a perfect symbol of eternity, that gift of the heavens by which the fabric of our lives is woven. We accept this gift with our hands stretched towards the sky in a gesture of prayer, for we children of the Earth know how to honor this gift, yes, and even to go beyond it to something more noble, through the secret we bear deep within us. The secret of humankind — the powerful masters of the world who fear Nature and whom Nature fears in return for this simple reason — is that we, in the vanity of our humanity and the eminence of our power, are the product of a seed that in the course of time will engender another finer and nobler seed, as surely as one generation succeeds another. This pattern constitutes its own unending time, above and beyond ordinary time, thanks to the work transmitted by human hands. I am referring to the achievements through which creativity, boundless and untrammeled, reaches heights that put it far beyond anything to be found in Nature.

When we think of the remains of past civilizations, we at once think of Syria. Everything then becomes clear — as luminous as crystal and bright as flashes of lightning, as brilliant as the sun and radiant as the sacred flame in which the angels are enveloped when their joyful wanderings through the gardens of heaven lead them through the shadowy regions of the eternal Paradise that has been promised to us. It is in the name of this Paradise that our dearest wishes take on the breadth of the distant horizon. Everything that is beautiful, as we know, or should know, can exist or will never exist.

Baron von Oppenheim described Syria as an archaeologists' paradise. The present traveling exhibition entitled *Syria, Land of Civilizations* enables scholars, researchers and everyone interested in this land to visit Syria without actually going there. For it is we who are coming to them, as if on a flying carpet out of *The Arabian Nights*, bearing our most sumptuous, astonishing and desirable treasures, so that others may learn more about the world's oldest civilizations through these signposts to the past. Just one example of such outstanding archaeological discoveries is the skeleton of a Neanderthal child buried 100 000 years ago in the Dederiyah cave in the Afrin region of northeast Syria. The long succession of civilizations known to Syria has quite rightly made our country a sort of historical encyclopedia, an indispensable source of information for those who study the emergence and development of civilizations, and who might be edified to a lesser or greater degree by this study.

Syria has thus had the privilege of contributing to the construction of a universal civilization and therefore constitutes the second homeland of all cultivated people throughout the world. At Ugarit, on the Syrian coast, the world's first alphabet was discovered in the fourteenth century BC. Tablets found in Syria and dating from the ninth century BC bear signs that are thought to be a form of embryonic writing. The temples built when Mari, Ugarit, Ebla, Palmyra and Bosra were in their glory are among the oldest such buildings known to history. The oldest sculptures in stone, clay, ivory, bone and bronze have also been discovered in Syria. These now famous sculptures include representations of the "mother goddess," the kings of Mari and Ebla, the gods of Ugarit and its princess, Greco-Roman divinities such as Venus, Mercury, Zeus, Leda and Cupid, as well as Nemesis, the goddess of justice and vengeance. There are also the majestic sculptures of Palmyra and the statues of Syrian emperors from the time of the Roman Empire, including the marble likeness of Philip the Arab, discovered in the city of Shahba in the Jebel al-'Arab.

But here I am merely skimming over a whole history of such complexity that the various art forms lending it tangibility are simply eloquent witnesses to the cultural activities and creativity expressed in its architecture, its glasswork, jewelry, rock painting, mosaics, drawings and engravings, as well as its innumerable tablets, which have preserved melodies and poetry along with intellectual illuminations, strategies of war and economic inspirations in flights of lyricism. Far from being exhaustive, *Syria, Land of Civilizations* is perforce symbolic. The present exhibition encompasses some 400 ancient objects selected from among the most important discoveries made in Syria — whether recently or in the past — related to the empires and kingdoms that developed there, reached great heights and then faded as the ages unfolded. The exhibition is intended to give visitors in host countries the clearest possible picture of Syria's exceptional history and civilization, whose importance to archaeology and science is unparalleled. The discoveries made in this land are guideposts to the history of humankind; they concern us all but are of particular interest to archaeologists, historians, anthropologists and all those who study the emergence and evolution of civilizations.

The principal goal of this exhibition, and those like it, is to promote communication on a cultural level. We consider this to be part of our duty to undertake "civilizational" and ethical exchange, based on our concept of heritage in its most universal sense. We must thus foster communication, for Syria, with its secular roots, believing in words and actions, and in dialogue between nations, expends considerable energy in this direction and consciously condemns the idea of confrontation between civilizations, which, rather than leading to progress, harmony and complementarity, brings destruction, isolation and divergence. It is strange but manifestly true that the great nations of today know barely anything of what they should know concerning smaller nations — which may be small in size but not in historical importance, despite the enormous progress made elsewhere in space exploration, computer science and electronic communications. For this reason, the Arab people — with the place they occupy in the history of civilization, with their deep roots in the natural sciences and humanities — are trying carefully and steadfastly to continue the mission that began when their knowledge was transmitted to Europe via Andalousia; they thus hope to remedy this lack of understanding and strengthen the foundations of communication between civilizations. Such communication, while maintaining our past in our present, has always been, and always will be, a priority for Syria. From the dawn of time, our Arab ancestors devoted themselves to establishing such contact, communication and understanding in order to enrich their knowledge through the means available to them, whether elementary or complex. In this regard, one only has to think of the Phoenicians, who developed and founded the most prestigious of civilizations on the Syrian coast, in particular, and then transported their culture to other places along the Mediterranean shores. It should also be mentioned that Arab culture, as an important synthesis of science and the arts, later transported these disciplines to African and European shores, and then to South America, with a generosity that is engraved in the memory of history.

This exhibition is a precious gesture, offered on behalf of the two past millennia towards a third one, at whose door we now knock, in the hope that we will be steadfast in our efforts throughout the next millennium to promote civilization and a culture that engenders human values. Such a culture would be "the culture of peace," in its most sublime and radiant sense, benefitting all those who endure oppression and attempt to defend themselves when faced with aggression, whether in its military, economic or cultural form, whether in the shape of colonialism, blockades or threats. The culture of peace in no way signifies submission and acceptance of a fait accompli, but rather seeks to put an end to aggression and the despoiling of the earth, its riches and its liberties. Such a culture works towards a just and honorable peace. It truly defends human rights, upholds the logic of justice and the law, rather than the logic of force, whatever its nature, and supports the brotherhood of mankind, praised by the old Syrian poet Meleager of the ancient city of Gadara in these terms: "Do not believe that I am a stranger, we are all sons of the same homeland, the Earth."

Has the time not come for us to aspire to a world without barriers between people, a world that eliminates the borders between civilizations and cultures, based on equality and fraternity, rather than on rivalry and hegemony? Is it not time to establish a culture that reflects the aspect and colors of the universe, open to all?

To conclude these few comments intended as a foreword to the exhibition catalogue, it gives me great pleasure to transmit to readers, viewers, visitors, archaeologists, specialists, researchers and all those with a passion for archaeology, those who engage in excavations, as well as the host museums and the people who spared no efforts in preparing this important exhibition, the salutations of the President of the Syrian Arab Republic, Hafez Al-Assad, who shows the deepest concern for antiquities, archaeological excavations, restoration and conservation. I would also like to express gratitude to the presidents and officials of the host countries for the reception they have given this exhibition. And lastly, I wish to praise the efforts of the archaeologists and archaeological missions that have come from so many parts of the world to work in Syria and thank them for their achievements in the areas of archaeological fieldwork and discovery, as well as research and scientific synthesis. Through their work, they provide an example of solidarity between nations, in the most sublime form of humanity and splendor.

DR. NAJAH AL-ATTAR
Minister of Culture, Syrian Arab Republic

It is not an exaggeration to call this exhibition "Syria, Land of Civilizations." Archaeological and historical research shows that Syria has been inhabited since the early Paleolithic era, around one million years ago. Exceptional archaeological and anthropological discoveries date from that period. It also appears that the first and most creative steps towards human civilization took place in Syria. It was here that the "Neolithic Revolution" occurred in the ninth millennium BC, when people began to build villages, cultivate cereals and domesticate animals. These crucial innovations developed steadily through the later millennia until Syria was once again the center of major transformation. This was the "Urban Revolution," which brought enormous changes, marked by the appearance of well-organized fortified cities, temples, palaces and other public constructions in the fourth millennium BC. Throughout the third, second and first millennia BC, Syria saw a succession of prosperous cities, states, kingdoms and empires, established by Sumerians, Akkadians, Amorites, Aramaeans and other peoples. These political entities are well known for their high social, economic and spiritual achievements in many fields, such as architecture, art, metallurgy, trade, religion and administration, not to mention the invention of writing. At the end of the first millennium BC and the beginning of the first millennium AD, Syria was an important part of the Greek, Roman and Byzantine empires. At the beginning of the eighth century AD, Syria became the heart of the first Arabo-Islamic, Umayyad empire. Syria continued to play a distinguished and primordial role as a crossroads of civilizations throughout the Middle Ages.

This exhibition aims to shed light on these facts. It traces the appearance and evolution of major human cultural innovations as evidenced through archaeological discoveries, many of which are recent and of exceptional historical value. The exhibition, which is to be presented in Switzerland, Canada and the USA, reflects our common interest in bridging the distance between us and our sincere desire to do so. We hope it will open the doors of dialogue and cooperation between our nations. The objects presented in this book clearly show that every one of us has roots in Syria and can find the basis of our beliefs there; we thus all share a common culture and heritage. This is the message for the new millennium that we want to address to the whole world through this exhibition. We are extremely honored and proud that the exhibition has the patronage of H.E. President Hafez Al-Assad, who always gives personal care, protection and encouragement to heritage. We also benefit highly from the continuous strong support of our Minister of Culture, Dr. Najah Al-Attar, who directs and follows our activities closely. The exhibition and the catalogue are the result of efforts on the part of many Syrian, Canadian, American and Swiss institutions and scholars, who have cooperated with admirable determination and shown great mutual understanding and respect throughout the organizational work. I would like to express my deepest thanks to all of them, especially Mr. Roland Arpin, Director-General of the Musée de la civilisation de Québec, whose vision and openness has made possible this exhibition and its tour. I am confident that this exhibition will be one of the most remarkable international cultural events of the beginning of the twenty-first century.

PROF. DR. SULTAN MUHESEN
Director-General of Antiquities and Museums, Syria

As human beings, we tend to take pride in our modernity. Our vanity about today's achievements often leads us to forget the vital contribution made by the hundreds of generations that preceded us. And, while we may be dazzled by the exceptional scientific and technological progress of the last few decades, there is also a need to humbly acknowledge our continuing indebtedness to ancient Eastern thought, even though it is separated from us by two thousand years.

The exhibition offered to us by the Musée de la civilisation allows us to transcend borders and cultures. It gives us an opportunity to contemplate a heritage that is shared by all human beings. What a fascinating experience it is for us, as North Americans, to look at a 12 000-year-old figurine and in its contours try to discern the hand of the craftsman, to imagine this person's life, joys and sorrows — knowing that the civilization in which the object was made flourished at a time when the northeastern part of America was entirely covered by a thick mantle of ice.

We are deeply grateful to the Syrian Arab Republic for devoting such effort to conserving this heritage, which is, of course, its own, but which is in many respects also the heritage of all humankind. We would also like to express sincere gratitude to Dr. Najah Al-Attar, the Syrian Minister of Culture, who has given this undertaking his support from the very beginning and has made it possible to carry out the project in optimal conditions.

AGNÈS MALTAIS
Minister of Culture and Communications, Québec

It was inevitable that one day the Musée de la civilisation would take on the challenge of attempting to illustrate the birth of civilization itself. Our museum was established 12 short years ago, but it has taken humanity 12 000 years to give meaning to the word that contains our raison d'être. Indeed, the path to civilization has been a long one, and through this exhibition you will be able to follow that path from the very beginning. What better time to reflect on our collective past than at the dawn of a new millennium? Indeed, at a time like this, we feel such reflection is essential.

This exhibition reminds us again just how much we owe to this mythic territory. The treasures that the Syrian Arab Republic has so kindly shared with us provide a brilliant demonstration of the high level of refinement reached by ancient civilizations. A lot of the things that we now take for granted we owe to our forebears, those men and women who with all their might and intelligence pushed the boundaries of life and learning.

Now it is our turn to contribute to the chain of human thought. In a thousand years, when others look back on our contribution, will we have done something of which we can be proud? Will our descendants see our era as a time when the quality of human life was enhanced or rather as a period of regression? The answer is entirely up to us.

In mounting this exhibition, we had the opportunity to build partnerships of which we are very proud. I would like especially to draw attention to the role of the Director of Antiquities of the Syrian Arab Republic, Prof. Dr. Sultan Muhesen, who was able to guide us, walk with us and, above all, put his confidence in us during the five years that we devoted to this remarkable project. I would also like to thank the Canadian, Swiss and American museums that collaborated with us in order for this project to come to fruition. We already have the proof that such collaboration leads to success.

ROLAND ARPIN
Director-General, Musée de la civilisation, Québec

INTRODUCTION

The passage from one millennium to another — so rare in human experience — is an ideal occasion to reflect deeply on the path traced by the human species from the moment that certain of its members decided to live in larger groups and adopted habits that went with this new lifestyle. Such reflection leads to all sorts of questions: How did the first human societies emerge? How were they organized? And how did they evolve?

If we wish to retrace the origins of civilization — that is, the establishment of a system that still influences social change, economic patterns and intellectual progress — we must go all the way back to the time when groups of humans had acquired efficient means of survival and began to take various steps that allowed a new culture to develop. Such developments took place so long ago that they can be observed only through objects that the members of these human societies left behind them, never imagining that one day their possessions and products would be used to interpret the way they lived. These objects bear witness to a bygone time in the history of humankind. But was this time so very different from ours? In many ways, our society may be seen as a prolongation of the first socioeconomic experiments undertaken by the human species.

Statue of a king of Mari.
Cat. 1

For the past 12 000 years, Syria has, more than any other place in the world, been marked by the birth and interaction of civilizations that changed the course of human history. With its cultural wealth and close links with neighboring peoples, Syria has truly played the role of a crucible in the development of ancient civilizations in the Near East, while these in turn, as this catalogue demonstrates, have had a marked influence on the Western world. The period covered by this exhibition begins with the first attempts to settle in villages on Syrian territory — the earliest villages known. It ends with a period of confrontation, when European knights came to Syria during the Crusades. To be sure, this period symbolizes a brutal contact between East and West, but it was also the starting point for intellectual exchange between the two. This moment of contact has been chosen as the time at which our chronological presentation draws to a close.

The dawn of the third millennium seems an appropriate time to look back at the past 12 millennia of the human adventure. The purpose of this exhibition is not simply to provide information about different aspects of the cultural process we call "civilization" or about the great civilizations that succeeded one another in parts of the Near East. Its purpose is also — perhaps above all — to present the various elements that make up the concept of civilization itself. It is hoped that this exhibition will inspire visitors to stop and reflect on the characteristics and foundations of the civilization in which they live — and even, if possible, lead them to turn towards the future and wonder what the civilization of tomorrow will look like.

In the Near East, the houses associated with the first civilizations were made of mud bricks that had been dried in the sun.

What is a civilization?

The term "civilization" appeared in the major European languages during the eighteenth century, but it was only towards the end of the nineteenth century that it began to acquire the sense we now associate with it — that is, a "complex whole which includes knowledge, belief, art, morals, law, custom and other capabilities and habits acquired by man as a member of society."

Specialists in different fields began to make pronouncements on the topic in the early nineteenth century. Some of them tried to determine exactly when and where the first great civilizations arose. They also attempted to define how the concept of civilization applied to these periods and what elements were essential components of the concept, a subjective one in many respects. Anthropologists proposed that the term "civilization" should apply to any state-governed society. According to this view, the defining criterion of civilization was a certain type of sociopolitical organization: a strong central government ruled by a political elite, not related by kinship, at the top of a social hierarchy in which there were several classes reflecting the specialization of labor, kept under control by a judicial system, such as a code of law. The economic and social structure of such societies was based on agriculture and stockraising.

In contrast, other authors felt that a civilization was defined by the complexity of its internal organization rather than by the type of organization it had. For archaeologists, evidence attesting to the existence of a civilization was to be sought in a society's material culture. For example, the presence of public buildings erected in cities implies that special technological skills were exercised by a certain number of the community's members, whose role was to carry out such tasks for a higher class. The members of the upper class were responsible for supervising economic production and therefore also had to see that food surpluses were redistributed among the members of the community, or traded for other goods, using management systems which often depended largely on writing.

CIVILIZATION AND THE ENVIRONMENT: A TIGHTLY KNIT RELATIONSHIP

Today's theorists accord much importance to the relationship that is established between a civilization and the environment in which it develops. All of the great civilizations arose in parts of the globe where irrigated farming was carried out on a large scale. To accumulate water and redistribute it fairly through a system of canals, which must be built, maintained and defended, requires central coordination. Thus, it is the centralization of activities related to irrigation rather than irrigation itself that fostered the development of a political structure in a community, so long as the economic advantages of such a system continued to grow.

There is also general agreement that irrigation made it possible to increase agricultural production and thus obtain the food surpluses required to maintain specialized workers who were part of the community but who did not help to provide food. As an added advantage, the irrigation canals could also be used for transportation and thus encouraged trade with other places.

Some believe that the development of a civilization is automatically accompanied by control of a widespread and complex trade network, since a well-structured, powerful central social organization is required to run such a network, especially when, as is usually the case, it covers a vast territory spreading beyond the natural limits of the ecological zone that gave birth to the civilization.

Consideration of such territorial constraints has led anthropologists to think that constant natural population growth in these early societies put pressure on them to expand their living space and thus engage frequently in war. Military operations, as well as being a means of obtaining new land while appropriating the wealth and integrating the population of conquered regions, favored the development of ever larger and more powerful states ruled by a class of military leaders.

However, most of the archaeologists who consider demographic pressure on a society to have been an influential factor in the development of civilization believe it more likely that this factor brought about changes in the society's internal organization: such pressure would have been accommodated by the adoption of a new socioeconomic stratification within an agglomeration known as the city. Certainly, the word civilization itself points in this direction, since it is derived from the Latin word *civis*, meaning "one who lives in the city." Archaeologists, who base their classification systems on artifact typologies that reflect the level of technological development acquired by their users, have for a long time treated the process of urbanization as the most evident symbol of civilization.

At present, more and more specialists recognize that the birth of a civilization cannot be attributed to any one factor but rather to a number of converging elements. In the end, all that can be said is that a civilization is distinguished by the diversity and variety of the experience and institutions shared by a group of humans.

Agriculture is the basis of civilization. Harvesting here is done with a sickle.

THE FIRST GREAT CIVILIZATIONS

According to what is known so far, the first great civilizations arose at various times in the early history of mankind and in quite different places on the globe. Composed of a hierarchy of socioeconomic classes, these civilizations were based on the creation and control of food surpluses that were administered by a small ruling class through complex management systems. The political elite used some of this surplus production to engage in trade with distant lands so as to acquire luxury goods that reflected social status. At home they used this surplus to have monumental architecture built by community members specialized in this field and to commission works of art intended to symbolize social cohesion. Religion, which was another potential source of influence on social relations, was also controlled by the state.

Researchers have generally found it appropriate to study the first great civilizations under three principal headings: politics, economy, and religion or abstract thought. The present exhibition is arranged around these three main themes.

With respect to politics, power was usually in the hands of a small group of people, the elite class or one member of the community. Positioned at the apex of a rigid social hierarchy, the rulers exercised power through a bureaucratic system that saw to the management of state matters such as collecting taxes, keeping public archives, controlling trade, overseeing construction projects, supervising specialized production and organizing military operations. In such hierarchical societies, belonging to a class was reflected by whether or not one

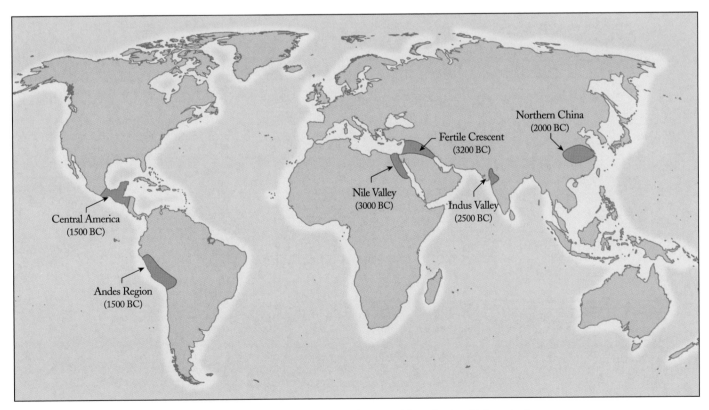

Cradles of civilization throughout the world with dates of first-attested form of sociopolitical organization

MAJOR STAGES OF DEVELOPMENT

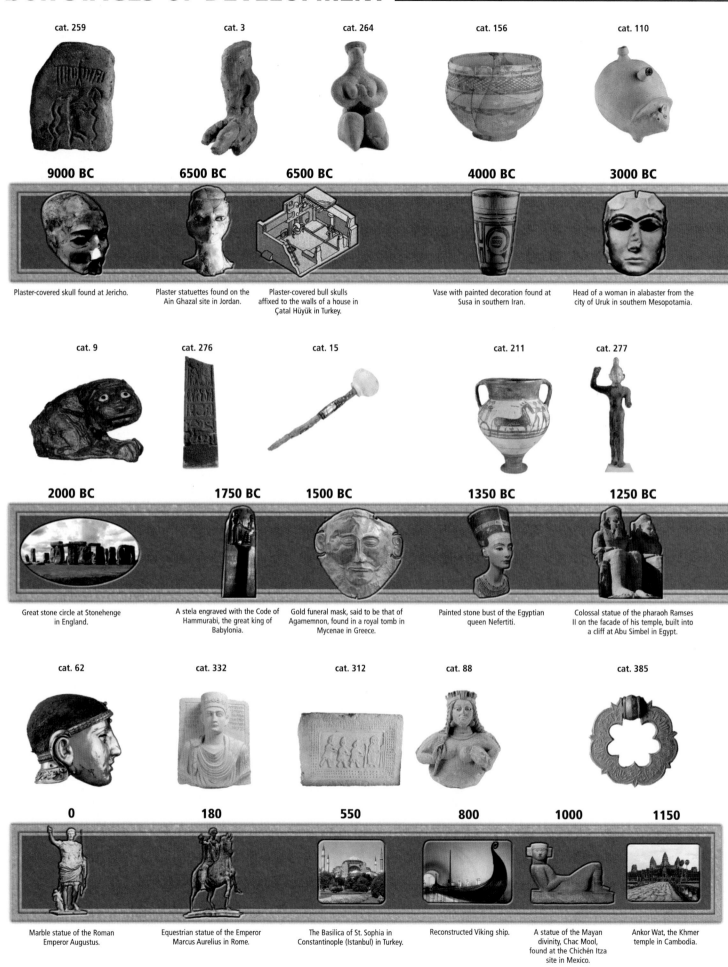

cat. 259

9000 BC

Plaster-covered skull found at Jericho.

cat. 3

6500 BC

Plaster statuettes found on the Ain Ghazal site in Jordan.

cat. 264

6500 BC

Plaster-covered bull skulls affixed to the walls of a house in Çatal Hüyük in Turkey.

cat. 156

4000 BC

Vase with painted decoration found at Susa in southern Iran.

cat. 110

3000 BC

Head of a woman in alabaster from the city of Uruk in southern Mesopotamia.

cat. 9

2000 BC

Great stone circle at Stonehenge in England.

cat. 276

1750 BC

A stela engraved with the Code of Hammurabi, the great king of Babylonia.

cat. 15

1500 BC

Gold funeral mask, said to be that of Agamemnon, found in a royal tomb in Mycenae in Greece.

cat. 211

1350 BC

Painted stone bust of the Egyptian queen Nefertiti.

cat. 277

1250 BC

Colossal statue of the pharaoh Ramses II on the facade of his temple, built into a cliff at Abu Simbel in Egypt.

cat. 62

0

Marble statue of the Roman Emperor Augustus.

cat. 332

180

Equestrian statue of the Emperor Marcus Aurelius in Rome.

cat. 312

550

The Basilica of St. Sophia in Constantinople (Istanbul) in Turkey.

cat. 88

800

Reconstructed Viking ship.

cat. 385

1000

A statue of the Mayan divinity, Chac Mool, found at the Chichén Itza site in Mexico.

1150

Ankor Wat, the Khmer temple in Cambodia.

THE WORLD'S FIRST CIVILIZATIONS

cat. 295

cat. 13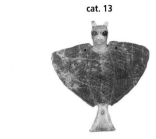

cat. 286

cat. 272

cat. 1

 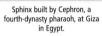

2500 BC   **2450 BC**   **2400 BC**   **2250 BC**   **2050 BC**

Sphinx built by Cephron, a
fourth-dynasty pharaoh, at Giza
in Egypt.

Gold helmet found in one of the
royal tombs of Ur in southern
Mesopotamia.

Stone bust of a man found at the
Mohenjo-Daro site in the Indus Valley.

Bronze head representing the grandson
of Sargon, the great king of Akkade,
who was the first to unify
Mesopotamia.

Basalt statue of a great king of the
Mesopotamian city of Telloh,
shown holding a spouting vase.

cat. 52

cat. 58

cat. 56

cat. 61

cat.149 a-c

1000 BC   **700 BC**   **600 BC**   **500 BC**   **200 BC**   **200 BC**

Colossal Olmec stone head from
La Venta in Mexico.

Winged bull that once decorated the palace of Sargon II at
Khorsabad in Assyria.

Reconstitution of ancient Babylon,
showing the Tower of Babel.

Bas-relief illustrat-
ing the birth of
Buddha in 556 BC.

Bronze Roman copy of a
Greek stone bust of the
philosopher Aristotle.

Marble portrait of
Alexander the Great found
at Pergamum in Turkey.

Modern village home built of unbaked brick with a stairway leading to a circular silo.

possessed certain symbols of social status, such as houses, fine clothing, jewelry and luxury objects. The clearest symbol of power, however, was represented by monumental architecture, which required a combination of technical skill, bureaucratic management and esthetic qualities. Indeed, certain artistic creations, although produced by lower-class craftsmen, were reserved for the enjoyment of the political elite alone. These works of art thus reflected the society's system of cultural values.

As far as economy is concerned, the first civilizations varied in the ways they adapted to their environment, depending on available ecological resources. However, they were similar in that they all institutionalized the right of the ruling class to appropriate food surpluses. And in every civilization, these rulers sought to display their power and authority publicly by building temples, palaces, storehouses and fortifications and by keeping an army to maintain order in the community. In short, these economies depended on the exploitation of social inequalities.

As for thought and religion, each civilization provided itself with a god or special divinities so that the benevolent forces of the supernatural might influence the reproduction of plants, animals and humans. In general, the king or the rulers acted as mediators between their subjects and supernatural forces. As well, some religions allowed ordinary people to play a role.

In short, the essence of a civilization lies less in tangible objects than in a whole set of intricate organizational processes affecting society. The existence of a civilization presupposes a complex type of sociopolitical, economic and intellectual organization.

Archaeology: a continuously evolving social science

ALMOST ALL THE OBJECTS presented in this exhibition were found by archaeologists in the course of scientifically conducted excavations. For archaeological researchers, the interest of these finds lies not only in their artistic value but also in the clues they provide to a past way of life that they must attempt to reconstruct through induction. The archaeologist's task is basically to try to see through the objects to the men and women who made them, used them and eventually left them behind. The discovery of objects on a site, as spectacular as it may appear, is actually just the collecting of data.

The fundamental problem facing archaeologists is that their main object of study — the human beings of the past — has disappeared. The only source of information about these humans is what they left, which may consist of mere traces of some activity. Then these remains must be interpreted, and interpreted properly.

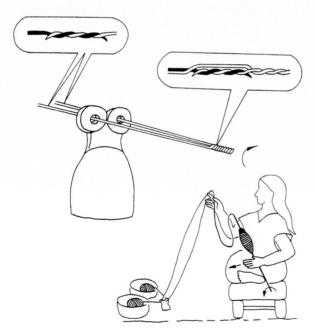

It should be kept in mind that even when the archaeological data available are tangible objects that can be observed and described, like those in the present exhibition, their interpretation remains strictly theoretical — and therefore debatable. The comments made in the following pages reflect the opinions shared by the majority of archaeologists, but this in no way implies that they are unanimously accepted by the scientific community. In any case, all science must be debatable and refutable, since the integration of new knowledge leads us to constantly adjust our vision of reality.

Certain thinkers have turned their attention to the very nature of archaeology, which, since the data are unchanging, appears to be an objective science. They have

This object, at first thought to be a symbolic representation of a deity, is now interpreted as an ordinary tool used in cloth making.
Cat. 124

found that archaeologists, without really being aware of it, allow their scientific interpretations to be colored to some degree by concepts that are particular to their own cultures. Indeed, those who study past human life are only human themselves.

Moreover, it can never be known how many human activities have taken place in the past without leaving a trace. Any archaeological or anthropological interpretation of a culture is necessarily incomplete, since it is based only on what has come down to us. This is why data are collected in the field using increasingly sophisticated techniques for ground reconnaissance, excavation and archaeometric analysis, which foster the development of constantly updated interpretative models.

As you visit this exhibition, keep in mind the people of long ago whose lives we experience through these objects, as well as those who today try to understand these people to the best of their ability.

An abandoned town southwest of Aleppo.

SYRIA, CRADLE OF CIVILIZATION

Some 12 000 years ago, in certain regions which are now part of Syria, people decided to live in places where the natural environment provided so much food for their survival in every season that they could settle there permanently. These new human settlements soon developed a way of working as a community. Then, as new situations arose and community activities became more diverse, this way of working together gradually evolved into different forms.

The early settlers engaged in economic activities which were at first centered on the food needs of community members, but later were aimed at accumulating agricultural surpluses that would free certain members to devote time to different tasks, such as crafts, and that could be used to trade for goods which were unavailable in the immediate environment. Such trade, however, necessitated more complex administrative structures.

Successful community life must be underpinned by a shared system of values, a dominant ideology and collective way of thinking. These affect how the supernatural is represented, how the conceptualization of abstract elements is given concrete expression and how beliefs are systematized in an institution like a religion. This aspect of community life also includes the rational explanation of the world and scientific thought, which blossomed in Syria during the Islamic period, leaving a legacy to which the modern Western world is largely indebted.

Syria is one of the most ancient places in the world where a new way of life, which may be considered revolutionary when compared to what preceded it, was tried by groups of human beings as early as 10 000 BC. The people who settled in the region made objects that today testify to the dawning of a civilization which would take various shapes over the centuries right up to the time of the Crusades, when the Islamic East and Christian West confronted each other.

SYRIA, LAND OF CONTRASTS

Certain features of the Syrian territory made it a place where the first agro-pastoral societies in the world could appear, leading eventually to the development of great civilizations. In discussing this territory, it is convenient to divide it into three main regions, not of equal size nor equally watered by the Euphrates, one of the two great rivers of Mesopotamia.

In the west, a narrow coastal plain lies along the Mediterranean, bordered on the east by a north-south mountain range called the Jebel Ansariyah, which causes moisture to precipitate before it reaches the interior and thus makes its climate a Mediterranean one, with plenty of rainfall on both east and west slopes. There are several passes in this mountain range, but the widest passage through it lies near the present-day city of Homs and it is here that contact between the coastal region and the interior is easiest. This region is naturally turned towards the Mediterranean; it was settled mainly in periods when Syria was more focused on the Mediterranean world, such as during the Crusades, when European forces conquered the coastal plain and built fortresses

The mountainous landscape along the coastal plain.

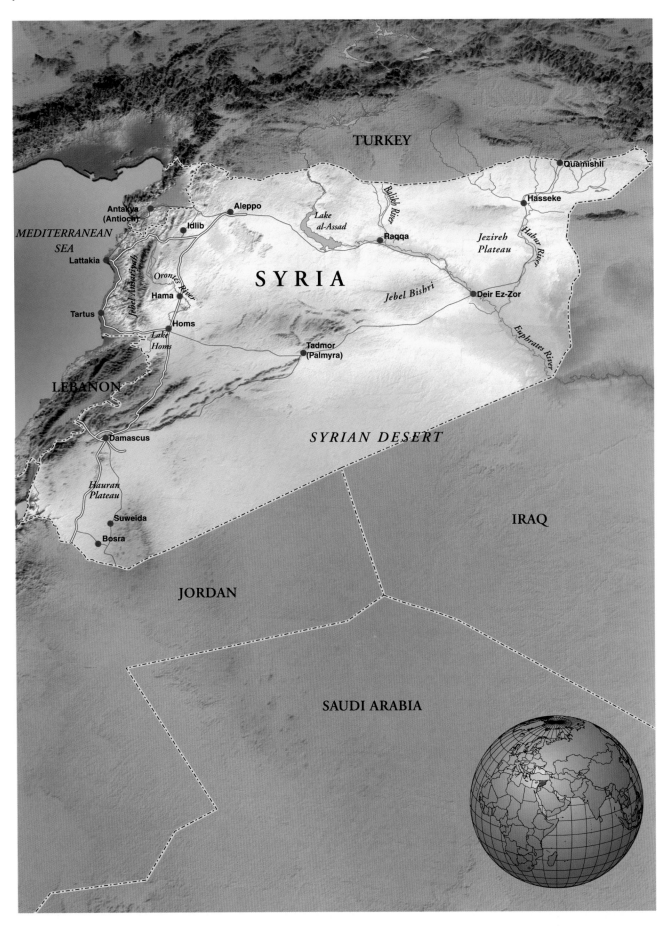

Modern Syria

SYRIA, LAND OF CIVILIZATIONS

on the heights of Jebel Ansariyah. The effort made to populate this region of Syria was not as intense as it was in the interior regions.

Elsewhere in Syria, the situation is very different. About 58% of the territory receives a yearly rainfall of less than 250 millimeters. This territory is semi-arid steppe land that is actually desert in some areas and does not really support agriculture unless it is irrigated. However, these dry regions are entirely suitable for raising cattle, sheep and goats, as well as for transhumance, or herding small numbers of these animals from place to place along the edges of the desert areas, never far from the watering places in the semi-arid zones. The only people to range farther than this were the camel breeders. Around 2000 BC, they began to venture into the desert with their caravans, stopping at oases like the one at Palmyra in order to survive on long-distance routes. This

semi-arid region is bordered on the north by two mountainous areas, one of which is the Jebel Bishri.

Lying between the two preceding regions is a zone of plains, valleys and plateaus receiving 250 to 500 millimeters of rain each year and thus supporting agriculture without irrigation. Contained in an arc-shaped area and fabled for its fertility, this region has come to be

Camels grazing in the semi-arid steppe.

The rich farmlands of the Fertile Crescent.

The wide meanders of the Euphrates.

known as the Fertile Crescent. It was here that the first agriculture was attempted and here that enough cereal could be grown to supply people living outside the area. The zone may be seen as composed of several sectors, from south to north: the Hauran Plateau, whose soil is fertilized by the decomposition of volcanic rock; the lowlands near the Homs "gap," which allows in masses of moist air from the Mediterranean; a valley irrigated by the Orontes River, with the Jebel Ansariyah to the west and the Jebel Zawiyah to the east; a wide plain around the present-day city of Aleppo, stretching eastward to the Euphrates; and beyond this river, a vast cereal-producing plain, the Jezireh, watered by two tributaries of the Euphrates — the Balikh and the Habur.

The Euphrates, one of the two great rivers of Mesopotamia, loses about one quarter of its water as it flows along its 500- to 600-kilometer course through Syrian land. This water nourishes a fertile alluvial valley in the middle of a high, flat steppe. Not only does the Euphrates irrigate the Syrian portion of the Fertile Crescent but it also provides a means of communication between the Mediterranean world (the city of Aleppo is about 150 kilometers from the coast) and southern Mesopotamia, through which it passes before flowing into the Persian Gulf, and on into the Indian Ocean.

A term to learn in Near Eastern archaeology: the tell

Tell 'Atij on the banks of the Habur River.

IN ARABIC, the word "tell" means "hill." The term is used in the archaeology of the Near East to designate a special kind of hill that dots the flatlands in these regions. These hills were not formed naturally, but rather developed gradually as debris from crumbling house walls accumulated. The houses built on such sites were made of sun-dried brick, which offers little resistance to the forces of erosion. When the walls eventually fell, the rubble was leveled out and a new house was built on the ruins of the old.

When archaeologists dig a tell, they must try to distinguish each of the superimposed buildings and the objects it contained when it was destroyed. Each building is called a "layer," corresponding to a stratum of different-colored earth. A vertical cross-section (or stratigraphy) of a tell excavated by an archaeologist displays the series of layers that make up the entire mound.

INTRODUCTION

catalogue

1

Statue of a king of Mari
Diorite
2200 BC

This statue represents King Ishtup-ilum, who ruled over the city-state of Mari. The sculpture was discovered in the palace of Mari at one end of the throne room where the statues of other dead kings no doubt stood, facing the throne of the living king on the other side of the room. Ishtup-ilum seems to have been a great king, for it was he who built the Temple of the Lions, dedicated to the King of the Land, next to the palace.
The king is shown in a solemn pose. His garments and the style of his beard reflect considerable refinement. Enhanced by the somber color of the stone, the monarch's powerful build and muscular arms convey a sense of quiet assurance that befits a great potentate.

TELL HARIRI, ANCIENT MARI: PALACE   147 x 44.2 x 40 cm
NATIONAL MUSEUM, ALEPPO   M 7882
SMC 130

THE ORGANIZATION OF society

THE ORGANIZATION OF society

As was seen in the previous passages, a civilization may be said to be distinguished above all by a complex, structured social organization, based on a hierarchical order of social classes, the highest of which is constituted by a political elite, or even a single leader, in whose hands lies all political power.

To start with, society was organized around village life, based on farming and animal husbandry; all the members of the community were related by kinship and enjoyed equal status. Then, as agricultural techniques improved and the population consequently increased, there grew a need to ensure that all the members of the community had enough food to survive, and the best way to meet this need apparently was to adopt a more organized social structure. This structure would someday develop into a fully formed political system, but at this point the interests of the community were managed by a chief or a ruling class, whose members were usually related to one another.

Head of a Hittite statue found at Ain Dara.
Cat. 56

Once this embryonic politico-economic organization was in place, social structures began to become more definite. The farming village consisting of a few families grew into a populous trading city that was ruled by one leader, supported in the exercise of power by a class of civil servants. Some cities, like Mari and Ebla, dominated and exploited neighboring territories to ensure that their own citizens had enough food even though these people were engaged in specialized, non-agricultural tasks. As the sphere of influence of these agglomerations grew, they became city-states. The trade they engaged in brought prosperity but also required that certain members of the community become specialized in management.

Previous page:
Statuette of an orant from Mari.
Cat. 286

THE MAJOR PHASES OF SYRIAN HISTORY

1 million BC
SETTLEMENT

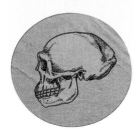

12000 BC
VILLAGES

6000 BC
CHIEFDOMS

3000 BC
CITY-STATES:
Ebla
Mari
Ugarit

Invasion of the
Amorites
2000 BC
Battle of Qadesh
1286 BC
Invasion of the
"Sea Peoples"
1200 BC

KINGDOMS

1000 BC
ARAMAEAN

1000 BC
HITTITE

745 BC

ASSYRIAN

EMPIRES

612 BC

NEO-BABYLONIAN

538 BC

PERSIAN

333 BC

HELLENISTIC

Death of Alexander the
Great 323 BC

64 BC

ROMAN

Reign of Queen
Zenobia in Palmyra
267-272

395

BYZANTINE

Hegira 622

636

ISLAMIC

Umayyad dynasty 661
Abbasid dynasty 750
Ayyubid dynasty 1171
Mamluk dynasty 1250

End of Crusades 1291

41

Later, Syrian lands, or rather various parts of this territory, were integrated, sometimes forcefully, into kingdoms that were usually controlled by some dominant ethnic group, whether Amorite, Assyrian, Hurrian, Hittite or Aramaean. These peoples were not necessarily newcomers to the territory they occupied, and their ways of managing society respected local interests. It was in this period that the first "Arab" populations appeared in Syria.

Later still, the Syrian territory as a whole was annexed to immense political structures encompassing several other regions as well. These structures were the empires. One after the other, Hellenistic, Roman, Byzantine and Islamic rulers imposed their centralized government control over the economy and politics. However, they also showed some flexibility in adapting to regional differences.

THE BIRTH OF VILLAGES

THE OLD WAY OF LIFE: THE HUNTER-GATHERERS

The Syrian territory began to be populated about one million years ago by members of the human species coming most likely from East Africa. Archaeologists call the era Paleolithic, meaning "old stone," since during this period, humans used stone, or more precisely, flint, to make their tools.

Until about 200 000 BC, the humans — that is, representatives of the species

The Dederiyah cave where the skeleton of a Neanderthal was discovered.

The peopling of Syria:
recent discoveries

THE FIRST EVIDENCE OF HUMAN presence in Syria comes from chipped flint tools found in a few sites in the valley of the Nahr el-Kebir on the Mediterranean coast and in the Orontes Valley. It appears that the first humans to enter Syrian territory, about one million years ago, were *Homo erectus*. These humans probably came from the south by one of two routes, since sites from this period are found along both the Mediterranean coast and the Syro-African rift. By about 500 000 BC, *Homo erectus* had spread to all the geographical regions of Syria. Despite the extraordinary richness of Syrian sites from the prehistoric periods, human remains are rare; nevertheless, those that have been found are extremely significant.

In 1996, a large skull fragment was discovered by a Syrian-Swiss team at the Nadawiyah Aïn Askar site in the el-Kowm region north of Palmyra. Examination of this parietal bone, which is the oldest human skeletal find to date in the Near East, revealed that it belonged to an adult *Homo erectus*. Nadawiyah Man, as he is called, was the first representative of the human race to be positively identified in Syria. It is estimated that he lived about 450 000 years before our era. The discovery raises interesting questions about the relation between Africa and Asia at this period and the role that the Near East may have played in the expansion of humankind towards the Asian and European continents.

In 1993, the skeleton of a Neanderthal child was found at a depth of 1.5 meters in the Dederiyah cave, 50 kilometers north of Aleppo. The cave was occupied by humans during the Middle Paleolithic period (100 000 BC to 40 000 BC). The child was found lying on its back, with its arms apart and its knees flexed; a flat stone lay under its head and a flint flake was on its chest, over the heart. These features are signs that the body had been deliberately buried. The 83-centimeter-long skeleton is almost complete, and all its anatomical parts are perfectly preserved and easily identified. The presence of teeth indicates that the child was about two years old at the time of death.

The child found at Dederiyah provides new data concerning the distribution of Neanderthals in the Levantine and offers clues to the chronological and phylogenetic relation between two human populations — Neanderthal and early *Homo sapiens*. Specifically, the discovery has a bearing on the theories about the relationship between these two populations, helping us to decide whether Neanderthals and *Homo sapiens* coexisted and were actually just two varieties of the *Homo sapiens* type, or rather met for the first time in the Near East, with the former arriving from Europe and the latter from Africa.

Another, less complete, skeleton was found at a depth of 3.5 meters in a grave at the Dederiyah site in 1997. An initial examination suggested that this child was also about two years old, but not as robust as the first child. Excavation of the cave also revealed the humerus of a six-month-old infant and over one hundred fragments of teeth. Comparison with other sites excavated in the Near East makes it possible to date the bone remains to about 60 000 BC.

Finally, in 1996, the Syrian-French team working on the Umm el-Tlel site in the el-Kowm region discovered a fragment of a Neanderthal man's skull in the layer dating from the Mousterian period (Middle Paleolithic). Another skull fragment was found on the same site in 1997, but it has not yet been identified.

While the stone tools found in Syria show that humans lived there one million years ago, the earliest human remains discovered so far date to about 450 000 BC. These discoveries contribute greatly to our understanding of the evolution and expansion of the very first human beings.

PROF. DR. SULTAN MUHESEN
Director-General of Antiquities and Museums, Syria (Damascus)

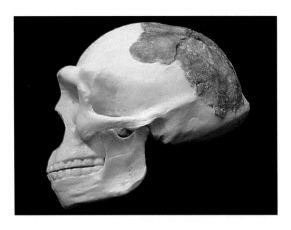

Homo erectus, or "standing-upright man" — living in Syria were cave-dwellers who survived by foraging for their food. They hunted wild animals and gathered plant food, adapting to the changing seasons. Near the end of this period, humans learned to control fire and use it. Then gradually, between 200 000 BC and 40 000 BC, these people, who were now Neanderthals, left their caves and rocky shelters and began living in the open near watering places. Between 40 000 BC and 12 000 BC, humans, now known as *Homo sapiens sapiens* like ourselves, continued to live by hunting and gathering the wild resources around them, but they had developed features for their stone tools that improved their efficiency. They lived in seasonal camps and left little behind in the soil for archaeologists to study. Still less can be surmised about their social organization; the very most that can be said is that it was probably based on the family group. Nonetheless, a recently discovered skeleton of a Neanderthal child whose body had been deliberately buried in a cave suggests that even at this very early stage the members of a group had some form of respect and esteem for the other members of their group. This respect seems to have extended to children, who might not yet have contrib-

uted to the survival of the group, but must have nevertheless represented a guarantee for the future of their families or clans.

A NEW WAY OF LIFE:
THE AGRICULTURAL REVOLUTION

Archaeological sites dating from about 12 000 BC reveal the first indications of a radical change — some authors go so far as to call it "revolutionary" — in the lifestyle of the people living in the Syrian territory. It was about this time that the climate changed. Around 15 000 BC, an era of cool temperatures was replaced by a period of global warming, bringing rain and humidity to the Near East. By 12 000 BC, the continuous warming trend had made the climate of this region about as dry as it is today. At this time, groups of hunter-gatherers started to establish permanent year-round settlements in areas where the natural food supply was so plentiful that moving from one camp to another was unnecessary. In these zones, the native flora included species of cereal plants that were eaten by humans and, more particularly, by animals. A relationship between humans, animals and plants was thus established.

These humans began to live in circular huts made with branches and animal hides. Their most distinctive feature was that they were partially sunk into the earth. In this way, the very first permanent villages took shape in Syria, as they apparently also did in other parts of the world. However, these settlements must be considered pre-agricultural since, as odd as it may seem, they were inhabited by people who were still foragers and not farmers. The village-dwellers took advantage of the natural

resources of this zone in the Syrian territory, living off an abundance of wild animals (gazelles, deer, boar and cattle) and plants (einkorn, polygonum and astragalus). Grain from such plants was crushed and ground with a new invention — tools made of polished stone. Archaeologists call this era the Neolithic period, meaning that of "new stone," in contrast to the preceding period, named the Paleolithic (meaning "old stone").

Dwellings are adapted to the new lifestyle

The early round huts, two to three meters in diameter, continued to be crudely built of perishable materials such as branches and daub, but at one point they were no longer sunk into the ground. Instead, near the huts, people dug out small hollows to make silos in which to store the seeds of wild plants gathered in the surrounding clearings. A little later, the walls of the circular homes began to be made of *pisé*, a mixture of mud and straw, which made the whole structure much more solid. Houses became roomier

and were even subdivided according to the various activities of its inhabitants. In addition, people built small rectangular stone structures, about one meter square, right beside the house. Here they stored the seeds that they were beginning to try to reserve for planting in the fields in spring. However, the principal means of obtaining food at this time was still fishing and hunting, especially for small game such as hare [105].

Houses continued to be built of *pisé*, but now in a rectangular shape, giving evidence of their permanent and well-planned nature [5]. The interior consisted of a few rooms laid out in three rows. Near the door was an area reserved for food preparation, with storage space and cooking facilities. The inner floor and walls were coated with a layer of plaster to make these surfaces more durable and to keep out the small rodents [114] that were attracted by the grains stored there. As village houses grew larger, they also grew more numerous. The villages seem to have been well planned, since alleys were laid between the houses for passing traffic. Some of the

Reconstitution of a Paleolithic landscape.

45

alleys even had a system for draining resid-
ual water, as exemplified by a channel, over
20 meters in length, discovered on a recently excavated site. Such public installations strongly suggest that a sense of community was developing in the villages.

Figurine.
Cat. 3

VILLAGE LIFE DEVELOPS

It was thus during the Neolithic period that
people in a few parts of the Syrian territory
first began to live in groups that extended
beyond the family or clan. A village could
have up to about 50 houses, with a family of
five or six living in each one. The inhabitants seem to have enjoyed equal status,
since no house was more imposing than another. It is believed that each village had a
leader who was the head of a family or an
ancestor of the clan who was revered even
after death. The skulls of such people were
kept and covered with painted plaster,
crudely modeled to represent their features
[4]. Some of these skulls were discovered
near headless human-shaped figurines,
which could have been used to support
them [3].

Women must have played a very important role, since from 10 000 BC they
began to be represented in stone and in
fire-baked clay, and from 9500 BC such
figurines, with very explicit female characteristics, became common [262].
According to the most widely accepted
interpretations, these figurines symbolized

Dwellings: from round to rectangular

THE SITE OF JERF AL-AHMAR provides a key to understanding the historic developments that led from the first round dwellings to later rectangular houses in the Near East. The some 30 houses brought to light at the site furnish all the elements required to study the process whereby the villagers went from living in round houses that were isolated from one another to living in houses with a rectangular layout. The later style of house encouraged a stronger village structure to emerge, laying the groundwork for the great urban agglomerations that would subsequently appear in Syrian territory.

Even during the very first occupation of the site, around 9000 BC, people seemed to want to build on level ground. Slopes were dug out so that slightly sunken, round houses could be constructed on them. Terracing became so extensive that the seventh village was built on at least four terraces. Several of the houses were joined to one another by low retaining walls along the terraces, indicating that a certain number of the community's members must have worked together on a common building project. The terrace seems to have been constructed and reinforced with retaining walls at the same time that a number of houses were erected; the coordination of such an undertaking would have required some form of centralization with respect to decision making and the organization of labor.

One of the later occupations of the site offers another picture of the inhabitants' organizational capacities. A dozen houses stand in an arc of a circle around a structure that is both a "village square" and community building. The "village square" is, in fact, simply the flat roof of a large round construction that is entirely subterranean. The building was used for storage, but human remains were also discovered. A headless skeleton was discovered lying on the floor of the central room and a skull was found set in a corner of a wall.

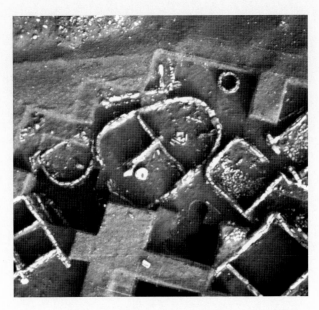

Aerial view of part of the site of Jerf al-Ahmar.

By the time of the final occupation of Jerf al-Ahmar, the change from round house to rectangular dwelling had gone as far as it would. Technical advances, especially where tools were concerned, made it possible to build walls that were truly perpendicular to one another. This by no means prevented people from constructing houses with rounded corners or from combining the two types of corners in the same house. The variations in house plans show that social pressure was not strong enough to impose a single model, as would be the case later on. The great architectural creativity that was expressed at this time — in the size and layout of constructions, the number and arrangement of rooms, and openings onto courtyards and extensions — reflects a diversity that contrasts with the standardization of villages in the eighth millennium.

DR. DANIELLE STORDEUR
Centre national de recherche scientifique (Lyon)

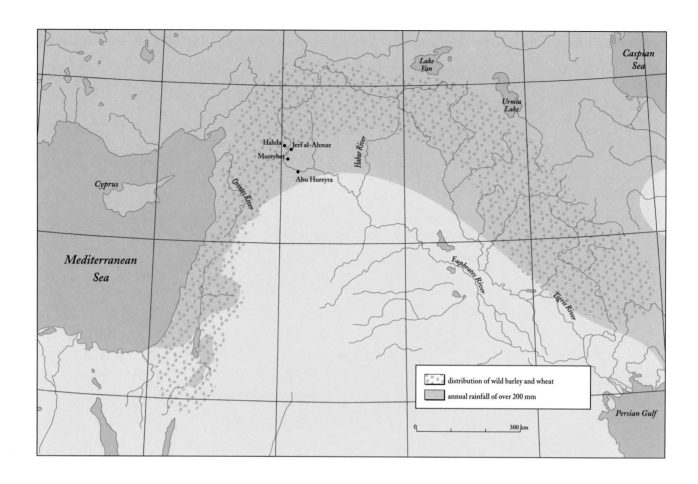

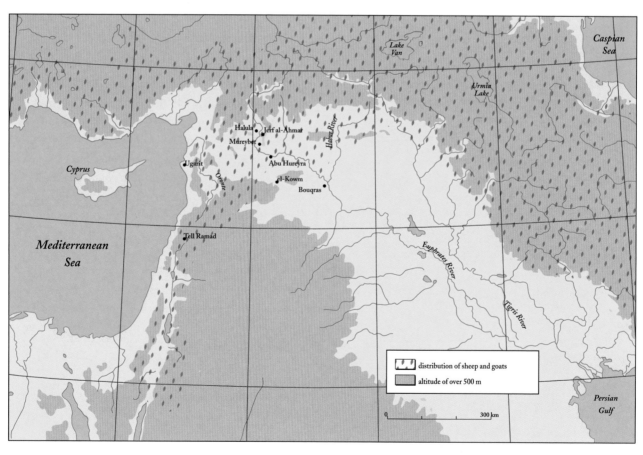

The first agricultural villages in the Fertile Crescent

SYRIA, LAND OF CIVILIZATIONS

the very principle of fertility at a time when human societies first attempted to control the reproduction of plants and animals. For, although there was no lack of natural resources, people suddenly adopted a new strategy for obtaining food, using cultivated plants and domesticated animals. However, it would be wrong to conclude that women's status was related solely to their reproductive role. The study of certain skeletal remains found in a house from this period has revealed that they were very active in household work. The women's bones displayed deformities that were probably caused by extended periods of sitting in the same position during the physically demanding task of grinding grain to make bread and other food. According to certain ethnographic studies, producing enough flour for a household's daily bread needs would have required two to three hours of grinding.

Chiefdoms: a sign of a new political order

By about 6000 BC, village life, based on agriculture and cattle raising, had become widespread in several regions of Syria, although some groups of people adopted this lifestyle later than others and some continued to follow a nomadic way of life. Ceramic from this period was decorated with painted motifs that might represent bulls' heads [99] or goats [101]. Goat figures were also sculpted in stone [108]. Sites from this period contain an abundance of terra cotta female figurines [264], symbols of the fertility that humans were attempting to control with ever growing success.

A little before 5000 BC, the Syrian agricultural villages came under the influence of a culture originating in southern Mesopotamia (present-day Iraq). The villages already practiced irrigation and fallow-field farming, but their social structure gradually grew more complex as a new hierarchical organization based on chiefdom was introduced. Elsewhere during this period, villages began to have certain houses, larger than the others, which are believed to have been the seats of an early form of government. Although such buildings have not yet been discovered on Syrian sites of this period, there is nonetheless evidence that the southern culture was present, since a painted ceramic typical of this culture has been found. In fact, on one Syrian site, a potter's workshop from the period has been uncovered, strongly suggesting the adoption of a new social order, in which it was possible for specialized craftsmen to devote themselves to work that was not related to farming.

Apart from the construction of buildings that were more imposing than others in a village, the Mesopotamian chiefdoms were notable for not being led by a single chief, but rather by a ruling body that made decisions affecting the community as a whole. This body was responsible for management, controlling agricultural production and storing surpluses in granaries constructed for this purpose, so that the extra food could, on the one hand, be redistributed — to specialized artisans in particular — and, on the other, be traded for luxury goods that would publicly proclaim the higher social status of the elite class.

CITIES AND STATES: AN UN-PRECEDENTED DEVELOPMENT

THE FIRST CITIES TAKE SHAPE

In southern Mesopotamia (southern Iraq) large urban agglomerations, like that of Uruk, gradually took shape in the fourth millennium before our era. Those who ruled these cities represented an entirely new social phenomenon. As part of their trade network, they set up other cities along the banks of the Euphrates to serve as strategically placed commercial posts. Some of these "colony cities" were quite large for the time, covering up to 10 hectares. Surrounded by thick defensive walls, they held dozens of houses, some of which were larger than the others and were embellished with mosaics made of baked clay cones [280] on their outer walls. These buildings were used as residences for the members of the social class that ruled the city, or as meeting places where this class of people could make decisions concerning the city's defence and economic life. The many public buildings in these towns also included large storehouses for goods that would eventually be traded or that had been acquired through such trade. The quantity (or weight) and the commercial value of these goods were determined, and then added up and recorded using a system of tokens, or *calculi* [233], and tablets inscribed with numerals [235]. These tools were used only by a special class whose members devoted their time to this type of management task. The person who occupied the highest position in this social hierarchy may have been the individual represented on the cylinder seals [29]. Archaeologists have called this figure dressed in a long robe a "priest-king." The ambiguity of this designation for such an important person may be attributed to the paucity of information available both about this individual and about his sociopolitical role. The same ambiguity colors the interpretation of some of the monumental buildings with richly decorated walls. Were they leaders' houses or temples? The beginnings of an explanation can be gleaned from sites dating from the following millennium.

THE BIRTH OF CITY-STATES: MARI, A COMMERCIAL METROPOLIS

During the third millennium BC, great city-states grew up in various places throughout Syrian territory. In the city of Mari, according to the archaeologists who excavated it, the oldest public building is a palace, and thus the seat of civil government. The building contained a throne room with two rows of three large pillars. It also housed a structure described as a sanctuary. This sacred precinct comprised a wide central area surrounded by smaller rooms, which in turn were encompassed by an outer corridor. The divinity, whose identity remains unknown, stood in the room to the south of the central area, where there was an altar. The architectural layout of this building provides helpful clues when it comes to defining the nature of royal power and its origin at this time. The two forms of power — civil and religious — may or may not have been in the hands of one person, but it is clear that they were placed together within a building that symbolized power.

Another significant architectural particularity of the Mari palace also reflects the new social order. One of the great courtyards that allowed people to circulate through the building housed a workshop where a craftsman did inlay work with mother-of-pearl.

Several unfinished pieces, panels ready to be inlaid, have survived. They show us scenes of war [37], offerings being made to the king and the sacrifice of a ram [303]. The presence of such a craftsman's workshop within the palace is a clear sign that a special relationship existed between those who held political power and those who carried out specialized tasks, particularly when these tasks were related to the artistic expression of symbols of that power in a material that had to be imported from distant lands, as was the case for mother-of-pearl in the city of Mari.

Eloquent testimony to Mari's connection with its faraway neighbors is furnished by a jar, also discovered in the palace, containing some 50 precious objects. They included a long lapis-lazuli bead [12] inscribed with the name

Mesanepada, a king of the first dynasty of Ur (whence the designation "Treasure of Ur" attributed to this find); a pendant representing a lion-headed eagle [13], or a bat according to a recent reinterpretation, made of lapis lazuli, gold, bitumen and copper; gold and silver toggle pins [8]; bead necklaces of lapis lazuli and carnelian [10 and 11], exotic materials from Afghanistan; and a series of cylinder seals imported from southern Mesopotamia. These opulent examples of material culture may have been costly gifts from other kingdoms or the valuable booty of war, but whatever the case, they reflected the power and prestige of the political authority that ruled from the palace.

The enormous number of masterworks discovered in the ruins of the Mari palace

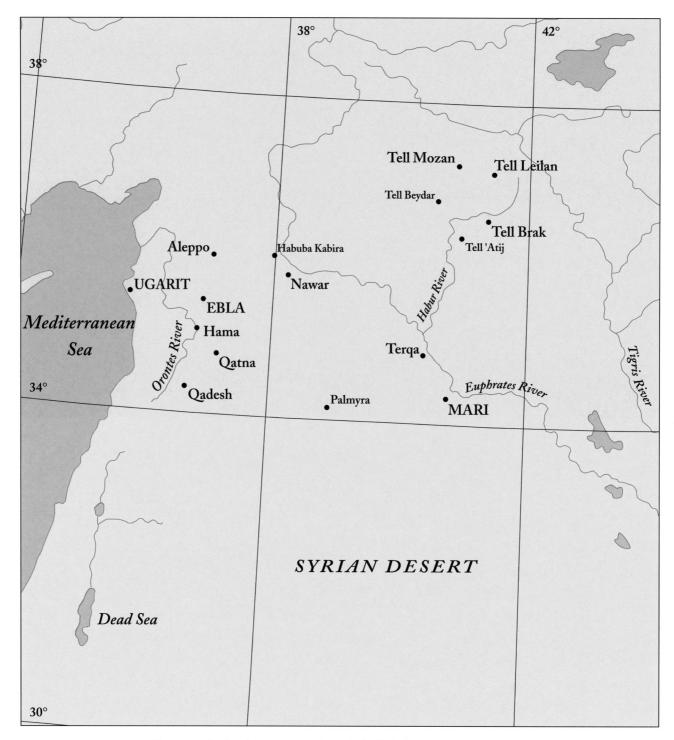

City-states and major urban areas in Syria during the fourth, third and early-second centuries BC

SYRIA, LAND OF CIVILIZATIONS

testifies as well to the city's great prosperity, a consequence of its control over river traffic between northern Syria and southern Mesopotamia. Its position on the right bank of the Euphrates was strategic rather than the result of chance. Mari was a new city. It had not grown from a village but had been created literally out of nothing towards the beginning of the third millennium BC by a political authority in charge of developing the region. The city was not founded as a farming centre, located as it was on a semi-arid steppe that could not support normal agriculture because of insufficient annual rainfall. Nonetheless, canals were dug from the right bank of the Euphrates, with one of them linked to a reservoir lake, so that an irrigation network could be used to ensure the sustenance of the urban population.

On the other side of the river, a canal was built for transportation between the Euphrates and its tributary, the Habur. Eleven meters wide and 120 kilometers long, the canal made it possible, even in the dry season, for boats to sail northward to the verdant plains watered by the Habur. This canal development gives some idea of the scale on which public works could be built by a powerful third-millennium city-state relying on a multitude of laborers and a few craftsmen with the right technical expertise. Just maintaining the canal once it was built would also have been a challenge. Year-round navigation through the man-made canal was important to Mari, for the Habur valley was where storage buildings had been constructed. The site of Tell 'Atij is a good example of such a supply post under the control of a powerful city-state.

Ebla, the ideal city-state

Ebla was another great urban center that existed at the same time as Mari, during the third millennium. The city itself took up 40 to 50 hectares (400 000 square meters), while its royal palace covered more than 2500 square meters. One of the most interesting parts of the palace was a large open space measuring 35 meters by 60 meters, with gateways on at least two of its sides. Archaeologists call it a "court of audience." It is believed that the king would sit on a podium under the court's north entrance to receive caravans, messengers, ambassadors and civil servants. So that the decisions taken during such audiences or other transactions would not be forgotten, their substance was inscribed on soft clay tablets that were not baked afterwards but simply left to dry in the air. The tablets were then stacked on shelves against the walls of a small room under the east gateway to the audience court. In 1975, about 15 500 tablets bearing 4000 to 5000 decipherable texts were discovered in this archives room, which has since become famous. The tablets have been beautifully preserved, since they were baked when the palace was destroyed by fire around 2300 BC. Writing no doubt represented a highly efficient management tool for a state administration, which is why it was developed in the first place. However, given the enormous number of symbols (1200) that had to be memorized in the first systems, only a limited number of scribes learned to write and keep the archives.

The way the palace of Ebla is situated perfectly expresses the important role it played in the city. It stands between the lower town, where the ordinary people lived, and the heights of the acropolis, where the princely class had residences. It should be emphasized that the role fulfilled by the palace was above all an economic one. The activities managed by the king and his corps of scribes and civil servants were related to production. The

Ebla: a model city-state

TELL MARDIKH, situated 60 kilometers south of the modern city of Aleppo, is the name given today to the site of the ancient city of Ebla. It offers an excellent picture of what a Syrian city-state was like in the third and second millennia before our era. Ebla might be said to serve as a model to which other Syrian city-states from the same period are to be compared.

Around 2400 BC, Ebla was the most important city of Inner Syria between the Euphrates and the Mediterranean. In it stood a royal palace that has provided us today with an extraordinary treasure of some 17 000 cuneiform tablets dealing with accounting, the economy, administration, law, diplomacy, rites, vocabulary and literature. The tablets belonged to the royal archives, which all great city-states had at the time. The relations that Ebla maintained with Egypt are confirmed by the presence of alabaster and diorite vases sent as gifts by the Egyptian pharaohs. Ebla was also in contact with other great Syrian cities, such as Mari (Tell Hariri), Tuttul (Tell Bi'a) and Nawar (Tell Brak). The city-state's outstanding importance is supported by both archaeological remains and epigraphic documents.

In the second phase of its history, Ebla was enlarged by 56 hectares and its lower town, which extended around the circular acropolis, was surrounded with a massive *pisé* rampart measuring 45 meters in width and 22 meters in height. Forts were built at various points along the wall, and it had a number of well-defended gates. The city's size and its defensive wall make it clear that Ebla was the most important political center in Syria at the time. Its exceptional status is confirmed by the presence of a whole series of impressive public buildings. There was one royal palace on the acropolis; another, called the northern palace, was the residence of the crown prince and was built above the royal necropolis. A temple on the acrop-

olis was sacred to the goddess Ishtar, while temples to the gods Shamash and Resheph stood in the lower town. The sacred area of Ishtar was also found in the lower town; it consisted of a temple and an impressive cult terrace where the sacred lions of the goddess were kept. It is evident that the temples and palaces represented two major poles in the sociopolitical organization of the time.

Ebla was destroyed in around 1600 BC and it ceased to be mentioned in written documents after 1200 BC. However, the entire city was preserved and remains accessible to archaeologists, since the surface of the site is occupied only by cultivated fields. Since 1964, the archaeological mission of the University of Rome "La Sapienza" has been involved in 35 excavation campaigns at Ebla under the direction of the author. But the site still holds many more secrets that will someday soon no doubt change the way we view the past.

PROF. DR. PAOLO MATTHIAE
Universita di Roma "La Sapienza"

Reconstruction of part of the palace of Ebla.

Aerial view of Tell Mardikh, ancient Ebla.

archaeologists who excavated Ebla think that the true locus of state power was in a group of rooms in the palace, which they have called the "administrative quarter." They comprise an inner courtyard with a small room to the north and a large room for holding audiences to the south. Excavations in the courtyard uncovered diorite and alabaster bowls imported from Egypt, small blocks of lapis lazuli from Afghanistan [203] and fragments of marble figurines that would have formed decorative friezes on furniture [39-42]. At the height of its political power, Ebla's sphere of cultural and commercial influence extended as far as Mesopotamia, Anatolia (present-day Turkey) and Egypt. The economy underpinning this influence was managed by the political power of the king and his dignitaries centered in the administrative quarter.

Like Mari, Ebla went up in flames in about 2300 BC when Sargon was expanding the short-lived empire he ruled from the capital city of Akkad in Mesopotamia. However, the Akkadian presence in Syria brought more than destruction. Naram-Sin, Sargon's grandson, built a palace on the site of Tell Brak on the plains of the Upper Habur in the northeast of present-day Syria so that he could follow developments more closely in this distant region of the Akkadian Empire.

THE AMORITE CITY-STATES:
CITIES OF NOMADS

Around 2000 BC, a new people established kingdoms of exceptional strength and power throughout Syrian territory, but particularly at Mari and Ebla. They were the Amorites, sometimes called the Hanaeans, which is another name for Bedouins. These were nomadic sheep-breeders who lived in northern Syria in a region called, in the cuneiform texts, Amurru.

Under the rule of Amorite dynasties, Mari once again, about 1800 BC, became an important city. As evidence of this development, a large new royal palace was built at the time, covering an area of two and a half hectares and comprising some 300 rooms or courtyards. The thickness of the clay-brick walls and their height — they still stand at four meters in places — indicate that the palace had an upper floor, which would have doubled the total number of rooms. The director of excavations at Mari also believes that terraces could have been built on the rooftops to provide havens of rest; they may have even been embellished with gardens. At the center of one of the two great courtyards stood a palm tree made of gold. This magnificent palace was unique at the time and was a perfect expression of the power wielded by the king of Mari.

The majesty of the site was further emphasized in the throne room, which held statues of the king's predecessors [1]. Its walls were painted with various scenes, including one in which divinities invest the king with royal qualities. Such propaganda art aptly expressed a very powerful form of authority; through the work of specialized craftsmen, it intended to proclaim divine protection of royal rights. As well, the palace contained a shrine in one of its corners and just outside it, on the east side of the palace, stood a complex of temples, including the lion temple [9], which was closely associated with royal power.

Additional evidence of the important role played by the government body based in the Mari palace comes from the 20 000 tablets discovered in its archives room. These documents may be grouped into two main categories — administrative texts and letters. Some dealt with daily life in the palace. For example, cer-

Drawing painted on a wall in the palace of Mari showing the king receiving royal attributes from a divinity.

tain texts were about the distribution of food rations to the specialized craftsmen who made instruments and jewelry [176] for the king and his court. Other texts show that letters were exchanged between the king and the governors of other cities in his kingdom concerning various developments and measures to be taken. Letters were sent as well to foreign sovereigns with a view to maintaining good relations with neighboring kingdoms, somewhat like diplomatic correspondence in an embryonic stage.

At Ebla, it was decided by some powerful political authority around 1950 BC that the city should be fortified with an impressive beaten earth rampart that was 45 meters thick at the base, 18 to 22 meters high and 2.5 kilometers long. It encompassed an area of 55 hectares. Four solidly constructed gates passed through it and fortresses were built on top of it and on its sloping sides. The decision to defend Ebla

with such an imposing wall underlines the military basis of royal power. At the time, a number of sumptuous palatial residences for the king and the members of his family stood in the city. Most of them were situated near temple complexes. One such temple was consecrated to the cult of royal ancestors and protected the royal necropolis, which contained the tombs of the king's family. Three of the tombs were particularly rich in jewels and other funeral goods — that of the "Lord of the Goats," for example, held an Egyptian ceremonial mace [15], costly jewelry [16, 18, 21 and 22] and fenestrated axes [169]. Such a concentration of riches used as grave goods to accompany a deceased king expressed a form of respect for royal authority. It is also an indication of the wealth that was accumulated by a social elite through commercial exchange and the labor of specialized craftsmen.

KINGDOMS ARE ESTABLISHED

The city-state of Mari was pillaged by the troops of King Hammurabi of Babylon in 1761 BC, when he integrated Syria into his empire. In order to standardize the application of justice in his vast empire, Hammurabi decreed his now-famous code of law. The city-state of Ebla was destroyed around 1600 BC by the Hittite king Mursili I, since it represented an obstacle to his political and commercial expansion towards the Levant and Mesopotamia. The destruction of these two major city-states by foreign powers in the middle of the second millennium BC was indirectly the outcome of a new development in the Near East during this period. Different groups, for whom we have names thanks to the written documents that were left by them from about this time on, began to constitute kingdoms that lasted for various lengths of time and covered territories of various sizes. This meant that fairly large areas of Syria belonged at one time or another to these different foreign kingdoms, ruled, for example, by the Assyrians or the Hittites. Elsewhere, the local populations grouped together and formed political entities (such as the Aramaeans and the Hurrians) as a counterbalance to the foreign occupation.

The Assyrians
and the city of Shubat Enlil

A little before 1800 BC, the Assyrians came down from the high plateaus of northern Mesopotamia and made Tell Leilan, in northeast Syria, their regional capital, giving it a name that honored one of their most important gods. They called it Shubat Enlil, or "the place where Enlil dwells." This is probably why they raised a magnificent temple on the highest point of the acropolis, decorating its thick mud-brick walls with columns sculpted directly into the surface. From the palace situated in the lower town the Assyrians ruled over part of the triangle-shaped territory formed by the many tributaries of the Habur River in this region.

Shubat Enlil was probably at the center of a state that derived its wealth from the crops grown by the Amorite populations who had moved to the surrounding plains, where dry-farming, that is, farming without irrigation, could be done. An archaeological survey has revealed an impressive number of villages — some 60 in all — dating from this period and located within a 15-kilometer radius of the city on which they must have depended. The Assyrian troops advanced as far south as Mari on the Euphrates in 1841 BC but did not destroy the city; instead, they placed an Assyrian governor on the throne there for a short period of time.

The Hurrians: horsemen of renown

Around 1500 BC, and perhaps even a little earlier, the same region of the Habur valley changed hands and became the center of the kingdom of Mitanni. It was populated mainly by Hurrians, whose presence in the area had been attested since the third millennium. The Assyrians, like many other groups, had to submit to their authority. The kingdom of Mitanni was actually a loosely knit union of different principalities ruled over by a king who essentially looked after the federation's foreign relations. The capital of this kingdom, Wassukanni, has not yet been found, but archaeologists have very recently identified some of its major cities: Urkish, discovered under the layers of Tell Mozan; and Nawar, found on the site of Tell Brak. The remains of palaces and temples attest to the significant presence of the Hurrians.

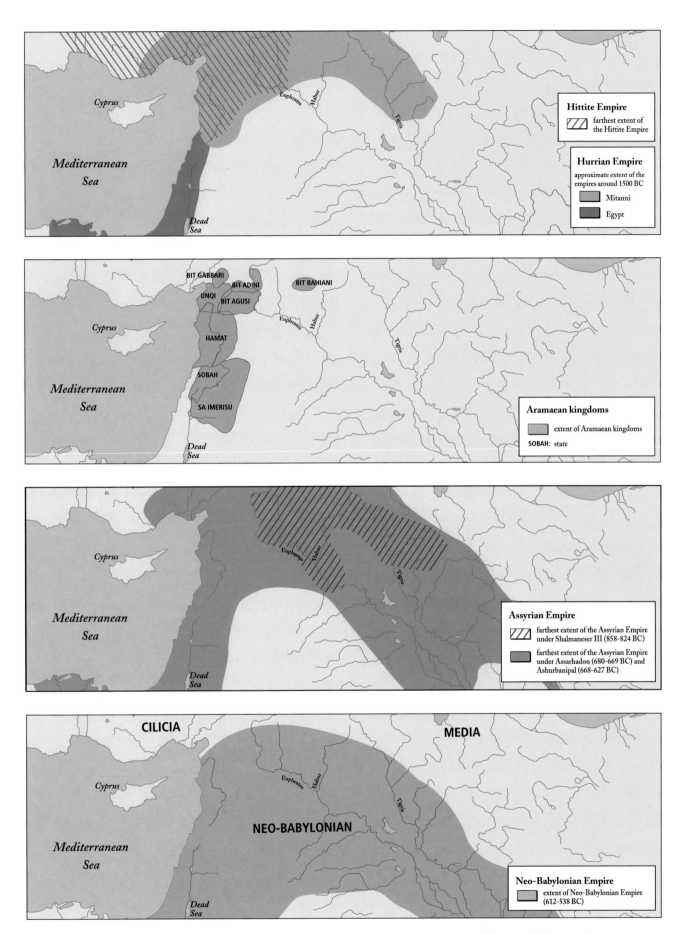

The kingdoms to which Syria belonged between about 1500 BC and 612 BC, when it became part of the Neo-Babylonian Empire

Tell Brak: A Mitanni city

THE MITANNI EMPIRE dominated North Syria from around 1550 BC until its collapse early in the thirteeth century BC. The people spoke Hurrian, but the names of their rulers and some of their gods were Indo-Aryan, which is related to Vedic Sanskrit. The actual origin of the names, however, remains obscure. The heartland of the Mitanni Empire lay along the upper reaches of the Habur River, where one of its cities, Tell Brak (ancient Nawar), has been excavated by a British expedition under the direction of Professor David Oates. At the height of Mitanni power in the fifteenth century BC, the Empire extended from the Mediterranean to the Zagros mountains.

The Tell Brak archaeologists found a palace and a temple from this period, together with residential neighborhoods that were inhabited right up until the end of the Bronze Age. Although the public buildings had been destroyed and burned by the Middle Assyrians early in the thirteenth century BC, the palace and the temple still contained broken remnants of their original fittings, as well evidence of the various craft activities that took place in the palace itself. These included the manufacture of glass objects, frit, faience and ivory, and the working of iron-rich copper. Indeed the Hurrians are believed to have invented the technique of core-moulding for the manufacture of glass bottles and beakers, examples of which were recovered from the palace.

The palace ground floor consisted of two very large reception rooms and some workrooms, while the residential rooms seem to have occupied an upper story. A limestone statue, the only surviving example of Hurrian sculpture, was found in one of the reception rooms along with a cuneiform tablet recording a legal case sworn in the presence of Tusratta, a Hurrian king well-known from the Egyptian Amarna letters. This tablet, and another dated from the reign of Tusratta's less known elder brother, were sealed with the dynastic seal of their ancestor Saustatar. The exact same seal had also been used at Nuzi.

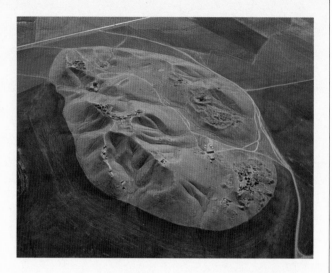

Aerial view of Tell Brak.

The pottery most characteristic of the Mitanni Empire is known as Nuzi ware, named for the site in eastern Iraq where it was first discovered. The designs are painted in white on a red or dark background. The residential district of Tell Brak has provided the first known evidence of the evolution of this very striking style from the painted Habur ware characteristic of the Middle Bronze Age. That style continued to be in use at least until the end of the fifteenth century AD.

The Mitanni are often equated with a "horse and chariot" aristocracy, but the evidence from Tell Brak and elsewhere shows that the fast spoke-wheeled chariot was in use in northern Syria long before the Hurrian presence. It was the discovery of a Hittite text on the training of horses, derived from a Mitanni source, that led scholars to think of the Hurrians first and foremost in terms of their horsemanship. Certainly, Mitanni military success owed much to their prowess not only in their use of chariots, but also of the composite bow, introduced about this time.

Prof. DRS. DAVID AND JOAN OATES
The McDonald Institute for Archaelogical Research (Cambridge, U.K.)

The Hurrian-language texts that have come down to us provide information about the kingdom's class system. There were at least three social classes among the Hurrians: the "laborers," who were peasants or prosperous craftsmen who could possess their own goods as well as having a community lot; "day workers," who owned little or no land; and "the exempt," who were specialized craftsmen, like wheelwrights, attached to the royal family. Above this social stratification came a military organization that included foot soldiers, archers and charioteers. The latter constituted a noble class, given the growing importance of chariots in the battles of this period. The Hurrians were famed for breeding and training horses. As well, they produced craftsmen of great talent; they are generally associated with copper work and glass making, using both powdered glass frit [180] and vitreous paste.

The Hittites: Anatolia and Egypt sign a peace treaty in Syria

The Hittites, an Anatolian people, took advantage of the decline of the Hurrians around 1380 BC and seized territory in the north of Syria. There they built new cities, including Emar, situated on the Euphrates. Its governor was responsible for surveying the valley from his palace, or *hilani*, perched on a man-made promontory overlooking the city.

Near the palace were four temples consecrated to local divinities, and living quarters comprising some 30 houses. A striking example of the archaeological material recovered from this site is provided by clay blocks moulded with the footprints of children [300 and 301]. The inscription written on these blocks tells us that the children were to be given to the temple priests when they were old enough to be educated and could serve the priests. The transaction was to pay a debt contracted by the children's father, who was too poor to honor it. It was common for debts to be settled like this at the time, since human life was considered to have a price. These children's fate was probably better than that of many others, as the priesthood enjoyed enviable social status and the children would have had a chance to become scribes — highly qualified work. Such training was often done in temples, at least in Emar, where a library was found.

The Hittites, a major power at that time, fought with the Egyptians for control over the Levant. In 1286 BC — the fifth year of the reign of Ramses II — the two kingdoms confronted each other in a battle on Syrian territory, at Qadesh in the Orontes valley. Neither side could claim victory. The conflict ended with a famous peace treaty, considered to be the oldest one of its kind in military and diplomatic history, which allowed both sides to withdraw without losing face.

Model reconstruction of the residential quarter in the Hittite city of Emar.

Next page:
Qadesh, in the Orontes Valley, where the Egyptian and Hittite armies clashed in 1286 BC.

Ugarit, a kingdom of Mediterranean commerce

While the Hittites' sphere of influence was restricted to Syria's interior regions, Egyptian interests were centered on the Mediterranean coast, where they maintained commercial relations with people living in port cities. At this time, the largest of these cities was Ugarit. It had been founded long before, but in the later half of the second millennium BC, it experienced great prosperity based on its maritime trade. Apart from a few objects brought from Egypt or made in an Egyptian style [210], there is nothing in the material culture of Ugarit to suggest that Egypt had a great deal of influence on city life. Ugarit retained its own character and independence. The city's division into neighborhoods indicates urban planning. It was surrounded by a great rampart pierced by an unusual postern, whose main gate faced the sea and was protected by a fortress. The royal palace contained a spacious throne room, residences for the royal family, living quarters, temples and carefully built tombs that held exquisite jewelry. But the community's most remarkable contribution was to perfect a new writing system using alphabetic cuneiform [253]. This system is known by the name of the language for which it was first used: Ugaritic. As well as administrative texts of all sorts and the usual letters received by the king of Ugarit as part of diplomatic relations, several tablets record mythological tales, sometimes at great length. These writings have enabled us to have a fairly good idea of the beliefs held by the inhabitants of Ugarit at this time.

However, about 1200 BC there was a great upheaval. Populations, who have been given the generic name of "Sea Peoples" for lack of agreement on the exact identification of the groups involved, started to migrate in vast numbers. Coming from southeast Europe, these populations passed through Anatolia and descended the Levantine coast, stopping only when they reached the frontiers of Egypt. In their wake, they left in ruins a number of urban centers, including some on the Syrian coast and in the Syrian interior.

Aerial view of Ugarit on the coastal plain.

THE NEO-HITTITE KINGDOMS SEEK THE PROTECTION OF THE GODDESS ISHTAR

While the "Sea Peoples" caused the Hittite Empire to fall as a political system, the Hittites themselves survived the devastation and grouped together in small independent kingdoms in western Anatolia and northern Syria. They reoccupied certain cities and made them the capitals of these new kingdoms. One such city was Ain Dara, which lay northwest of Aleppo. Here, a great temple was constructed with huge blocks of skillfully cut basalt. It stood atop the 30-meter

Ain Dara, in the heart of a Neo-Hittite kingdom in northern Syria.

lite cities and little villages that supplied the urban population with food. Their borders fluctuated with the political vicissitudes of the times, sometimes making way for other peoples from within the Syrian territory.

THE ARAMAEANS, A DIVERSIFIED PEOPLE

A little before 1000 BC, tribes of nomadic Bedouins who had been living in Mesopotamia since 2300 BC could be found in a dozen settled kingdoms with diversified populations on the western and northern plains of Syria. These people were called the Aramaeans because they lived in the "country of Aram," according to some texts that have come down to us. The tribes were led by chieftains, who were somewhat like hereditary sheikhs, surrounded by an aristocracy based on lineage. The rest of the members of the tribes were, at first, on an equal footing. However, a hierarchy eventually developed, the classes consisting of large landowners, craftsmen, farm workers and slaves.

Families, ruled over by a patriarch, were small (four or five members) because of high infant mortality. Women's tasks included preparing meals and caring for children, but they were also responsible for producing

acropolis, which overlooked a lower town that covered 59 hectares. The temple was dedicated to the warrior goddess Ishtar. Protectress of this mountainous region, her lover was the God of the Mountain. Several of the great blocks of basalt were finely sculpted with decorative motifs like the heads of lions and sphinxes. To symbolize divine protection, the main entrance was flanked by carved lions, animals which are often associated with Ishtar. Human representation, however, was fairly rare [56].

The situation was not very stable for these small states, which consisted of a capital surrounded by a few autonomous satel-

cloth. In the Aramaean army, soldiers were armed with bows and arrows, and were known for their use of cavalry and chariots [52]. However, the Aramaeans often avoided pitched battles by falling back to their well-defended citadels, where the attacking army, normally Assyrian, had no choice but to lay siege.

The capital of one of the Aramaean kingdoms was Guzana, a city near the source of the Habur River on the present-day site of Tell Halaf. In it stood a palace with an impressive facade, held up by enormous columns in the shape of animals and human beings. Along the base of its walls were 178 blocks of basalt carved with hunting or battle scenes showing Aramaeans represented in profile. Similar bas-relief carv-

ings have been discovered very recently at the base of the walls of a temple excavated on top of the citadel of Aleppo.

An Aramaean city called Burmarina, which was mentioned in the military annals of an Assyrian king because it had resisted him for so long, has just been identified on a site excavated by archaeologists on the banks of the Euphrates. Its identification was made possible by the discovery of clay tablets on which the name of the city was written. One of these tablets, which recorded a money-lending contract, is the longest document in Assyrian Aramaic discovered to date [249]. The Aramaeans eventually disappeared as a political entity, but Aramaic was to become the international language of the Near East, especially for commercial transactions and

Facade of the National Museum at Aleppo, with a reconstruction of the entrance to the Aramaean palace of Guzana.

New discoveries
at the citadel of Aleppo

Aerial view of the citadel of Aleppo.

SINCE THE AUTUMN OF 1996, a Syrian-German team of archaeologists has been conducting excavations on top of the citadel of Aleppo, ancient Halab. The mission has set itself two main objectives:

- To collect archaeological evidence about the early second century BC, a period during which Halab was the political center of the kingdom of Yamhad. After the destruction of Mari by King Hammurabi in 1761 BC, Halab began to play an important role in northern Syria and continued to do so until the Hittite king Mursili I captured it around 1600 BC.

- To discover the city's main temple, which was sacred to the storm god and is mentioned in texts as early as 2500 BC. Our working hypothesis was that the temple and palace buildings stood on the highest point of the citadel hill, which today rises to 60 meters and covers an area measuring 280 meters by 160 meters. The central city would have spread out around the summit of a natural promontory that offered protection from floods along the Kuwaik River and a view of the surrounding region. The place-name "Halab" refers to this geographical situation.

Previous to the arrival of the Syrian-German team, only one test excavation had been carried out on the citadel. Between 1929 and 1932, George Ploix de Rotrou had found a basalt relief sculpture representing two winged genies, along with a crescent moon and a solar disk. In was in this area that we began excavations.

During the first excavation campaign, an orthostat building — that is, with large stones set on one of their shorter ends — was discovered. Its exceptional size leads us to believe that it was a temple. Its total width is estimated to be 28 meters, while its length is still unknown. The building was constructed at the time of the Yamhad kingdom, but it was modified at the beginning of the first millennium BC and furnished with a dais wall embellished with relief sculptures. This wall has been cleared along 10.9 meters, and it is expected that nine to ten meters remain to be excavated. Its relief decoration represents divinities, in particular the storm god, shown as a human in a chariot drawn by a bull, as well as two oxen on either side of a tree of life, a lion and a fabulous mythological figure.

The central figures are clearly in the Hittite tradition; in fact, two of them bear inscriptions confirming that this is the case. The others, notably the lion and the bird-headed figure, belong to the Assyrian tradition. These relief sculptures reflect the cultural symbiosis that existed between the Hittites and Aramaeans at the beginning of the first millennium BC in northern Syria.

WHALID KHAYYATA
Director of Antiquities in the Aleppo Region
PROF. DR. KAY KOHLMEYER
Fachhochschule für Technik und Wirtschaft (Berlin)

The storm god in a chariot.

Mythological figures.

diplomatic relations. As the most widely spoken language in the Near East, it was also the tongue in which Christ preached and in which the books that comprise the Old Testament were initially written.

Another discovery has provided the oldest Aramaic inscription to date and the first Assyrian-Aramaic bilingual text. It was found on a life-size statue of a certain Hadad-yisi, uncovered near Guzana at Tell Fekheryah. From a historical point of view, it is interesting to note that in this inscription, Hahad-yisi gave himself the title of king in the Aramaic text, which was intended for his subjects. But in the part that would be read by the Assyrians, however, he presented himself simply as a governor! His ruse is a good indication of the ambiguous political loyalty of certain cities and regions at this time.

THE NEO-ASSYRIANS, EMPIRE-BUILDERS

While the Aramaeans were becoming politically and socially organized by establishing small independent kingdoms, the Assyrian kings sought a foothold in the north of Syria from which they could better defend themselves against attacks coming from this area [58]. Consequently, in 856 BC, King Shalmaneser III took Til Barsib, a city belonging to the Aramaeans, or, according to some, to the Hittites, so that the Assyrians would have a place where they could cross the Euphrates and therefore be able to carry out raids in the rest of the Syrian territory beyond the river. The city was renamed Kar-Shalmaneser ("Port Shalmaneser") in honor of its conqueror.

Shortly after this conquest, the Assyrians built a palace whose walls are decorated with painted murals testifying to the presence of Assyrian dignitaries in the city [57]. Further to the east, Hadatu (present-day Arslan Tash), another Aramaean city, was captured by the Assyrians and a new palace was built there as well. Its excavation has revealed many decorative pieces of ivory [53 and 54] that had once been part of inlay work embellishing the furniture taken as war booty from the Aramaean princes. In the Near East, Aramaeans were considered to be masters of the very specialized art of working ivory. Being very rare and used only for inlay work, ivory was a luxury material that was highly prized by the political and economic elite.

The Assyrians' rule over Syrian territory was not solely political and coercive. It also brought certain changes that contributed to the welfare of the local population. In the lower valley of the Habur, in a region quite

Assyrian dignitaries presenting themselves to the king, in a frieze painted on the walls of the Assyrian palace of Til Barsib, the site of present-day Tell Ahmar.

Dur Katlimmu, the Assyrian capital, on the banks of the Habur.

close to the Assyrian Empire, the new rulers transformed a city called Dur Katlimmu, corresponding to the present-day tell of Sheikh Hamad. They enlarged it and gave it a four-kilometer-long defensive wall so that they could use it as an administrative and economic center, which would include a palace and dignitaries' residences. To feed the 7000 people living in a city spread over 55 hectares, they carried out an innovative plan, creating an irrigation system along both sides of the Habur. To do so required knowledge of

sophisticated techniques. This development showed, for example, that they knew how to exploit the natural slope of the land over long distances and how to bypass obstacles.

In 745 BC, the Assyrians completed their conquest of Syria and thoroughly subdued the Aramaean kingdoms, going so far as to deport some local populations to Assyria. Those in the region of Hama, which had been the capital of an important kingdom, were especially affected. The whole Syrian territory was divided into 20 provinces, each

The Assyrian presence in northeast Syria

IN THE EIGHTEENTH CENTURY before our era, when Babylonian troops led by King Hammurabi conquered southern Mesopotamia, the Assyrian king, Shamshi-Adad, expanded his empire westward into northern Syria. During his reign, he made Shubat Enlil (Tell Leilan) the new seat of royal power in this region.

In the course of the next four centuries, the Assyrians lost control of northern Syria and were dominated first by the Babylonian Empire and then by the Hurrian Empire (the Mitanni kingdom). However, in the second half of the fourteenth century BC, the Assyrian kings won back their independence and the Middle-Assyrian Empire arose. It ruled over the eastern part of the Jezireh, the region of northeast Syria between the Tigris and Euphrates rivers. With the return of the Assyrians, the whole region was reorganized politically and economically. The political center of the new Assyrian province was the city of Dur Katlimmu (Tell Sheikh Hamad), in the lower region of the Habur valley. In a monumental building standing on the western slope of the Dur Katlimmu citadel, an archives room was found containing over 550 cuneiform texts. The texts confirm that Dur Katlimmu was a regional administrative center at the time. The city authorities were responsible for the distribution of farmland and played an important role in the development of commercial transportation.

In the following centuries, the Assyrian Empire again underwent difficulties, but in the ninth century BC, it attained new heights. In this period, the main administrative centers in the Jezireh were Shadikanni (Tell Ajajah) and Dur Katlimmu, which once more became a great city. Archaeological excavations on both sites have provided information that makes it possible to reconstruct in detail the way the cities were organized and the roles they played. At Shadikanni, the remains of a palace complex were brought to light. Part of the palace consisted of a long hall entered by a doorway decorated with sculptures of winged bulls with human heads (Lamassu). The hall would have been used for receptions. Three stelae were found outside the hall in what was probably a courtyard. The first one represents a winged genie under the symbols of the gods Shamash, Sin, Sibittum and Ishtar. The second shows a winged bull in front of a stylized palm tree. On the third is a genie carrying a goat. The style of both the architecture and the relief decorations was strongly influenced by that of other palaces in Neo-Assyrian capitals.

During the eighth century BC, Dur Katlimmu tripled in size. The city had a citadel and a lower town, both of which were surrounded by a four-kilometer-long rampart. A palace stood in the northeast corner of the lower town, while several noble residences occupied the central area. The residences had large inner courtyards with floors paved with stone, plastered walls and frescoes painted on the interior walls of great reception rooms. The peasants who lived around the city were able to use a system of irrigation canals that made it possible to farm land that was far away from the river. In the city itself, the houses were equipped with drains to eliminate wastewater.

ASSAD MAHMOUD
Director of Antiquities and the Deir Ez Zor Museum

ruled by a governor of Assyrian origin, aided in his task by a body of administrators.

Since explicit texts on the subject are lacking, it is difficult to say how the Aramaeans adapted to this subjugation. They were no doubt occupied with the job of daily survival but were also called upon to work as specialized craftsmen in the service of the new rulers. However, in the regions from which people had been deported, it is easy to imagine how unstable the climate must have been. To add to the insult, the Assyrian kings replaced the deported populations with Assyrians. At the same time, not all the people living in the Syrian territory were subjected to Assyrian rule. Nomadic peoples were probably little affected, since their activities kept them far from the cities. However, they must have felt the Assyrians' influence eventually,

since it was the Assyrians who first used camels to travel in caravans across the desert.

THE ARABS AND NOMADIC LIFE

The Assyrian kings occasionally had to fight off "Arab" tribes, as they were called in the writings of this period. As far as can be made out, the people referred to in the texts as Arabs were traders who raised camels and cattle, living in the Hauran region and in southern Syria. At that time, the term "Arab" referred to a nomadic lifestyle; the word was introduced by the peasants and city-dwellers to identify a way of life that contrasted with their own. Apart from the fact that these people are mentioned for the first time in the documents of the time, almost nothing is known about them in this early period. Their role in the history of Syria is better documented in later periods.

A Bedouin camel-raiser and his herd traveling across the semi-arid steppe in Syria.

SYRIA BECOMES PART
OF THE GREAT EMPIRES

THE PERSIAN EMPIRE AND THE USE
OF ARAMAIC AS THE OFFICIAL LANGUAGE
In 612 BC, Syria was integrated into an empire that had just been formed in Babylonia
by the father of Nebuchadnezzer II; however, this essentially political and administrative operation left no trace whatsoever in the
material culture.

Then, in 538 BC, the Achaemenid Persians arrived from what is now Iran, over-
came Syria peacefully and made it a satrapy
of their immense empire. This satrapy was
called Aber Nahr, which in Aramaic meant
"beyond the river" (the Euphrates), and
Damascus became its capital. The Persians
wanted access to the Mediterranean and appreciated Syria's geographic situation, as
well as its forests and coasts. They therefore
treated the local Syrian dynasties as allies

rather than as vassals. The Persians' toler-
ance, although motivated by commercial
interests and strategy, meant that Syria enjoyed considerable autonomy. On the other
hand, small kingdoms sprang up, so that the
territory was politically splintered. The great
cities of Syria continued their commercial
activities uninterrupted, establishing colo-
nies along the Mediterranean coast. The
Persians constructed roads, which became
the backbone of the postal service they set
up to ensure communication between the
heart of their empire and the Syrian coast.
As well, they fortified the coastal cities and
defended them with a navy of 300 warships.
One of these ports was 'Amrit, called Marathus at the time; here, impressive tower
tombs were built, a sign that the local population enjoyed a certain prosperity. In the
coastal cities, people continued to use the
Canaanite language, but everywhere else in
Syria, Aramaic soon became the language

Sanctuary in the
port city of
Marathus, the site
of present-day
Amrit.

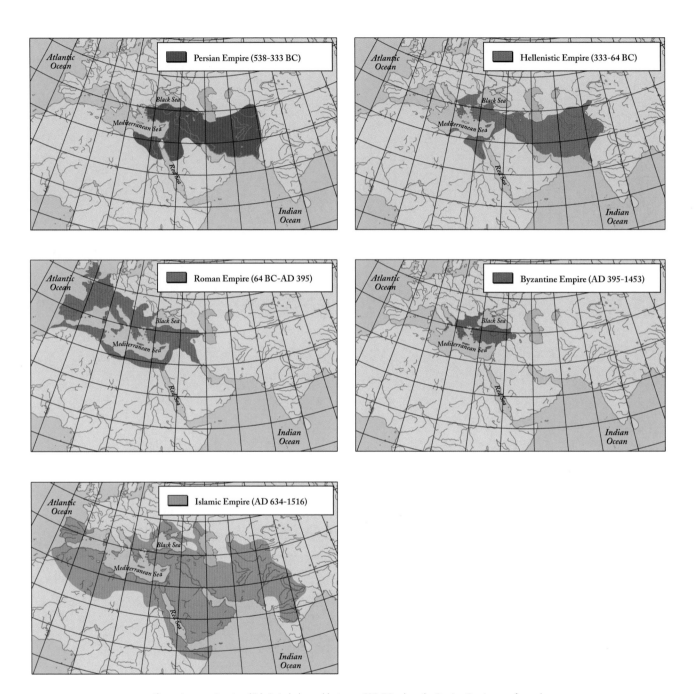

The various empires to which Syria belonged between 538 BC, when the Persian Empire was formed,
and AD 1516, when it became part of the Ottoman Empire

spoken. It even was adopted as the official language of the Persian administration in the eastern provinces, where documents in Persian were translated and retranscribed. Hebrew, a dialect of Canaanite, was also in use. As for the Arab dialect, it was spoken by a good part of the population of the desert regions of Syria, but there was not yet a writing system for it.

Alexander the Great and his successors: the influence of Greek culture in Syria

In 333 BC, Alexander the Great defeated the Persian armies. His death in 323 BC was followed by a violent struggle for power among his generals, which ended in 312 BC, with Syria in the hands of Seleucus I, named the "Victorious" (Nicator). He made Syria the heart of his empire, which stretched from the Mediterranean to India, and established Antioch-on-Orontes as its capital. The name "Syria," whose etymology remains uncertain, seems to have begun to be used in the Hellenistic period to designate a territory corresponding more or less to modern-day Syria. Around 300 BC, Seleucus founded a number of new cities to control the trade route that went along the Euphrates and then entered the Orontes valley to reach Antioch and the shores of the Mediterranean. In fulfilling this role, these cities — for example, Apamea in the valley of the Orontes and Dura-Europos on the banks of the Euphrates — grew rich and became richer still during the following period.

The Seleucids — the descendants of Seleucus — were obliged to defend the southern part of Syria and the Mediterranean ports against the repeated attacks of the Lagids of Egypt, who wished to extend their power. Thanks in part to advice given by Hannibal, the Carthaginian general who had sought refuge in Syria, a Seleucid king won a great victory. But even more credit for the victory is due to the use of elephants trained for war. His

The great colonnaded street at Apamea.

successors had less luck in battles in the eastern regions with the Parthians, who were daunting semi-nomadic horsemen and archers from northern Iran, southwest of the Caspian Sea. In 250 BC, they began to take over the eastern provinces of the Seleucid Empire and, in 113 BC, they occupied the frontier city of Dura-Europos.

The small local Arab principalities took advantage of the disruption caused by these foreign problems by declaring their independence and thus initiating the political disintegration of the Seleucid Empire, which, in any case, was in the throws of a struggle for succession. The Hellenistic dynasties had played a limited role in Syria. The Greek language never managed to supplant Aramaic, and Arabic was becoming the language of southern Syria and the eastern steppe.

UNDER THE ROMAN EMPIRE:
THE ORONTES FLOWS INTO THE TIBER
The final blow to the Seleucid Empire came from the west. The Romans had seen their sea trade threatened by the appearance of pirates in the eastern Mediterranean, a result of the political anarchy that reigned in the Seleucid Empire. In 64 BC, they sent their armed forces to subdue the pirates and from there, under the leadership of General Pompey, went on to occupy Syria. Pompey made Syria a province of the Roman Empire, although for the time being this did not affect the Nabataean kingdom [67] to the south of Damascus. It would join the empire only later. During 400 years of Roman rule, the province was administered by a succession of some 100 governors. One of the first was the wealthy Crassus, who was persuaded by the lure of rich booty to engage the Parthians in a war, which led to his

death in 53 BC. The Parthians continued to incite local potentates to revolt against the Roman presence, which created a climate of instability in Syria. It was only in AD 68, when Vespasian was declared emperor by the legionaries posted in Syria itself, that the region began at last to enjoy an enduring peace that allowed the province to become Romanized and enter the empire's economic and social sphere.

The Roman presence [63] was soon felt as numerous bridges, new roads and public buildings were constructed, irrigation projects carried out, entire regions surveyed, and tracts of land cleared in sparsely populated areas. Unlike the rest of the Empire, Syria was not organized in a way that gave cities dominion over the countryside, even though they controlled vast areas of the land surrounding them. On the contrary, the cities' purpose was to support the inhabitants of scattered farms in numerous small villages. The cities were not independent social and economic centers as they had been before. Although some, like Palmyra, for example, grew through commerce, this was never at the expense of their primary role. Even urban social organization was affected by the structure of indigenous tribes, as is reflected in the appearance of a great variety of temples in the cities.

Between the first and fourth centuries of our era, Romanized Syria experienced considerable demographic growth in the countryside. The villages where the peasants lived varied in size, but such differences cannot be related to any particular hierarchical organization. Within the villages themselves, the houses seem to have been laid out without any planning; there are no streets or public squares, but only uneven empty spaces between the houses. Each house corresponded to a social unit, the family, and to an economic unit, a piece of land or farm. Society was thus essentially agrarian. Some of the villages were surrounded by a wall, no doubt as a defence against attacks by nomads. For there were herders — erroneously termed the "Safaitics" — in the basaltic desert in the south of Syria. Evidence of their presence has come down to us in the form of graffiti and drawings engraved on large stones [221].

The craftsmen in these villages enjoyed considerable social importance and were or-ganized in guilds. Their handiwork, typical of Roman Syria, include blown glass [190]; purple-dyed cloth [354]; textiles, like those discovered in the tombs of Palmyra and Dura-Europos; pottery, bronze and stone sculptures, like the funeral stelae of Palmyra [332 to 337]; and masterworks in precious metals.

In AD 106, the Emperor Trajan took over the Nabataean kingdom, part of which lay in southern Syria, and made it into a Roman province, giving it the name of Arabia. Two of its major cities were Suweida and Bosra, its capital.

Bosra's famous theatre is still used today for cultural events.

New information
about Roman Suweida

SINCE 1997, the Directorate General of Antiquities and Museums in Syria has worked with French and German teams on an archaeological research project in the city of Suweida, which lies about 100 kilometers south of Damascus. The project began with a study of archival documents containing descriptions, drawings and photographs left by travelers who visited the city and its monuments in the nineteenth century.

The project continued in the field with a systematic survey to list, photograph and draw the archaeological remains that are visible on the surface, including the stones with architectural decorations or inscriptions in Greek, Latin and Nabataean that are preserved inside present-day houses. A detailed record was made of each monument, whether it had been known for a long time, recently discovered or hidden in the basement of a modern house. This information was transferred onto a computerized topographic map, which makes it possible to find the precise location of any monument and understand the way various structures are related within the city.

In the final stage of the project, archaeological excavations were carried out in certain monuments. On the basis of the initial results, it seems likely that the city had existed from the Bronze Age to the Hellenistic period, but that it reached its full development in the Roman Empire. During this time, the city was renamed Dionysias in honor of the great god Dushara, who was associated with the Greek and Byzantine Dionysus. A neighborhood was built, which included a number of Roman monuments. One of these buildings was a nymphaeum with a dedication inscribed on its facade, stating that it was constructed under the governorship of Cornelius Palma, the first Syrian legate (106-109) at the time of the Emperor Trajan. It was destroyed in 1860.

Other buildings of note are an odeum with a diameter of 24 meters, a theatre with a diameter of 96 meters, and churches, including a great basilica (the cathedral) dating from the sixth century and measuring 69 meters by 48 meters. The odeum and the arch of a fifth-century church (the Mashnaqa) were the object of excavations and test pits, which shed light on their roles. The odeum was probably not used for musical performances, as the name would suggest, but rather a hall in which the city council met. The arch, which is well known to the inhabitants of Suweida and was previously thought to be one of the city gates, was revealed to be actually the sole surviving vestige of a church that was destroyed.

Carrying out a survey is not a simple enterprise in an urban environment, but this project was successful, thanks to the cooperation of the city's inhabitants, the support of the Syrian Directorate General of Antiquities and Museums and the contribution of different international teams.

HASSAN HATOUM
Director of Antiquities and of
the Museum of Suweida

The arch of a fifth-century church in Suweida.

A little later, the Emperor Marcus Aurelius (162-180) extended the province of Syria by incorporating the Jezireh, a territory lying beyond the Euphrates and considered until then to represent the eastern frontier of the Empire. Under the emperors of the Severian dynasty (193-235), the country enjoyed a period of exceptional prosperity, reflected in the architectural renovation of most large cities. During this period as well, in 212, the constitution of Caracalla bestowed Roman citizenship on all free inhabitants of the Empire. Following the assassination of Caracalla, three Roman emperors came from Syria itself. Their names were Elegabalus (218-222), Alexander Severus (222-235) and Philip the Arab (244-249). The Emperor Philip organized spectacular festivities to mark the 1000th anniversary of Rome's founding and transformed his native city, Shahba, into a typical Roman city and renamed it Philip-

popolis. Syrians were no longer simply a conquered people living in a subjugated province. In one of his satires, the Roman poet Juvenal wrote that the Orontes flowed into the Tiber, referring to the enormous influence of Syria in Rome. For example, at the time, all the Roman senators of Near Eastern origin were Syrian.

During this time, however, the Sassanids, a dynasty that succeeded the Parthians in Iran, began to make raids against Syria, unintimidated by the Roman army. Palmyra, an oasis-city and a stopping place for caravans, was particularly affected by this threat to trade routes from the east, and its king, Odainat [64], eventually managed to push the raiders back. He twice — in 262 and 267 — pursued them right up to the gates of Ctesiphon, their capital in Iran, a bold initiative that won recognition from Rome. His brilliant wife, Queen Zenobia [65], succeeded him and

The ruins of Palmyra, the caravan city where Queen Zenobia reigned for a time.

through shrewd strategy took over a kingdom that extended from Anatolia to Egypt and the northern Arabian peninsula. However, her territorial and political claims prompted the Emperor Aurelian to set off with an army to safeguard the territorial integrity of the Eastern Roman Empire. Queen Zenobia was captured following the siege of her city in 272.

In the reign of the Emperor Diocletian (284-305), the eastern frontier of the Roman Empire was reorganized and a peace treaty was signed with the Sassanids in 297. It was vital that commercial relations with distant Asian countries providing the Empire with silks and spices should not remain troubled. To better integrate Syria with the Empire, Diocletian increased the number of administrative districts, and thus the number of civil servants, while raising the taxes paid by citizens. As a result, new administrative careers opened up for the Syrian elite.

In 313, the Emperor Constantine granted freedom of religion to all the citizens of the Roman Empire. Then, during the reign of Theodosius (379-395), the last emperor to rule over an undivided empire, Christianity was declared the state religion. When he died, the Roman Empire was separated into two parts: the Western Roman Empire and the Eastern Roman Empire, which would soon be known as the Byzantine Empire.

The Byzantine Empire: built on religious quarrels

With the division of the Roman Empire in AD 395, Syria became part of the eastern empire. Its capital, Constantinople, built by the Romans on the site of the Greek city of Byzantium, had already been declared the capital of the whole former Empire in 330 by Constantine I, the Great. Battered by bar-

barian invasions, the Western Empire fell in 476, and Europe entered the Middle Ages. The Byzantine Empire, however, would survive for another thousand years, falling only in 1453, when Constantinople was taken by the Ottomans, who renamed it Istanbul and made it the capital of their new empire.

The Eastern Empire had some 50 provinces distributed among five dioceses, each of which was directed by a bishop. This empire suffered great epidemics and violent earthquakes, but it was weakened above all by religious quarrels, or heresies, some of which led to bloodshed. The Christians of Asia held beliefs that were judged to be heretical by the Patriarch of Constantinople. These beliefs, in fact, reflected the social opposition of regional Eastern forces to the centralizing Greco-Latin government and were therefore viewed as a threat to the political cohesion of the Empire.

With the triumph of Christianity in Syria, it was not only the bishops' spiritual power that grew, but also their political and social power. Monks became increasingly numerous and respected, and had a strong influence on the people. For example, they promoted Syriac culture and preferred the Syriac language (a later form of Aramaic) to Greek, which was used by the imperial administration. Some of these monks were hermits, like St. Simeon Stylites (390-459), who lived atop a 15-meter column. He attracted crowds of pilgrims, who brought back souvenirs, called eulogias, from such pilgrimages [314]. Since St. Simeon had received such devotion throughout his life, a large sanctuary was built on the site soon after his death so that pilgrimages might continue. Other buildings were erected nearby, including a baptistery and a majestic cross-shaped church that housed a relic of the Saint's column under its dome.

Before Christianity became the state religion, many martyrs gave their lives for their faith. The city of Rusafa, situated on the steppe between Palmyra and the Euphrates, is linked with the martyrdom of St. Sergius in about 300, following his refusal to abjure his Christian faith. From the fifth century on, this small military town underwent a remarkable transformation as veneration for the tomb of St. Sergius grew. Four monumental basilicas were constructed, along with several chapels and, of course, inns for lodging the pilgrims. The city was given the name of Sergiopolis. In the sixth century, the city's rectangular rampart — measuring two kilometers long and 15 meters high, and guarded by 50 towers — was renovated to improve its defences against repeated raids by the Persian Sassanids' army.

In Syria, this period was one of prosperity and demographic growth, as people settled in previously unoccupied land. The population consisted mainly of peasants who were fairly well-off and free of state oppression. There were many populous cities; one of these was Apamea, with more than 100 000 inhabitants; another was the capital, Antioch. Some of the city-dwellers were professional workers belonging to well-defined organizations that provided public services. Basic necessities were available as well as luxury products. As well, there were all kinds of craftsmen who were regulated by a sort of professional code.

However, under the reign of Justinian (527-565) and his immediate successors, Syria was troubled by a number of wars with the Sassanids. These Persian-Syrian wars grew more intense between 611 and 639, when the Sassanids began an occupation of Syria.

The city of Rusafa, surrounded by the wall that protected it in its days of glory when it was known as Sergiopolis.

THE ISLAMIC ARAB EMPIRE:

AN EMPIRE CENTERED ON RELIGION

In 634, two years after the death of the Prophet Muhammad, Arab tribes started to attack Byzantine Syria. Certain Arab tribes were already living in Syria and had done so for some while; at the time, however, they were Christians. The country offered only weak resistance and, in certain regions, the newcomers were even given a warm welcome! Damascus fell in 635 and the Muslims settled there permanently. The Syrian Arabs converted to Islam in great numbers without any real force being used by the conquerors.

Syria was divided into four regions (*jund*), over which the governor of Damascus had military and administrative control. As of 647, these governors came from the Umayyad branch of the Arab tribes, named after the Prophet's grandfather. This branch was therefore related to that of the Prophet himself, and one of its members usually occupied the position of caliph of the Empire. In 660, the governor of Damascus succeeded in being named caliph, and the following year, the city became the capital of the Umayyad Empire (661-750). This empire controlled a territory that extended westward to the Maghreb, the Spanish peninsula and present-day southern France, eastward to the borders of India and China, northward to the mouth of the Volga and southward to the cataract of the Aswân River in Egypt. Military governors ruled the provinces of this empire, aided by tax managers and supported by the local population.

While the countryside had been quite independent in the Byzantine period, it now was economically and socially dominated by the cities and controlled by the military. For the purposes of standardization in this vast empire, Arabic was made the official language for documents drawn up by any administrative bureau. (These were called *dîwân* in Arabic, a term that has given us the word "divan," since the administrative bureaus, council rooms and reception rooms were furnished with cushion-covered benches.) As well, existing tax registers were translated from Greek and Persian into Arabic. The homogeneity of the far-flung empire was shaped not only by Arabicization, but also by the practice of a single religion, Islam; it was first an Arab, and then an Islamic, empire. The new administrative system was soon reflected in architecture. Mosques sprung up, representing the seat of religious power and a place where people could gather and worship, and richly decorated palaces were built for the new elite to live in, embodying the new esthetic values of the ruling class.

The Umayyad dynasty was soon contested and, in 750, power passed into the hands of a new dynasty, that of the Abbasids — named for one of the Prophet's uncles, Abbas. They established themselves in Iraq and ruled the empire from the new capital, Baghdad, which they founded there in 762. Damascus thus became a former capital and fell out of favor with the new dynasty. Central and southern Syria were neglected by Baghdad. Northern Syria alone received some attention, especially during the reign of caliph Harun al-Rashid (766-809), the famous hero of several stories in *The Arabian Nights* and a contemporary of Charlemagne. He moved his residence to Raqqa, on the Euphrates.

In 850, the Abbasid dynasty began to decline, and parts of Syria were dominated by a series of other Arab dynasties, including the Fatimids of Egypt, starting in 969, and the Turkomans and Seljuks from Asia Minor, starting in 1076. The Syrian territory became even more disjointed in 1097 with the arrival of the Crusaders, who established themselves in certain places considered strategic for their mission in the Holy Land. These Christian warriors, wearing a cross — the symbol of Christianity — sewn on their clothing or painted on their armor, had left Europe in 1096 with the intention of delivering Jerusalem from the Turks, who had conquered the Syrian-Palestinian corridor in the second half of the eleventh century. These invaders from Turkestan had made it

difficult for Christians to visit the Holy Land, so, in 1095, Pope Urban II called on the knights of Europe to wage a holy war.

At the beginning of the second millennium of our era, the whole of the Syrian territory was affected by a new system set up to pay mercenaries in the army. Large tracts of land were owned by a single military officer. The officer would be granted the property taxes paid by the peasants in a region so that he could use them to pay his soldiers' wages. These military landowners had little interest in their property, and as a result the land was underused and the peasants sank into poverty. This marked the end of a free society based on small peasant farms and the establishment of a society based on the power of large landholdings.

Agricultural products were sold in the city, in markets near the *sûq*, which was a street or series of streets where craftsmen worked with a few salaried slaves in small workshops, with crafts of the same nature concentrated in the same area. Weavers,

Raqqa, the Abbasid capital built by Harun al-Rashid.

The Crusades as viewed by the Arabs

THE OPINION OF ARABS REGARDING the Crusades was strongly influenced by the impressions they had of the behavior of the first Crusaders. When the European soldiers suddenly appeared on the Antioch plain on October 20, 1097, the Arabs at first thought they were faced with an army from the Byzantine Empire. The Byzantine army was a determined, powerful enemy, and a threat to Islam, but relations between the Empire and the Arabs were marked by respect for customs that provided a certain normality. However, the Arabs were soon made aware of their error, for the behavior of the Crusaders was radically different than that of the Byzantines. To begin with, they were fanatical, inflexible and bloodthirsty; they massacred Muslim prisoners and harbored such hatred towards Islam that they attacked the very symbols of the Eastern religion. As well, after the capture of Ma'arat an-Nu'man, hunger drove some of the Crusaders to eat human flesh; they roasted children, before devouring them.

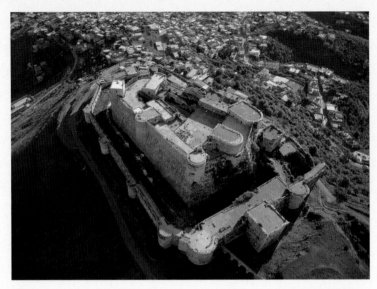

Crac des Chevaliers.

To be sure, not every Crusader engaged in such savage practices. The knights, who belonged to the aristocracy, generally attempted to protect their prisoners. However, the commoners who took part in the Crusades committed acts of great barbarity. Some of them, called Tafurs, fought with simple cudgels and used them to beat Muslims to death, believing that this would gain them entrance to Paradise.

The capture of Jerusalem in July 1099, was accompanied by the worst excesses. Even among the knights, few showed self-control and humanity. The Muslims were massacred, the city was systematically pillaged and the Muslim holy places were desecrated during two entire days. In the months that followed the seizure of a city, the Crusaders would expel the Muslims and force them into exile. Throughout the Islamic world and the Byzantine Empire, the behavior of the Crusaders caused indignation; at first, however, it led only to disorganized and fragmentary reactions that ended in failure.

The children born to the Franks who settled in the East grew up to be quite different from the Europeans, who scornfully referred to them as *poulains*, or "colts."

The members of this second generation showed more respect towards the Muslims and their customs and beliefs. And the Muslims, for their part, considered them to be different. They learned to admire the courage and military valor of the Franks but continued to disapprove of their fanaticism, insolence, ignorance and coarse manners. They ridiculed the Franks' primitive medical practices and, above all, they detested those whom they saw as brutal, perfidious invaders who did not keep their word. They particularly hated the knightly orders, the Templars and the Hospitallers. During the twelfth century, the Muslims were mobilized under Nûr al-Dîn and then under Salâh al-Dîn, who united Egypt, Syria, northern Iraq and Yemen under his command. In 1187, his troops won a decisive victory at Hattin and took over virtually all the territory held by the Franks. The Third Crusade (1187-1193) ended with Salâh al-Dîn allowing the Franks to live on a narrow strip along the Mediterranean, leaving them just enough of a foothold that they would not feel the need to start a new Crusade. However, at the end of the thirteenth century, the Mamluks, coming from Egypt, expelled the Franks once and for all.

DR. GEORGES TATE
Centre national de recherche scientifique (Paris)

goldsmiths and bankers tended to have shops close to the main mosque. There were no true professional corporations. The craftsmen might sell their goods directly to the public or through small shops run by merchants. These merchants also retailed goods from distant lands, obtained by large-scale traders and stored in government warehouses (*funduq*). A civil servant was appointed to see that public morality and administrative regulations were respected, and especially to ensure that weights and measures were exact.

Cities also had an administrative quarter where the administration's employees lived and worked, and at times a citadel and a military quarter. At the geographical heart of large cities stood a principal mosque, or *djâmi'*, where solemn Friday prayer took place, while smaller mosques, or *masdjid*, were found in various neighborhoods. The

city as an entity is closely associated with Muslim civilization, but curiously, it has no legal status in Muslim law. Cities grew up despite the absence of formal institutions. De facto hierarchies also developed. Important merchants and civil servants were at the top of this social pyramid, with soldiers forming a new aristocracy. Most of the cities in the Islamic era had been founded long before, but certain new cities were established during this period.

In 1153, a Turkish emir named Nûr al-Dîn (1146-1174) recaptured the city of Damascus; from there he attempted to reunite Syria and expel the Crusaders. His project was finally achieved by one of his generals, Salâh al-Dîn — known in the West as Saladin (1137-1193). He managed to unify Syria and Egypt in 1171, crush the Crusaders' army in 1187 (marking the end of the Second Crusade) and found a new dynasty,

Entrance to the citadel of Aleppo built by the famous Salâh al-Dîn (Saladin).

THE ORGANIZATION OF SOCIETY

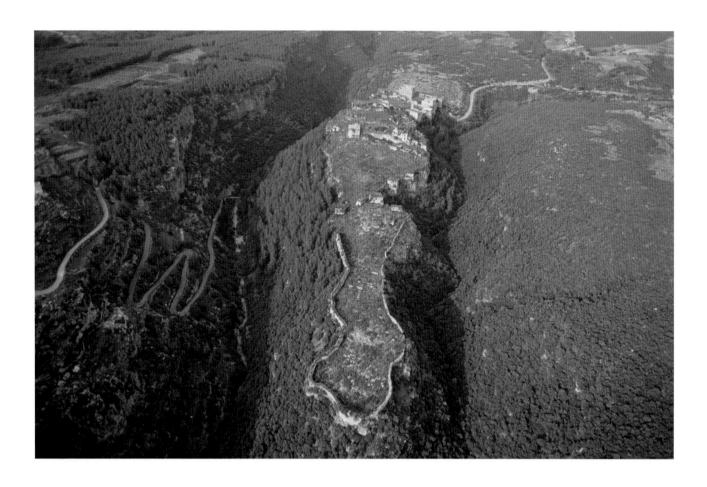

Qalat Salâh al-Dîn
(the fortress of
Saladin) built on
the heights of a
mountain chain
along the
Mediterranean
coast.

that of the Ayyubids. Salâh al-Dîn and his successors adopted a more neighborly policy towards the Christians. They were now free to go on pilgrimages to Jerusalem, just as were Muslims, for whom the city was also a holy place. The Ayyubid authorities built new cities and restored old ones, constructing citadels in a number of cities, such as Damascus and Aleppo. These citadels proved useful at the time of later Crusades, the last of which took place in 1291. For Syria, this was a golden age, a time of exceptional intellectual and artistic flowering.

In 1260, Syria was overrun by Turkish mercenaries coming from Egypt. They were known as Mamluks, from an Arabic word meaning "bought," since they were the children of slaves originally bought on the Black Sea market. These "Men of the Sabre" chased out the Mongols, who had just sacked the cities of Damascus and Aleppo. They also expelled the European knights for good around 1291, putting an end to the Crusades. From then on, the most deserving officers in this powerful army were each awarded a coat of arms — which in Arabic was referred to as a "color" — that displayed their personal crests. The Mamluks' economic policies encouraged the export of typical Syrian goods, such as glass, metalwork and silk goods, to Italy and Spain. Fond of pomp and luxury, they carried out major building projects. This was a period of great prosperity for Syrian craftsmen.

Around 1400, Syria was invaded by Tartar troops under Tamerlane and eventually was unable to withstand the pressure of Ottoman imperialism. In 1516, when the last Mamluk sultan was killed, Ottoman occupation of Syria began.

The Grand Baron Hotel in Aleppo

AT THE BEGINNING of this century, the Grand Baron Hotel was a pied-à-terre for Western archaeologists in Syria. T. E. Lawrence, who later became a legend under the pseudonym of Lawrence of Arabia, often stayed in this hotel in the year 1909 while he was doing research on the castles of the Crusades for his doctorate in archaeology. He returned here as well between 1911 and 1914 when he joined the British Museum's archaeological mission.

Twenty years later, the hotel was still a gathering place for archaeologists. Max Mallowan stayed there with his wife, the novelist Agatha Christie. Although she was an active member of the archaeological team, she never stopped writing mystery stories. On the contrary, she drew inspiration from her new environment. *Murder in Mesopotamia,* for example, is set in an archaeological excavation, and the book presents a colorful but accurate picture of the microcosm in which the members of an archaeological team live as they toil away in an isolated region, enduring quite Spartan living conditions. The novel's plot, which involves the murder of one team member by another, unfolds in true Agatha Christie style.

Modern-day view of the famous Grand Baron Hotel in Aleppo.

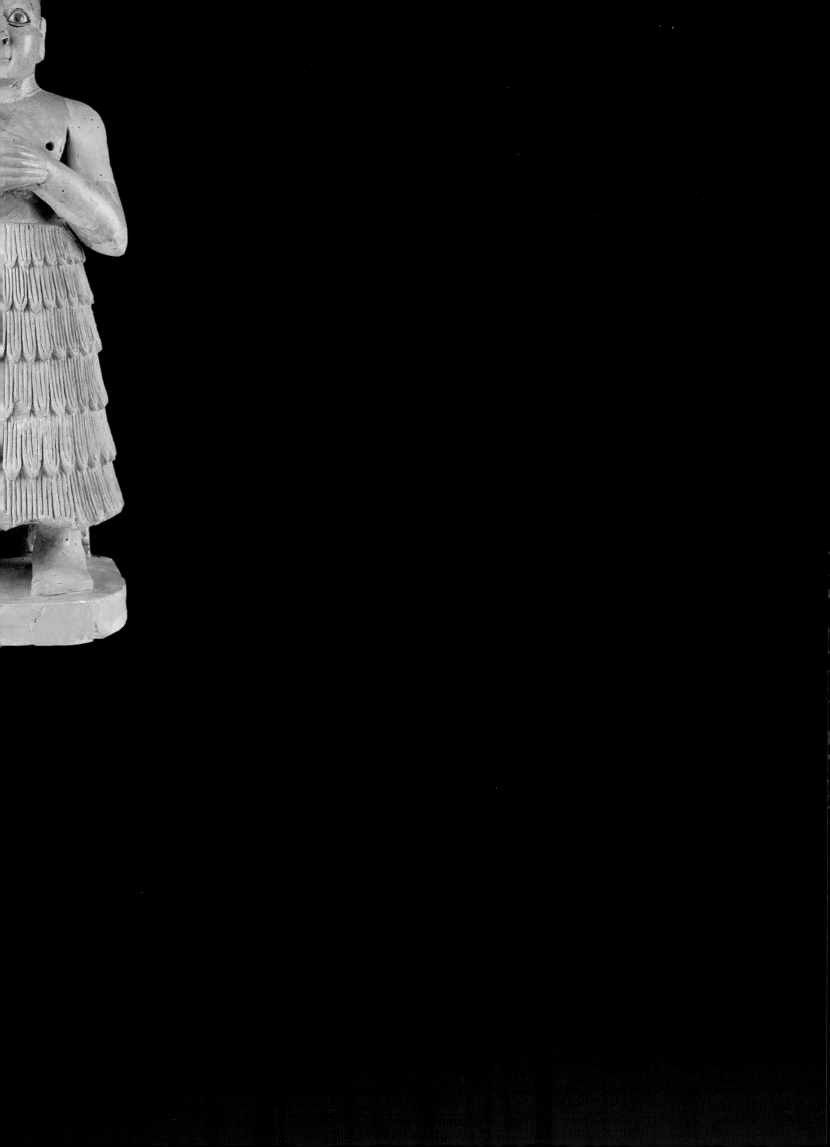

2
Hand ax
Flint
500 000 BC

This somewhat crude tool, made by removing large flakes
from both faces of a rough-hewed flint cobble, belonged
to one of the first inhabitants on Syrian territory. At the
time, humans lived solely by hunting and gathering food,
using implements of this type. Almost nothing is known of
their social organization. Stone tools are the only vestiges
of their presence that have come down to us.

LATAMNE   22 x 10 x 7.5 cm
NATIONAL MUSEUM, DAMASCUS   LT.216

3
Figurine
Clay
6000 BC

This large, schematically represented figure lacks a head. It is believed that the figurine was used to support a skull with features modeled in plaster **[4]**, since it was found near one of these skulls.

TELL RAMAD   25 x 15.5 x 8.5 cm
NATIONAL MUSEUM, DAMASCUS   1121   *SMC* 52; *BAAL* 55

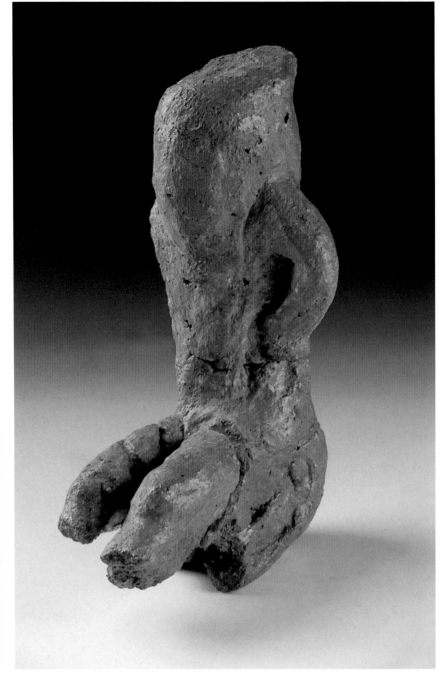

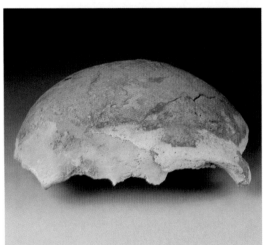

4 a-b
Fragments of a skull and jaw
Bone and plaster
6000 BC

The skulls to which these fragments belong are unusual in that they were covered with plaster that was moulded and painted in order, it is believed, to represent the features of the deceased person. Such special treatment was reserved for the skulls of only a few, and it seems to be related to a sort of ancestor worship. People who in life had played a particularly important role in their communities, or had perhaps ruled over them, were venerated in this way after death.

TELL RAMAD   11 x 10 x 5.5 cm/10 x 10 x 4.5 cm
NATIONAL MUSEUM, DAMASCUS   R 66.415/R 66,4

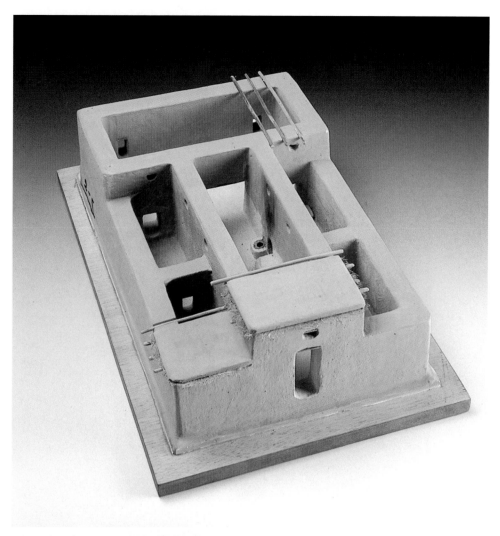

5
Model of a house (reconstitution)
Plaster
Modern

Sedentarization is a pivotal social development in the appearance of a great civilization. The phenomenon is reflected in the construction of permanent dwellings. The first houses that prehistoric Syrians lived in were round; later houses became rectangular, with rounded corners. However, by around 6000 BC, at least on the site of el-Kowm, near Palmyra, people were living in three-part rectangular houses like this one. Their houses had plaster floors and were equipped with storerooms for keeping food and hearths for cooking it.

46 x 30 x 15 cm
PALMYRA MUSEUM

6
Figurine
Stone
9000 BC

This is the earliest representation of a human face found in Syria. Originally it was painted. The aquiline nose suggests what the people living at the time might have looked like. However, some specialists have also interpreted this carving as a symbolic representation of a bird of prey, which was the object of a cult in this period.

TELL JERF AL-AHMAR   4.4 x 3.6 x 2.4 cm
NATIONAL MUSEUM, DAMASCUS   1204

7
Statuette
Gypsum
2400 BC

This statuette was found in 1934, only one month after archaeological excavations had begun at the Tell Hariri site. It was unearthed in the remains of a temple and represents a person who wished to be immortalized in an attitude of prayer. The inscription borne by the statuette made it possible to identify the person as one of the kings of Mari and thus to infer that the site was the ancient city of Mari itself. The inscription, covering the left shoulder and part of the back, reads: "Lamgi-Mari, King of Mari, chief ensi of Enlil, his statue to Inanna-ush, has dedicated." The statuette displays royal attributes in two of its features: the arrangement of the hair and the long wavy beard. Unlike other statuettes of the same type, this one has eyes that are sculpted. In back, a protuberance suggests the tail of an animal.

TELL HARIRI, ANCIENT MARI: TEMPLE OF ISHTAR
27.7 x 10.3 x 11.5 cm
NATIONAL MUSEUM, ALEPPO   M 10406   *BAAL* 91; *SMC* 107

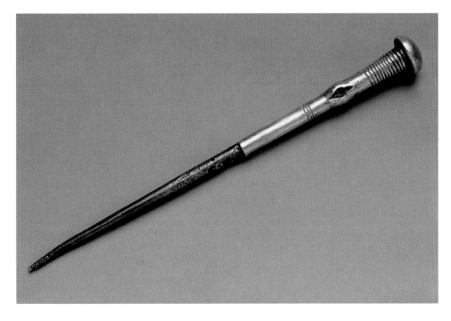

8
Toggle pin
Gold and silver
2500 BC

This type of pin with a broad head and an eye in the upper part was generally used to hold clothing in place. Toggle pins were usually made of bronze, but the one shown here is instead made of silver, with the upper part covered in gold leaf. As well, parallel grooves form a decoration above and below the eye. It is therefore a luxury object. The pin was also part of the "Treasure of Ur."

TELL HARIRI, ANCIENT MARI: PRE-SARGONIC PALACE   12.6 cm
NATIONAL MUSEUM, DAMASCUS   2395 (M 4428)
BAAL 106

9
Lion sculpture
Copper
1800 BC

This copper sculpture shows only the front part — the pronome — of a lion with its jaws open. It comes from a temple located near the palace and dedicated to the King of the Land, a divinity that has not yet been identified. The lion was accompanied by another lion that was identical to it. The two once stood against a wall inside the temple at the entrance to the inner sanctum, so that they appeared to be leaping out from the wall, ready to pounce on visitors. The eyes are inlaid. The animal's body was formed by cold-hammering sheets of copper over a sculpted wooden form, which has since disappeared, and fixing them to the wood with nails.

TELL HARIRI, ANCIENT MARI: TEMPLE OF THE LIONS
70 x 54 x 40 cm
NATIONAL MUSEUM, ALEPPO   M 7906   *SMC* 132B

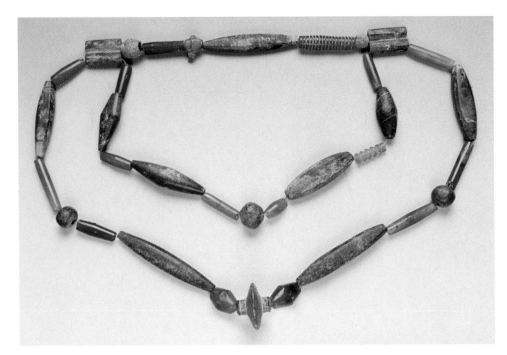

10/11
Necklaces
Lapis lazuli and carnelian
2500 BC

The beads in these two necklaces (33 in one and 21 in the other) were made of two kinds of semiprecious stone. The blue stone is lapis lazuli and the red is carnelian, both of which came from the far-off mountains of Afghanistan, a country with which the city-state of Mari maintained relations. These materials were often used to make pieces of jewelry, which were luxury items reserved for a political elite, worn as an expression of social status. These necklaces were part of the "Treasure of Ur."

TELL HARIRI, ANCIENT MARI: PRE-SARGONIC TEMPLE
NATIONAL MUSEUM, DAMASCUS
M 4431/4435 4430/4434 *BAAL* 108

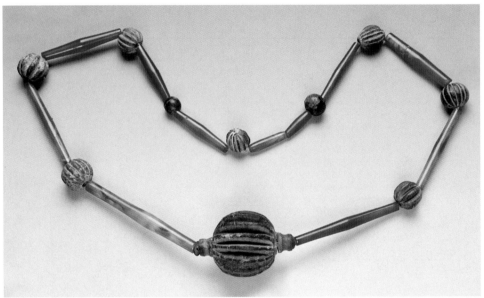

12
Bead
Lapis lazuli
2500 BC

Although this elongated bead is well worn, it was possible to decipher the inscription it bears: "To the divinity GAL, Mesannepada, King of Ur [this] slender bead G[an]a[u d] being King of Mari has dedicated." The bead was discovered in a jar, along with about 50 other precious objects, in a burned layer marking the destruction of the palace of Mari. The archaeologist who discovered this trove designated it the "Treasure of Ur" on the basis of the inscription. It is now thought, however, that the jar and its contents were placed in the earth as a ceremonial deposit when the palace foundations were built, rather than being a collection of gifts sent by one of the kings of Ur with whom the king of Mari had to maintain diplomatic and trade relations.

TELL HARIRI, ANCIENT MARI: PRE-SARGONIC PALACE
11.8 x 1.9 x 1.7 cm
NATIONAL MUSEUM, DAMASCUS M 4439 *BAAL* 103

Next page:
13
Breastplate
Lapis lazuli, gold, copper, bitumen
2500 BC

There are three holes in this lapis lazuli breastplate engraved with the body and wings of an eagle. This suggests that it was intended to be worn. The eagle's head and tail are made of gold and attached to the lapis lazuli with copper wire, with the whole set on a bitumen core. The eagle-headed lion was a common image in the land of Sumer, where it bore the name of Anzu and was used as an emblem for the god Ningirsu. The divinity may have been imported to Mari. However, some researchers, on studying this unique Mesopotamian object, have argued that the animal represented is, in fact, a bat. However it is interpreted, the breastplate is clearly an exceptional ornament and must have been worn by a high-ranking Mari dignitary who was probably male, since the object is extremely heavy. The breastplate was also part of the "Treasure of Ur."

TELL HARIRI, ANCIENT MARI: PRE-SARGONIC PALACE
13 x 12 x 1 cm
NATIONAL MUSEUM, DAMASCUS M 2399 *SMC* 114; *BAAL* 104

14

Statue of a high-ranking dignitary
Basalt
1850 BC

This statue cannot be identified as that of a king, since the figure is not wearing a tiara or royal mantle; however, it very likely represents a high-ranking dignitary belonging to the ruling class in Ebla. This interpretation is supported by the fact the statue was found in the vestibule of a very important temple in the city, along with fragments of other basalt statues representing a seated king and a standing queen. All these statues must have originally stood in the lower town's great temple, dedicated to the goddess Ishtar, who was associated with the divine protection of royalty. The statue is especially precious since it survived the devastating raids carried out by the Hittite king Mursili I around 1600 BC and the systematic pillaging of the city that ensued.

TELL MARDIKH, ANCIENT EBLA: TEMPLE P2   105 x 47 x 31 cm
IDLIB MUSEUM   3304 (TM.88.P.627)
SMC 146; *EBLA* 254; *FESTSCHRIFT STROMMENGER* p. 111-128

15

Ceremonial mace
Marble, ivory, silver and gold
1750 BC

There could be no better testimony to the relation between Ebla and Egypt than this ceremonial marble mace with an ivory handle. It seems to have been a gift from the Pharaoh Hetepibre Hornedheryotef, one of the first rulers in the Thirteenth Dynasty of the Middle Kingdom. The recipient was an Eblaite king whose identity is still unknown but whom archaeologists have named the Lord of the Goats because of the pictures of these animals on the pottery found in his tomb. The pharaoh called himself "Son of the Asiatic," and the idea of his sending such a gift to Eblaite royalty suggests that he might have come from northern Syria himself, perhaps even from Ebla. It is also possible that the gold jewelry **[16-23]** discovered in this tomb was part of the present to this Eblaite king, who seems to have had close links with the pharaohs of the Thirteenth Dynasty.

TELL MARDIKH, ANCIENT EBLA: TOMB OF THE LORD OF THE GOATS   19 x 2.4 cm/5.6 x 4.4 cm   IDLIB MUSEUM 3484+3170 (TM.78.Q.453-461)
SMC 145; *EBLA* 383-384

This exquisite jewelry was part of the funeral goods placed in the tombs of members of the royal family of Ebla. The tombs were found in a hypogeum built under one of the palaces in the city, which was the capital of a small state at the time. The jewelry clearly belonged to members of the elite class in this city-state, whose prosperity was largely based on trade and the agricultural productivity of the fertile land in its immediate surroundings.

MARDIKH, ANCIENT EBLA
NATIONAL MUSEUM, ALEPPO

16

Cylindrical element
Gold

This object is ornamented with tiny spheres of gold that have been melted together on the surface of the cylinder in a technique referred to as granulation in goldsmithing. The cylinder may have been a handle on a ceremonial object like the mace offered by a pharaoh to a king of Ebla **[15]**.

TOMB OF THE LORD OF THE GOATS   6.7 x 2.2 cm
M 10587 (TM.78.Q420)
EBLA 385; *SMC* 150

17

Necklace
Gold, amethyst, lapis lazuli

This piece is very likely the central part of a necklace. It is made of pomegranate-shaped gold beads on either side of a rectangular gold plaque inlaid with a cabochon of lapis lazuli.

TOMB OF THE PRINCESS   10.2 x 2.5 cm   M 10591
SMC 149; *EBLA* 393; *BAAL* 157; *ED* 107

18

Necklace
Gold

This necklace is made in three sections. From each one there hangs a circular pendant decorated with granulation to represent a six-pronged star with a dot between the prongs.

TOMB OF THE LORD OF THE GOATS   10.3 x 4.4 x 2.5 cm
M 10783 (TM.79.Q250 A-C)
EBLA 396

19

Stick pin
Gold

This pin would have been used to hold garments in place. Its head, in the shape of an eight-pronged star, is attached by a hemispherical cap. The upper third of the pin is marked by a ring with engraved lines on either side of it, and above this mark the pin is twisted.

TOMB OF THE PRINCESS   17.6 x 3.8 cm   M 10784
EBLA 392; *BAAL* 156; *ED* 104

20

Ring
Gold

This ring could have been worn through a hole in a nose or an ear. The lozenges decorating its surface demonstrate extraordinary mastery of the granulation technique.

TOMB OF THE PRINCESS   3.2 cm   M 10786 (TM.78.Q 366)
EBLA 394; *BAAL* 155; *ED* 106

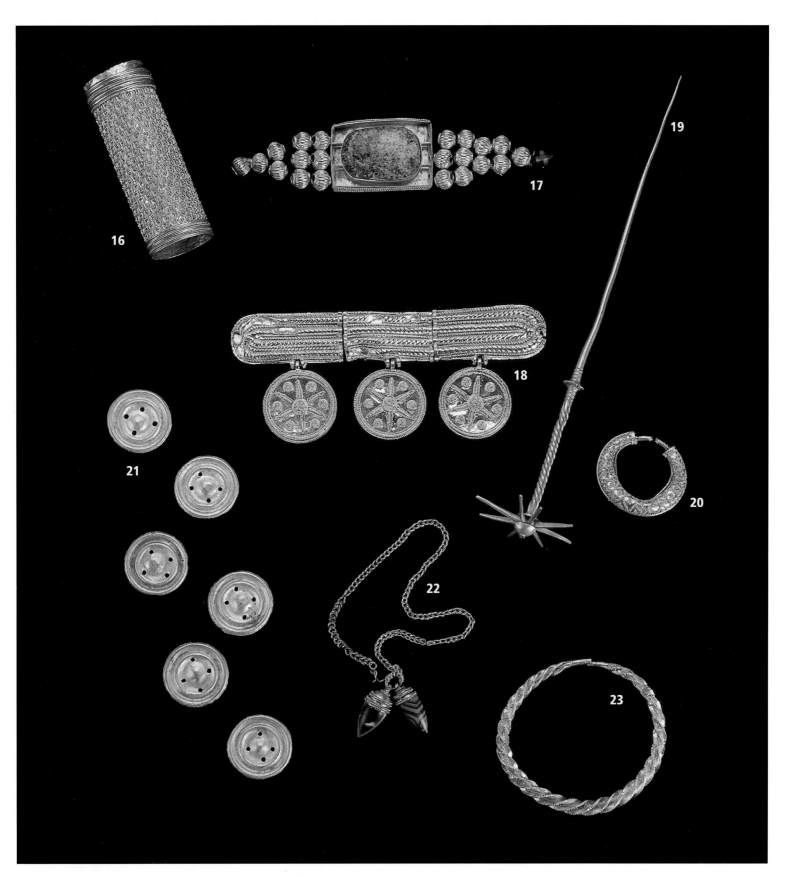

21 a-f
Buttons
Gold

These six four-holed buttons made of gold were probably sewn onto royal garments, which unfortunately have not survived the passage of time.

TOMB OF THE LORD OF THE GOATS   2.4 cm
M 10798 (TM.78.Q411)
EBLA p. 403

22
Necklace with two pendants
Gold, rock crystal, greyish-green translucent stone

Two beads made of semiprecious stones hang from a gold chain with very fine links.

TOMB OF THE LORD OF THE GOATS   22 cm
M 10790 (TM.78.Q407)
EBLA 398

23
Bracelet
Gold

This bracelet was one of six such items found on the skeleton of a young girl who had been buried in one of the numerous small caves, or hypogea, hollowed out beneath the surface of a courtyard in one of the city's palaces. Like the other bracelets, this one is twisted and decorated with tiny golden balls.

TOMB OF THE PRINCESS   5.6 cm   M 10785 (TM.78.Q370)
EBLA 391; *BAAL* 154; *ED* 105

24
Cup
Gold
1300 BC

The decoration on this masterpiece of Syrian goldsmithing suggests that it might well have been part of the furnishings in a palace of Ugarit. The hemispherical gold cup is entirely covered with embossed and engraved motifs, arranged in three concentric friezes. The motifs do not form any narrative; there are simply sequences of animals and hybrid beings set symmetrically on either side of palmettes, with ibexes leaping here and there.
There is a scene showing two men killing a lion, but it blends into another scene, representing lions attacking bulls. The decoration on this exceptional example of the goldsmith's art suggests that it could have been a precious object related to royal authority.

RAS SHAMRA, ANCIENT UGARIT   17.5 x 4.7 cm
NATIONAL MUSEUM, ALEPPO   M 10129
BAAL 178; *UGARITICA* II p. 1-48 and Pl. 3-5

25
Ceremonial dagger
Gold
1300 BC

There were many goldsmiths in the city of Ugarit. A large number of objects made of precious metal have been found in well-demarcated areas scattered throughout the city. One such object is this elegant dagger of solid gold (200 g), with its flattened handle engraved in a decorative palm-branch design. It was discovered in a collection of items, also made of precious metal, which had been hidden with other pieces in a terra cotta jar. Ugarit derived great profit from the Mediterranean trade and, it is thought, especially from trade in the luxury metal products fashioned by its skillful craftsmen.

RAS SHAMRA, ANCIENT UGARIT   27.2 x 3 x 0.4 cm
NATIONAL MUSEUM, DAMASCUS   3587 (RS 25.470)

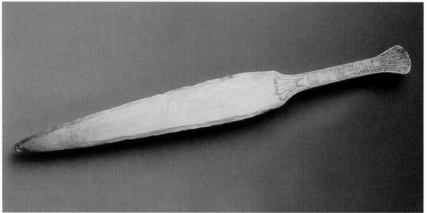

26
Ceremonial ax
Iron and copper inlaid with gold
1500 BC

This weapon represents one of the first attempts to produce steel in Syria. This makes the piece quite exceptional, even though the technique involved was not yet perfected. The ax blade was made of steel — iron with carbon added to it. The smith cast a copper flange, or socket, at the heel of the ax so that it could be fitted onto a haft. The flange is decorated with animal motifs in relief. The forequarters of a reclining boar can be seen on the back of the flange and two lion heads hold the blade in their jaws. Gold wire hammered into incised lines highlights certain details of the animals' anatomy as well as the floral motifs around them. This unique ax was discovered in the northwest area of the city in a small building that has been interpreted as a sanctuary.

RAS SHAMRA, ANCIENT UGARIT   19.5 x 6.4 x 4 cm
NATIONAL MUSEUM, ALEPPO   M 10127   *BAAL* 203

27
Statuette of the god Baal
Silver and gold
1800 BC

The metal figurines found at Ugarit, whether flat or in the round, were usually made of bronze. This one, however, was cast in silver and ornamented with gold; the figure wears a golden loincloth and necklace, or torque, and carries a golden mace in its left hand. The statuette has generally been identified with the god Hadad or Baal, the "Master," especially since it was found in a store of votive idols near the great Temple of Baal. It is known that Baal bore a mace as a sign of his power and used it to see that his commands were carried out.

RAS SAMARA, ANCIENT UGARIT   28 x 5.5 cm
NATIONAL MUSEUM, ALEPPO   M 8162
UGARITICA II p. 71-85 and Pl. 17-19

28

Cylinder seal

Steatite

1800 BC

The scene engraved on the surface of this cylinder-shaped seal is a perfect reflection of the nature of civil power in Syria at the time. The scene shows a king walking in front of a goddess, who is presenting him to another divinity seated on a throne and holding symbols of power — a rod and a circle — which she prepares to hand over to the king. While the scene attests to the divine nature of the power held by the king, the cylinder seal itself is an object that would have been used in the administration of trade matters, under the strict supervision of government authorities, with the king at their head.

TELL ASHARA, ANCIENT TERQA   2.7 x 1.6 cm   DEIR EZ ZOR MUSEUM   10372 (TQ 11 Fi30)   *L'EUFRATE* 293

29

Cylinder seal and its imprint

Alabaster and plaster

2400 BC

A person wearing a short skirt places one foot on a stylized mountain and extends his left hand to a figure with two faces representing Isimud, the vizier of the Sumerian god Enki (Ea in Akkadian), who is shown seated to the right of the scene. Between the god and his vizier is what appears to be an altar with a plant above it. Enki was the god of sweet underground water (Abzu); he was associated with wisdom, magic, incantations, crafts and the arts. He was often represented with a long beard and dressed in tufted robes, receiving worshippers or devotees bearing offerings.
The cuneiform inscription reads as follows: " My god is just (name of the person) scribe. "

TELL HARIRI, ANCIENT MARI   3 x 1.6 cm
NATIONAL MUSEUM, DAMASCUS   M 3951   *SCEAUX-CYLINDRES DE SYRIE* 25

30

Cylinder seal and its imprint

Columella and plaster

2600 BC

This cylinder presents a scene of animals and humans fighting. The design is unusual because if you look at the picture one way you see a nude man holding an antelope on its hind legs in either hand, while if you turn it around you see a naked man and a man with a bull's head and tail standing back to back, each of them attacking a rearing lion.

TELL HARIRI, ANCIENT MARI   3 x 1.7 cm (seal)/12.2 x 4.5 cm (imprint)
NATIONAL MUSEUM, DAMASCUS   M 4452   *SCEAUX-CYLINDRES DE SYRIE* 12

31

Cylinder seal and its imprint

Columella and plaster

2600 BC

The scenes represented on the two friezes of this cylinder seem to be related to a ritual ceremony conducted to mark the solemn opening of temple or place of worship. In the lower frieze there is a ziggurat, or terraced tower, with a figure on either side; four other figures are shown nearby, two of them using straws to drink what might be beer from a jar. The upper frieze presents a banquet scene with a schematic representation of a table.

TELL HARIRI, ANCIENT MARI   3.7 x 2 cm (seal)/15.5 x 5 cm (imprint)
NATIONAL MUSEUM, DAMASCUS   M 4445   *SCEAUX-CYLINDRES DE SYRIE* 18

32

Cylinder seal and its imprint

Columella and plaster

2600 BC

This cylinder has a frieze of battling animals, with two lionesses and a lion attacking a gazelle. The end of the scene is marked with two horizontal lines and, below them, a vertical scorpion. Above the lines is a blank space in which the owner's name could be placed.

TELL HARIRI, ANCIENT MARI
3.2 x 1.9 cm (seal)/13.5 x 4.6 cm (imprint)
NATIONAL MUSEUM, DAMASCUS   M 4448   *SCEAUX-CYLINDRES DE SYRIE* 15

THE ORGANIZATION OF SOCIETY

MOULDS AND THEIR IMPRINTS

Terra cotta
1800 BC

Some 50 terra cotta moulds were extracted from the debris of a palace room in the city-state of Mari. Since this room was close to the kitchens in the domestic quarter of the "king's house," it is thought that the moulds may have been used in the production of dairy products like cheese or, more probably, for making bread and pastries served at the royal banquets described in texts. The most common forms are circular and shallow.

TELL HARIRI, ANCIENT MARI: PALACE
NATIONAL MUSEUM, ALEPPO

Mould **33** has seven concentric circles, three of which are embellished with a total of 24 birds.

27 x 3.8 cm   M 7872   *BAAL* 130

Mould **34** belongs to a type of mould with geometric designs.

25.2 x 4.7 cm   M 7866

Mould **35** is shaped like a fish and has scales that are represented in a very realistic style.

30.2 x 11.2 x 5.7 cm   M 7862   *BAAL* 133

Mould **36** is rectangular in shape and is decorated with a deer-hunting scene. A man is returning from the hunt with a stag, which he leads by the antlers, while a dog rears up in front of him, as if to inspect the animal. In the background, in the upper left-hand corner, is a smaller stag, perhaps a younger deer accompanying his captured father.

23.5 x 19.2 x 7.7 cm   M 10105

101

37
Plaque with inlay
Shell, schist, bitumen
2400 BC

A Mari soldier wearing a long tunic uses his left arm to push along a naked prisoner with his arms bound to his torso. Along with many other similar plaques found at Mari, this would have been part of a mosaic in several panels intended to commemorate an important victory by the city's king. However, the picture should be seen not as narrating a specific event, but rather as expressing the idea of victory through the symbolism of a captured enemy. This interpretation is supported by the fact that the plaques were discovered in a temple and not in a room within the palace. This piece was made of mother-of-pearl and schist stuck onto a schist base with bitumen.

TELL HARIRI, ANCIENT MARI: PALACE   12 x 10.3 cm
NATIONAL MUSEUM, ALEPPO   M 5113   *L'EUFRATE* 256

38
Engraved plaque
Limestone
2500 BC

A helmeted warrior carries a spear in his left hand, while with his right hand he holds up a large shield that is made of rushes and curved back at the top. Behind him stands an archer, preparing to let an arrow fly. The archer's body is protected by a garment that gives the impression of being rigid (perhaps a tunic made of leather or even metal). The enemy is shown in the background, reclining (or perhaps dead) and, as was often the case, naked. While the antagonists cannot be identified, this combat scene is interesting because it demonstrates an early use of shields, previously thought to have been invented by the Assyrians between 900 BC and 800 BC.

TELL HARIRI, ANCIENT MARI   15 x 9.8 x 1.4 cm
DEIR EZ ZOR MUSEUM   11233

Next page:
39/40/41/42
Inlay parts
Marble
2400 BC

These four small marble plaques are finely engraved with scenes of war, or, more specifically, pictures of soldiers conducting captives. The plaques would have been inserted into long wooden planks that once decorated a wall in a palace of Ebla. The decoration must have been part of an exceptional monument of at least three meters in height, with a dozen panels placed one above the other. The monument was no doubt intended to publicly celebrate a military victory won by the king of Ebla and would have been set against a wall some place in the palace where distinguished visitors would see it and be impressed by the war-like power of the Eblaite ruler.

TELL MARDIKH, ANCIENT EBLA: PALACE G   13.9 x 11 x 0.8 cm/
14 x 10.8 x 0.8 cm/13.5 x 8 x 0.8 cm/13.6 x 9.3 x 0.7 cm
IDLIB MUSEUM   3260/3247/3248/3245   *SMC* 103; *EBLA* 20-23

THE ORGANIZATION OF SOCIETY

CITIES AND STATES: AN UNPRECEDENTED DEVELOPMENT

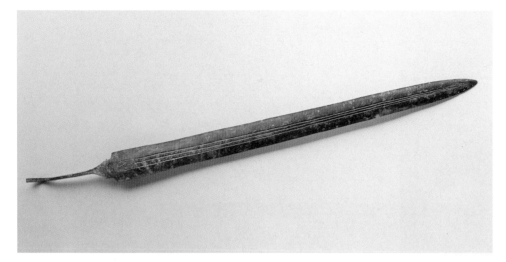

43
Sword
Bronze
1200 BC

This sword bears a cartouche of Pharaoh Merneptah (1224-1204 BC), the son and successor of Ramses II, confirming the essentially commercial contacts that existed between Ugarit and Egypt. The sword has a long double-edged blade and a narrow extension, called a tang, which would have been fitted into a wooden hilt. The weapon was probably made locally for the pharaoh's army, which was not familiar with this type of arm. It was discovered in a residential quarter of Ugarit, in a house that may have belonged to an armorer.

RAS SHAMRA, ANCIENT UGARIT   74.5 x 5 x 0.5 cm
NATIONAL MUSEUM, DAMASCUS   3591   *BAAL* 205

44
Ceremonial weapon
known as a sickle sword
Bronze
1300 BC

The sickle sword is a weapon with a curved blade at the end of a long straight handle, the two parts being cast as a single piece. The handle on this one was decorated with an inlay of some organic material — ivory, perhaps — that has since disappeared. At the time, the privilege of bearing such a luxurious and relatively rare weapon was reserved for gods, heroes and kings. The sickle sword was the mark of the king's status as a warrior and a dispenser of death. It was also the sign of might when borne by war-like divinities. In the king's hands, it symbolized the divine origin of his authority and the control he had over life and death.

RAS SHAMRA, ANCIENT UGARIT   58 x 5 x 2.4 cm
NATIONAL MUSEUM, ALEPPO   M 10136   *BAAL* 204

45
Spearhead
Bronze
1800 BC

From the middle of the second millennium BC, Urkish became a great city in the kingdom of the Mitanni and was peopled by Hurrians, who had begun to move into the northeast region of present-day Syria by the end of the third millennium BC. The spearhead would have been attached by its tang to the shaft of a spear. The weapon was found in a tomb and probably belonged to a member of the noble warrior class that headed the entire social organization of the kingdom. The Hurrians were distinguished for their skill in working copper and are also credited with the introduction of the battle chariot, from which such spears could be hurled as projectiles.

TELL MOZAN, ANCIENT URKISH   27.5 x 2.8 x 2 cm
DEIR EZ ZOR MUSEUM   (A2.124)

46

Spearhead with socket

Bronze

2000 BC

This spearhead has a socket at its base so that it could be fitted onto a shaft. It was the product of a totally new metallurgy technique in Ugarit at the time. The archaeologist at Ras Shamra believed that this advanced technology was introduced to Syria, along with previously unknown types of metal weapons and other objects, by a newly arrived population, which he named *porteurs de torque,* or the "torque wearers." Torques — a kind of twisted neck band — were found in great quantities in these people's tombs and are also represented around the necks of certain figurines **[27].** This example of the new type of weapon would have been a luxury good, belonging to a member of the city's elite class.

RAS SHAMRA, ANCIENT UGARIT   3.2 x 41 x 3.1 cm
NATIONAL MUSEUM, DAMASCUS   6495   *UGARITICA* II p. 49-57

47

Dagger

Bronze

1800 BC

Having been found in a great city that controlled overland travel and in particular the route to the Mediterranean, this dagger may have belonged to a set of ceremonial arms that came into the king's possession at the time of his coronation. In 1286 BC, a famous battle took place outside this city's walls, when Pharaoh Ramses II fought with the Hittites who had come down from Anatolia and with their Syrian allies. The dagger still has one of the rivets that held the tang in the hilt.

TELL NEBI MEND, ANCIENT QADESH   27.5 x 5.3 cm
HOMS MUSEUM   756

48

Dagger

Bronze

1300 BC

The double edge on this weapon distinguishes it as a dagger rather than a knife, which is classified morphologically as having only one cutting edge. The blade and the hilt were cast in one piece. The dagger is interesting because you can see how the hilt was designed to receive inlay of wood, bone or ivory. Luxury weapons decorated in this way were part of a very long Near Eastern tradition associated with the exercise of royal power.

RAS SHAMRA, ANCIENT UGARIT   37.5 x 5.7 x 1.8 cm
NATIONAL MUSEUM, DAMASCUS   3820

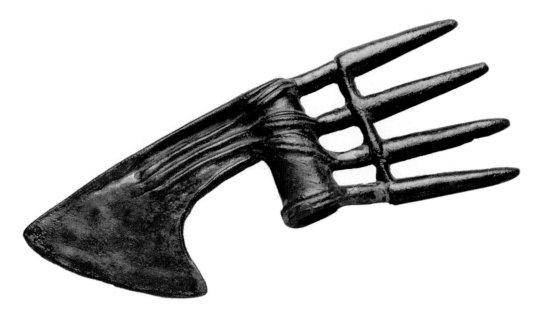

49
Flanged ax
Bronze
1300 BC

This ax has a flange for fitting it onto a handle. The exterior of this flange is decorated with reeding that extends in four long points beyond the heel of the ax. The cutting edge of the blade is sharply curved. Such an elaborate weapon may be considered to have been a symbol associated with the exercise of power.

UNKNOWN   18.5 x 6.8 x 2.2 cm
NATIONAL MUSEUM, DAMASCUS   6823   *Cf. SMC* 182

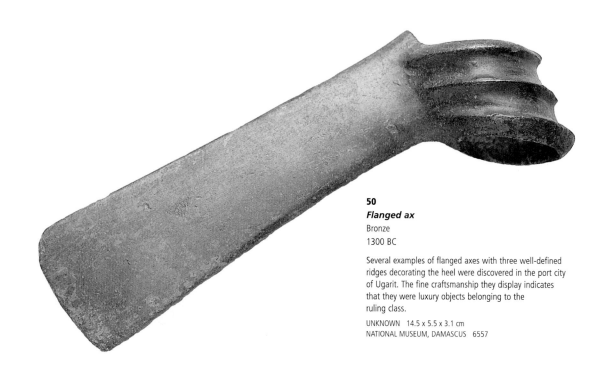

50
Flanged ax
Bronze
1300 BC

Several examples of flanged axes with three well-defined ridges decorating the heel were discovered in the port city of Ugarit. The fine craftsmanship they display indicates that they were luxury objects belonging to the ruling class.

UNKNOWN   14.5 x 5.5 x 3.1 cm
NATIONAL MUSEUM, DAMASCUS   6557

51
Figurine of the god Teshub
Bronze
1800 BC

Syria produced a great number of bronze votive figurines
meant to be placed in sanctuaries. According to a recent
study, three quarters of the 2000 figurines that have come
down to us represent gods, almost all of them male,
shown in war-like poses. This one, which was cast in one
piece using the lost-wax method, represents the Hittite
god of war Teshub. He bears a bow in his left hand and a
curved sword in his right.

UNKNOWN 12.5 x 5 x 3.5 cm
NATIONAL MUSEUM, DAMASCUS 112

53
Decorative plaque with sphinx
Ivory
800 BC

This ivory plaque was used to ornament a piece of ceremonial furniture. It was discovered in a palace of the
Assyrian governor of the city of Hadatu on the Upper
Euphrates, where the Assyrian Empire had its seat in
northern Syria. It has been established, however, that the
plaque was not made there but had been taken as plun-
der, along with other plaques of the same type, from the
princely palaces in Aramaean cities when they were conquered by the Assyrian army, and particularly during the
sack of Damascus in 732 BC. One such plaque even bears
the name of Hazael, "King of Aram," who reigned in
Damascus from 845 BC to 805 BC. Hazael was known for
his fierce resistance to the Assyrian invaders.
The sphinx, a winged lion with a human head, is a figure
borrowed from the Egyptian repertoire. Its use demonstrates
the way Aramaean craftsmen were able to integrate themes
originating in the countries with which they had contact.

ARSLAN TASH, ANCIENT HADATU   7.9 x 5.8 x 1 cm
NATIONAL MUSEUM, ALEPPO   M 833   *BAAL* 249

52
Statue of an Aramaean king
Basalt
900 BC (?)

Since it was found out of context, this massive statue
sculpted in the round is difficult to date with precision.
However, several features point to the possibility that the
statue represents an Aramaean king: the material used;
the stocky, geometric style; certain details like the hair-
style and beard; and the figure's pose, with hands held
out close straight in front. This interpretation is supported
by the fact that comparable statues have been found on
well-identified sites. Aramaean sovereigns were frequently
represented in this pose so that they could receive the offerings of their successors or be placed in a chariot as if
they were hunting.

UNKNOWN   180 x 45 x 38 cm
NATIONAL MUSEUM, ALEPPO   M 11444

54
Plaque with genies
binding papyrus stalks together
Ivory
800 BC

Here is a good example of how iconographic themes were
borrowed from Egypt. The plaque shows the Nile gods of
Upper and Lower Egypt symbolically binding stalks of
papyrus into the same bundle to represent the unification
of Egypt.

ARSLAN TASH, ANCIENT HADATU   10.7 x 10.4 x 1.6 cm
NATIONAL MUSEUM, ALEPPO   M9785   *BAAL* 249

55
Frieze of sculpted figures
Ivory
600 BC

Although the Aramaean city of Til Barsib was annexed by the Assyrian king Shalmaneser III in 856 BC, local crafts-manship continued to develop, especially in ivory work. This frieze, recently discovered in the debris of a palace occupied by Assyrian dignitaries, is a fine example of such work. However, according to some specialists, ivory pieces like this one were no longer made by Aramaean crafts-men after the city fell to the Assyrians, but since such work was greatly valued, it was saved and reused by the conquerors. The frieze has tenons on the upper and lower edges, indicating that it was inlaid into a wooden panel that would have decorated a piece of ceremonial furni-ture. The procession of musicians and men carrying provi-sions was probably part of a larger composition illustrat-ing a royal banquet.

TELL AHMAR, ANCIENT TIL BARSIB   34 x 10 x 0.8 cm
NATIONAL MUSEUM, ALEPPO   M 10982 (TAH.94.C481789)
AJA 101 (1997) p. 440-442

56
Head of a statue
Basalt
700 BC

This impressive head of a woman, with her horned crown and rosette-embellished diadem, was found in the Temple of Ishtar. The temple was built on the site of Ain Dara by Hittite settlers who came from Anatolia to set up indepen-dent kingdoms in northern Syria at the beginning of the first millennium, after the Hittite Empire had fallen to the invading "Sea Peoples" around 1200 BC. The sculpture is an interesting vestige of the Hittite presence in Syria.

AIN DARA   36 x 28 x 56 cm
NATIONAL MUSEUM, ALEPPO   M 11123   *AIN DARA* Pl. 55-56

57
Painted mural: two Assyrian dignitaries
Fresco on mud plaster
750 BC

In 856 BC, the city of Til Barsib, the capital of the Aramaean kingdom of Bit-Adini on the Middle Euphrates,
was captured by Shalmaneser III of Assyria (859-824 BC),
who renamed it Kar Shalmaneser, meaning "Port Shalmaneser." He and his successors used the city as a base
from which to launch attacks on the rest of Syria. They
consequently established an official residence there. The
walls of the throne room in this palace were decorated
with painted murals. The fragment shown here represents
two Assyrian dignitaries in court dress. They are wearing
checkered robes, earrings, and headbands embellished
with rosettes. The fragment was once part of a larger picture, which was copied at the time of its discovery. In the
original painting, the two dignitaries were leading a vanquished enemy before the Assyrian king, who was seated
on a throne surrounded by his courtiers.

TELL AHMAR, ANCIENT TIL BARSIB   41 x 38 cm
NATIONAL MUSEUM, ALEPPO   M 7509   *BAAL* 247

58
Stela: two men in a chariot
Basalt
800 BC

This stela presents two male figures dressed in the Assyrian fashion, standing in a chariot drawn by a pair of horses. Since the two-wheeled chariot was used only in battle
or for victory parades, a monument of this sort is a clear
sign of the Assyrians' military presence in northern Syria
from the ninth to the seventh century BC. However, the
Assyrians did not simply subjugate the local populations.
This stela itself shows that there must have been exchanges of some type between the two groups, since,
while it represents a subject that is definitely Assyrian, the
style of the relief work is typical of that done in the workshops of local sculptors.

NEAR TELL AHMAR, ANCIENT TIL BARSIB   96 x 56 x 17 cm
NATIONAL MUSEUM, ALEPPO   M 10172
L'EUFRATE 384; *FESTSCHRIFT STROMMENGER* p. 94-95

59
Vase of Shalmaneser III
Alabaster
850 BC

It is rare to find an archaeological document that illustrates political relations between two nations. Military victories are usually represented with scenes of war. However, the central decorative panel on this stone vase shows two kings shaking hands, surrounded by their courtiers. The scene thus commemorates an agreement that was reached peacefully, without recourse to arms. The vase was discovered by chance in the territory of northern Syria, and this location suggests that the Assyrian kings may have been able to conclude friendly treaties with the indigenous kings. The pictorial theme was already an established one, since it was also sculpted on the base of the throne of Shalmaneser III in his palace of Nimrud in Assyria.

JEZIREH REGION   20 x 19 cm
NATIONAL MUSEUM, DAMASCUS   7491
L'EUFRATE 368; *AAAS* 38-39 (1987-1988) p. 1-10;
FESTSCHRIFT STROMMENGER p. 29-32

60
*Stela to the god Sin
(recto/verso)*
Limestone
700 BC

This stela is interesting because it shows Sin, the god of the Moon (note how his crescent-shaped symbol has been repeatedly integrated into the design), dressed as an Assyrian and standing in front of a carefully drawn fortress with two crenellated square towers. The other side of the stela represents a winged genie of the type often sculpted on the walls of Assyrian palaces, guarding the main entrances. The stela attests to the Assyrians' military occupation of northeast Syria at the beginning of the first millennium BC. The lower section of the stela was recently found in one of the collections at the Louvre.

TELL AHMAR, ANCIENT TIL BARSIB   38.7 x 28 x 7.3 cm
NATIONAL MUSEUM, ALEPPO   M 4526
L'EUFRATE 372; *FESTSCHRIFT STROMMENGER* p. 99-100

111

61
Sarcophagus
Terra cotta
500 BC

During the period when Syria was a satrapy in the great Persian Empire (from about 538 BC to 333 BC), the coastal cities enjoyed considerable economic prosperity as a result of their active role in eastern Mediterranean trade. They were particularly well-situated to act as places of transit for certain goods being shipped to the heart of the empire in Iran. The wealthy people who profited from this lucrative trade and those who held important administrative positions in the Achaemenid satrapy had themselves buried in terra cotta sarcophagi with the top section of the cover moulded in the shape of a human head.

'AMRIT, ANCIENT MARATHUS   55 x 51 x 16.5 cm
TARTUS MUSEUM   64   *DAM* 10 (1998) p. 120

62
Helmet with mask
Silver and iron
AD 50

This helmet consists of a visor to protect the face and a shell covering the rest of the head. It is made entirely of iron coated with silver except for the crown area, which was originally covered with fabric; the material has disappeared but the imprint of its fibres is visible in the rust. This luxury object, with its polished silver mask and finely sculpted diadem and rear peak, was probably used for parades. However, it was also made to be worn in battle, since there is a hinge above the forehead that attaches the visor to the helmet. As well, holes have been made under the eye openings so that the wearer could look down to see where he was going. The helmet must have belonged either to an Arab king of Emesa, or at least someone close to the king, since it was discovered in the city's royal necropolis. The Roman historian Arrian relates that the auxiliary cavalry of the Roman army took part in tournaments in which the adversaries wore masked helmets. This helmet was probably made in the workshops of Antioch, which were famous for their precious metal products. It is very likely that the silversmith modeled the mask's features to resemble those of the person who would wear it.

The city of Emesa (present-day Homs) was very important in the Roman period, since it controlled a network of trade routes. The local dynasty that ruled the city and its territory no doubt profited greatly from this economic prosperity.

HOMS, ANCIENT EMESA   25 x 20 x 20 cm
NATIONAL MUSEUM, DAMASCUS   7084
AAAS 2 (1952) 101-108; *SYRIA* 36 (1959) 184-192

63
Statue of a soldier in a breastplate
Basalt
AD 200

In 64 BC, Syria became a Roman province. Roman rule lasted for 400 years, and during this period some one hundred governors were appointed to run the province. However, the territory was not truly integrated into the Empire until AD 68, when troops stationed in Syria proclaimed Vespasian emperor. Romanization was beneficial in that it brought enduring peace to the Near East, especially along the Empire's eastern borders. This statue of a man wearing a breastplate made to look like torso muscles, his short cloak attached on the right shoulder with a round fibula, is a symbolic expression of the public administration that Rome established in the province of Syria.

DHAKIR   125 x 60 x 40 cm
SUWEIDA MUSEUM   341
LE DJEBEL AL-'ARAB 7,22

64
Head of a statue of King Odainat
Marble
AD 251-267

During the third century, Rome's control over the Syrian region of the Empire was weakened by repeated attacks on the part of the Sassanids, who had succeeded the Parthians in Iran. This created an unstable situation, which several Near East principalities tried to turn to their advantage by seeking independence. Odainat thus turned the oasis-city of Palmyra into a nearly autonomous kingdom. He managed to remain loyal to Rome and at the same time safeguard his caravan station's busy trade with the East by counterattacking the Sassanid troops and driving them back to the gates of their capital, Ctesiphon, in Iran. This valor earned him Rome's gratitude. He was assassinated in AD 267. His wife, Zenobia, who was rumored to have plotted this murder, succeeded him as ruler of Palmyra.

TADMOR, ANCIENT PALMYRA   45 x 24 x 27 cm
PALMYRA MUSEUM   B2726/9163

65
Coin with the effigy of Zenobia
Bronze
AD 267-272

After the death of King Odainat in AD 267, Queen Zenobia continued her husband's work. She was so successful that in AD 270 she led her army into Egypt and then turned her attention towards Anatolia. But Aurelian, the Roman Emperor, struck back and forced her to retreat to Palmyra; he lay siege to the city and captured it in August AD 272. Zenobia was taken prisoner and, depending on the author, either died in captivity or was paraded in chains at Aurelian's triumph in Rome and then, after the triumph, was either exiled to Trivoli or beheaded. Legends soon grew around this episode of Roman history, in which a strong-willed, brave and ambitious woman for a time stood up to the might of Rome. Here Queen Zenobia appears in profile on one of the rare coins she had minted during her short but ever so eventful reign.

TADMOR, ANCIENT PALMYRA: VALLEY OF THE TOMBS   2.4 x 0.2 cm
PALMYRA MUSEUM   102/9114   *SMC 242*

66
Head of a statue of Philip the Arab
Basalt
AD 250

According to some specialists, this head of a clean-shaven man could be the portrait of the Roman Emperor Philip the Arab (AD 244-249), since it was found not far from Shahba, the village where he was born. During his reign, Philip the Arab transformed his native village into a city endowed with all the public facilities normally found in Roman towns (baths, aqueducts, a theatre, temples, ramparts, monumental gates and streets paved in checkerboard patterns) and renamed it Philippopolis.

DHAKIR   32 x 25 cm
SUWEIDA MUSEUM   346
LE DJEBEL AL-'ARAB 7,28

67/68
Heads of statues
Basalt
AD 100

When Syria became a province of the Roman Empire in 64 BC, the Roman general, Pompey, did not try to integrate the kingdom of the Nabataeans, which included the southern area of Syrian territory. It was only later, in AD 106, under the Emperor Trajan, that the Nabataean kingdom was made into a Roman province called Arabia. The Nabataeans, who were of Arabian origin and had lived as pastoral nomads before settling down as farmers, derived considerable profit from the caravan trade.

SUWEIDA REGION   22 x 18 cm/22 x 16 cm
SUWEIDA MUSEUM   79.106/863.761
LE DJEBEL AL-'ARAB 4,25

69
Funerary stela
Basalt
AD 300 (?)

The Greek inscription on the lower section of this stela reads as follows: " Boades, daughter of Thaimos, aged 15 years. "

SOUTHERN SYRIA   95 x 35 x 17 cm
SUWEIDA MUSEUM   1/76
LE DJEBEL AL-'ARAB 7,09

71
Window
Basalt
AD 400 (?)

This basalt panel was used as a window in a Byzantine church. Light came in through the large circular holes arranged in a ring and through the small elongated holes in the center. The decorative program of a Syrian church around AD 350 normally included such windows. While the provenience of this window is not certain, it may have come from Halabiyya, since this city is located in a region that is rich in basalt.

HALABIYYA, ANCIENT ZENOBIA   72 x 62 x 12.5 cm
NATIONAL MUSEUM, DAMASCUS   34905

70
Plaque
Marble
AD 1000

One of the faces of this square marble plaque is sculpted in relief with three Byzantine crosses, each mounted on a support. On either side of the smaller crosses there is an inscription in Syriac, a language that developed out of Aramaic and that is still spoken today in the Christian communities of the Near East. The inscription reads as follows: "Made by David, the hermit monk, pray." The plaque was discovered recently standing against the north wall of a mortuary chapel built in about the year 1000 at Tell Tuneinir, on the Habur River. The chief archaeologist at Tell Tuneinir believes that the David mentioned in the inscription was the founder of this modest Syriac Orthodox monastery.

TELL TUNEINIR   25 x 20 x 5 cm
DEIR EZ ZOR MUSEUM
(S993/1861 TNR 98/933005)

72
Bowl with cross decoration
Glazed ceramic
AD 600 (?)

In about AD 300, a Roman officer named Sergius was martyred at Rusafa, an isolated fort in the middle of the desert between Palmyra and the Euphrates. In the fifth century, as more and more pilgrims made their way to the site, it became a large Byzantine city. It was renamed Sergiopolis, and four monumental basilicas and several chapels were built there. One of these basilicas, which was dedicated to the Holy Cross, has recently yielded a treasure of sacred vessels [316-320]. Since the pilgrimage site had become so important, the Emperor Justinian (AD 527-565) took it under his protection. The bottom of this bowl was decorated with a medallion in which a Greek cross was painted, its four equal arms ending in a heart-shaped motif.

RUSAFA, ANCIENT SERGIOPOLIS   20 x 17 cm
NATIONAL MUSEUM, DAMASCUS   29318   *SMC* 288

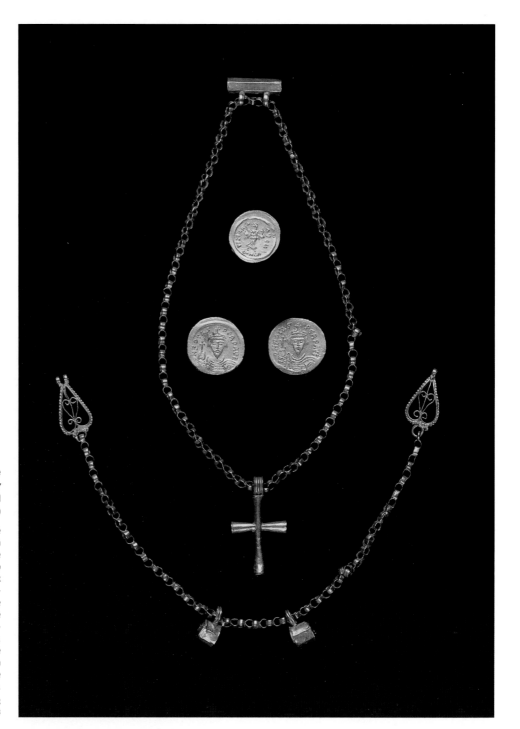

73 a-e
Treasure of coins and jewelry
Gold
AD 400

Discovered by chance in 1987, this tiny treasure trove consists of two necklaces and three coins that had been hidden in a small ceramic jar. Precious belongings were often concealed in this way when people wanted to keep them out of the hands of pillagers, invaders or even tax collectors. During the Byzantine period, coins of remarkably stable value were widely circulated throughout the Empire. The Byzantine monetary system was based on the gold pound (327 grams), from which 72 coins, called nomismata, were minted. Being worth their weight in gold, these coins were hoarded. The chain necklaces, also made of pure gold, are representative of the period. One has a cross, symbolizing the triumph of Christianity, and the other has a finely worked clasp.

AL-KENIAH, JISR AL-SHOQHUR
IDLIB MUSEUM   246, 247, 1091/1,1091/2,1091/3

74
Capital
Limestone
AD 500

It was not until about AD 250 that Christian communities in Syria began to construct the buildings they called churches with a large rectangular room in which the faithful could pray together. To set these churches apart from other large public buildings, people began to decorate them by sculpting geometrical motifs in the limestone mouldings around the doors and windows. A little later on, plant-like patterns became popular and, by around 400, leafy designs were being sculpted on capitals. Architectural decoration in churches increased markedly after 475, with the construction of the sanctuary dedicated to St. Simeon Stylites. Capitals, in particular, were ornamented with acanthus leaves that appeared to be ruffled by the wind. Usually the medallions in the corners of the capitals were sculpted with Greek crosses, whose arms are all of equal length.

AL-BARA, NEAR ALEPPO   73 x 95 x 27 cm
IDLIB MUSEUM   1191

75/76/77/78
Candelabra/Lamp with cross/
Eagle-shaped lamp/Scales
Bronze

AD 600

All of these objects were recently found by accident in a cache in a bronze-worker's shop. The craftsman must have intended to melt them down, since they all show signs of having been damaged. The lamp with a handle in the form of a cross is very typical of the Byzantine period. A hole in the base of the lamp indicates that it was meant to be set on the candelabra found in the cache as well. Lamps suspended by small chains were also popular in this period. The scales represent a fairly rare find; they are a reminder of the importance of trade in the economic life of the time.

JENDEÜRES (NEAR ALEPPO)
27.5 x 7.5 cm/14 x 12 cm/20 x 12.5 cm/25 x 8 cm
NATIONAL MUSEUM, ALEPPO   C1955/C1953/C1951/C1952

SYRIA BECOMES PART OF THE GREAT EMPIRES

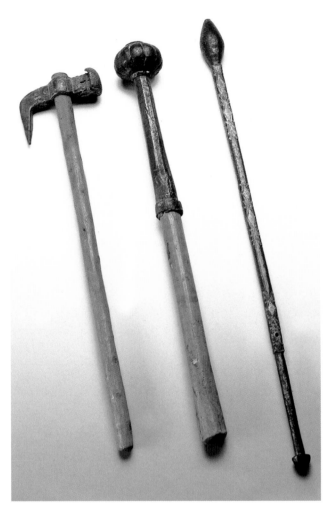

79/80/81
Maces and spearhead
Steel
AD 1200

Here are examples of the maces and spearheads used by the Muslim soldiers during the Crusades. These weapons come from the citadel of Aleppo, which was constructed by the great Muslim general, Saladin — or Salâh al-Dîn in Arabic — who fought fiercely against the Crusaders. Looking at these arms, one cannot help but think of how ferocious combat must have been when the two armies clashed.

ALEPPO: CITADEL   58 cm/50.5 cm/48 cm
NATIONAL MUSEUM, DAMASCUS   471 A, 474 A, 473 A

82
Helmet
Iron with brass mountings
AD 1400

This simple conical helmet with a visor is an example of the armor worn by the Mamluk soldiers who vanquished the Crusaders. The upright band in the middle would have been lowered in battle to protect the soldier's nose; the drop shape at the end indicated the owner's rank. The helmet originally also had protectors for the neck and cheeks.
The bronze workshops of Syria were known for their production of weapons and armor under Mamluk rule, but after the Tartar invasion of about 1400, they were reduced to making simple vessels with a little incised decoration. However, the workshops continued to produce a small quantity of armor ornamented with gold and jewels; these weapons were taken to Istanbul as war booty after the Ottoman conquest of 1516.

ALEPPO (PURCHASE)   26 x 21 cm
NATIONAL MUSEUM, DAMASCUS   1555/5132 A   *ED* 280

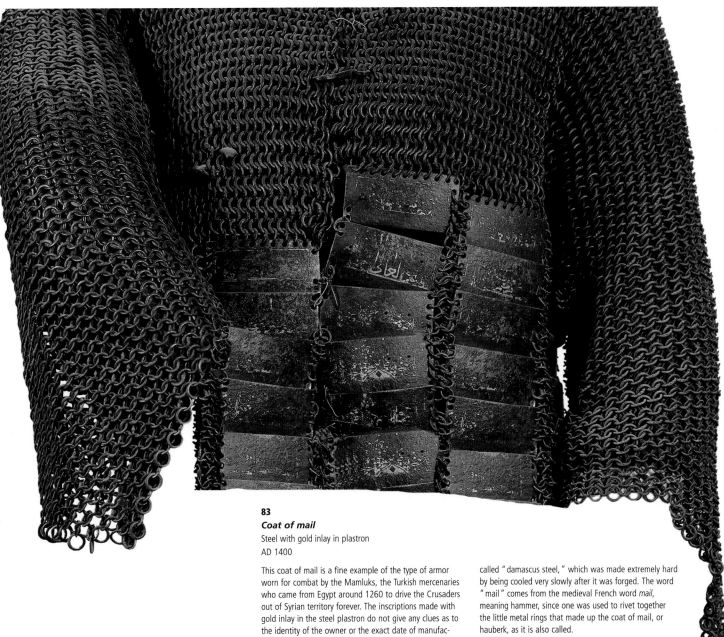

83

Coat of mail

Steel with gold inlay in plastron

AD 1400

This coat of mail is a fine example of the type of armor worn for combat by the Mamluks, the Turkish mercenaries who came from Egypt around 1260 to drive the Crusaders out of Syrian territory forever. The inscriptions made with gold inlay in the steel plastron do not give any clues as to the identity of the owner or the exact date of manufacture. It is known, however, that under the Mamluks, the city of Damascus specialized in making armor and swords. The city's name is associated with a famous type of steel, called "damascus steel," which was made extremely hard by being cooled very slowly after it was forged. The word "mail" comes from the medieval French word *mail*, meaning hammer, since one was used to rivet together the little metal rings that made up the coat of mail, or hauberk, as it is also called.

DAMASCUS   111 x 48 cm

NATIONAL MUSEUM, DAMASCUS   6788 A   *SMC* 382

84

Sword

Steel

AD 1200 (?)

This long, straight-bladed sword is probably of Islamic make, since the groove in the center of the blade and the decoration on either side of it are motifs commonly found on twelfth-century Syrian vessels made of ceramic. Damascus was renowned for its production of very strong swords. The city's armorers often ornamented their swords with elaborate, delicately incised motifs; this type of weapon was called a damask sword. Contrary to popular belief, Arab swords were straight rather than curved. The swordsmiths of Damascus became the victims of their own reputation, since after the Tartar invasion led by Tamerlane in about 1400, they were deported to Samarkand. This virtually put an end to the making of the swords that many a Crusader had taken back to Europe, where they were highly esteemed.

UNKNOWN (PURCHASE)   91.5 x 10.2 cm

NATIONAL MUSEUM, DAMASCUS   472 A

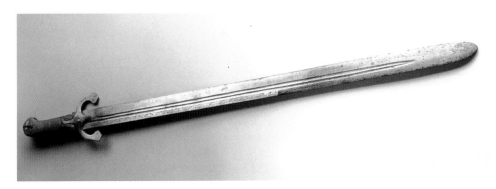

85
Bust of a young man throwing a ball
Sculpted stucco
AD 728

Over 50 000 fragments of stucco sculptures like this one were found in the ruins of the castle called Qasr al-Hayr al-Gharbi, which was built by the Umayyad caliph Hisham ibn 'Abd al-Malik (723-742) in the Syrian steppe, about 60 kilometers southwest of Palmyra around 728. It is often difficult to determine what parts of the castle were decorated by these sculptures. Part of the main facade of the castle has been reconstituted and now forms the monumental entrance gate to the National Museum of Damascus. Although stucco sculptures appeared during the Umayyad dynasty, the fashion for decorating public buildings, especially mosques, with sculpted stucco developed principally during the Abbasid dynasty.

QASR AL-HAYR AL-GHARBI   27 x 17 cm
NATIONAL MUSEUM, DAMASCUS   31770 A   *SMC* 304

86
Bird
Sculpted stucco
AD 728

This fragment was part of a sculpted decoration composed of a multitude of people and animals in a hunting scene. Hunting was one of the favorite pastimes of the caliph and his court; they could indulge in this sport in game parks close to their castles, where, surrounded by walls that sometimes reached three meters in height, many animal species roamed free.

QASR AL-HAYR AL-GHARBI   41 x 26 cm
NATIONAL MUSEUM, DAMASCUS   31769 A   *SMC* 302

87
Statue of a man
Sculpted stucco
AD 728

This statue once embellished a balustrade on the upper level of the portico leading to the courtyard of an Umayyad castle. The man's short curly hair and bearded face were inspired by the Roman portraits that figure so prominently in the art of Palmyra. Another sign of Roman influence is the fact that the man is dressed in a toga.

QASR AL-HAYR AL-GHARBI   54 x 26 cm
NATIONAL MUSEUM, DAMASCUS   31767 A   *SYRIEN* 99; *BAAL* 327

88

Bust of a crowned woman

Sculpted stucco

AD 728

This bust of a woman was set into a spandrel between the arches of a tower on the principal facade of the castle called Qasr al-Hayr al-Gharbi. She holds a braid in her right hand and a bird, perhaps a dove, in her left. The pose is reminiscent of that given to the figures on the funeral stelae of Palmyra, a nearby city that the caliphs would have known of.

QASR AL-HAYR AL-GHARBI   41 x 28 cm
NATIONAL MUSEUM, DAMASCUS   31768 A
SYRIEN 98; *BAAL* 326

89
Bust of a young man holding a palm
Sculpted stucco
AD 728

The Umayyad castles consisted of a complex of various buildings, the largest of which was the palace. Although located on the edge of the Syrian desert, the castle of Qasr al-Hayr al-Gharbi had a park that measured 1050 by 442 meters and was surrounded by a three-meter-high wall guarded by towers at the corners and along the sides. Palm trees were probably grown inside, giving the park the appearance of an oasis like Palmyra. At al-Gharbi, water was brought to the park and to the palace through an underground clay conduit that led from a masonry-dammed reservoir lake a few kilometers away.

QASR AL-HAYR AL-GHARBI   22 x 21 cm
NATIONAL MUSEUM, DAMASCUS   31771 A   *SMC* 306

90
Commemorative plaque
Marble
AD 1082

This inscription of 16 lines is sculpted in relief on a marble plaque that was set on a pillar on the southern facade of the Umayyad Mosque in Damascus. One of the events commemorated by the plaque was the construction of a *maqsûra*, or enclosed area in a mosque reserved for the ruler, under the reign of Sultan Malikshâh. Since according to the Koran it was forbidden to represent God or living creatures, monumental inscriptions developed into an element of Islamic art. The Cufic script used for this inscription soon became the type of writing in which all such inscriptions were done.

DAMASCUS : THE UMAYYAD MOSQUE   123 x 65 cm
NATIONAL MUSEUM, DAMASCUS   86/5A   *SMC* 299

91
Capital with cross and vine leaves
Marble
AD 500 and 800

Given the small size of this capital, it was probably originally part of a ciborium, or sort of canopy that covered the tabernacle of the high altar in early Christian churches. It was very likely imported from a region of Asia Minor (Turkey) where this style of capital was developed. On each of its four faces there is a sculpted representation of either a Latin cross with splayed ends or a five-lobed vine leaf. However, the church to which it belonged was destroyed, along with many other buildings, when the Abbasid caliph Harum al-Rashid transferred the capital of his empire from Baghdad to Raqqa and had much of the city rebuilt (AD 796-808). The architectural detail shown here was integrated into an Islamic building, which is why the topmost arm of the cross has been removed.

RAQQA (PURCHASE)   30 x 26 x 30 cm
NATIONAL MUSEUM, DAMASCUS   9560 A
MUSÉE NATIONAL p. 255; *BAAL* 322; *ED* 228

92
Dish
Monochrome faience (blue)
AD 1200

The medallion in this dish's basin bears an inscription that says quite simply: " al-Malik" (the King). The inscribed plate was probably made to honor the first caliph of the new Ayyubid dynasty, which took over the running of state affairs in Syria in 1171. The founder of this dynasty was the famous Salâh al-Dîn, known in the West as Saladin. He was a Kurdish officer and a fierce adversary of the Crusaders and, in particular, Frederick I Barbarossa. He re-vitalized Arab culture and developed international rela-tions, thus placing Syria back in the center of Muslim world for a while, at least until the end of his dynasty in 1250. Ceramic production under the Ayyubids of Syria came, for the most part, from Raqqa.

RAQQA   33 x 8 cm
NATIONAL MUSEUM, DAMASCUS   1387 A

93
Box with cover
Brass with silver inlay
AD 1338

With its cupola-shaped cover, this box (perhaps for jewelry) is thought to have been made to resemble a mausoleum. According to the cursive inscription that decorates the outer sides, it belonged to a Mamluk named Turghây, who was appointed governor of Aleppo in 1338. The text reads: " His High Excellency our master, the great emir, champion of the faith, the honorable one, defender of our borders, aided by God, the victorious one, the helper, the hero, the peerless one, the counsellor, belonging to the sovereign, the glorious one, the very illustrious Jamâl al-Dîn Turghây, may his prosperity endure ! "

UNKNOWN   23.6 x 22 cm
NATIONAL MUSEUM, DAMASCUS   5380 A   *SMC* 377

Bracelet
Gold
AD 1200

This bracelet is formed by a large hollow ring decorated with embossing. Inscribed on the diagonal bands that spiral around it are wishes for happiness, success, power and long life addressed to the owner, who apparently had no need of being wished riches. The elaborate flat clasp was decorated with little spheres of gold and filigree set with precious stones, of which all but the middle one have since disappeared. It is rare that such jewelry is found, since much of it was melted down even in antiquity. This was a means of safeguarding and transporting personal wealth; the custom still exists today in certain Near East countries where worked gold is sold by the pound. Bracelets like this one were worn in pairs at the ankle or upper arm, over the sleeves of clothing.

RAQQA   13 cm
NATIONAL MUSEUM, DAMASCUS
2800 A   *Cf. SMC* 363; *BAAL* 343

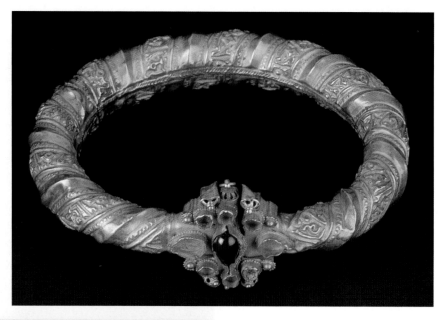

95 a-b/96
Earrings and necklace
Gold
AD 1200

The earrings consist of a delicate web of round filigree, ornamented on one side by tiny spheres; finely worked gold beads dangle from three little chains. The necklace is made of large round gold beads separated by cone-shaped elements to which smaller beads are attached with rings. This jewelry was found at Palmyra, but in Islamic tombs. The funeral busts of Palmyrene citizens of the Roman period make it clear that it was customary for the dead to be buried with their jewelry, as a symbol of their material wealth during their earthly lives and perhaps to guarantee a similar style of life in the hereafter. This custom was abandoned by both the Christian and Islamic religions.

PALMYRA   3 cm (diameter)/50 cm (length)
NATIONAL MUSEUM, DAMASCUS   3974 A/3967 A   *SMC* 360

97
Amulet box
Gold
AD 1300

This splendid box is made entirely of gold wire fused together in a technique called filigree. The inscription engraved on one of the box's faces wishes its lucky owner the following blessing: "Eternal glory, good fortune and long life to the possessor." The degree of perfection displayed by certain pieces of Islamic jewelry, like this one, attests to the great mastery of the Arab goldsmiths in the practice of their art.

ALEPPO   8 x 7 cm
NATIONAL MUSEUM, DAMASCUS   1054 A   *SMC* 367

98
Earrings
Gold, turquoise and pearls
AD 1200

Anyone looking at this pair of earrings will find it easy to understand the renown of the Islamic goldsmiths and their mastery of the techniques developed by their predecessors, particularly the Byzantines. This tradition and the reputation it earned are perpetuated even today in the elaborate pieces of jewelry offered in the souks of Damascus and Aleppo. Each of these earrings consists of a sort of birdhouse with a bird perched on top, and four other birds dangling from lengths of fine chain attached to each corner of the house. The sides of the birdhouse are decorated with filigree motifs and set with small turquoise stones. The earrings are the epitome of ostentation.

ALEPPO   18 cm/16 cm
NATIONAL MUSEUM, DAMASCUS   1057/3802 A   *SMC* 364

THE ORGANIZATION OF
the economy

THE ORGANIZATION OF
the economy

H uman societies may adopt very different social structures, but their first priority is always to ensure that the community has enough food to eat, since this is essential to the survival of the species. Thus, if any group of humans wants to increase and diversify its activities, it is obliged to invent and intensify agricultural practices; it can no longer rely on hunting and gathering food resources from the immediate environment.

Syria was the place where humans first experimented with cultivating cereal plants and raising animals, two activities that are fundamental to the emergence of a civilization. The yields thus obtained grew so rapidly that surpluses resulted. Even though these surpluses were at first intended to ensure the reproduction of plants and animals from one year to the next regardless of seasonal constraints, they led to the possibility of redistribution, so that some people were free to specialize in tasks that were unrelated to farming and thus produce non-agricultural goods. In every period, even those marked by the establishment of sophisticated political systems, agricultural production remained the foundation of the whole economy.

The Syrian territory was naturally suited to farming and herding, but it also offered raw materials, such as flint, clay and gypsum. These could be used to make tools, instruments and utensils that simplified certain tasks, especially those linked to the community's food needs. But the first village-dwellers of Syria were not interested only in utilitarian objects. They soon began to produce luxury items, fashioned at first from local materials and later from imported materials. Over the centuries craftsmen learned to fully exploit the potential of these exotic commodities.

Phoenician coin.
Cat. 257

Previous page:
Mycenaean vase.
Cat. 211

Such luxury materials could be acquired by trading local goods such as agricultural produce. Thus, farming became further intensified in order to create agricultural surpluses for use in commerce. In addition, long-distance trade routes in the Near East almost inevitably passed through Syrian territory, given its geographical position and the waterway provided by the Euphrates.

The great increase and diversification of trade-related activities soon made it necessary to establish means of controlling and managing commerce. Simple methods, such as marking traded goods with a seal, continued to be applied even as new, more sophisticated, tools were developed. At first, small clay tokens were used to reckon the quantity of various goods. Then the system was improved so that the type of product, rather than just the quantity, could be identified. The symbols employed represented the first steps towards writing. The trading cities of Syria have provided a vast quantity of cuneiform tablets, giving not only lists of products but also information on administrative, political and legal activities. Eventually, cuneiform writing was simplified and made more efficient through the adoption of an alphabetic system developed in a Syrian port city.

The landscape of the Fertile Crescent.

THE INVENTION
AND INTENSIFICATION
OF AGRICULTURE

It is the opinion of many researchers that agricultural production is an essential condition for any great civilization, since it enables human beings to free themselves from a constant preoccupation with finding daily food. Certain authors go so far as to say that the invention of agriculture in the Neolithic period represents a revolution in the history of humanity.

Even if settlement preceded the development of agriculture, a settled society could not develop unless people had learned to perfect agricultural techniques. The very development of a village into a city means that city-dwellers are dependent on others to produce at least some of the food that they need.

It is true, of course, that agriculture cannot be practiced without favorable environmental conditions to start with. Certain combinations of soil types and sufficient annual rainfall are essential. But recognition must also go to the active role played in the process by the human beings who, for reasons that are still not really understood, decided to benefit from certain plants and animals and try to affect their reproduction so as to have more control over them and increase their production. The research to date suggests that the very first attempts by humans to manipulate the reproduction of plants and animals occurred in Syrian territory. Similar experimentation, which also led to the invention of agriculture, took place later and quite independently, in places like Egypt, India, China, Central America and South America.

EARLY AGRICULTURAL PRACTICES
AND THE BEGINNINGS OF VILLAGE LIFE

Around 10 000 BC, following a period of global warming, permanent villages, the first of their kind in the world, began to be established in a zone that covered a good part of modern Syria. Today we refer to it as the Fertile Crescent because it provides such a favorable environment for agriculture. Cereal and leguminous plants were found here in their wild state, as were the ancestors of certain species of domesticated animals. The region received enough annual rainfall for cereal plants to grow without human intervention. The presence of such plants, and especially barley, attracted grazing animals of various species, depending on the season. At first, the people living in the villages contented themselves with gathering the fruits of the earth, which were so plentiful in this fertile earthly paradise. These first settlements are thus called pre-agricultural villages, and their inhabitants were hunter-gatherers rather than farmers.

A little after 9000 BC, that is, earlier than anywhere else in the world, the people who had settled in villages began to use the meadows around them to cultivate certain plants, such as barley, einkorn and emmer wheat, which had until then grown wild. These crops spread quickly across the Fertile Crescent. They were cultivated along with the wild ancestors of certain other plants, like rye, and with legumes, such as peas, lentils and chick peas. It is difficult to say exactly when this primitive form of agriculture began, since it took several generations before the cultivated plant species started to display the genetic mutations that resulted from domestication. Archaeologists interpret the appearance of storage pits dug

into the floors of village houses as a conclusive sign that the inhabitants had adopted a new way of life based on agriculture.

It also took many generations for morphological changes to show up in the skeletons of animals as a result of domestication. At present, however, it can be convincingly argued that there is evidence of goats being raised in Syria in around 8000 BC, and that a few centuries later, in around 7500 BC, sheep were being bred. When the raising of goats and sheep became widespread, in about 7000 BC, pigs and cows began to be domesticated. The dog, which was useful for rounding up herds, was domesticated as early as 10 000 BC. At the same time that they practiced agriculture, the villagers continued to obtain food by hunting gazelles, aurochs, hemions and small game using arrows [102] and slingshots [103]. Craftsmen represented animals in figurines made of terra cotta [115], polished stone and even bone [108], and painted animal motifs on vases made of stone [105] or ceramic [99 and 101].

The adoption of agriculture as a means of subsistence had an observable effect on villages and houses. Villages grew larger, covering up to 12 hectares, or four times more than they had previously. Houses were usually separated from one another by alleys that enabled people to circulate through the village. The alleys converged on courtyards, which indicates a certain degree of planning. The houses were rectangular in shape, rather than round, and had several communicating rooms. The walls and floors were made of unbaked bricks rather than *pisé*, and their surfaces were coated with lime. Rooms were laid out differently according to their use. One of them would have contained domestic equipment such as ovens, fireplaces and bins to store food. In some houses, the surfaces of the walls and even the floors were decorated with painted motifs; archaeologists have found representations of cranes, a human head and female figures. One village even had a defensive wall with gates as well as a three-meter-high earthwork rampart built with drystone.

Such public works, which were quite novel at the time, must have required considerable social coordination and meant that the villagers had a certain amount of free time to devote to community needs.

By 7000 BC, all of Syria had joined the Neolithic age. The domestication of plants and animals seems to have been well established in the more hospitable zones of the Near East. It was then that farmers and stockraisers moved onto the semi-arid steppe. The dryness of its climate — with an annual precipitation of less than 200 millimeters — makes it probable that its inhabitants practiced some primitive form of irrigation, since dry-farming was impossible. This hypothesis is confirmed by a study of the plant remains collected on archaeological sites from the period; they contain adventive plants, or weeds, which are not planted but take advantage of irrigation to establish themselves. As well, a collection of faunal remains from the period include the bones of a type of rodent, the antelope rat [114], which normally lives in irrigated fields.

Another agricultural innovation has recently come to light through microscopic examination of certain elements of this society's material culture. To make harvesting more efficient, people constructed sickles by fitting flint blades into crude hafts made of wood or bone. As more and more plants were harvested, a new system was developed for removing grains from the ears of cereal plants. A tribulum, which consisted of a wooden platform with a multitude of flint blades inserted into its lower surface, was dragged repeatedly over sheaves of plants laid on the ground. The tearing action of this instrument not only removed grain but also broke up the plant stalks and thus produce chopped straw. This was used to make *pisé* and, later, mud bricks, which, in turn, were used to build houses. Thus we see clearly the link between intensified agricultural practices and the development of architecture.

The houses in this period were laid out with an 11-meter-long T-shaped room,

Modern reconstruction of a Neolithic sickle.

Reconstruction of an old tribulum drawn by a horse.

Modern reconstruction of an ancient tribulum, based on information provided by old texts.

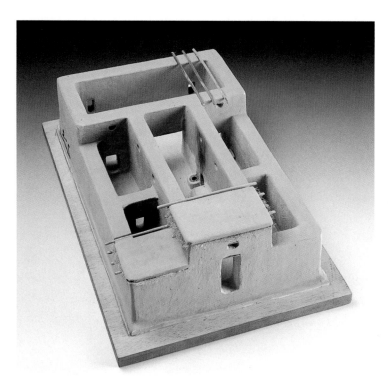

Modern model of a Neolithic house. Cat. 5

The oldest representation of a human face found to date in Syria. Cat. 6

which these houses stood gradually became vast mounds, as new houses were built over old ones and demolition material accumulated. The work of leveling old housing sites to make way for new ones represented a new practice at the time. The attention devoted to how homes were built is an indication of their permanent nature.

AGRICULTURAL SURPLUS
AS AN INSTRUMENT OF POWER

By around 6000 BC, village life based on agriculture and animal husbandry had become widespread in Syria. Villages grew into denser agglomerations with rectangular houses that now had some 20 small rooms, which may be interpreted as indicating that the inhabitants' lifestyle was becoming more complex. Some of these houses also had a second floor which was used for private rooms, unlike the ground floor, which held rooms for receiving people and for preparing food. However, the most significant architectural innovation was the appearance of small circular structures. About three meters in diameter and built aboveground outside the large two-story houses, they probably served as community granaries.

According to several researchers, the granaries point to the existence of some political system, somewhat like a chiefdom, in which the accumulating of agricultural surplus was controlled and food products were redistributed in exchange for services rendered by specialized craftsmen or for imported items considered to be luxury goods. To increase yields, it was probably necessary to expand the area of the land under cultivation, provide the

flanked on either side by small rooms in which various goods were stored [5]. Near the entrance was a hearth built against a wall, while a niche for keeping food was made in another wall nearby and a sort of brazier was dug in the floor. These houses also had systems for draining wastewater: channels in the plaster of the floors ran from one room to another or through doorways, drainage holes passed through walls, and beneath the floors there were even true encased drains. The sites on

right amount of irrigation and allow the soil to recuperate through fallow periods. In short, agricultural work had to be planned.

By-products of animal husbandry and agricultural diversification

During the fourth and third millennia, another important step was taken in agricultural production. The people who raised livestock began to find uses for their animals besides killing them for meat. For example, they learned to use milk, wool (from sheep), hair (from goats), traction (by oxen) and transportation (by ass).

Other changes affected cultivation methods themselves. Farmers began to use plows pulled by animals instead of cultivating the earth with digging sticks and primitive, man-drawn plows. Metal instruments probably made it easier to build the irrigation canals that had become necessary now that agriculture was being practiced in dry zones. A use was found even for the steppe regions, which, although not very suitable for agriculture, were an ideal territory in which to pasture herds of sheep and goats, watched over by nomadic shepherds.

The nomads were at first pastoral people but gradually became part of a nomadic

Beehive-shaped community store-houses in a village of the Fertile Crescent in Syria.

Loom weights. Cat. 126

Reconstruction of a warp stand.

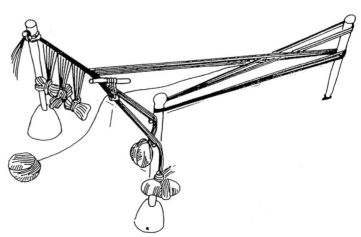

trading society. They obtained raw materials from distant regions in exchange for unprocessed agricultural goods (such as grains, animals or hides), or, better still, in exchange for goods made from the by-products of animal husbandry, such as textiles and dairy products. Cloth making was no doubt an important activity at this time, but very few vestiges of this production have come down to us, given the fragility of the material. During the third millennium, linen cloth, made from flax, began to be replaced by woolen textiles. This led to an intensification of sheep-raising and semi-nomadic pastoral practices in the zones that lay outside the

Livestock enclosures built by nomads using surface stones.

true agricultural areas but that were ideal for pasturing animals. Certain authors consider the change to woolen textiles to have had revolutionary effects. As herds of animals that produced milk increased, ways of conserving this abundant and nutritious food were probably developed. But since the product of such inventions would have been highly perishable, we can only guess what they might have been.

Urbanization meant that some of the available manpower in the community was directed towards accomplishing specialized tasks in the cities. As well, a new social class arose that was responsible for managing the community's activities. Consequently, even more effort had to be made to increase agricultural yields in order to meet the food needs of those members of the community who did not participate in farming activities. The city-state of Mari, for example, had gardens within the city itself but was situated in a fairly unproductive territory. Thus it relied

on food imported from regions in the zone where dry-farming could be practiced. To store this food, large granaries were constructed along the banks of the Habur River, a major tributary of the Euphrates, on whose banks Mari stood.

Cultivation of the land grew more diversified at the same time that it became more intense, and new products began to appear. Texts dating from the third millennium BC and discovered in Ebla mention that certain fruit trees were grown and that olive oil and wine were produced. This was the first instance of vines and olive trees being planted in Syria. From Ebla, they spread to the rest of the Syrian interior and especially to the coastal regions, where the soil and climate were much more suitable for vineyards and olive groves. Meanwhile, in the regions towards the east, where barley grew, people began to produce beer.

INSTITUTIONALIZED AGRICULTURE

The Habur region seems to have been used as a bread basket for the city-state of Mari as early as the third millennium BC, and even more so in the first millennium BC, when the Assyrians established themselves there. They set up an elaborate irrigation system on both sides of the river to extend the area of land under cultivation beyond the fertile valley and into the surrounding semi-arid steppes. The Assyrians also introduced the use of the Arabian dromedary for transporting goods along trade routes in these dry regions. Elsewhere in the country, olive oil and wine was produced by the Aramaeans.

Under the rule of the Achaemenids of Persia, agriculture in Syrian territory was promoted through the establishment of private and public projects, to which references may be found in official texts. A new species of vine was even introduced in Damascus, and the pistachios for which Aleppo became famous began to be grown there.

An olive grove in the Ebla region.

Irrigated fields along the Habur.

The Romans systematically developed the cereal-growing lands in their Syrian province, particularly to grow wheat, even in regions where harsh conditions required the installation of an irrigation system relying on water that was transported from the mountains through specially constructed canals to community cisterns. The mountain slopes in the northern and southern regions were well suited to olive trees and vines, and from them oil and wine were made. The coastal regions supplied figs, pears and apples. The importance of textile making suggests that there was a large sheep population, which would have been put to pasture in the semi-arid steppe and guarded by nomadic shepherds. In short, the economy of Roman Syria was based on agriculture and not on caravan trade, as has long been maintained by certain authors who were impressed by the vast ruins of the caravan station of Palmyra.

As for the Byzantine era, there exists a detailed study of 700 villages of the period, about 60 of which have been well preserved, with ruins standing as high as eight meters in some

Reconstruction of a winepress.

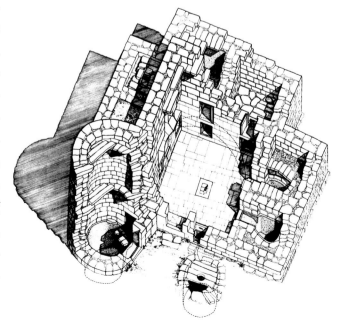

places. Some of the peasants who lived in these villages practiced diversified farming based on vegetables and fruit trees, but most specialized in one of two main agricultural activities. The first was olive oil production and wine making, both of which are evidenced by the discovery of numerous family-owned and community presses. The second was the raising of sheep and cattle, which is reflected in the great number of stone mangers found in the villages. The products of these activities were sold in the cities, and it appears that the farmers did very well from such sales, since quantities of coins have been found in the villages where they lived.

In the sixth century (AD 527), the situation changed dramatically. Syria was exposed to repeated attacks and pillaging by the Persians. In the countryside, suffering was caused by earthquakes and epidemics like the plague.

Food crises were rampant. After the prosperous Byzantine period, with its conquest of new farmland and rapid population growth, the sixth century ushered in a long and steady decline, which impoverished the peasants.

The decline in agricultural production was accelerated by the establishment of the first Islamic dynasties in Syria, despite the use of new irrigation techniques like the noria. This waterwheel irrigation was in fact invented somewhere in the Near East as early as 200 BC according to the Roman author Vitruvius, but it became widespread only during the Islamic period.

In Syria, the Islamic dynasties encouraged the cultivation of crops, such as cotton and flax, that had industrial uses and could be used to increase foreign trade. The villages were ruled by the cities and treated as resources to be exploited. A civilization that

An abandoned town southwest of Aleppo.

141

The norias: a traditional irrigation method in the Hama district

THE CITY OF HAMA, situated 120 kilometers north of Damascus, is the best place to see norias, the waterwheels that have been used to irrigate fields since antiquity. In *The History of Abul al-Fida,* a book written by Sultan Abul al-Fida (1273-1331), it is said that "Hama is eternal, like Ash-Sham (Damascus); it is one of the most beautiful cities in the land of Damascus, with magnificent castles on the citadel and norias along the Orontes River that irrigate the gardens."

There were two types of wheels at Hama: the maddar was turned by an animal, while the noria was activated by water. The first type has disappeared and only norias still exist today. The noria is a wooden wheel with buckets in its outer rim. Set upright in a river, the wheel is turned by the current and the buckets are filled with water. The action of the wheel carries the buckets upwards, and at their highest point the water in them is poured into an aqueduct. As the wheel continues to turn, the now empty buckets are carried down to the river, where they are refilled. The largest known noria, called the Al-Muhamma-Diyyah noria, has 120 buckets.

The earliest representation of a noria found to date is in a mosaic dating from AD 469 discovered at Apamea. The mosaic is now displayed in the new museum at Hama.

Between the city of Ar-Rastan, 20 kilometers south of Hama, and the village of Acharneh, 40 kilometers north, there are more than 100 norias along the Orontes. In the city of Hama itself, there are 17 norias still in use today. The biggest one, the Al-Muhamma-Diyyah noria, stands in the western part of the city and measures 27 meters in diameter. It was built by the city's governor in 1361. The second largest is the Mamuriyyah noria, which was built in 1453, near the Azem Palace.

Most of the norias, including the Al-Muhamma-Diyyah, are now in ruins. For the past few years, The Directorate General of Syrian Antiquities and Museums has been working on their restoration, giving special attention to the towers, dams and aqueducts that were used with them. The norias of Hama that are still turning along the Orontes are a source of fascination not only for the eyes but also for the ears, since friction of wood on wood fills the air with a haunting rhythmic groan.

ABDELLAZAR ZARZOUQ
Director of the Hama Museum and Antiquities in the Hama Region

Norias in the Hama region.

had been based on village life became urban and was no longer concerned with cultivating the rich soils of Syria. It is significant that the farmland abandoned at the time of Umayyad rule was returned to cultivation only in the twentieth century.

MASTERY OF MATERIALS

As human beings first struggled to survive then attempted to improve the way they lived, and eventually sought to prosper, they took materials from the world around them — whether nearby or far away — and used them to make weapons, tools, instruments, utensils, containers and ornaments. They learned simple ways to turn raw materials into needed objects. With time, however, they discovered how to exploit the different properties of an increasing number of materials. In the following pages, we will look at a few of these materials; they have been selected because they seem to contribute significantly to an understanding of the nature of civilization.

STONE OBJECTS: THE FIRST TRACES OF HUMAN ACTIVITY

During the Paleolithic era, hunters made weapons by taking large flint pebbles and striking their edges with other, harder, pebbles. Flakes of stone would be chipped off the large pebble creating sharp edges. Since this technique resulted in a tool that was worked on both faces, it is called a biface [128].

Someone then had an ingenious idea: the toolmaker could take a block of flint and strike off flakes that could themselves be used as tools. This represented a considerable technological breakthrough at the time, since in-

stead of producing a single tool by chipping flakes off a flint core, people could now make dozens of tools at a time by carefully controlled flaking. At this point, we can talk of a true lithic industry ("lithic" coming from "lithos," the Greek word for "stone"). The flakes produced with this technique were used as arrowheads, which enabled people to hunt from a distance, and as scrapers [131] for cutting up animal carcasses.

Later on, in the Neolithic era, flakes of flint in the shape of long blades were fitted into grooves made lengthwise in wooden sticks or long animal bones; these tools were

How blades were flaked from a flint core.

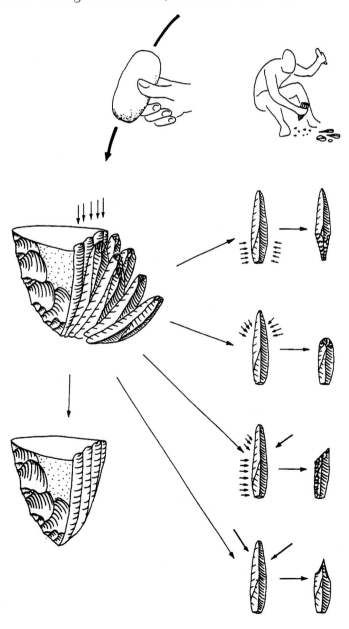

the first sickles, used for harvesting the plants that people were beginning to cultivate. The stone component was held in the groove with pitch, or bitumen, which seeps up through the ground in several regions of the Near East where petroleum deposits lie close to the surface. Pitch was the first glue used by human beings

The appearance of sickle blades in prehistoric man's tool kit is a clear sign that human beings were now exploiting their natural environment more thoroughly and were increasingly interested in plants as a source of food. The sickle was accompanied by another type of stone object — one that had never been seen until then and an indication that a new way of life was being adopted. This was the quern, which was used to grind the grains of plants harvested with a sickle for human consumption. The quern, made of basalt [121], a

very hard volcanic stone, also represented a significant technological innovation in the history of mankind, since this instrument was fashioned not of flaked stone but rather of polished stone. In fact, the Neolithic, or "new stone age," is so named because it was the period in which the new technique was developed. Although the flaking technique required great dexterity, it was very fast. In contrast, polishing stone was long and laborious work. A quern could take more than a month to make. With use, the grinding instruments were gradually worn into different shapes [119].

People began to use polished stone to make other types of tools that had previously been made of flaked stone, tools such as axes [138] for cutting down trees for firewood or for beams supporting house roofs. As well, vessels were painstakingly fashioned

out of limestone, marble and gypsum. Since they had to be hollowed out, their presence implies that the drill had been invented. Furthermore, great skill and patience were required to polish them so evenly. Craftsmen were even able to create stone vases in the shape of animals [106].

It should not be supposed that the new technology of stone polishing immediately replaced flint toolmaking. The technique of flaking stone indeed went on to be further refined, and both techniques coexisted throughout the Neolithic period and even beyond it, since they were used for different purposes. One new use of flint was the tribulum, which consisted of a flint blade [118] placed on the lower face of a wooden plank. When dragged over sheaves of cereal plants, it served to separate the grains from the stalks. Flaking was also adapted to a newly discovered material, obsidian, a vitrified vol-

canic stone that could be worked like flint but that produced a sharper edge and did not become blunt as quickly [135]. Since deposits of this stone are found in only a few locations, especially in eastern Turkey, its presence in Syria makes it one of the first materials, if not the very first, to have been traded over considerable distances.

BONE, IVORY AND SHELL: THE CRAFTING OF LUXURY ITEMS

Hunting obviously supplied Paleolithic man with another material to work with — animal bones. By the time the first permanent villages were formed,

Stone vessels from the Neolithic period.
Cat. 139, 140 and 141

How the surface of stone vessels was polished.

145

The origins of the first tools in Syria

AS THE HUMANS KNOWN as *Homo erectus* moved from eastern Africa and gradually conquered Eurasia, their route necessarily passed through the Near East. In Syria, the earliest tools discovered so far are over a million years old. They were found mainly in the valleys of the Nahr el-Kebir and the Orontes. The tools consist of crudely flaked pebbles and a very few thick, irregular bifaces.

During the Acheulean period (1 000 000 BC to 200 000 BC), which was characterized by the predominance of biface tools, humans spread throughout most of Syria. From the earliest phases come handaxes and long massive bifaces, both of which were always flaked with stone hammers. In a large deposit at Latamne, in the Orontes Valley, several levels of human occupation dating from about 800 000 years ago have been found; they contain tools of this type in association with rich faunal remains displaying African traits.

In 1996, the remains of an early *Homo erectus,* dating from about 500 000 years ago, was brought to light in the Nadawiyah Aïn Askar deposit (el-Kowm, in central Syria), in the lowest level of an Acheulean sequence. This discovery confirmed that the desert regions of today once played an important role in the human conquest of the Old World. This sequence, a 25-meter-thick accumulation that represents about 600 000 years of prehistory, is one of the largest in the Near East. The Acheulean can be divided into six cultural phases distributed among 24 archaeological layers. The earliest phase is distinguished by bifaces showing extremely fine flaking work, while the middle and later phases are characterized by bifaces that are thicker and much less standardized, along with an increase in lighter tools represented by microbifaces and cleavers.

Unexpectedly, the bifaces in the oldest layers, estimated to be 400 000 to 500 000 years old, display ex-

The site of Nadawiyah Aïn Askar.

ceptionally fine craftsmanship. They have perfectly symmetrical forms and beautiful pure lines. Tools did not have to be "beautiful" to be useful, but the concern for aesthetics that went into making these pieces is undeniable. It is evident that a symbolic element had entered the making of tools and that *Homo erectus* was expressing the first stirrings of artistic creativity.

At this site, *Homo erectus* lived on the edges of a circular lake, at the bottom of a sinkhole surrounded by steppe country. On the steppe, vast stretches of herbaceous plants grew and there were several species of gazelles, antelopes, equids and archaic dromedaries that the early humans could hunt. A fragment of a *Homo erectus* skull was discovered in the site's eighth layer, which contains an abundance of finely chipped oval bifaces. A series of comparisons has shown that Nadawiyah Man presents characteristics that are very archaic and that he belonged to a group of classic *Homo erectus* of the Asian type.

PROF. DR. JEAN-MARIE LE TENSORER
University of Basel

bone carving was well established and would not change for the next four or five millennia, or until around 3000 BC, when bone was replaced by copper. Bone was used chiefly for utilitarian objects like awls, needles and pins for working leather, although more elaborate items were also made, such as pins with heads carved into a simple design [147] or symbolic objects with human [146] or animal forms.

Craftsmen also prized another bony animal part — the teeth of hippopotamuses or elephants, commonly known as ivory. Both these species apparently lived in Syrian territory long ago — the hippopotamus near the coast and the elephant in the steppe. Ivory from hippopotamus was used for everyday objects, while elephant ivory was reserved for luxury items. Between the tenth and eighth centuries BC, ivory-carving developed to the point that different schools of this art can be identified. The reputation of the Syrian carvers (who were actually Aramaeans at this time) spread throughout the Near East. For the most part, craftsmanship was centered on sculpting pieces that were used to decorate furniture [53]. Around 700 BC, the elephant disappeared from Syrian territory, perhaps as a result of having been overexploited for its ivory, and from then on craftsmen had to rely on tusks imported from Africa or India.

Shells were brought from the Persian Gulf and the Red Sea. They were pierced for use as simple pendants; sawed in two for use as ceremonial vessels; or cut into pieces for inlay in decorative panels. For shell inlay — an inexpensive version of ivory inlay — only the mother-of-pearl mantle of the oyster shell was used. Made of calcium carbonate, mother-of-pearl has the same composition as pearl. Shells and ivory were worked by specialized craftsmen in workshops associated with palaces or temples. The raw material was imported and the finished hand-crafted product was exported.

CLAY: THE ALL-PURPOSE MATERIAL

The first vessels made of a material that was baked in a fire were not fashioned out of clay, as we might assume, but rather of plaster. The first Syrian villages were located in regions where the substratum is formed by a thick layer of gypsum, a material that is easily made into powder. When gypsum powder is mixed with water, there is a chemical reaction and the mixture hardens as it air-dries. Gypsum plaster was used in the first dwellings to coat the floors and walls and to make household equipment such as basins, vessels [153] and rectangular bins for storing grain. Such containers, which originated in Syria, are called "white vessels" by archaeologists because of their appearance. Some of them show the imprint of basketwork [152], which represented another category of containers at this time.

Clay is also found throughout the Near East. It was used in about the same period to shape female figurines [151] and animals, as well as tiny vessels, or pots. But such objects were merely slightly hardened in a fire; they were not really baked.

Vessel made out of a shell.
Cat. 298

Statue of a potter
working on the
wheel.
Cat. 166

Between 6500 BC and 6000 BC, the first true ceramic — that is, clay vessels baked in a hearth at temperatures of 500°C to 800° C — made its first appearance in Syrian villages. The earliest baked clay vases were made by stacking up small slabs of clay and shaping them into simple, often rounded forms. The clay was not pure, but mixed with water and straw to make it more resistant as it dried. Surfaces were smoothed to remove traces of modeling and a thin coating of very diluted clay (slip) was poured over the object to make it even more uniform. A slip of a different color than that of the paste could be applied with a brush to decorate the surface of the vase [155]. These techniques gave birth in the Near East to a long tradition of painted ceramic, which, because of the diversity of motifs and forms, has been elected by archaeologists as the most distinctive element in the material culture, regardless of the period, the region or the community that produced it.

A little before 4000 BC, ceramic-making reached a new stage. Vessels were still shaped by hand but were now made out of long

rolled coils. The paste was purified and mixed with fine sand to temper it. The surfaces were decorated with geometrical designs painted in reddish-brown, black and purple [156]. However, the most significant innovation at this time was that pottery was baked in kilns that could reach a temperature of 1200°C and thus produce true ceramics. Some 15 kilns of this type have been discovered recently on a site in Syria. They are associated with a potters' workshop that still holds the craftsmen's tools.

Between 3500 BC and 3000 BC, Syrian potters began to shape their ceramics on a wheel, which was simply a circular disk turning on a small pivot on the bottom side, set on the ground or with the pivot fitted into a socket in the floor of a house [165]. The wheel had to be spun by an apprentice while the potter kept both hands on the vase. This was not a true potter's wheel, which allows the craftsman to shape the vase as he turns the wheel with his feet. Such wheels appeared only during the second millennium BC. Although the primitive wheel was slow, it nonetheless provided

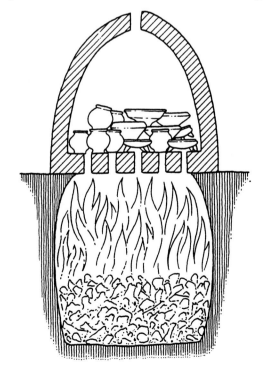

potters with a means of making vases in greater quantities and more uniform shapes. Not all ceramic was turned on a wheel; some of it was made in moulds [163].

When Syria was integrated into a succession of great empires (from the seventh century BC on), the ceramic used by its inhabitants resembled that found elsewhere in the empire, although there is evidence of some local pottery-making. In the Roman period, huge quantities of ceramics, especially roof tiles, were produced. It is thought that the need for wood to fuel the kilns was so great that it led to the deforestation of Syria's wooded regions. The loss of woodland was hastened in the Islamic period, when baked bricks began to be made. Raqqa was the first city to produce these bricks, starting in about AD 800. Another type of Islamic ceramic, characterized by a vitrified surface, will be dealt with further on, in the section entitled "Glass and vitreous products."

Metal, a sign
of technological progress

Mineral deposits on Syrian territory were not rich enough nor close enough to the surface for metal to be extracted in antiquity. It should not be concluded, however, that all the metal objects found in Syria

were made in other countries. The fact that raw materials were imported and transformed by local craftsmen is confirmed both by ancient texts and archaeological discoveries.

A distinction must be made between precious metals, like gold and silver, and base metals, like iron, and copper (which, with the addition of a little tin, becomes bronze). Gold was the first precious metal to be used, since it exists in a natural state in regions near Syria and also because it is easy to work and can be cold-hammered, being malleable and extremely ductile. However, very few early gold objects have survived to this day because, even in antiquity, they tended to be melted down for reuse. Gold artifacts are generally represented by jewelry and ornaments. At that time, gold was thought of as a precious material to be reserved for the adornments of a sociopolitical elite or for extravagant offerings in temples. There were a number of ways that gold could be worked, depending on its eventual use. It could be melted and cast in moulds [174]. It could be processed into fine threads that could be braided into bracelets, coiled into decorative designs for jewelry (filigree) [176], or used in weaving to produce damask cloth (a textile that takes its name from the city of Damascus). It could also be transformed into tiny spheres or grains that could be delicately fused together (granulation). Or it could simply be hammered into gold leaf and shaped on a wooden form [177] or decorated with embossed motifs using a punch. Gold was sometimes combined with silver in a proportion of between 20% and 50% to produce an alloy called electrum.

Unlike gold, silver was rarely found in a natural state. It had to be sought in deep mines where the ore was so pure that merely melting it was sufficient to extract silver. The silver used in the Near East came from the ores of eastern Anatolia, which were rich in lead. Until other methods were discovered, the lead was simply melted, leaving the silver behind. The first silver objects, mainly ornaments, appeared around 3500 BC. Silver quite soon took on another type of value, for it was used as a standard of measurement in commercial exchanges. At first its value was based on its weight, but later this value came to be related to symbols marked on the faces of small silver disks, or coins. The polished silver *Helmet with Mask* from Emesa [62] is an outstanding example of an ornamental object made of this precious material.

True metallurgy began with the use of copper, another native metal that is widely found on the earth's surface, especially in the mountainous regions of Anatolia, north of Mesopotamia. It was here that the Syrian craftsmen obtained their supplies. Copper can be cold-hammered, which increases its hardness but causes it to become less malleable, to the point of brittleness. It becomes elastic again if it is gently heated (to around 400-500°C) and then allowed to cool slowly. It is essential that copper be hardened if it is to be used for tools and weapons with cutting edges. It can also be made harder by combining it with another metal. Copper is often already mixed with another metal in naturally occurring ores. In the Near East, this metal is usually arsenic, which can constitute up to 15% of the ore. However, the most common man-made alloy is obtained by adding tin in a proportion of 9% to 17%; this produces what we call bronze. Tin is fairly rare, and

specialists still debate its source in antiquity. While written sources from Mari and Ebla mention convoys of asses laden with tin coming through southern Mesopotamia from Afghanistan, recent field research seems to indicate that the mines and even the metallurgists' workshops were located in certain mountainous regions of present-day Turkey, close to Syrian territory.

Copper and its alloy, bronze, were used to make a vast array of objects. Most of them were cast in single open moulds [167] of stone or clay, which were sufficient for making simply shaped weapons or tools in one piece [171]. Two-piece moulds [170] were used for more complex objects such as axes with shaft holes [49] or fenestrated blades [169]. Figurines [51], on the other hand, were made using the lost-wax technique. The model was shaped out of bees' wax and covered with clay. The object was then baked in an oven; this caused the wax to melt and escape through holes made for this purpose in the clay shell. The same holes were used for pouring molten metal into the mould, where it filled the space previously occupied by the wax. Large sculptures, on the other hand, were made of metal sheets [9] that were riveted at their ends or even welded together.

Around 600 BC, new techniques were found that made it easier to produce iron than bronze, and in Syria, as in other parts of the Near East, the age of bronze gradually ceded to that of iron. It would actually be closer to the truth to speak of the age of steel, since pure iron was never produced in antiquity; during the smelting process, it was inevitably combined with carbon produced by the wood charcoal that had to be used as fuel to reach the high melting point of iron (1537°C, compared with 1084° C for copper). If allowed to

Modern artisan hammering a copper article.

cool slowly, this mixture of iron and carbon (between 0.5% and 1.5%) became a very strong metal that was harder than bronze and kept a sharpened edge longer. It was thus an ideal material for tools and weapons that required cutting edges and was mainly used to make such items. However, since iron ore contains between 30% and 40% useless gangue, it took some time for the technology to develop to make possible its usage. The first attempts at smelting iron ore were made in the mountainous regions of the Near East in 1200 BC.

Through experimentation, metalworkers eventually realized that they could produce an iron blade that was much harder and required less sharpening if they reheated it in a charcoal-burning hearth, hammered it while it was still hot (which is actually forging) and then cooled it by plunging it into water. At the time of the Crusades, Damascus was producing a carburized, hardened steel known as "Damascus steel," which was used to make straight rather than curved sword blades and whose fame spread as far as Europe. The tradition had existed long before the Crusades, but this growing reputation led to the industry's downfall. During the Tartar invasions of 1400, Tamerlane had the swordsmiths of Damascus deported to Samarkand, his capital. Certain authors think that "damask work" was actually just the decorative inlay that the Damascus craftsmen applied to swords made of steel imported from other lands such as India.

GLASS AND VITREOUS PRODUCTS

Frit is considered to have been the first step in the pyrotechnical developments that led to glassmaking. It is a man-made material produced by mixing a powder of finely ground quartz with a small quantity of sodium or potassium and lime, and then heating the mixture to the point that it sticks together in a well-amalgamated, compact mass. However, since the components do not melt completely, the paste obtained, which is usually a whitish color, may vary in texture, ranging from soft and crumbly to hard and solid, depending on how thoroughly the different elements bonded in different heating conditions. Objects made this way do not have a glassy coating, and this characteristic distinguishes frit from what is known as faience.

Faience is made with the same ingredients as frit, but the process involves much higher temperatures, which cause a proportion of the components to melt and become fused with one another. As the mixture cools, it turns into a material that is similar to glass in hardness and appearance. In fact, a thin glaze of glass forms on the surface of faience objects, and glass inclusions may be found scattered here and there in the paste itself. Since, in antiquity, faience required comparatively sophisticated technology, the material was reserved for making luxury products that could be exchanged between the political elites of different regions. The first objects to be made of faience in the Near East were beads for necklaces. They appeared as early as 5400 BC, while vessels in faience were not in use until about 3000 BC.

Unlike faience, glass has a homogenous, non-crystalline structure, since the elements composing it are heated until they are completely fused. To produce glass, Syrian craftsmen used a mixture of silica (about 75%), which is found as grains of quartz in sand, and an alkali modifier (between 15% and 20%), obtained from the ashes of plants growing in a saline desert environment and containing sodium, potassium, lime and manganese. The addition of a modifier was necessary because it

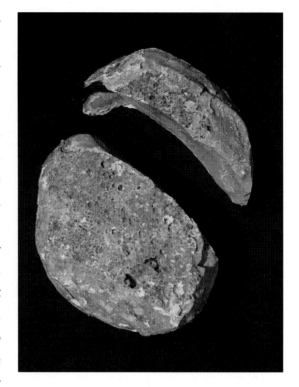

lowered the melting point of the silica, which normally is 1700°C, to a temperature that could be reached by the furnaces of the time. A third ingredient was calcium oxide in the form of lime (around 10%); it acted as a stabilizer to give the glass more resilience.

Mineral pigments — metallic oxides — could be added to make the glass opaque, translucent, tinted or transparent. The process consisted of mixing all the ingredients together and heating them in a special furnace. At 1400°C, the mixture melted and turned into a viscous liquid. It was kept at this temperature for a few hours and then allowed to cool slightly to 1100-1300°C to make it stickier and thus easier to handle. However, this phase could not last for more than a few minutes, since as it cools, molten glass can become solid very suddenly. Furthermore, if it cools too quickly, it is likely to break or at least remain very fragile. It may therefore be necessary, during the cooling process, to reheat the glass and soften it up again in a compartment of the furnace made for this purpose.

Frit bowl from Tell
Brak.
Cat. 180

None of the glass artifacts found so far in the Near East predates the middle of the second millennium before our era. Syria appears to have played a very important role in developing and perfecting glassmaking techniques. Interesting evidence of this is supplied by the recent discovery of glass ingots in a palace built at Tell Brak, in northeast Syria, in the sixteenth century BC. The existence of glass ingots strongly suggests that glass was traded in this unfinished form so that it could be later remelted in workshops that were specialized in producing glass objects rather than in making glass itself. Craftsmen living on the eastern shores of the Mediterranean in the seventh century BC are thought to have been the inventors of clear glass. This type of glass resulted when they decided to use antimony as a bleaching agent.

Apart from simply shaping glass by hand, which was in any case never very common, the first real method of making glass objects was to take strands of viscous glass and coil them smoothly around a vase form which had been made of a clay and sand mixture and attached to the end of a rod. The glass-wrapped clay core was placed in a furnace hole and the coils soon fused together. Held on the rod, the vessel was then gently rolled on flat, smooth surface (marvering) to obtain even walls of uniform thickness. In this period, such glass objects were usually decorated with threads of colored glass that were applied to the surface while it was still viscous so that they melted into it.

When parts like handles were added, they were made separately and simply pressed onto the surface before it cooled. Gradual cooling allowed the object to become hard and solid. At this point, the clay core was chipped away with a pointed instrument; the product of this glassmaking method is therefore called "core-formed glass."

Glass objects could also be made by pouring molten glass into open moulds, but this method was rarely practiced. The invention of glassblowing is attributed to Syrian glassmakers in the first century before our era. In this method, a lump of viscous glass was stuck at one end of a long hollow rod and the craftsman shaped it by blowing into the other end. According to Latin texts, Syrian glassmakers were in great demand almost everywhere in the empire because of the uncommon skill they had developed in this art. They kept this reputation in the Islamic period, when both Damascus and Aleppo were major centers of blown-glass production.

In a parallel development, starting about the middle of the second millennium BC, Syrian craftsmen are believed to have tried out a new technique for coating the surface of baked clay objects, especially ceramics, with a clear or tinted vitrified glaze made of the same ingredients as glass. It was not until much later, between AD 750 and AD 900, that potters began to add fluxes to the composition in the form of tin oxide (to produce tin glaze, which typically gives an opaque creamy-white appearance) and lead (to produce lead glaze). A

Glass vessel.
Cat. 181

Steps in making a glass flask by coiling strands of viscous glass around an unbaked clay core.

Glassblowers still practice their art in Damascus and Aleppo.

paste instead of an earthenware paste in fashioning their ceramics, covering it with a white slip and a transparent overglaze. The resulting ceramic is known as Islamic faience. It was also at this time that decorative motifs in blue and white became popular. The blue glaze was obtained from cobalt, which came from a region in Iran. Later, Arab potters exported this material to China, where it was called "Muhammadan blue." The Arab potters also developed a remarkable firing technique that gave ceramics a lustrous metallic coating. This technique produced a finish in which particles of silver or copper were diffused into the surface of a previously fired glaze. To obtain this effect, potters applied a red-ochre paste containing salts of silver or copper and a little vinegar onto the surface of a vase that had been already glazed and baked a first time. The vessel was baked a second time, but at a lower temperature and in a reducing atmosphere (that is, without oxygen) so that the carbon monoxide produced by the fire broke down the silver or copper oxides in the paste, freeing the metals. When the firing was done, the

flux is any substance, like lime, wood ash or fern ash, which, when combined with clay, fuses during firing and thus produces a vitreous glaze. The glazing mixture could be painted on the previously baked ceramic object with a brush or poured over its surface. The object was then returned to a kiln and baked with an oxygenated fire at a relatively low temperature until a vitreous coating formed and was fused to the surface of the clay, giving it a glossy appearance.

At about the same time, a little before AD 800, some potters began to use a silica

Blown-glass fish.
Cat. 190

red-ochre paste was washed off, but particles of the metal it had contained would remain, transferred into the original glaze. The technique produced varying effects of tone depending on the quantity and type of metal oxide used. Most of the metallic lustreware made in Syria between AD 1100 and AD 1260 came from kilns in the workshops of Raqqa, which were later destroyed by the invading Mongols. Another well-known type of ceramic was earthenware decorated with motifs incised on a slip that was highlighted with green-, yellow- and brown-tinted glazes. It was then coated in a transparent lead glaze [**193**].

Under the Mamluks (thirteenth and fourteenth centuries), ceramic production tended to be concentrated in two major categories, depending on whether the decoration was incised or painted. Some incised decorations were made on a white slip with a transparent lead overglaze tinted with yellow, ochre, brown or bottle green, while others were scratched out more deeply, forming relief patterns in the colored glaze, which varied greatly in thickness. The other category, often erroneously called "enameled ceramic," was characterized by its painted designs, which were usually blue on white. Islamic ceramics were traded throughout the Near East and Europe.

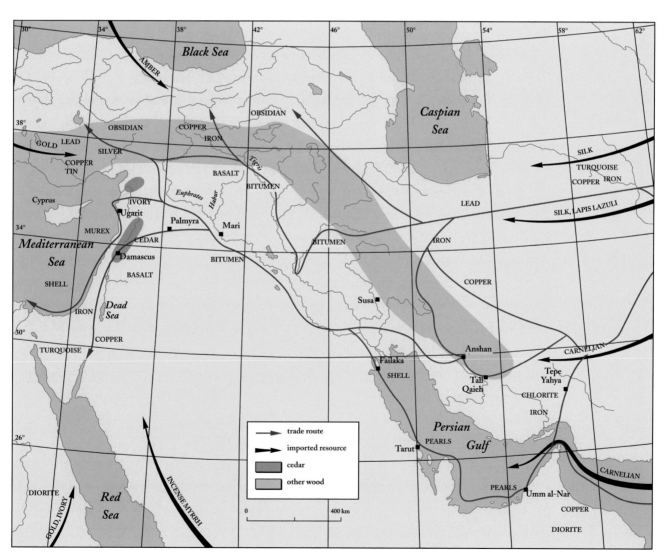

Principal trade routes in the ancient Near East and known sources of some of the raw materials used for everyday items and luxury objects

THE CREATION OF SURPLUSES AND THE DEVELOPMENT OF TRADE

Surpluses were first accumulated and kept in communal storehouses as a safeguard against irregular harvests, but this excess produce also provided farming villages with a commodity that could be traded for goods or raw materials which were not available in the immediate environment. Such trade developed rapidly as different modes of land and water transportation were explored.

Throughout the Neolithic period, the people who worked stone on Syrian territory found ways to obtain obsidian, a glassy black volcanic stone that was found in large deposits in certain regions of eastern Turkey and which could be used to make very sharp blades. Although local flint was available, these people also tried to get pieces of flint with different colors and textures than that in their own environment and sometimes even sought out Canaanean blades — a type of flint blade that had already been chipped in a certain way. Querns and other grinding instruments were made of basalt, which was readily available in deposits on Syrian territory. Given the widespread occurrence of these highly useful artifacts in Neolithic sites, it is clear that there must have been an established trade network within the territory for basalt, and perhaps even for the objects. Even in the Neolithic period, when stone tools constituted practically the entire material culture, it is clear that trade played an essential role in the cultural evolution of Syria's first inhabitants.

Trade therefore began very early on, indeed as soon as people started living year-round in one place, and it appears to have been fairly well organized. Archaeological excavations of a fifth-century site on the Habur River, a waterway that rises in Anatolia to the north and flows into the Euphrates to the south, have brought to light a terra cotta model of a small boat, which indicates that the inhabitants of the region were familiar with this means of transportation. The original boat would have been made with bundles of reeds joined together at either end and coated with bitumen to make it watertight. Such boats could still be found until very recently in the southern marshlands of Iraq. Contacts between the Habur region in northern Syria and northern Mesopotamia are also supported by similarities in the way the pottery of both regions is decorated.

TRADING COLONIES AND RIVER COMMERCE

Commercial relations grew more important around 3500 BC, or perhaps a little earlier, when merchants from southern Mesopotamia set up trading centers — some of them as large as cities — along the Euphrates in northern Syria. In these centers they built large warehouses for storing the goods that were exchanged. To control how the goods were shipped out, received and transported, the doors of these warehouses were sealed.

During the third millennium BC, at a date that is still not certain, there appeared new cities whose economy was based entirely on commerce. Well-known examples are Mari, on the Euphrates, and Ebla, on the plains south of Aleppo.

In this period, trade goods were almost always transported by water, since this represented the quickest and least costly means. The Euphrates was by far the most important waterway; with its tributaries it covered some 500 to 600 kilometers of Syrian territory

Mari, a transit city

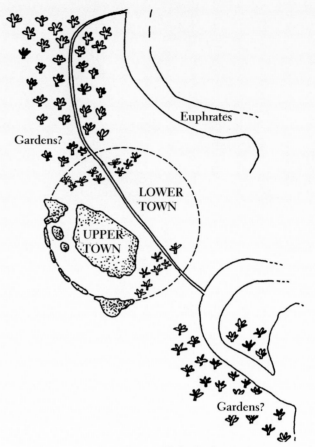

The location of Mari in relation to the river.

THE SYRO-MESOPOTAMIAN BASIN is drained by the Euphrates, which flows from northwest to southeast, linking the mountain ranges of eastern Anatolia with the Persian Gulf. At the river's southern limits in Syrian territory it passes through a vast alluvial plain with enormous agricultural potential. Here, in the second half of the fourth millennium, there arose a powerful urban civilization, the first of its kind. The river's two tributaries, the Balikh and the Habur, facilitate contact between the northern area of the basin and the mountainous regions. The river thus constituted an important line of communication and played a pivotal role in linking two regions whose economies differed fundamentally but complemented each other.

The situation was perfectly clear to the region's inhabitants at the beginning of the third millennium, around 2900 BC. They decided to put these advantages to good use and founded the city of Mari. They chose a site for it near a natural narrowing of the river called Abu Kamal (Baghouz in antiquity), where boats using the river were obliged to pass. It was thus an ideal location for controlling river traffic and collecting taxes. The city undertook a huge project to develop the valley. On the right bank a network of irrigation canals was constructed, covering several dozen kilometers and fed by a reservoir lake. The water was used to grow enough wheat to meet the population's needs. The city authorities also decided to encourage trade between Mesopotamia and northern Syria by building a 120-kilometer-long canal, a project that involved considerable construction work and even the excavation of part of the plateau. The canal was perfectly regular in shape and reduced the length of the trip by eliminating meanders and making it easier to haul the boat on the way back downstream.

At first, it was the Habur plain that profited the most from these developments. In the middle of the third millennium BC western Syria, with its access to Anatolia, the Mediterranean Sea and inland Syria, entered Mari's sphere of influence and thus reinforced the city's wealth and power. Timber felled in the forests of the Taurus (in present-day Turkey) and shipped south no doubt accounted for some of the heaviest traffic along the Euphrates. Mesopotamia's great need for wood must have stimulated river trade, but

it is impossible to say what volumes were involved. At the beginning of the third millennium BC, and perhaps even a little before, copper extracted from the Taurus Mountains took the same route. It is well known that mastery of this metal was in part responsible for Mesopotamia's supremacy at this time. As well, a certain amount of tin, which is a necessary component of bronze, may have come from the Taurus, although at a later date it is known to have been imported from Iran. Commodities from Mesopotamia and Syria, including farm and animal products, pitch and stones, also passed through Mari.

As the main trade routes were transferred closer to the foothills of the Taurus Mountains and as overland travel became more common, thanks to draft animals and pack saddles, the waterway lost its status. The partial abandonment of the Euphrates as a trade route led to the disappearance of Mari at the beginning of the second millennium BC.

PROF. DR. JEAN-CLAUDE MARGUERON
École pratique des hautes études (Paris)

Collecting salt in a salt marsh not far from Mari. Salt was traded in antiquity.

Goods were transported up and down the river on rafts made of timber and branches lashed together with tamarind bark and floating on sheepskins inflated with air. Modern calculations show that 200 of these skin floaters together could support a load of five tons; 800 of them could carry up to 36 tons. But other types of craft were used. For example, an outline drawing of a barge with sails appears incised on the wheel of a miniature cart found at Tell 'Atij, where, incidentally, large granaries and stone anchors [219] were also discovered. Furthermore, texts from a slightly later date mention boats weighing 40 tons each. Goods were transported in animal-skin bags, cloth sacks, woven reed baskets and ceramic jars in a range of shapes and sizes, often designed for a certain type of merchandise. As will be seen further on, all these containers were sealed during transport.

The city of Ebla, located halfway between the Euphrates and the Mediterranean coast, was a station on overland trade routes. Certain texts describe the convoys of

and provided a link between the Mediterranean (which is only 150 kilometers away at one point), Anatolia (where its source lay) and southern Mesopotamia, with its ports for boats arriving from the Persian Gulf and the Indian Ocean. Mari's administrators had an 11-meter-wide canal dug for 120 kilometers along the banks of the Euphrates to the mouth of the Habur, so that navigation would be easier and less dependent on the water level of the river. Ancient texts mention teams of haulers who worked in relays along the banks of this canal.

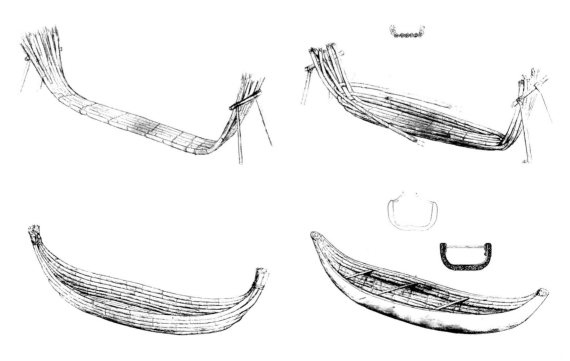

Reconstruction of the type of boat used for trade on the Habur, based on a recently discovered clay model.

asses that were used to transport goods on these routes. However, this type of trade was much less profitable than river commerce, since it took a convoy of 500 asses to carry the cargo of just one 40-ton boat.

Port cities, like Ugarit, appeared along the western coast and, through them, Syria had contact with the Mediterranean world.

Overland trade
and beasts of burden

The first beast of burden to be used in the Near East was the ass, domesticated a little after 4000 BC. Previously, small loads had been carried short distances on the backs of human beings. The ass could transport a load of 50 to 90 kilograms in all sorts of terrain and cover a distance of 20 kilometers a day in steppe country. When carrying a load, this animal went at speeds of only 3.6 to 5.4 kilometers per hour for four or five hours. It was not fussy about what it ate, but it had to drink large quantities of water — 40 liters a day — and had to be al-

lowed to stop at a watering place at about every 20 kilometers. Consequently, it was impossible to venture into desert regions with this pack animal. As well, the weight of the load being transported had to be distributed equally on either side of the animal's back, and this meant that someone was obliged to continually keep an eye on the state of the pack during the trip. The pack saddle, which is a device made of wood and leather that can be placed on an animal's back and have a load attached to it, did not appear until the beginning of the Christian era.

The next animal to be domesticated was the horse. Although specialists have not yet determined exactly when this happened, it was sometime in the third millennium BC. It was then possible for humans to breed the mule, which is the offspring of a horse and an ass. This animal could carry one and a half times the weight borne by an ass. It could also travel more rapidly — 4.8 to 6.4 kilometers per hour — and for longer distances, covering 32 to

The mule-drawn cart remains a practical means of transportation.

Terra cotta model of a cart. Cat. 215

per day. The animal also required a great deal of fodder and water, which complicated using it for transportation.

Only with the camel was it practical to used the most direct routes in Syria, which entailed traveling through the desert and arid steppe. However, in the second millennium BC, according to texts found at Mari, caravans of asses used such a route. It went northward from Mari via Palmyra to Qatna (Homs) and then through the Homs gap to the Mediterranean coast. Thence it led southward to Damascus. But desert horizons truly opened up when the Arabian camel, or dromedary as it is often called, began to be used as a beast of burden in Syria around 2000 BC. The animal had probably been domesticated in southern Arabia between 3000 BC and 2500 BC, and its arrival in Syria coincided with the period in which the country began to import Arabian incense. In fact, the camel is associated with this type of commerce. The animal began to be more common in Syria after 1100 BC. In the following centuries, it was frequently represented in the bas relief decorating the palace walls of the Assyrian kings; camels were shown wearing a sort of pack saddle to which goods could be secured. However, camels really began to be used only in the Persian era, at the end of the sixth century BC, when, with their Aramaean drivers, they transported the aromatic products of Arabia throughout the vast Persian Empire.

As a pack animal, the camel was impressive. It could carry twice as much as the cartload that could be drawn by oxen, and it could do so over uneven ground where carts could not pass, covering 32 to 40 kilometers per day. It could travel at a speed of five kilometers per hour even when loaded and, above all, it could go without water for 10 to 14 days, and sometimes even longer. It was the only pack

40 kilometers each day. This was a definite improvement. But mules also had to have access to water at the end of each day. The horse was never used for transporting merchandise. From the time of its domestication, the horse was associated with social and military prestige and was only used for riding. As well, the traction power of a horse cannot be exploited without a harness system and this had not been discovered at the time.

The ox, which had been domesticated since around 7000 BC, was widely used as a draft animal in the Near East. It was slow-moving, going only 3.6 kilometers per hour on average, and could work little more than five to six hours a day. At first, the ox was used to drag sleds over the ground, but it was not until around 3000 BC, when the wheel was invented, that the animal's traction power could truly be appreciated. The ox was attached to four-wheeled carts, which are frequently represented in the artifacts of the period. The carts were sometimes covered with a kind of sheet to protect the merchandise inside. The cart, of course, could be used only in regions where the terrain was not too uneven and, ideally, where cart trails had been laid out. It is calculated that an ox pulling a cart could go no farther than 15 kilometers

animal that could travel such long distances in dry regions. It could do more trips in a year than any other beast of burden and lived four times longer than an ass or a mule. It also was more tenacious, had more endurance and cost less to maintain. As well, a camel caravan did not need to be watched over by the drivers as much as a caravan of asses did. From the time it was adopted until very recently, the camel's many advantages have made it the ideal pack animal for desert regions. However, it was not really used for riding in antiquity.

TRADE NETWORKS
AND THE IMPORTANCE OF CARAVANS

The camel thus became the traders' pack animal of choice during the Hellenistic period (fourth to first centuries BC), while cities like Dura-Europos, Halebiyya-Zenobia, Palmyra and Apamea were founded as points along a new trade network where goods unloaded from convoys of boats on the Euphrates were reloaded on the backs of camels and transported to the Mediterranean.

When Syria became part of the Roman Empire, it also became part of Rome's vast trade network. Syria's most sought-after product was cereal. To promote cereal production, roads and bridges were built, irrigation systems were installed and arable land was meticulously surveyed. In southern Syria, there were pastoral nomads (called "Safaitics" because they were often in the Safa Desert) who moved from place to place on the backs of camels. They were part of the trade network as well, and left engravings of camels on large basalt stones to mark their passage through the desert [221]. There were also, of course, the many

The city of Dura-Europos on the Euphrates, the place from which camel caravans left for Palmyra.

THE ORGANIZATION OF THE ECONOMY

The city of Palmyra and its oasis. In the Roman period, the city earned its name from the abundance of palm trees growing there.

Camels engraved on stone, found in the Safa Desert. Cat. 221

The Tariff of Palmyra.

caravans that came through Palmyra. In the past, some scholars were so taken by the romantic picture of these desert caravans stopping off at the oasis city that they described the whole of Roman Syria as a "transit country," its prosperity based entirely on caravan trade. Although this is now known to be an exaggeration, the fact remains that such trade was extremely profitable. In Palmyra, with a population of 200 000 at the time, wealthy private citizens endowed the city with many fine public buildings and had magnificent tombs built for themselves.

In AD 137, the city's fiscal law, called the Tariff of Palmyra, was engraved on a large block of stone, recording the rules for trade in common goods, including olive oil, animal fat, salt fish, grains, wine, animal fodder, pinecones, camel skins and live camels, animals for butchery or breeding, aromatic oils and perfumes. However, there was no law concerning luxury products like silk, spices or incense. Merchandise of all sorts was transported in goatskins on the backs of camels or asses. In the rest of the Roman Empire, Syrians had a reputation of being great merchants.

In the Byzantine era (fifth to seventh century of our era), commerce once again began to expand and city life became important. Many cities, including those that had

been newly founded, grew rich because the great international trade route still passed through Syrian land, although now it no longer went through Palmyra but further north. Boats came to the port of Halabiyya-Zenobia on the Euphrates to unload cargoes of luxury products like silk, ivory, spices and precious stones, which came from the Far East. From there, caravans set out for Antioch on the Mediterranean coast, passing through Rusafa-Sergiopolis, Aleppo or Apamea-on-Orontes. There were extraordinary profits to be made, but the government siphoned off part of them by collecting taxes on commercial transactions. The cities'

prosperity was thus based on distant trade rather than on agricultural goods produced in the surrounding countryside. The farmlands benefitted from this trade indirectly, since city-dwellers who grew wealthy through commerce were consumers of the farmers' goods, especially wine and olive oil.

Long-distance trade in the Islamic period

The Umayyad caliphs had an extremely liberal economic policy and did not take any measures that would allow the state to interfere with production or commercial transactions. Nevertheless, trade declined slightly at

The city of Zenobia, at the site of present-day Halabiyya, controlled trade on the Euphrates and redirected it by camel caravan to Palmyra.

The island of Arwad, off the shores of Tartus, was used for maritime trade in the Islamic period.

Underwater excavation of an Islamic shipwreck near the port of Arwad.

the beginning of the Islamic period. Under the Abbasids, who succeeded the Umayyads, the center of commerce shifted to Baghdad, the new capital of the empire in Iraq. Syria regained its commercial importance only when the Ayyubids came to power in AD 1076. It

then became a prominent player in the Mediterranean commercial world, along with the Italian city-states, of which Venice was a prime example. There was a strong demand for brocades of damask silk, copper work, inlaid wood (marquetry), gilded glassware, glazed ceramics, enameled tiles and fine leather goods. In the largest trading cities, Damascus and Aleppo, complexes called caravansaries were built, serving as a combination of warehouses, wholesale outlets and inns.

Economic activity was slowed down by the Mongol invasions of 1260 but resumed under the rule of the Mamluk knights, who prized fine weapons and horse harnesses. In this period, Syria and the other Near East countries exported a wide variety of goods to Europe: silk brocade; garments of embroidered cotton or linen; harnesses for horses; glassware, which was usually gilded; finely worked jewelry; and arms of all sorts, including the renowned damask swords. Syrian merchants also imported an array of foreign

goods: horses; furs, amber and wax from the Baltic; slaves, gold, rare woods and ivory from Africa; precious stones and metals from India for armor and equestrian equipment; and silk, spices, dyes, medicines and ceramics from the Far East. These luxury products began to be available in the specialized city markets called souks. New caravansaries were built. Towards the end of the Mamluk period, trade with the Far East declined as the threat of the Ottomans loomed. Eventually, in 1516, the Ottoman Empire conquered Syria, but by that time, trade with the Far East no longer necessitated overland transport, for Vasco de Gama had opened a sea route when he discovered the way around Cape Horn in 1498.

Long-distance trade in the Islamic period focused on luxury products that were relatively light-weight but extremely valuable, or on products of secondary consumption for urban aristocrats. The purpose of this commercial activity was not so much to stimulate exports of local finished products made with imported raw materials but rather to make the highest profits possible by speculating on prices and thus reinforce the power and comfort of those who provided financial backing for the trade

expeditions. Since everyone wanted to benefit from this lucrative business, the authorities levied taxes on goods brought across the country's borders and taken into the cities where the merchandise was sold. The state thus derived great benefit from this trade and, in some cases, even operated monopolies. Consequently, the merchants, who were not necessarily Arab or Muslim and who did not specialize in any given product or market, formed groups to reduce their risks. The practice of using credit developed, and some people began to draw up contracts that set out the details of certain transactions in advance, especially those related to the textile trade. Arabic tended to be the language of commerce. This was the period when the camel began to replace the ox-drawn cart as a means of transporting goods overland, since this animal could cover great distances without water. However, at regular intervals along the caravan routes there were caravansaries, or *khâns*, where the caravan drivers and their camels could stop and rest. The caravansaries were fortified and encircled by walls. Inside was a vast square courtyard surrounded by halls, sleeping quarters and stables for the merchants and their animals.

The remains of an ancient *khân*.

165

MANAGING PRODUCTION AND COMMERCIAL EXCHANGE

From the time of the very first exchanges, people felt the need to make some record of their transactions and keep accounts of a kind. As the volume of trade increased between distant communities and even between neighboring groups in the Syrian territory, it became essential that administrative systems be set up to manage trade effectively. A number of processes for recording commercial exchanges were developed.

TOKENS, THE FIRST ACCOUNTING TOOLS

The earliest management method to be developed in the Near East was a system using small tokens of various forms made of unbaked clay. They were marked with symbols that identified the type of goods traded and their quantity. They were called *calculi* [232] because they were used to make calculations as part of a management system based on numbers — a sort of primitive bookkeeping. According to many authors, the token symbols were the precursors of writing.

Unbaked clay tokens were used as calculation aids when goods were traded.
Cat. 233

WRITING AND THE FIRST ALPHABET

The *calculi* accompanied the goods to the place where they were traded. Tokens with holes in them were probably threaded onto cord. In the fourth millennium, those without holes began to be encased in a hollow ball of clay, called a bulla [234], on which marks were made with a reed stylus to symbolically represent the value of the tokens inside. The bulla was then imprinted with a seal so that it could not be tampered with before arriving at its destination. It soon became evident that with this new system, the tokens were no longer necessary; the symbols representing the value of the tokens could be used on their own. These symbols consisted of very simple dots and lines stamped or incised on a bulla that had been flattened into a little disk of clay [236]. Since these disks bore essentially numerical symbols, they are called "numeral tablets." They no longer carried the imprint of a seal, since a tablet does not contain any objects and cannot be broken into.

The number of signs used soon began to increase until there were 1200 of them, each with its own meaning. At first, a wooden or reed stylus with a pointed end was used to make the symbols, since it left clear marks when pressed into the surface of a wet clay tablet. But before long, it is thought, scribes began to use styli whose ends were whittled into a triangular shape and held at a slant so that the resulting characters consisted of little wedge-shaped marks. Western travelers seeing examples of this writing system for the first time gave it the name of "cuneiform," from *cuneus*, the Latin word for wedge.

A writing system thus grew out of a need to remember facts and record information related to commercial exchanges. This is why most of the early texts in cuneiform script were economic in nature, consisting of lists of goods stored in warehouses, delivery and reception notes, accounts of all kinds, contracts [245] and lists of food rations distributed to specialized craftsmen [242]. There was also a category of texts that were meant to record political accords, such as letters between rulers and treaties [254]. A third category consisted of what might be termed intellectual texts. These were lists of symbols [253], lists of words [248], exercises for pupils [241], scientific texts [237] and mythological tales.

As an ever growing quantity of information had to be processed, this method of writing became unwieldy. In the fourteenth and thirteenth centuries BC in the port city of Ugarit on the Mediterranean coast, scribes adopted a new system of cuneiform writing whose origin is still not known. Texts were read from left to right and only 30 symbols were used, each corresponding to a letter of an alphabet. This revolutionary system was much easier to learn than the previous one because of the small number of signs that had to be learned. It eliminated the need for long apprenticeship, and was thus more accessible and democratic. The alphabetic writing first adopted by the Greeks between the tenth and eighth centuries BC was used to devise alphabets for the European languages. (The word "alphabet" itself comes from the first two letters of the Greek alphabet: *alpha* and *beta*.) The Egyptians adopted Coptic writing, which was also based on the Greek alphabet, while the Aramaic alphabet served as the basis for the alphabets used in the Arabic, Syrian and Hebrew languages. By the beginning of the new era, cuneiform writing had become obsolete.

The physical medium on which writing was done also changed over time. At first, scribes used flattened bits of wet clay that were later allowed to dry in the air. They were not baked, unless it was by accident, as sometimes happened when the place they were kept in burned down. Clay was found in deposits throughout the territory and was easy to obtain. The tablets were often no bigger than the palm of one's hand, although the tablets varied greatly in shape. This was not deliberate;

Archives room
of the city of Ebla.

their differences are simply the effect of when and where they were made and what they were used for.

Syria did not have access to Egyptian papyrus until the Hellenistic period. At that time, the papyrus market was a monopoly controlled by the Ptolemies, an Egyptian dynasty of the third century BC. The scrolls (*volumen*) in the library of Alexandria were made of papyrus. Then, at Pergamum, in 200 BC, a new writing support was developed to replace papyrus. Made from the skins of goats and sheep, parchment was pliable and could be used on both sides, unlike papyrus. As well, sheets of it could be assembled into a book (*codex*) which could contain more written text than a scroll. The new system was adopted in the Byzantine Empire in the fifth century AD. The scroll continued to be used, although it was now unrolled vertically, rather than horizontally. Finally, the secret of paper making was learned by the Arabs from the Chinese who had been taken prisoner when the Chinese army was defeated by Islamic troops at Samarkand in 751. It was in the twelfth century AD in Spain, in the emirate of Cordoba, that the Arabs introduced paper to Europe. From there, the use of paper spread through the Christian West over the next two centuries. The existence of paper made it possible to invent printing, and the resulting dissemination of ideas on paper has continued to grow to this day.

Cylinder seal decorated with simple linear motifs.
Cat. 223

SEALS AS MANAGEMENT TOOLS

The authorities in the public administrations of the Near East, like their counterparts today, appreciated the usefulness of stamps. They discovered that they could control the security of traded goods in transport by marking them with a stamp seal or, later, with a cylinder seal. The motifs incised on the surface of these seals corresponded at first to the distinctive signs of various administrative units. The use of a seal to establish the identity of a private person came later.

In the Near East, the stamp is the oldest method of authenticating ownership of a possession. Stamps were used as early as the Neolithic period, long before writing was invented. The stamp was generally made of a small piece of stone, often sculpted into the shape of an animal [228 and 229] or into a simple geometric form, with a handle by which it could be grasped [226]. On its flat bottom surface were engraved geometric [225] or figurative motifs that left a relief pattern when the stamp was pressed on wet clay. Stamps were mostly used on clay stoppers that plugged jar openings or on clay envelopes that covered an object requiring a seal [227]. Some of the stamp seals, especially those in the shape of animals, have holes in their handles, indicating that they were worn like pendants around their owners' wrists or necks.

A little before 3000 BC, the stamp seal began to be replaced by the cylinder seal, whose appearance heralded the advent of cuneiform writing. In comparison with the stamp seal, the cylinder seal offered a larger surface for engraving a design and could be rolled indefinitely. The scenes represented on seals became increasingly complex and diversified. Another advantage of the cylinder seal was that there was no limit to the size of the surface that received the impression. Cylinder seals were always bored lengthwise so that they could be worn as pendants [224].

To seal a jar closure with a cylinder seal, a piece of cloth was placed over the jar opening and pulled taut with a length of string tied around the vessel's neck. The string was covered with wet clay, which was then imprinted by a cylinder seal rolled on its surface. For goods transported in bundles and cloth sacks tied with cord, lumps of clay were simply applied to knots and then marked with a cylinder. We know about these methods of sealing things because of the marks of string and cloth left on the underside of clay seals found on the floors of warehouses where they were tossed into careless heaps as the containers used for transport were unsealed after reaching their destination.

Most of the seals that have survived to this day were used as part of a system for keeping storehouse doors closed. This is not surprising, since the administration of the time was based on the centralized storage of goods and products to be redistributed or traded. They were kept in palaces or specially-built warehouses under the strict

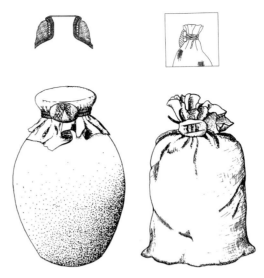

supervision of civil servants. Each worker had his own distinctive seal and was responsible for the security of one or several storerooms. Texts inform us that a storeroom could be opened only by the civil servant responsible for it and, once opened, it was resealed by him. The most common closing system consisted of attaching one end of a cord to the door and rolling the other end around a knob of wood or baked clay [230] set into the adjoining wall. Clay was applied to both ends of the cord and imprinted with a cylinder seal.

The sealings used to secure the doors of warehouses are very informative documents in many respects, since they give the names of potentates, display symbols representing the deities worshipped and can help to identify the name of the city that once stood where the seals have been discovered.

Since sealing was a way for people to establish legal ownership of their possessions and guarantee their identity, seal imprints soon began to appear at the end of cuneiform texts inscribed on tablets, especially when they represented contracts or wills. Sometimes cylinder seals were even rolled in a way that actually sealed a letter in a clay envelope [245].

How doors were sealed.

Knob used for sealing a door.

The royal storehouse of Urkesh

The imprint of a seal from Tell Mozan with an inscription bearing the name of Urkesh.

THE IDENTIFICATION OF MODERN archaeological sites with ancient cities can only come as the result of written documents found at the site itself. We had proposed that Tell Mozan might be the site of ancient Urkesh on the basis of inferential evidence, and the excavations were to bear this out in a most unexpected way. It was no stone statue as in Mari, no clay tablet as in Terqa, but the tiniest fragments of clay sealings no bigger than your thumbnail.

We were digging a cluster of rooms that were undistinguished except for two things: a very symmetrical architectural layout and rather messy floors! In the accumulation left behind on these floors, we began to find clay sealings that had evidently been dropped after the container they had sealed was opened. Some of these seals were inscribed. When the total reached 170 during our first excavation campaign, we decided to devote an entire season to the excavation of just one room. And it paid off! With almost 2000 sealings found to date, we have been able to reconstruct a very vivid picture of what was happening in those rooms and to confirm that this was indeed the site of ancient Urkesh!

Why should these little scraps of clay be so important? And why should the discovery of Urkesh have attracted so much interest? These two questions — and their answers — are intertwined. The sealings represent a variety of scenes from the royal court B: the king, the queen, the crown prince, his nurse, the cook of the queen, etc. We know with certainty about all these details because of the cuneiform inscriptions that identify the main characters, just as captions do for photos. The title for a king is given in Hurrian: "endan Urkesh." This title is not used in any other Hurrian city. The fact that the sealings were found on the floor implies that the goods they sealed were related to the people named. We assume they served as identifying both the landowner and the person to whom the item was addressed: goods were brought in from neighboring farms and kept in reserve for their beneficiaries. Thus it seems that our modest rooms served as the storehouse attached to the royal palace itself.

These seals date from about 2200 BC. The use of the Hurrian language in royal titles at such an early time attests to a Hurrian ethnic presence in the area several centuries before it was generally thought. But we can go even further back in time. Since there is a substantial stratigraphic continuity at the site, and since we have monumental architecture from the early part of the third millennium, we can infer that Urkesh was a major Hurrian city some 1500 years before Hurrians were otherwise thought to have first appeared on the scene. When Hurrian mythology preserved in later texts speaks of the father of the gods, Kumarbi, residing in Urkesh, they reflect this awesome truth. Therein lies the wonder and beauty of archaeology; from hardly recognizable scraps of physical evidence we can come to recognize the imprints of the gods!

PROF. DR. GIORGIO BUCCELLATI
University of California (Los Angeles)

Next page: *View of a part of a souk in modern-day Damascus across from the Great Mosque of the Umayyads.*

Weight as a system of measurement

Any system of trade must have its system of measures. In particular, a system based on weight is required for goods that cannot be counted. It is therefore very probable that people had a system for weighing goods at the very beginning of trade activities in the Near East; however, it is difficult at present to say what elements of their material culture might have served this purpose. The first weights were simply pieces of stone of different sizes and in a great variety of shapes that were finished to varying degrees. The people who used them had no doubt agreed to give them values based on a system that is almost impossible to guess at today unless one finds a complete set of different-sized weights belonging to the same system. Such a set was found at Ugarit [255]. This set, which was in use around 2000 BC, is particularly interesting because of the weights' unusual shapes and because they are made of metal, a material that was not generally used for this purpose until a thousand years later. A few weights have survived with their unitary value inscribed on the surface and sometimes even the name of the person who owned them. In the Byzantine and Islamic periods, glass weights were used, especially in jewelry-making, because they were more precise.

Coins as instruments of trade

The first coins are now known to have appeared only around 650 BC in a region to the west of Asia Minor (present-day Turkey). The ruler of Lydia, the famous King Croesus, had them made out of an alloy of gold and silver called electrum. It was not until much later, at the end of the sixth century BC, that a money system began to be used in Syria as a result of its integration into the Persian Empire. The Achaemenid kings of Persia minted quantities of coins in gold (*darics*) and silver (*siglos*) to manage trade between the different satrapies of their empire. However, cuneiform texts of Ebla dating from long before, in about 2500 BC, refer to transactions in which goods were paid for with certain amounts of silver — which did not occur naturally in Syria — measured by weight. In Mesopotamia as well at that time, silver was becoming a standard material for payments and trade. The word "silver" came to mean "money." There soon appeared silver rings whose weight had been previously established and even bits of silver ingots in standard shapes and weights. But their value was always based directly on their weight rather than on a currency value guaranteed by a ruler whose symbol was marked on them. Nevertheless, these various forms of silver had one of the practical advantages of money — they could be hoarded. Stores of silver have been found in certain treasuries dating back to the second millennium BC [256] and even the third millennium BC.

Under Alexander the Great, all coinage was standardized to match the value of Athenian currency. Coins included pieces of gold, silver and bronze, all of which bore the name of Alexander and the heads of different gods and goddesses. The uniformity of this new coinage reflected a systematic monetary policy that was maintained without any real change after Alexander's death and even during the political confusion that ensued. In fact, coins bearing Alexander's image continued to be minted after his death. The Seleucid kings who succeeded him in Syria retained the Athenian standard and the imperial coinage with the goal of uniting disparate populations not only through economic links, but also through shared cultural and political values. The new rulers hoped that their subjects would feel that they all belonged to the Hellenistic world if the faces of their coins bore Greek inscriptions and representations of great Hellenic gods and that they owed allegiance to the king if his portrait appeared on their money. In Syria, these coins were minted in over 20 workshops.

Roman rule did not mean that these numerous mints disappeared, since the first emperors wisely gave the local governments a certain latitude in this field. As a result, a provincial coinage developed. However, in the second century of this era, an imperial currency was created with the aim of reinforcing economic links between the different regions of the empire. This monetary system also made it easier to pay the wages of the soldiers stationed throughout the empire's vast territory. The only mint in Syria to continue operations was that at Antioch, the capital.

The Emperor Diocletian increased the tax burden of the empire's citizens and began to conduct a general census of people, animals and property so that the central administration in Rome could collect taxes more efficiently. In Syria, this census was taken between AD 293 and AD 305, using a fiscal unit called a *caput*, which could be used for counting a person, an animal or an area of cultivated land.

In the third century, there was a monetary crisis and silver began to be replaced by gold for minting. By the fourth century, with the *solidus*, the coin minted by Constantine the Great, gold had become the enduring standard. Bronze was seldom used for minting in the rest of the empire, but in Syria bronze coins continued to be struck in large quantities. The inscriptions were now in Latin and the figure on the face of a coin was always that of the Emperor, represented as a soldier, a consul or a hero. Coinage had become a means of propaganda.

Great quantities of coins from the Byzantine era have been found in village sites dating from that time, evidence that the villagers were wealthy enough to accumulate cash and that this was a period of considerable economic activity. The basic unit of value was a pound of gold (327 grams), which was minted into 72 coins, called *nomismata*, of nearly pure gold (4.54 grams each). This currency remained stable for a very long time and suffered significant depreciation only in the eleventh century.

When the Arab dynasties first came to power in Syria, Byzantine gold *denarii* and Sassanid silver *drachmas* continued to be used as before. A little later, they began to be marked with an Islamic sign and then with the image of the caliph. Around AD 700, the figure of the caliph was replaced by extracts of texts from the Koran [258], accompanied by the date and place of the minting and the name of person who struck the coin. The Islamic monetary system was based on the gold *dinar* (4.25 grams) and the silver *dirham* (2.91 grams), but an official means of determining the equivalence between the two coins was not established until the end of the ninth century. These coins were valued not only in the Near East, but also in the Mediterranean and southern Europe, where they were hoarded in immense treasure rooms.

Scene of slaves being weighed at a slave market. Miniature by al-Hariri. Baghdad, 1237. (Paris, Bibliothèque nationale de France)

the economy
catalogue

99
Painted sherd: bull
Ceramic
5500 BC

The bull's head was a very common motif on the pottery of this period. It is believed that such representations are linked to the symbolic role played by the bull in the concept of reproduction.

TELL HALULA   6 x 4.5 cm
NATIONAL MUSEUM, ALEPPO
1555 (HL 5118.c1a10)

100/101
Painted sherds: fish and gazelles
Ceramic
5000 BC

While people hunted animal species like the gazelle, which was found throughout Syrian territory, they also fished wherever the environment permitted. For villagers living along the rivers of Syria, fish was part of their normal diet. These two fragments of pottery coming from the same archaeological context show that, where it was possible, people consumed both meat and fish.

TELL KASHKASHUK I   6.5 x 5 cm/10.5 x 7.5 cm
NATIONAL MUSEUM, ALEPPO   1553 (KK 91.95+75)

103 a-e
Slingshot balls
Terra cotta
3500 BC

These balls are evidence of another weapon used for hunting wild animals — the slingshot. While these slingshot balls are made of terra cotta, stone balls were used as well.

JEBEL ARUDA   3 to 4.7 cm in diameter
NATIONAL MUSEUM, ALEPPO   M 10477 (JA 429/JA 77-203)
L'EUFRATE 123

102
Arrowhead
Flint
7000 BC

Arrowheads constituted a large proportion of the stone tools produced by human communities in this period. As a hunting instrument, this arrowhead represents an improvement on the models that preceded it since it has a stem at one end, making it easier to fix onto the shaft of an arrow.

TELL HALULA   8 x 2.3 x 0.7 cm
NATIONAL MUSEUM, DAMASCUS   1381 (HL.2D.951.350)   *Cf. SMC* 45

104
Aurochs horn
Horn
7000 BC

This horn of an aurochs, or wildon, comes from the site of Tell Halula. This is one of the sites where, although the animal bones unearthed there have been analyzed, it is difficult to say whether the animals they belonged to were domesticated or not. These animals were in fact in the process of being domesticated, but the change in the way they lived had not yet affected their morphology. Although cattle were not the first animals to be domesticated in the Near East, the wild bull had a symbolic role in the development of domestication. Several sites predating the appearance of animal-raising have revealed a great number of aurochs horns, which are thought to have represented the male aspect of reproduction.

TELL HALULA   39 cm
NATIONAL MUSEUM, ALEPPO   1554

105/106
***Vessels in the shape of a hare
and a hedgehog***
Alabaster
7000 BC

The hare is common throughout the Near East. For the humans living there, hares were small game that continued to be hunted even after certain animal species had been domesticated.

TELL BOUQRAS   18 x 9 x 8.5 cm/14.5 x 8 x 7 cm
DEIR EZ ZOR MUSEUM   2136 (BJ 100)/2138 (BJ 119)
BAAL 48 and 49

107
Hedgehog figurine
Terra cotta
2500 BC

The remains of hedgehogs, small insect-eating mammals that are covered with needles, are frequently found on sites of various periods, but in very small quantities. Vessels in the shape of animals were not for everyday use, but rather luxury items or cult-related objects.

NERAB   6.5 x 5.6 x 4.2 cm
NATIONAL MUSEUM, ALEPPO   M 7656

108
Gazelle figurine
Bone
7000 BC

Bone analyses of animal remains found at Syrian archaeological sites indicate that the most widely hunted wild animal was the gazelle. Since this species came from Africa, it was well-adapted to living in stony desert regions. On the basis of vestiges found at Abu Hureyra, a village on the banks of the Euphrates dating from 9500 BC to 5000 BC, archaeologists have even been able to determine that the first villagers were primarily gazelle hunters. They established their village on one of the migratory routes used by these animals and hunted them every spring. The figurine shown here may have decorated the end of a tool handle.

TELL BOUQRAS   3.5 x 3.5 x 0.6 cm
DEIR EZ ZOR MUSEUM   2159 (BJ 121)
L'EUFRATE 53; *BAAL* 46

109
Vessel in the form of an ostrich
Ceramic
800 BC

In the Near East, the natural habitat of the ostrich was the Syrian steppe, extending from the borders of Mesopotamia to the plains of Antioch. Certain texts report that these birds were even seen near Palmyra by visitors to the region in the mid-ninth century BC In the Neo-Assyrian period, which was when this vessel was made. Ostrich-hunting was a royal sport that certain kings could not refrain from boasting about. King Assurbanipal II wrote a letter in which he claimed to have killed 140 ostriches in a single hunt. The bird was used as a motif for luxury objects. After this period, illustrations of ostrich-hunting became rare, for the species was probably on the brink of extinction.

TELL AHMAR, ANCIENT TIL BARSIB   39 x 19.5 x 17.7 cm
NATIONAL MUSEUM, ALEPPO   M 7565

THE ORGANIZATION OF THE ECONOMY

110
Vessel in the form of a pig
Terra cotta
3200 BC

In Syria, the pig was domesticated at the same time as cattle, in about 7000 BC, when goat and sheep raising was already well established. Wild pigs lived in marshy regions receiving more than 300 millimeters of rain each year and in wooded areas. Hog raising spread quickly, since the pig is the fastest-breeding domestic animal and represents an important source of protein. However, as the Near East was deforested and complex societies developed, pork consumption diminished. With the introduction of religious precepts prohibiting pork, people stopped eating it altogether.

JEBEL ARUDA   30 x 25 cm
NATIONAL MUSEUM, ALEPPO   M 10167 (JA.DD.300)
L'EUFRATE 118; Cf. *BAAL* 66

111
Sculpted vessel in the form of a ram's head
Alabaster
3000 BC

This is a unique piece. It represents the right side of a ram's head, recognizable because of the horn that curves around the back of the head and up to the animal's eye. The other side of the object is hollowed out to form a vessel that would have been used for practicing some cult, for it was discovered in a foundation deposit of a temple at Mari. The hole just below the upper part of the horn goes right through the object, suggesting that the vessel was meant to be suspended. The sheep was the second animal to be domesticated for its meat in the Near East. This happened in about 7500 BC, some 500 years after the first goats were domesticated.

TELL HARIRI, ANCIENT MARI : TEMPLE OF NINHURSAG
14 x 9.8 x 4.7 cm
DEIR EZ ZOR MUSEUM   19071 (TH 97.129)

112
Bas-relief
Limestone
AD 200

This bas-relief presents a rider — the god Arsu, the protector of caravans — mounted on a camel with a saddle, and also shows part of a horse wearing a harness and reins, suggesting that it, too, has a saddle. The camel was used for transporting merchandise and was rarely mounted, but the opposite was true of horses. The earliest representations of animals being ridden date to about 2000 BC; they show people mounted directly on the back of asses without any saddle. During the second millennium, a saddle of sorts appeared. Shortly after 1000 BC, bas-reliefs show horsemen sometimes riding bareback and sometimes mounted on a saddle. From then on, the use of saddles spread rapidly. With the Persian Empire, the saddle became established throughout Syria.

JEBEL BAL'AS   49 x 38.5 x 10 cm
NATIONAL MUSEUM, DAMASCUS   2624/5.247
ANTIQUITÉS GRÉCO-ROMAINES p. 38 and Pl. 16:1

113 a-b
Animal figurines
Terra cotta
2200 BC

Although there is evidence that the horse was domesticated in Syria during the third millennium BC, it could not be used as a draft animal until the second millennium BC, when a suitable harness system was developed. These two horse heads distinctly show bridles made of several parts. The figurines are probably the earliest representations found so far in Syria illustrating this harness element, which was fitted onto horses' heads so that their movements could be better controlled. After 1000 BC, the Assyrians introduced a sort of bit which, instead of going across the inside of the animal's mouth, was placed under its neck. Reins were also attached to the bridles. In the Near East, the horse was used for riding much more than for pulling chariots. The first saddle appeared during the second millennium BC.

TELL BRAK   5.5 x 5.5 x 2 cm/7.2 x 6.5 x 4.2 cm
DEIR EZ ZOR MUSEUM   5897/4204 (TB 9063/TB 6185)

114
Head of a small rodent
Alabaster
5800 BC

In this period, the people living in the newly formed villages started to keep immense quantities of grain in community storehouses. There is no doubt a relation between their new way of life and the appearance of ornaments, like this pendant, in the shape of small wild animals, for all kinds of little grain-eating rodents seem to have been attracted to the granaries. The archaeological remains of such buildings reveal numerous skeletons of these animals, which seem to have taken advantage of humans' agricultural activity from the very beginning.

EL-KOWM   3 x 1.5 x 1.5 cm
PALMYRA MUSEUM   9231   *SMC* 34

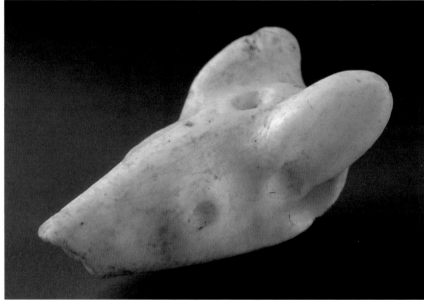

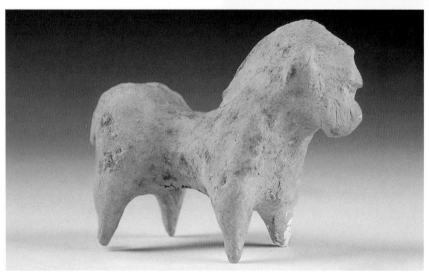

115
Animal figurine
Terra cotta
2500 BC

The horse was domesticated in the Near East during the third millennium BC. One of the characteristics of the domesticated horse is its long flowing mane, very unlike the short, stiff mane of the wild horse. This figurine shows an animal with a long mane and thus is one of the first representations of a domesticated horse in Syria.

TELL CHUERA   7.7 x 3 x 5.5 cm
RAQQA MUSEUM   309 (TCH 76/69)

116 a-b
Hoes

Limestone
1500 BC

To make the holes in the ground for sowing seed, the first farmers used simple digging sticks with pointed ends that had been hardened by fire. In later periods, farmers were able to break up the soil more thoroughly with hoes like these, attached to wooden handles. It is also possible that pieces like these were used as plowshares in a primitive kind of plow pulled by an ox (domesticated by 7000 BC). Plowing is attested as early as around 4000 BC and perhaps even 5000 BC, on the basis of bone deformations displayed by certain cattle skeletons.

TELL MISHRIFEH, ANCIENT QATNA   25.5 x 19.5 cm/26 x 19.5 cm
HOMS MUSEUM + 922   923 (MISHRIFEH 383 + 380)

117
Animal trap

Terra cotta
1200 BC

Storage areas for grain attracted small rodents [114] in such numbers that people had to think up ways of keeping them out. For example, they plastered the inner walls of the silos and made traps to catch them. The size of the holes in this trap suggest that it was intended to catch rats.

TELL MESKENE, ANCIENT EMAR   37.5 x 13 cm
NATIONAL MUSEUM, ALEPPO   M 10443   SMC 154

118 a-f
Blades

Flint and bitumen
2800 BC

Before the appearance of metal, sickles for harvesting plants were made with a wood or bone handle with a groove into which flint blades were inserted and held in place with bitumen (photo). Microscopic examination of the cutting edge on the blades shown here has revealed that they were not used on a sickle but were rather fixed to the underside of a wooden platform, called a tribulum. This implement was pulled over heaps of freshly harvested plants not only to thresh the grains from the ears, but also to chop the stalks into bits of straw that were mixed with mud to make bricks.

TELL 'ATIJ   2.2 to 4 x 1 cm
DEIR EZ ZOR MUSEUM
ATJ 87. 194 + 236/ATJ 88. 166 + 210 + 119 + 148

119
Mortar and pestle
Basalt
1500 BC

Materials were crushed by the movement of the hand-held pestle against the motionless mortar. This method was used to crush small quantities of grain or bits of minerals in order to obtain pigments that entered into the composition of paints or cosmetics.

TELL BAZI 21 x 7/27 x 12 cm
NATIONAL MUSEUM, ALEPPO M 11128/M 11129

120
Circular millstones
Basalt
1500 BC

This type of milling instrument, with one circular stone set on another, represented an improvement on the quern and rubbing stone because grain could be poured onto the grinding surface through the space near the central pivot at the same time that the upper stone was being rotated to produce flour. The ground flour escaped from the sides and fell onto a piece of cloth or basketry that was placed under the millstones.

TELL BAZI 15 x 10 cm
NATIONAL MUSEUM, ALEPPO M 11127

121
Saddle quern and rubbing stone
Basalt and limestone
7000 BC

Harvested grains were ground with a crudely shaped rubbing stone. It was pushed back and forth over grain that had been placed on the surface of a wider, heavier stone, called a quern, which was set in the ground. Alveolate basalt was an ideal stone for making querns because it has a very rough surface and is very hard.

ABU HUREYA 44 x 24 x 8 cm/21 x 7.5 x 4 cm
NATIONAL MUSEUM, ALEPPO 716: 1 + 2 (AH 73.28 + 3425)

THE ORGANIZATION OF THE ECONOMY

122
Template in the shape of a foot
Limestone
5500 BC

Certain archaeologists have interpreted this type of object
as a cult-related item that would have been placed in a
temple, but the archaeologist at Tell Halula believes that,
given the object's size and the context in which it was
found, it is more likely to have been a form used for making shoes. It is an eloquent reminder of the applications of
leather obtained by tanning animal skins.

TELL HALULA   15 x 6 x 9.2 cm
NATIONAL MUSEUM, DAMASCUS   1397 (HL 46.281)
Cf. L'EUFRATE 109

123/124
Twining devices
Terra cotta
4000 BC/2800 BC

One of these objects was once thought to be an idol with
eyes, but recently they have been interpreted as being instruments for making cord out of wool or linen threads
spun with a spindle **[125].** By twisting two or three
strands together, a cord maker could produce a much
stouter type of thread.

TELL ABR/TELL KASHKASHUK   21 x 17.5 x 13/21.8 x 12 cm
NATIONAL MUSEUM, ALEPPO   M 1149 (ABR III 87.lev.4)/1113
L'EUFRATE 108

125 a-f
Spindle whorls
Terra cotta
5000 BC

These little spherical objects were used as weights in the process of spinning threads. A whorl was slipped onto one end of a short wooden stick called a spindle to act as a weight. The person spinning pulled strands from a hank of animal or plant fibre and twisted them into a thread that wound about the spindle as it was made to twirl up and down. In Syria, flax was the first fibre to be spun (into linen), predating the use of sheep's wool. According to some authors, the change from plant fibre to animal fibre during the third millennium constituted a revolution in the production of textiles in the Near East.

TELL ABR   4.5 to 2.5 x 3 to 1.5 cm
NATIONAL MUSEUM, ALEPPO   1156 (*ABR* II/A5/B7/B6/C5/B5/C4)

126 a-c
Loom weights
Limestone
3200 BC

When plant or animal fibres were woven on a loom, even a primitive one, the weaver used weights like these, ranging from 800 to 1000 grams. She — for it seems that weaving was done by women in the home — would wind the ends of groups of threads around the weights, which were grooved so that the threads would stay in place. Thus attached, the weights ensured that the cloth or band being woven was held taut during weaving. The weft thread unwound from a shuttle that was slipped back and forth between the warp threads. There is evidence that weaving started in the Near East as early as the seventh millennium BC.

TELL HABUBA KABIRA   9.3 x 7.8 cm/7.4 x 6.2 cm/8.9 x 7.2 cm
NATIONAL MUSEUM, ALEPPO   M 10497/M 10498/M 10499
L'EUFRATE 148

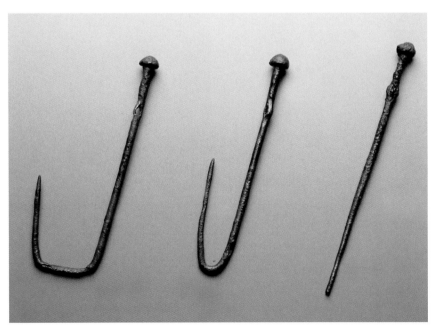

127 a-c
Toggle pins
Bronze
2500 BC

Sturdy pins like these, with an eye in the upper third and a bulbous head, were used to attach lengths of cloth together so that they could be worn as full robes or cloaks.

TELL MUBAQAT   11 cm/12.5 cm/11 cm
NATIONAL MUSEUM, ALEPPO   M 8990/M 8993/M 8994

129
Hand ax
Flint
1 million BC

This artifact was chipped out of a river pebble and represents what is called lithic industry. It is an example of the earliest evidence we have of humans (*Homo erectus*) being present on Syrian territory. This heavy tool had a variety of uses. The only technique known at the time involved chipping away at one piece of flint until a coarsely shaped tool was obtained.

TELL SITT MARKHO   16 x 10 x 6.5 cm
NATIONAL MUSEUM, DAMASCUS   1142 (2640 : 76)   *SMC* 1

128
Biface
Flint
400 000 BC

This type of Paleolithic tool was shaped out of a good-sized flint nodule that was skillfully struck a few times with a hammerstone to remove large flakes. The cutting edges thus obtained along the long sides of the tool may seem rudimentary but were very efficient. Since such a tool was flaked on both sides, it is called a " biface. " It was not fitted onto a shaft but rather held directly in a person's bare hand.

ARD HAMAD   12.8 x 6 cm
NATIONAL MUSEUM, DAMASCUS   1208 (A.H.1989)   *SMC* 10

130
Blade
Flint
40 000 BC

The oldest known traces of bitumen in the world can be seen on this piece. The bitumen was used as a glue to hold the blade in a groove made in a handle. Bitumen is a heavy, sticky form of petroleum found in various spots in the Near East where there are oil deposits. Oil may even flow with water out of certain springs, and the film that forms on the surface of the water can be collected.

UMM EL-TLEL   8.6 x 4.8 x 1.6 cm
NATIONAL MUSEUM, DAMASCUS   1135

131
Scraper
Flint
100 000 BC

The end of the Early Paleolithic period and the beginning of the Middle Paleolithic is marked by the appearance of a new type of flint tool that was used to cut up animal carcasses and scrape skins. The way this type of tool was made represented a true innovation: instead of being shaped from a single flint nodule, it was rather one of the short, thick flakes removed from a core.

YABRUD   6.5 x 4.2 x 1.8 cm
NATIONAL MUSEUM, DAMASCUS   1206   *SMC* 12

THE ORGANIZATION OF THE ECONOMY

132
Adze
Flint
8500 BC

An adze such as this one would have been fixed to a handle and used for working wood. This type of tool appeared at the same time that people began to settle and live in permanent houses built in part with wooden beams. A little later, adzes were made of polished stone.

MUREYBET   12 x 6 cm
NATIONAL MUSEUM, ALEPPO   1005 (MB 71.1521)   *SMC* 13

133
Blade
Flint
100 000 BC

Specialists of lithic industry attribute the blade-tool tradition to *Homo sapiens* and normally date this particular type of blade to about 35 000 BC. However, this example was found in a much older context, corresponding the period when *Homo erectus* lived. Either the tool was made by these early humans or *Homo sapiens* was already in Syria at the time. The cutting edges of this tool were chipped to make it sharper.

EL-HUMMAL   12 x 3 x 0.9 cm
NATIONAL MUSEUM, DAMASCUS   1207 (HU 182.1a)   *SMC* 13

134/135/136
Core and blades
Obsidian
7000 BC

These three pieces give a good idea of how the tool-makers of Syria removed flakes from an initial core and shaped the flakes into blades with smooth or toothed cutting edges. This technique represented a great innovation in flaked toolmaking, since it enabled people to obtain several blades from a single core instead of producing just one tool from one nodule. Obsidian is a vitrified stone formed by volcanic eruptions. The people living on Syrian territory could find this stone in outcroppings in the mountains of eastern Anatolia, just north of Syria. Obsidian was a highly valued material in antiquity and great skill was required to work it.

TELL BOUQRAS   11.8 x 1.8 cm/7 x 10.3 cm/5.5 x 1.4 x 0.7 cm
DEIR EZ ZOR MUSEUM   2075/1154/11884
BOUQRAS, Fig. 43

137/138
Adge and ax
7000 BC

Eventually, instead of being made out of flaked flint, certain tools began to be shaped from hard stone that was polished with an even harder stone, like emery. Polishing a stone ax could take four to eight weeks according to modern ethnographic studies. These tools had to be fitted into a shank made of antler before they could be fixed to a handle and used. Small use marks on the cutting edges are the only clues we have as to whether the tool was used to strike wood horizontally (an ax) or vertically (an adze).

TELL BOUQRAS   12.4 x 4.6 x 3 cm/7.3 x 4.8 x 1.2 cm
DEIR EZ ZOR MUSEUM   2088 (BQ 2773)/2081 (BQ 3506)
BOUQRAS, Fig 60:2 and 58:5

139/140/141
Vessels
Polished stone
7000 BC

The people who made these stone vessels went to the trouble of selecting veined or marbled rock that would add an interesting decorative element to their work. The site of Tell Bouqras, where the vessels were found, yielded a large number of such objects. They were clearly receptacles, but it is unlikely that they were used for cooking. At other sites, vessels of this type were included with funeral goods, but in this case the context did not allow such a conclusion to be drawn. Producing these vessels was extremely time-consuming; they were ground into a shape with a harder stone fixed to one end of a bow-drill. On the other hand, the result was worth the effort, judging by the sleek surfaces and elegant forms obtained. Certain vessels even had small feet.

TELL BOUQRAS   5.5 x 4.5 cm/5.7 x 3.5 cm/11 x 10.7 cm
DEIR EZ ZOR MUSEUM
2146 (BJ-102)/2105 (BJ-133)/2100 (BJ-91)
BOUQRAS, Fig. 73, 76 and 150

142
Bowl
Chlorite
9000 BC

This bowl, which has been reassembled from fragments, is remarkable because its surface is not only polished but also decorated with an incised design consisting of a band of triangles filled with oblique lines between two thick wavy lines. It is the oldest bowl of its kind to be found in Syria.

TELL JERF AL-AHMAR   12 x 9 cm
NATIONAL MUSEUM, DAMASCUS   1195

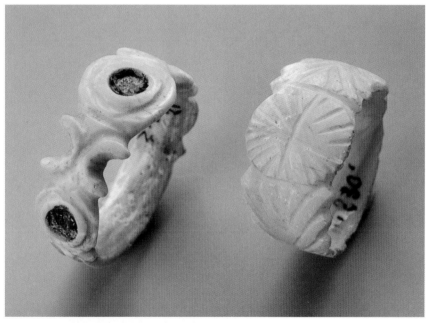

143/144
Rings
Shell
1200 BC

It has been established that the shells used to make these rings must have come from the shores of the Indian Ocean. One of the rings is simply decorated with incised motifs, but the other is carved with circular depressions that would have been inlaid with precious stones, held in place with bitumen.

TELL HARIRI, ANCIENT MARI   2.5 cm/2.3 cm
NATIONAL MUSEUM, ALEPPO   M 4404/ M 4384
BAAL 231; *L'EUFRATE* 258

145
Ornament in the shape of a bull
Shell
2500 BC

This ornament is made of a shell that was cut into the shape of a bull. A few incised lines on the surface of the shell indicate certain details. As a material, shell was always used for non-utilitarian goods. Ornaments made of shell reflected the wearer's social status.

TELL 'ATIJ   5 x 4.5 x 0.4 cm
DEIR EZ ZOR MUSEUM   6384 (ATJ.87.187)   *L'EUFRATE* 174

146/147/148
Figurine/Ornament/Awl
Bone/Bone and turquoise/Bone and bitumen
7000 BC

Animal bones were used very early on to make objects of all sorts. Bone is a material that is readily found, inexpensive and easy to work. Objects made of this material were generally utilitarian, like this awl, which was used to make holes in animal skins before sewing them together. The craftsman gave the awl a handle by sticking a lump of bitumen on one end of the instrument. Bone was also sometimes used to made non-utilitarian objects such as this ornament in the shape of a human head with turquoise inlay and holes pierced through it. The large human figurine was carved out of a long tubular bone and was incised with groups of parallel grooves to represent parts of a garment. The figurine's arms are raised in an attitude of prayer.

TELL BOUQRAS   14 x 5.2 cm/3 x 3 x 0.2 cm/4.7 x 1.6 cm
DEIR EZ ZOR MUSEUM   (SA 4090226)/2164/2195

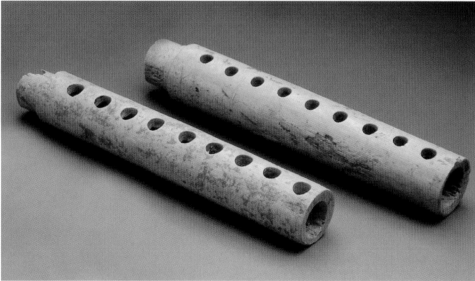

149 a-c/150 a-b

Cosmetic equipment/Flutes

Ivory

200 BC

The ivory used to make these objects came from elephant tusks imported from the Indian subcontinent. Elephants had once lived on the Syrian steppe but had been over-hunted and finally died out in about 700 BC. Hippopotamus teeth were also a source of ivory for Syrian craftsmen. The hippopotamus was another animal that at one time lived on Syrian territory, along the Mediterranean coast, but it, too, had been hunted into extinction. Hippopotamus ivory was whiter than that obtained from elephants and was therefore more highly valued. In Syria, the production of ivory objects reached its apex at the beginning of the first millennium BC, when the Aramaeans made splendid ivory inlay for furniture; the disappearance of the elephant from Syrian territory was a consequence of the growth of this craft and the popularity of its luxury product.

LATTAKIA   3.1 cm/10.5 x 0.3 cm/3.6 x 3.9 cm/11.2 x 1.9 cm
LATTAKIA MUSEUM
264/246, 263, and 245

152
Basketry imprints
Gypsum plaster
5800 BC

Before ceramic began to be used, Neolithic societies developed the skill of making utilitarian containers out of vegetable fibre. Basketwork is attested in the Near East as of the ninth millennium BC. Since the materials used were perishable, what is known about the basketry of the period comes from imprints of baskets left in plaster. Fragments like this one suggest that baskets may have been used in the preparation of plaster.

TELL EL-KOWM 2   11 x 9 cm
PALMYRA MUSEUM   929/9232 (K2.P97.17)

151
Female figurine
Terra cotta
7000 BC

In the Near East, clay was worked more than any other material except flint. The oldest objects made of clay are hand-modeled female figurines that were hardened in fire.

ARWAD   5 x 2.3 x 1.9 cm
NATIONAL MUSEUM, DAMASCUS   M 9   *SMC* 61

153
Dish
Gypsum plaster
5800 BC

In the Near East, plaster was used as a material for making vessels before clay was. Plaster was obtained by grinding gypsum into a powder and then mixing it with water. The advantage of plaster is that it becomes solid simply by drying in the air and does not really need to be baked. That is why a plaster coating was applied to the walls and floors of houses. Plaster was used especially to make vessels in the villages of the arid regions, such as el-Kowm, where no clay is found. In these regions, plaster continued to be used even after ceramic appeared at other sites.

TELL EL-KOWM 2   24 x 19 x 8 cm
PALMYRA MUSEUM   930/9233 (K.2.B.94.18)

154/155
Fragments of vessels
Ceramic
5800 BC

The fragments shown here are among the oldest examples of ceramic vessels known in the Near East. The earliest pieces discovered in Syria so far date to about 6500 BC. The word "ceramic" comes from the Greek *keramos,* which means "burned material" or "baked earth." Ceramic is clay that has been baked in a hearth or preferably an oven in which temperatures of 900°C to 1200°C can be reached. Clay that is hardened in this way remains porous, however, since such temperatures are not high enough to vitrify it. Ceramic is considered the first synthetic material to be made by humans, since it is the result of mixing clay, water, air (during drying) and fire (during baking) to obtain a new material that is solid and durable. Ceramic is a godsend for archaeologists because it is found in large quantities in archaeological excavations and can be used to classify sites. One of these sherds is part of the rim of a cooking pot that was entirely covered with a red "slip," that is, a coating of diluted clay. The other piece was decorated with red stripes on a white background.

TELL EL-KOWM 2   13 x 13 x 1.4 cm/13 x 10 x 1.3 cm
PALMYRA MUSEUM   1461/9237 (K2.S97.41)/1460/9236
(K2.Q97.76)

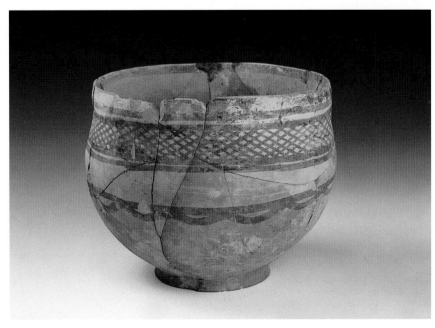

156
Deep bowl
Ceramic
4000 BC

A potter's workshop equipped with kilns was unearthed on the site where this bowl was found. This is why the site yielded such an abundance of bowls with almost all the same shape and decorated with a limited repertoire of painted motifs. At this period, vessels were still shaped by taking coils of clay and laying them in spirals to form the sides. The surfaces were then trimmed with a flat instrument to obtain a smooth finish.

TELL ABR   15.5 x 13 cm
NATIONAL MUSEUM, ALEPPO   1119   *SMC* 77

157
Bowl
Ceramic
5000 BC

As agro-pastoral village civilizations gradually developed, there were changes in the production of pottery, which took on various shapes and adopted different types of decoration over time. The changing shapes and decoration of ceramic can be used to reconstruct the chronological sequence of pottery production for a given site or region, and therefore for the communities that made and used such wares.

TELL KASHKASHUK   20.5 x 5.5 cm
NATIONAL MUSEUM, ALEPPO   M 10166   *L'ÉCRITURE* 9

158
Small bowl with beveled rim
Terra cotta
3200 BC

It is surprising to find such simple, roughly moulded bowls being made in a period when pottery techniques were quite well advanced. Although produced without much care, these bowls were nonetheless baked properly in kilns that could reach high temperatures. Specialists do not agree on the function of such vessels, which are found in abundance in virtually every Mesopotamian site dating from the end of the fourth millennium BC.

TELL BRAK   16.5 x 7 cm
DEIR EZ ZOR MUSEUM   11997 (TB 12216)
Cf. *SMC* 83 ; *L'EUFRATE* 122

159
Stemmed bowl
Ceramic
2700 BC

This is a fine example of the first types of vessels that were shaped on potters' wheels in Syria and northern Mesopotamia. It is easy to believe that such vessels were considered to be luxury products at the time and were often included with the grave goods that were placed in the earth along with the body of a member of the elite class.

TELL LEILAN   28 x 27 cm
DEIR EZ ZOR MUSEUM   2813 (L 77-288)   *L'EUFRATE* 158

160
Mug with lion-head base
Ceramic
1300 BC

The base of this one-handled mug was modeled into the shape of a lion with a threatening, open-jawed mouth. The mug does not have a hole in the bottom and is therefore to be distinguished from a rhyton, which often has a base shaped like an animal's head but is always perforated. Both types of vessel may have been used for making libations, for a mug that is similar to this one has been found with an inscription indicating that it was offered to a god. This vessel was most certainly intended for some special purpose, since the orbits of the lion's eyes once held an inlaid material, which has since disappeared.

RAS SHAMRA, ANCIENT UGARIT   16.2 x 14.5 cm
NATIONAL MUSEUM, DAMASCUS   4217 (RS 52.16.52)
BAAL 193; *ED* 140

161
Filter for watercooler
Ceramic
AD 1200

Decorative filters placed inside jugs, pitchers and watercoolers began to be used some time before, but it was in the twelfth century that this custom really developed in the Islamic world. Almost all the known examples are made of ceramic without any type of glaze so that the material would remain porous. The liquid such vessels contained would thus remain cool. Filters are often decorated as this one is, with animal motifs and abstract designs.

UNKNOWN   27.5 x 20 cm
NATIONAL MUSEUM, ALEPPO   S 521

162
Bowl with relief decoration
Ceramic
AD 100

The relief decoration on this bowl was applied to the surface just after the vessel was shaped, while the clay was still damp. Using small coils of clay, called barbotines, the potter wrote the following phrase in Greek: "Hail, pot merchants!" Under the bowl there appears a Greek letter, also in relief, in a medallion surrounded by large dots.
After the vessel had dried, but before it was baked, the surface was coated with a red glaze made of very pure diluted clay that would produce a lustrous finish. This type of ceramic was produced mainly in the potters' shops of Arezzo, a town in Italy, and exported throughout the Mediterranean area. However, the large quantity of vessels like this one found in Syria suggests that some of them could have been made in local potters' shops.

MANBIJ, ANCIENT HIEROPOLIS   12.7 x 5.8 cm
NATIONAL MUSEUM, DAMASCUS   2117/4479
ANTIQUITÉS GRÉCO-ROMAINES p.83

163
Mould for ceramic vessel
Ceramic
AD 1300

The fact that the inside of this bowl-shaped object is decorated with concave, or intaglio, motifs indicates that it was actually a mould. It was used to make bowls and a certain type of jug in which only the top part was decorated this way. The bottom part of these jugs was made in another, undecorated mould, while the neck, foot and handles were simply added once the parts of the main body were assembled. The clay that was used to make a vessel in a mould had to be very fine-textured and of good quality to ensure that it filled all the depressions in the design completely. The use of this technique implies that such vessels were produced on an almost industrial scale. The city of Raqqa was a center of this type of production in the Islamic era.

NORTHERN SYRIA 16.7 x 8.7 cm
NATIONAL MUSEUM, DAMASCUS 6876 A
BAAL 346; *ED* 268; *Cf. L'EUFRATE* 446, 447 and 448

164
Mould for lamp
Terra cotta
AD 600

Ceramic lamps were at first wheel-made, but as of the second century BC they began to be made in moulds. A mold consisted of two parts, corresponding to the upper and lower halves of the lamp. Each half was moulded separately and then fitted together. A handle was added and, finally, the filling hole and wick channel were made. This object is only the upper part of the lamp mould. The crosses in the medallions identify it as a Christian lamp. Since a mould could be used over and over again, identical models of lamps were produced in large numbers.

UNKNOWN 15 x 12 x 5.5 cm
NATIONAL MUSEUM, DAMASCUS 24021 *SYRIEN* 27

165
Potter's wheel
Basalt
1800 BC

This is not a true potter's wheel, but rather a slow wheel, similar to what is today called a banding wheel, for the potter could not work the device and shape the vessel at the same time **[166];** he needed an apprentice to turn the wheel. The slow wheel is made of two parts; the upper part is equipped with a pivot that fits into a circular mortise in the bottom part. The upper part, or wheel head, can thus be rotated on a central axis while the lower part provides stability. One can still see the wear marks on the surfaces of the rough stones despite the fact that they would have been oiled to reduce friction.

TELL KANNAS   18 x 14 x 12.7 cm
NATIONAL MUSEUM, ALEPPO   M 9117   *L'EUFRATE* 132

166
Statue of potter working at a wheel
Basalt
AD 100

The first potter's wheel was introduced in Syria at about the end of the fourth millennium, but it was slow **[165].** This statue shows us a true potter's wheel, which is activated by a lower flywheel that the craftsman turns with his foot while shaping the clay placed on the upper wheel head. The movement of the flywheel is transmitted to the wheel head by a central shaft. The potter's wheel made it possible to produce vessels with even shapes and very smooth walls. This statue was no doubt a funeral monument commissioned by a potter who wished to be represented working at his trade.

SUWEIDA   40 x 35 x 32 cm
SUWEIDA MUSEUM   143/68   *LE DJEBEL AL-'ARAB* 3,12

167/168
Mould for axes and daggers/Dagger
Limestone/Bronze
1300 BC

Since there are no copper-bearing geological formations on Syrian territory, this metal had to be imported from the mountains of eastern Anatolia (Turkey). The copper ore underwent initial processing in the form of crushing and extraction near the mine. Ingots of the metal were then shipped to cities, where craftsmen melted it down and cast it in moulds like this one to make tools and weapons. During the melting process, the metalsmiths added other elements to the copper to produce more resistant alloys; for example, tin might be added to obtain bronze. Metallurgy in Syria entailed not only technical knowledge, but also the establishment of a supply network since metal deposits were found only in certain regions that were isolated from settled areas and since metal itself is such a heavy material that it is difficult to transport.

TELL BAZI   24 x 13 x 6.5 cm/29 x 3.7 x 1.2 cm
NATIONAL MUSEUM, ALEPPO   M 11304 (BZ 24/35.15)/M 11302
DAM 9 (1996) p. 37-44 Fig. 14

169/170
Fenestrated ax/Two-part mould for ax
Bronze/Limestone
1800 BC

The type of ax shown here is called "fenestrated" because the blade has two small openings that looked like windows to the first archaeologists to describe such objects. It was a ceremonial arm rather than a real weapon. Kings and soldiers were often represented with such an ax in their hands. This ax was found in the tomb of a high-ranking dignitary and must have been considered a sign of his social status. A handle went through the perpendicular socket at the heel of the blade.

TELL MARDIKH, ANCIENT EBLA   7 x 6 x 0.9 cm/15.3 x 12.7 cm
IDLIB MUSEUM   3450 (TM.78.Q.495)/3211 (TM.84.G.30a-b)
SMC 147a; *ED* 118; *EBLA* 297

171/172/173
Adze/Ax/Saw
Bronze
3000 BC/2800 BC/1800 BC

These bronze tools were used to work wood — to shape, square and saw it. The saw has a handle made of ivory, a material that was usually reserved for luxury goods. The squaring ax and the carpenter's adze would have been provided with wooden handles. It is somewhat rare to find everyday metal objects, since their metal was usually melted down when the tool broke. Woodworking was an important aspect of Eastern civilizations. When public buildings began to be constructed, a demand grew for the wooden beams that supported roofs and upper floors. Texts mention timber-laden rafts descending the Euphrates to Mari, whose lumber needs were considerable. It is believed that the region began to be deforested at this time, not only for building purposes but also because metallurgy required huge amounts of charcoal.

JEBEL ARUDA/TELL KASHKASHUK/TELL ASHARA, ANCIENT TERQA
11.7 x 4 cm/37.5 x 8.3 cm/36.5 x 6 x 3.3 cm
NATIONAL MUSEUM, ALEPPO M 9107 (JA 77.219)/1287:1
DEIR EZ ZOR MUSEUM 1513 (TQ 3-100)
L'EUFRATE 227

174 a-b/175
Moulds for jewelry
Chlorite
1300 BC

The stone used to make jewelry moulds like this one is often called steatite by archaeologists, but it is actually chlorite. It is an ideal stone for moulds, since it does not crack or break on direct contact with heat and can be finely sculpted into shapes for beads, rosettes and other delicate gold items. The moulds shown here would have had a matching part. The two halves were placed one on top of the other and held in place with staples that fit into holes at the corners. Then the molten metal was poured through the little channels that run from the sides to the jewelry forms.

RAS SHAMRA, ANCIENT UGARIT/TELL BAZI
9 x 7 x 2 cm/8 x 4.2 x 1.2 cm
NATIONAL MUSEUM, DAMASCUS 5209
NATIONAL MUSEUM, ALEPPO M 11303 (BZ 25/3650)
DAM 9 (1996) p. 38 Fig. 12

176
Necklace
Gold, lapis lazuli, agate, blue glass paste
1200 BC

This necklace comes from one of the tombs dug by the Assyrians at what might have been a military post built on the ruins of Mari, which by that time had completely eroded away. The necklace is made up of 21 elements. Beads with four spirals, like the gold ones shown here, have been found from the Aegean to the Indus. Apart from lapis lazuli and carnelian, agate was the most popular semiprecious stone in Mesopotamia, especially for making necklace beads. Agate was imported into Syria from eastern Iran or India.

TELL HARIRI, ANCIENT MARI: TOMB 125
NATIONAL MUSEUM, ALEPPO   M 10113   *BAAL* 230

177
Mask
Gold
AD 50

Since gold is an extremely ductile and malleable material, goldsmiths could use hammering, embossing and chasing techniques to make a portrait with it. This is a unique piece, since no other like it has been found, and it is poorly documented, having been discovered by chance. Despite a lack of contextual information, it is almost certain that such a luxury item belonged to a king or an important dignitary.

HOMS, ANCIENT EMESA: TOMB 1   19 x 18 x 8.5 cm
NATIONAL MUSEUM, DAMASCUS   7206
SYRIA 29 (1952) Pl. 26

178
Necklace
Frit
2350 BC

Frit was produced by heating up a quantity of sand (quartz) mixed with salt. This glassy material is very similar to what is called faience except faience has a vitrified surface, while frit does not. The first objects made of frit or faience were beads — in the Near East the oldest such beads date back to the middle of the sixth millennium BC. To make beads like those shown here, viscous frit was applied around a thin rod or wire to form a tube of frit. Before the frit mixture cooled and became solid, the tube was cut into lengths of various sizes. This technique provided holes for threading but tended to produce oddly shaped beads because it was difficult to spread the viscous frit evenly. Once the beads were cut and hardened, they could be decorated with tiny threads of more viscous frit, incised with a burin, or sculpted into a rounded shape and sanded smooth.

TELL HADIDI
NATIONAL MUSEUM, ALEPPO M 10524
L'EUFRATE 283

179
Vessel with foot
Faience
1300 BC

Faience and frit are terms that are often confused, since in the Near East they both refer to forms of melted quartz that are chemically different from glass because they have a crystalline structure. However, faience objects are distinguished from frit by having a sort of glassy coating, so that the object seems to have a tinted, vitrified surface. This vessel, which comes from a temple in the city of Emar, is thought by archaeologists to have been used for religious ceremonies. It is significant that the vessel was found at this site, since many of the city's inhabitants were Hurrians. Although the very first examples of faience dishes in the Near East appeared as early as the fourth millennium, it was only during the later half of the second millennium that such wares became widespread, as trade flourished in the commercial empire of the Hurrians.

TELL MESKENE, ANCIENT EMAR   12.3 x 11 cm
NATIONAL MUSEUM, ALEPPO   M 10533   *L'EUFRATE* 343

180
Bowl
Frit
1500 BC

This bowl was described by the archaeologists at Tell Brak as the most beautiful blue frit object discovered at the site. The bowl was reconstituted with fragments that had been damaged by the fire that destroyed the building in which it was found. Faience is white in color and was sometimes coated with a tinted glaze, which gave the material a glass-like appearance. Frit, on the other hand, needed no coating since the material itself colored the surface of objects. This bowl was made with a simple open mould in a shape that was common for frit vessels.

TELL BRAK   19 x 7 cm
DEIR EZ ZOR MUSEUM   5557 (TB-8205)
EXCAVATIONS AT TELL BRAK 1: p. 87 (No. 79) 244-245

181 a-c
Flasks
Glass
800 BC (?)

The oldest known glass receptacles date to the middle of the second millennium BC and were discovered in Syria. This is evidence of the important role played by the Syrian region from the very beginning of glassmaking as a craft. In fact, certain authors have even claimed that the Syrians themselves invented glass for making vessels. The three flasks shown here are fine examples of the oldest method of making small glass containers, which were used to transport and store precious fluids such as perfumes and oils. Glass produced by this method, which remained in use until the first century of our era, is called core-formed glass. The method, which consists of circling coils of hot glass around a core, may have been developed in Syria (although conclusive evidence is still lacking).

UNKNOWN   12 x 6 cm/15 x 6 cm/14 x 3.5 cm
NATIONAL MUSEUM, DAMASCUS   15656/6769, 13732/5949, 1477
AAAS 10 (1960) p. 103

182/183/184
Bowls
Glass
100 BC

The surface of these bowls shows that the term "mosaic glass" is an appropriate one for designating the type of glass they are made of. The earliest examples of objects made with this technique date to the middle of the second millennium BC. Mosaic glass is obtained by making a bundle of different-colored glass canes and slicing it widthwise into little rounds. These are set one beside the other in a mould that is then placed in a kiln. This glass-moulding technique continued to be used until the first century of our era but was eventually supplanted by glass-blowing. Glass receptacles were not used as everyday objects until that time.

HOMS/ALEPPO/UNKNOWN   10 x 4.5 cm/10 x 3.7 cm/10 x 4.5 cm
NATIONAL MUSEUM, DAMASCUS   5738/5572/5433
ANTIQUITÉS GRÉCO-ROMAINES p. 160 and Pl. LVII

185
Bowl
Glass
AD 800

Although the invention of clear glass has been attributed to the Syrians living in the first millennium BC, the question is still under debate. Raqqa was an important glass-producing center in the Islamic period, especially during the reign of the Abbasid caliph Harun al-Rashid, who resided there between 796 and 808 and in that time built an industrial complex where glass was manufactured. This bowl was found at Raqqa in the course of recent excavations which made it possible to unearth glassmakers' workshops equipped with kilns. Chemical analyses carried out on the sherds found there show that Raqqa glass was made with magnesium 50 years earlier than such glass was previously thought to have been invented. It is even possible that the new recipe for glassmaking spread from Raqqa, in Syria, to the rest of the Islamic world.

RAQQA: NORTH PALACE (ROOM 15)   12.5 x 8.5 cm
RAQQA MUSEUM   1754 (Ra-OINK-104 1987)

187
Bottle
Glass
AD 800

This bottle was not blown by swinging and turning the molten glass but rather it was blown into a two-part mould, which left traces on either side. Syria won renown for its blown glass when this technique was invented in the first century BC. According to some, the technique was even invented by Syrians. During the Roman period, Syrian glassmakers established workshops in the rest of the Empire, where their skills were much appreciated. Their reputation was maintained in the Islamic era as well. Damascus especially was known as a major glassmaking center at this time.

UNKNOWN   17 x 13.5 cm
NATIONAL MUSEUM, DAMASCUS   7411 A

186 a-c
Birds
Glass
AD 1200

These birds were made by the core-form method, that is, with coils of molten glass rolled around a core of clay mixed with sand. Strands of glass in different colors were added to decorate the birds' bodies after the shapes had solidified.

UNKNOWN   11.5 x 5 x 4 cm
NATIONAL MUSEUM, DAMASCUS   9772/6621/3652 A

188
Long-necked bottle
Glass
AD 1300

This bottle, which was blown in a mould, is interesting because of its gilded and enameled decoration. Gold dust was mixed with a resin or some other organic adhesive so that it would stick to the surface of the bottle and produce a gilt finish. The enamel decoration was obtained by applying powdered glass of different colors. Syrian enameled glass was much admired by the Crusaders, who brought back many examples to Europe. Such glass was also exported to China as a luxury product. The multifoil arcs and lotus flowers represented on this bottle show a certain Chinese influence. The main production centers for enameled glass were Damascus, Aleppo and Raqqa, and Syria was the principal supplier of this type of glass in the Islamic world.

ALEPPO   21 x 11.5 cm
NATIONAL MUSEUM, DAMASCUS
4575/13097 A   *SMC* 341

205

189
Beaker
Glass
AD 800

The blue color of this Islamic beaker formed in an open mould probably comes from mixing a bit of powdered cobalt ore with the glass when it was being made. Blue was always the favorite color for glass and older materials like frit. It is thought that translucid tinted glass of this type was intended to imitate semiprecious stones, such as lapis lazuli [203], which was used to make great quantities of beads as early as the third millennium. Some archaeological excavations have unearthed ingots of bluish glass that were perhaps going to be melted down or, more probably, carved into beads.

RAQQA: ABBASID PALACE   14 x 5 cm
RAQQA MUSEUM   947 (Ra-OINK-82)

190
Flask in the shape of a fish
Glass
AD 200

This is an excellent example of glass blown in a mould. The mouth and eyes of the fish are represented in relief. The fish's body is decorated with strands of glass applied to the surface, a technique that fell out of favor by the middle of the second century. This small bottle was called an *uguentarium* and once held perfumes or oils. It was used as an offering to the dead; for the Romans, the fish had symbolic connotations related to reproduction.

TAFAS   28.5 x 11.5 x 5.5 cm
NATIONAL MUSEUM, DAMASCUS   1436/3065
MUSÉE NATIONAL p. 105, Fig. 40;
ANTIQUITÉS GRÉCO-ROMAINES p. 111 and Pl. L

191
Floor tile
Glass
AD 800

Glass was not only used to make receptacles — it also served as a flooring material. One side of this tile is smooth-surfaced. The other side, however, is covered with little knobs that would have stuck to the coating on which the tile was set. Such tiles were used only in royal residences.

The glassmaking industrial complex at Raqqa, recently excavated by a team of British archaeologists, also manufactured translucid glass tiles like this one, particularly for the palaces of the Abbasid caliph Harun al-Rashid, who lived in this city from 796 to 808. The archaeologists advanced the hypothesis that glass may have been exported to other centers in the Empire in the form of such glass blocks, since they were practical for shipping purposes.

RAQQA   13.2 x 11.7 x 1.3 cm
NATIONAL MUSEUM, DAMASCUS   16026 A
BAAL 337

192
Jar
Faience
AD 1150

When speaking of ceramics, the term "glaze" refers to a glassy film that is applied by brush or simply poured over the surface of a vessel after it has been baked. The procedure was known as early as the sixteenth century BC, invented, probably in Syria, by glassmakers who had developed certain skills in the preparation of vitrified products. However, glazing did not become widespread until the Islamic era. In a later development, lead was added to the glazing substance to obtain a transparent finish.

UNKNOWN   23.5 x 18 cm
NATIONAL MUSEUM, DAMASCUS   5382 A

193
Bowl with hare
Ceramic
AD 1200

Sgraffito, from the Italian word for "scratched," is the term used by specialists to designate this type of decorated ceramic, which appeared in the Islamic world at the beginning of the tenth century. This type of ware was very widespread in Syria. The large central motif — in this case, a hare — is quite typical of this pottery.

QASR AL-HAYR AL-SHARQI   23 x 11 cm
PALMYRA MUSEUM   1195/8126   *SMC* 348

194
Cow suckling a calf
Ivory
800 BC

In the Near East, cows, as well as other animals such as goats, sheep and camels, were raised for their milk. This food is rich in fat, and fat was essential to the health of a population who, by our standards, lived very harsh lives indeed. On the basis of modern ethnographic studies, it appears likely that the people of the Near East developed simple methods of conserving milk products early on in their history, since such food goes bad very quickly in a hot climate. Fresh milk was turned into yogurt so that it could be kept for a few days. While the milk products themselves have disappeared, of course, the utensils used to prepare them have survived [198].

ARSLAN TASH, ANCIENT HADATU   11.5 x 5.7 x 1.6 cm
NATIONAL MUSEUM, ALEPPO   M 817   *BAAL* 249

195
Sculpted lintel
Basalt
AD 100

The two vine branches with great bunches of grapes sculpted in this door lintel are a reminder of the vineyards that flourished in the Hauran region during the Roman period. The mineral-rich soil of this region, formed by disintegrating basalt, is especially well suited to vine growing. The region had two other assets that were necessary for viticulture: the forest had been cleared by this time and the mountains would have been terraced. In the houses of Hauran villages, archaeologists have found great quantities of grape seeds and underground cellars full of large storage jars. The courtyards contained screw-operated winepresses, surrounded by settling tanks. The wine production of southern Syria was well-known in the rest of the Empire and exported there.

SOUTHERN SYRIA   110 x 40 x 27 cm
SUWEIDA MUSEUM   162/313   *LE DJEBEL AL-'ARAB* 3,09

196
Vessel with sieve
Ceramic
800 BC

This vase with a spout has a sieve incorporated in its upper opening. It was probably used for making a liquid product that had to be filtered, such as wine to which herbs and spices had been added to help conserve it.

TELL AHMAR, ANCIENT TIL BARSIB   22.4 x 14.7 cm
NATIONAL MUSEUM, ALEPPO   M 7581

197
Child's tunic
Linen
AD 600

Linen was made from flax, a plant that requires a good deal of moisture and grows wild on the shores of the Mediterranean in the Near East. Flax provided the first plant fibres that were used to weave cloth for garments in Syria, in about 7000 BC. Plant fibres were spun and woven before animal fibre, like sheep's wool or goat hair, was used. It is believed that the child who wore this tunic was killed with his family after they had sought refuge in one of the tower tombs in the necropolis at the time of the Sassanid invasion of 610.

HALABIYYA, ANCIENT ZENOBIA   66 x 57 cm
NATIONAL MUSEUM, DAMASCUS   6523

198
Jar
Ceramic
3400 BC

According to a recent study, such a jar could be interpreted as a churn for making butter. The vessel would have been filled with milk and rocked to and fro on its base. When milk is shaken, the particles of fat that it contains tend to collect together. It took from half an hour to two hours of churning to produce butter. In the Near East, butter was made with yogurt because it kept better. Butter could become rancid very fast in the heat. Herders who raised dairy animals had to clarify their butter by heating it gently for an hour or two, until the water it contained had evaporated. This product is still commonly used for cooking in many parts of the East and is sometimes referred to in cookbooks as "ghee."

TELL HABUBA KABIRA   33 x 28 cm
NATIONAL MUSEUM, ALEPPO   M 10514   *L'EUFRATE* 138

199
Statuette of a couple embracing
Gypsum
2400 BC

In this statuette, the surface of the woman's robe and the man's skirt has been carved to look like sheepskin, represented by highly stylized tufts of fleece. Such clothing is somewhat surprising for the period, since animal fibres had been used for weaving cloth for a while at least. Sheepskin was perhaps used for a type of traditional ceremonial garment worn by worshippers when they presented offerings to a divinity in a temple.

TELL HARIRI, ANCIENT MARI: TEMPLE OF ISHTAR
12 x 9.5 x 8.5 cm
NATIONAL MUSEUM, ALEPPO   M 10104   *SMC* 110

200 a-b
Wall tiles
Enameled ceramic
AD 1430

At the beginning of the fifteenth century, the walls of most large public buildings in Turkey, Egypt and Syria were embellished with enameled ceramic tiles whose blue-on-white decorations were very similar to those shown here. In Damascus, these tiles were put on the walls of the Umayyad Mosque when restoration work was done on it between 1420 and 1423. Given the large quantity of tiles that were required for this work, it is believed that Damascus had its own specialized workshop for the production of ceramics. It is also thought that this workshop was managed by a traveling craftsman, who probably was in charge of similar restoration projects in Cairo, a few years before, and in Turkey, a little later, since the same kind of tiles dating from the Islamic period are found in both these places.

DAMASCUS: UMAYYAD MOSQUE   19 x 16.5 x 3 cm
NATIONAL MUSEUM, DAMASCUS   607 + 608 A
DAM 3 (1988) p. 203-214

201
Wall tile
Enameled ceramic
AD 1430

This square tile is decorated with a coat of arms in three bands: the upper one shows a white pen holder on a blue background, the middle one presents a blue goblet flanked by two white goblets on a maroon background, while at the bottom there is a white diamond on a dark brown background. This coat of arms belonged to the Mamluk sultan, al-Asraf Barsbay, who reigned in Damascus from 1422 to 1438.

DAMASCUS   21 x 19.5 x 2 cm
NATIONAL MUSEUM, DAMASCUS   1458 A
DAM 3 (1988) p. 209 and Pl. 40a

202
Block of obsidian
3500 BC

Obsidian is found only in certain deposits of volcanic origin. Archaeometric studies to determine provenance demonstrate that this vitrified material was imported into Syria from eastern Turkey, where it could be mined from outcroppings. These regions, lying just north of Syrian territory, could be reached by going up the Euphrates towards its source. The appearance of this block makes it clear that obsidian was imported in its raw form and was carved by local craftsmen when it reached its destination. Many specialists consider that nomadic people were involved in trading this material, which they could obtain when they migrated with their flocks in search of summer pastures in the mountains.

TELL BRAK   15 x 12 x 11 cm
DEIR EZ ZOR MUSEUM   TB-13178
IRAQ 55 (1993) p. 174

203
Piece of lapis lazuli
2300 BC

Lapis lazuli is no doubt the semiprecious stone that was best known in the ancient Near East. It was synonymous with splendor and prestige, associated with the gods, and therefore used to make cult-related objects. Lapis lazuli began to be imported to Syria about 4000 BC, probably from a region of Afghanistan that was later mentioned by Marco Polo in his account of his travels. The stone was traded in the form of blocks like this one by overland routes. It was then carved into small ornaments, amulets and cylinder seals. It seems to have been widely used by about 2500 BC. Finding a block of lapis lazuli at Ebla is very significant, since certain cuneiform texts from the city may be interpreted as saying that Ebla controlled the trade in lapis lazuli coming from Afghanistan on its way to Egypt.

MARDIKH, ANCIENT EBLA   13 x 5.5 x 4.5 cm
NATIONAL MUSEUM, ALEPPO   M 11299/1

204
Vase in the shape of a truncated cone
Steatite
2500 BC

The temple dedicated to the goddess Ishtar at Mari has yielded an abundance of luxury vessels sculpted out of a soft gray or green stone, which is commonly called steatite but is actually chlorite. This material is found in a mountainous region of eastern Iran, where such vessels were sculpted before being exported. In fact, a workshop (Tepe Yahya) was discovered near the quarries a few years ago. This type of vase was distributed over a wide area, from the Euphrates to the Indus. The outer surface of this fragment is decorated with a lion fighting a serpent. The small hollows in the animals' bodies were once filled with precious stones which have since disappeared.

TELL HARIRI, ANCIENT MARI: TEMPLE OF ISHTAR   14.5 x 13 cm
NATIONAL MUSEUM, ALEPPO   M 7829   *SMC* 119

205
Cloth
Chinese silk
AD 100

Cloth goods represented a considerable part of the merchandise that passed through Palmyra. The foremost of these goods was silk, made by a technique known only to the Chinese, who jealously guarded the secret for centuries. Palmyra was an important stopover along the Silk Road, just before the route reached the Mediterranean. By examining the silk cloth in which certain rich Palmyrene citizens had themselves buried, specialists have been able to ascertain that some of these pieces came from fabric imported directly from China, while others had been made and dyed locally, in Syria itself, using imported raw silk or silk thread. Dye was obtained from a plant called madder, which was also imported but from India.

TADMOR, ANCIENT PALMYRA (TOMB 40)   40 x 30 cm
NATIONAL MUSEUM, DAMASCUS

211

206 a-b
Necklaces
Carnelian
1800 BC

Carnelian, a kind of quartz with microcrystalline structure, was the second most popular semiprecious stone used in Mesopotamia to make beads and amulets. It is found here and there throughout the Near East in the shape of pebbles in alluvial deposits that exist in various places between Iran and India, as well as in the Arabian peninsula and Turkey. However, it is not found in Syria and had to be imported there.

TELL ASHARA, ANCIENT TERQA
DEIR EZ ZOR MUSEUM   3039, 3052 (TQ-245/TQ5-208)
L'EUFRATE 296-297

207
Necklace
Amber
1300 BC

Amber is the fossilized resin of coniferous trees. It varies in color from yellow to brown, is smooth to the touch and polishes well. Since the stone is not very hard, it is easy to work and, especially, to drill holes through. It produces static electricity and acts as a magnet when rubbed, and because of this was considered to have magic powers. Medical virtues were also attributed to it. Amber was used exclusively to make beads in the Near East, and only in small quantities. True amber comes from the shores of the Baltic Sea and was introduced to Syria by the Mycenaeans of Greece, who traded the stone during the late bronze age, that is, in the later half of the second millennium. Previously, Syrian craftsmen had used a resinous substance that was similar to amber, but which originated in Lebanon.

RAS SHAMRA, ANCIENT UGARIT
NATIONAL MUSEUM, ALEPPO   M 8202

208
Necklace
Rock crystal
2600 BC

Rock crystal is a sort of colorless quartz. Because of its hardness and fragility, it is more difficult to work than other semiprecious stones. However, it was commonly used in Mesopotamia as early as the sixth millennium. Although Pliny says in his *Natural History* (XXXVII, 23) that the most beautiful rock crystal came from India, the stone is found near Syrian territory, in Iran and in Turkey.

TELL KASHKASHUK III
NATIONAL MUSEUM, ALEPPO   M 10556
L'EUFRATE 224

209
Necklace
Carnelian, lapis lazuli, rock crystal, turquoise, frit
2300 BC

Although turquoise owes its name to Turkey, which was a source of the stone for Europe, it actually comes from Iran, Afghanistan and the Sinai, where it is found in the form of compact lumps or fillings in the cracks of altered rocks. It appears on the surface of the ground in places where there are outcroppings of copper-bearing stones like malachite, which accounts for the range of blue-green shades that make it so attractive. It is an easily worked stone.
Frit is a man-made product, with a composition similar to that of glass. It was used in place of semiprecious stones for making necklace beads.

JEZIREH
NATIONAL MUSEUM, ALEPPO   M 7822

210 a-b
Fragments of a vase with an Egyptian cartouche
Alabaster
1400 BC

In the later half of the second millennium, the Mediterranean area of the Near East was controlled by major political powers. Around 1450 BC, Ugarit was a small kingdom that formed a sort of satellite in the Kingdom of the Mitanni in northern Syria. When the pharaohs of the mighty Twenty-eighth Dynasty came to the throne in Egypt, Ugarit found itself in the this country's sphere of influence, as is attested by the cartouche of an Egyptian ruler on these vase fragments. Ugarit remained under Egyptian control until about 1350 BC, when the Hittites imposed their suzerainty on the little kingdom. In general, the Egyptians were content simply to visit the port cities along the coast to attend to their commercial interests.

RAS SHAMRA, ANCIENT UGARIT   13 x 7.5 x 3 cm/12 x 8 x 3 cm
NATIONAL MUSEUM, DAMASCUS   4155 and 4156

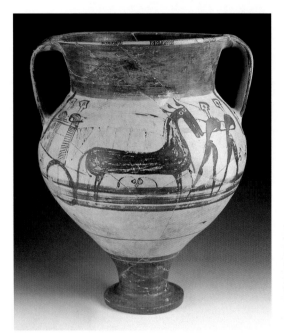

211
Vase with a cart
Ceramic
1300 BC

This type of vase, which is also called a crater, was produced by the Mycenaeans of pre-classical Greece. It illustrates the contacts Syria maintained with the Aegean world. The Mycenaeans are thought to have been responsible for the trade in amber, which came from the shores of the Baltic Sea and was used in Syria to make beads for necklaces [207].

RAS IBN HANI   47.5 x 36 cm
NATIONAL MUSEUM, DAMASCUS   6806   SMC 197

212
Bowl with two women
Faience
AD 1200

This bowl has a central decoration with two women sitting on either side of a tree, each holding a goblet. At the foot of the tree, a pool with scattered floral elements is represented in a stylized manner. This is an example of a frequently painted theme in Persian art. The bowl attests to the contacts between Syria and Iran at the time, not only in the field of crafts but above all in science and, especially, medicine.

HAMA   26 x 6.5 cm
NATIONAL MUSEUM, DAMASCUS   17900 A
HAMA IV: 2 p.182-187

213
Sarcophagus cover
Terra cotta
500 BC

The face represented on this sarcophagus cover is of distinctly Egyptian inspiration. The style reflects the strong contact between the Syrian ports and Egypt in the period when Syria was a satrapy in the Persian Empire (538 BC to 333 BC) and supplied the rest of this empire with goods traded from the Mediterranean.

'AMRIT, ANCIENT MARATHUS   55 x 49 x 16 cm
TARTUS MUSEUM   645
DAM 10 (1998) p. 121

214/215/216/217

Wagons

Terra cotta

2500 BC

Carts were developed towards the end of the fourth millennium. At first, they were drawn by asses or oxen, which were preferable for transporting heavy loads. The two-wheeled model is called a cart. The merchandise carried in four-wheeled wagons was protected with a cover. These wagons were pulled by four animals attached to either side of the pole that projected from the main body. As a means of transportation, wagons were slow, going no more than 15 kilometers per day, and could be used only on fairly flat land. Because of these disadvantages, it was more profitable to transport goods on the backs of asses, since these animals could travel over uneven terrain and cover a distance of 20 kilometers in a day. However, their loads had to be distributed in bags on either side of their spine, since the saddle pack for carrying goods directly on an animal's back was not invented until a little before our era.

UNKNOWN/TELL CHUERA [217]

16 x 13 x 12 cm/14.9 x 13.5 x 10.9 cm/12.5 x 10 x 10.5 cm/
10 x 8 x 5 cm

NATIONAL MUSEUM, DAMASCUS   6089/6814/6815/196

SYRIEN 162

218
Amphora
Ceramic
AD 1200

Three kilometers off the coast near Tartus sits the island of Arwad. Known as Arados in antiquity, it was active in the maritime trade of the Mediterranean throughout its history. This amphora, a vestige of the island's role, was discovered in a wreck recently excavated by a Japanese team. The shells encrusted in the surface of the amphora are evidence of its long stay underwater. This type of container was very practical, since its tapered shape meant that the weight of its contents was evenly distributed over the entire surface of the walls, rather than concentrated at the base, which might have given way when the container was handled. As well, amphorae were easy to stack against the sloped walls of a ship's hold.

ARWAD, ANCIENT ARADOS   70 x 32 cm
NATIONAL MUSEUM, DAMASCUS   19647

219
Anchor
Gypsum
2500 BC

In the ancient Near East, most merchandise was transported by water. Syria was a hub in the trade network, because goods coming from the Indian Ocean and the Persian Gulf could be sent to the Mediterranean world via the Euphrates, which runs the length of Syria and at one point is only 150 kilometers away from the Mediterranean coast. Land transportation was comparatively unprofitable, since boats were not only able to carry more merchandise than convoys of asses or wagons, but also faster. Boats navigated the Euphrates and its tributaries, especially the Habur. This anchor was found on a site near the Habur, 200 kilometers from where it flows into the Euphrates. The site, Tell 'Atij, was a depot for grains at the time that Mari was developing river traffic and sought food supplies in the northern regions.

TELL 'ATIJ   34 x 18 x 11 cm
DEIR EZ ZOR MUSEUM   ATJ 88.46
L'EUFRATE 176

217

220
Bas-relief of the goddess Allat
on a dromedary
Basalt
AD 200

The dromedary, which originated in southern Arabia, began to be used in Syria as a beast of burden for overland trade only in the second millennium, when the country became involved with the commerce in aromatic Arabian plants. Since one dromedary could transport twice the load of a wagon in one third the time and could go for 10 to 14 days without water, it was soon adopted as an ideal means of transportation in desert conditions. But its advantages were not fully exploited until the time of the Persian Empire (around 500 BC), when the Aramaeans began to use caravans. This Roman bas-relief shows the Greek goddess Nemesis, who was worshipped widely in Syria and was associated with the great Arab goddess Allat. She is represented here riding sidesaddle on a dromedary, an animal that must have played an important role in her cult.

RHANA SAHER (NEAR ALEPPO)   95 x 53 x 26 cm
NATIONAL MUSEUM, ALEPPO   C 686
SYRIA 84 (1971) p. 116 Fig. 2

221
"Safaitic" graffiti
Basalt
AD 200

"Safaitic" is the name given to the nomadic people who roamed the Syro-Arabian desert between the first and fourth centuries of our era. This drawing, scratched with flint on a block of very dense basalt, clearly shows a mounted horseman with a spear in one hand attempting to capture a one-humped camel and a dromedary. The words inscribed all around the scene say: "May the goddess Allat ensure good booty" [to whoever leaves this inscription untouched but] "may the goddess Allat make blind and mute" [whoever destroys it]. The nomads who lived in the Safa Desert at this time were stockraisers who specialized in camel-breeding and, given their knowledge of the region, played an active role in trade.

AL-EISAWY, SAFA DESERT REGION (SOUTHWEST OF DAMASCUS)
70 x 45 x 29 cm
SUWEIDA MUSEUM   852

222
Bowl with camel
Ceramic
AD 1200

The camel was a symbol of wealth for Arabs, for the animal had enabled merchants to become rich by forming caravans that transported luxury products, like silk and spices, over great distances. This vessel comes from Raqqa, which is situated on the Euphrates at a place where merchandise brought by boat from China and India via the Persian Gulf was unloaded and put on the backs of camels, which then set off for Aleppo and Antioch.
This type of ceramic, with its painted, dark blue decoration under a transparent turquoise glaze, was common in Syria during the Ayyubid period, and Raqqa was the largest center of production. It was widely held at the time that turquoise could ward off disease, which explains why the color was so popular.

RAQQA   27 x 7 cm
NATIONAL MUSEUM, DAMASCUS   13423 A   *BAAL* 351; *ED* 269

223
Cylinder seal
Feldspar
2500 BC

The advantage of the cylinder seal was that it could be
rolled and thus leave an imprint on a comparatively large
surface. The first cylinder seals were inscribed with very
simple geometric motifs. When the seal was rolled on wet
clay, these motifs created a decorative strip on
the clay's surface.

TELL 'ATIJ   3 x 2.6 cm
DEIR EZ ZOR MUSEUM   6337 (ATJ 86.61)
L'EUFRATE 177

224
Cylinder seal
Carnelian and gold
1900 BC

There was a tendency to use attractive stones to make
seals, since their owners often wore them as jewelry,
hanging on a cord. The sides of this cylinder seal are decorated with a scene of a hero (Gilgamesh ?) fighting a bull
with a man's head. The picture is carved in intaglio so
that the imprint it leaves is in relief. Cylinder seals of this
sort constitute an inexhaustible source of pictorial information about mythological stories.

TELL HARIRI, ANCIENT MARI (A TOMB OF SHAKKANAKKU)
3.5 x 1.5 cm
DEIR EZ ZOR MUSEUM   13162 (TH-23)

225
Stamp seal
Terra cotta
2300 BC

Seals were rarely made of terra cotta like this one; they
were usually carved from stone. The hole in the narrow
end shows that it was worn on a cord around the owner's
neck or wrist. The seal would have left an imprint of concentric circles, which was a common design at the time.

TELL BRAK   5.8 x 3.8 cm
DEIR EZ ZOR MUSEUM   10287 (TB 10033)

226
Seal
Stone
5800 BC

The first seals appeared in Syria a little after 6000 BC, when people began to store agricultural surpluses in community storehouses and wanted to control access to these buildings. The seals took the form of stamps, like the one shown here.

RAS SHAMRA, ANCIENT UGARIT   5.1 x 4.3 cm
NATIONAL MUSEUM, DAMASCUS   56 (RS 36.36)

227
Container with its seal
Stone and clay
5200 BC

Seals were used for securing any receptacle in which the owner wanted to conceal something. This is a stone container, covered with a coating of clay, which was then stamped with seals.

TELL SABI ABYAD   13.5 x 7 x 4 cm (container)/11.5 x 9 x 5 cm (seal)
NATIONAL MUSEUM, DAMASCUS   (SAB S91-55 and 1557)
L'EUFRATE 59

228/229
Seals in the shape of animals
Stone
3200 BC

People who owned seals had to have them handy at all times to carry out their responsibilities and therefore wore them as pendants. This gave people the idea of carving seals in animal shapes.

TELL BRAK   3.7 x 2.2 x 1.6 cm/2.7 x 1.9 x 2 cm
NATIONAL MUSEUM, ALEPPO   M 7725/M 7720   *Cf. BAAL* 77-80

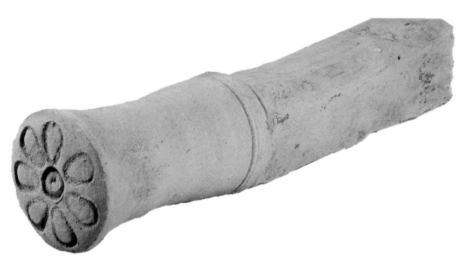

230 a-b
Knobs for doorways
Terra cotta
2500 BC

Knobs of this sort — with a square bottom end and a cylindrical handle — were set into walls beside doorways.
The item was part of a system for keeping doors shut.
One end of a cord was tied to the knob anchored in the
wall, while the other was attached to a handle made in
the wooden door. To control access to a room that had
been shut in this way, the two ends of the cord were covered with wet clay, on which a cylinder seal was rolled or
a stamp seal was impressed (illustration). This system was
commonly used in public buildings like palaces, where
there were storage rooms for surplus production and
goods acquired through trade.

TELL BI'A, ANCIENT TUTTUL   24 x 6.4 cm/27 x 6.2 cm
RAQQA MUSEUM/NATIONAL MUSEUM, DAMASCUS
546 (B124/46:8 90B:10)/547 (B124/46:7)
L'EUFRATE 268; *MDOG* 125 (1993) p. 113-131

231 a-o
Sealings
Unbaked clay
2300 BC

Fragments of unbaked clay like these are often found in
great quantities near the doors of the storehouses that
once stood in palaces. A civil servant who was responsible
for safeguarding a storehouse was careful to keep the
door sealed at all times (using the device explained in
230). When the storeroom was opened, the sealing, or
lump of clay with the imprint of a seal, was broken and
the fragments were thrown on the floor in a corner of the
room. Each civil servant in charge of a reserve had his
own seal, which was something like his piece of identity
in the administrative system of the palace.

TELL BRAK   3 x 1.7 cm
DEIR EZ ZOR MUSEUM   (TB 14073)

232 a-e
Tokens (calculi)
Terra cotta
3200 BC

Small clay objects like these are found in abundance on the sites where writing was eventually developed (around 3000 BC). People seem to have used them to represent merchandise for accounting purposes. When goods were traded, the person responsible for transporting them wore these tokens threaded on a string and gave them to the receiver, who knew how to decipher them. The quantity of the merchandise being traded was given by the number of lines, and its nature was symbolized by the shape of the token itself. These lines and shapes were eventually reproduced two-dimensionally on tablets and are thus thought by many to have been the precursors of writing.

TELL HABUBA KABIRA   2 x 1.5 cm (on average)
NATIONAL MUSEUM, ALEPPO   M 10576-9 M 8535   *SMC* 87

233 a-q
Tokens (calculi)
Unbaked clay
2500 BC

These tokens, which were also used to keep track of traded goods, were found on a site that postdates the appearance of writing. This shows that the new system did not replace the old one all at once. Since the tokens lack holes on which they could be threaded, they had to be placed in a hollow clay ball called a bulla **[234].**

TELL 'ATIJ   2.5 x 1.7 cm
DEIR EZ ZOR MUSEUM   (ATJ 87.244)
L'EUFRATE 178

234
Bulla (clay envelope)
Unbaked clay
3200 BC

Tokens, or *calculi,* were concealed in a hollow clay sphere like this one and then imprinted with a cylinder seal rolled on the surface. Large notches were made on the outside of the sphere to indicate the number of tokens it held. A bulla was never baked, of course, because the person who received the goods it accompanied had to be able to break it open and count the number of tokens sealed within.

TELL HABUBA KABIRA   6.3 cm
NATIONAL MUSEUM, ALEPPO   M 10170
SMC 88; *BAAL* 69

THE ORGANIZATION OF THE ECONOMY

235
Numeral tablet
Terra cotta
3200 BC

It soon became obvious that marking the number of *calculi* inside a bulla **[234]** on the clay ball's surface was somewhat redundant. People began to mark flat unbaked-clay tablets with the symbols for quantity — that is, notches and circular depressions — that had been previously provided by tokens. This type of tablet had to accompany the goods it quantified, since their nature was not indicated.

JEBEL ARUDA   9 x 8 x 2.8 cm
NATIONAL MUSEUM, ALEPPO   M 10169
SMC 90; *BAAL* 71

236
Numeral tablet
Unbaked clay
2500 BC

Over time, the symbols on the numeral, or numerical, tablets — used to help people keep track of numbers — gradually diminished in size and eventually became simply plain little dots and lines. The code they represented has not yet been deciphered.

TELL 'ATIJ   5.5 x 4 x 1.7 cm
DEIR EZ ZOR MUSEUM   (ATJ 87-246)
L'EUFRATE 179

237
Tablet: mathematical exercise
Terra cotta
2300 BC

Scribes were scholars as well as administrators, and they acquired all kinds of useful knowledge in addition to writing, especially if it could be applied in their work. The left-hand column of this little tablet presents a list of the highest numbers in the sexagesimal system, based on the number 60. The scribes were very interested in mathematics because they needed a system that would simplify the task of remembering certain quantities and doing mental calculations with them so that administrative transactions would be accurately accounted for. We still see traces of the sexagesimal system developed by the Mesopotamian scribes in our way of measuring time in hours, minutes and seconds.

TELL MARDIKH, ANCIENT EBLA   6 x 5.8 x 1.7 cm
NATIONAL MUSEUM, ALEPPO   M 10824 (M 347 TM.75.G.1693)
L'ÉCRITURE 133

238
Tablet: list of professions
Terra cotta
2300 BC

Lists like this one, enumerating titles and the names of professions, are known as lexical lists. They give all sorts of terms that are presented in a certain order, based on various themes or word forms, depending on the scribe who composed them. These lists were used above all in training scribes to write and increase their written vocabulary. The apprentice scribes learned to copy the elements that figured in the lexical lists, concentrating on certain themes or certain words that began with the same cuneiform sign. In doing so, they transcribed lists of words for objects, professions, animals and geographical places, grouped together according to criteria that varied depending on the purpose of the writing exercise. Today these lists represent an inexhaustible source of information on the society of the period and its institutions.

TELL MARDIKH, ANCIENT EBLA   16 x 15.5 x 2.5 cm
IDLIB MUSEUM   183 (TM.75.G.5259)   *L'ÉCRITURE* 142

239
Tablet: annual report on metal
Terra cotta
2300 BC

The various expenses incurred for gold and silver in the course of a year were recorded on large summary tablets at the end of this period. These tablets, constituting annual reports on precious metals, could have more than 20 columns on each side. Expenditures related to textiles, being more frequent than those related to precious metals, were summed up on a monthly basis **[240]**. This tablet is remarkable for its large size.

TELL MARDIKH, ANCIENT EBLA   30 x 28 x 2.5 cm
IDLIB MUSEUM   648 (TM.75.G.1860)   *L'ÉCRITURE* 141

240
Tablet: monthly expenditures for textiles
Terra cotta
2300 BC

Textiles seem to have had great economic value in ancient Eastern societies. On this large tablet, the scribes of the palace of Ebla drew up a list of the expenses incurred by the king for the purchase of textiles and clothing. These goods were offered to the gods, given to the palace functionaries or other subjects, and presented to foreign ambassadors. Since buying cloth entailed considerable expense, the palace chancellery produced lists like this one every month. Cloth was the only good for which monthly lists were made; expenditures for other materials were reported only annually.

TELL MARDIKH, ANCIENT EBLA   19 x 16.5 x 3.8 cm
IDLIB MUSEUM   85 (TM.75.G.1300)   *L'ÉCRITURE* 136

241
Tablet: school excerise
Terra cottta
2300 BC

This simple writing exercise dealing with a few important cuneiform signs illustrates the way scribes had to learn their skill. Essentially, they devoted themselves to copying other texts in order to memorize some 1200 signs in the cuneiform writing system. They began by copying out syllabaries, followed by lists of lexical items classified by theme. Then they could launch into complete texts, such as proverbs, which were easy to memorize because they were rhymed, and short extracts from well-known literary works. Finally, they would write out entire compositions, like hymns and epics. This training did not take place in a real school, however, but was rather offered by the literate in their homes.

TELL MARDIKH, ANCIENT EBLA 6 x 5.5 x 1.5 cm
IDLIB MUSEUM 477 (TM.75.G.1692) *L'ÉCRITURE* 148

242
Tablet: list of food rations
Terra cotta
2400 BC

The civil servants in the palace of Mari were responsible for seeing that food rations were distributed to the specialized craftsmen working for the king and his court. This tablet records the distribution of grain and beer rations to people who were designated by the trade they practiced at the palace. There were three carpenters, one felt maker, one potter, three curriers, two fullers and one gardener. On other tablets of this type, people are also designated by their place of work.

TELL HARIRI, ANCIENT MARI 6.6 x 6.6 x 3 cm
DEIR EZ ZOR MUSEUM 3210 (TH.80.102) *L'ÉCRITURE* 152

243
Tablet: list of food rations
Terra cotta
2400 BC

This list of monthly grain rations refers to 160 people who were dependent on the palace of Beydar. Among them were the four scribes to whom we owe this tablet and the others like it recently discovered at the Beydar site. These tablets are inscribed with essentially administrative texts — lists of employees, farm teams and animals that were allocated certain rations. Accounting on clay tablets was done on a monthly basis. At the end of every year, the information contained in these statements of expenditure was summed up and compiled in a register that constituted an annual report. Since the report made the monthly lists obsolete, they were discarded. Tablets like these were unearthed in the foundations of a house wall and inside a room of the same house, where they had been used as fill during construction.

TELL BEYDAR 7.6 x 7.6 x 2.6 cm
DEIR EZ ZOR MUSEUM 13039 (BEY 93-31) *L'ÉCRITURE* 162

244
Tablet sealed in an envelope
Unbaked clay
1700 BC

Contracts of various types, particularly those concerning the purchase of property, were recorded on tablets, which were then placed in envelopes. The text of a contract was rewritten on the outside of its envelope, and witnesses rolled their seals over the surface to secure the contents.

TELL ASHARA, ANCIENT TERQA (PUZURUM ARCHIVES)   16 x 9.2 cm
DEIR EZ ZOR MUSEUM   2364/2366 (T-97)   *L'EUFRATE* 299 and 300

245
Tablet in an envelope
Terra cotta
1300 BC

The tablet is a legal document relating to an inheritance. In accordance with the custom at the time, the tablet was concealed in an envelope on which the same text was transcribed. If one of the two parties concerned came to believe that the other had falsified the terms of an agreement, the envelope was opened by a judge so that he could compare the provisions written on the tablet with those given by the text on the envelope.

TELL EL-QITAR   11 x 8.5 x 4 cm
NATIONAL MUSEUM, ALEPPO   M 10471 (EQ-124 1.83)
L'EUFRATE 325

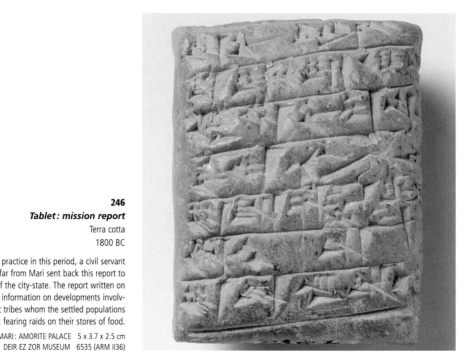

246
Tablet: mission report
Terra cotta
1800 BC

Following common practice in this period, a civil servant posted in a region far from Mari sent back this report to Zimrilim, the king of the city-state. The report written on this tablet provided information on developments involving various nomadic tribes whom the settled populations still distrusted, fearing raids on their stores of food.

TELL HARIRI, ANCIENT MARI: AMORITE PALACE   5 x 3.7 x 2.5 cm
DEIR EZ ZOR MUSEUM   6535 (ARM II36)

THE ORGANIZATION OF THE ECONOMY

247
Tablet: musical staff
Terra cotta
1400 BC

The oldest known musical staff was transcribed in cunei-form writing on the lower part of this tablet, under the double line. The six-line text in the Akkadian language gives the names of the intervals followed by a number. At present, no one is really sure about how these numbers should be interpreted or how they might be transposed onto a modern musical staff. Consequently, it is impossible to play the melody that has been transmitted to us in clay. The four-line inscription on the upper part consists of the words to a hymn that makes reference to the gods. This is therefore a complete text, with both words and music.

RAS SHAMRA, ANCIENT UGARIT   17 x 6.3 x 2.5 cm
NATIONAL MUSEUM, DAMASCUS   3916   *L'ÉCRITURE* 427

248
Tablet: lexical list
Terra cotta
1300 BC

In three columns on either side of this tablet, a scribe transcribed lists of Sumerian words that began with the same cuneiform sign or that were related from a thematic point of view. At the time that the tablet was inscribed, Sumerian was a dead language, but apprentice scribes continued to learn it as part of their education, just as Latin used to be learned in the Western world. The reason for this was that Sumerian was the first language to have been written in the Near East, around 3200 BC. The writing system employed was called cuneiform (from the Latin word cuneus for "wedge") because the signs were made up of wedge-shaped marks. Cuneiform writing is comparable to our Latin alphabet in that it was used to transcribe several languages.

RAS SHAMRA, ANCIENT UGARIT   22.3 x 15 x 3.4 cm
NATIONAL MUSEUM, ALEPPO   M 8220   *L'ÉCRITURE* 422

249
Tablet: contract in Aramaic
Clay
800 BC

The Aramaeans used an alphabet, but they wrote it with a system of cuneiform signs that had been simplified by the Assyrians (450 ideograms instead of 1200). Their language became common throughout the Assyrian Empire following the conquest of Syria by Shalmaneser III in 856 BC and then spread through the Persian Empire after 538 BC. The Aramaean language outlasted the Aramaeans themselves and for a long time continued to be used as an international language for commercial transactions. It is believed that Jesus preached in this tongue so that he would be understood by the multitudes. In a few of the villages in Syria, there are even some communities that still speak Aramaean today. The text inscribed on this tablet covers 21 lines and represents a contract for a loan of money between two people. By deciphering the text, epigraphists have been able to identify the city in which the tablet was found as Burmarina.

SHIOUKH FAOUQÂNI, ANCIENT BURMARINA
5.8 x 3.5 x 1.5 cm
NATIONAL MUSEUM, ALEPPO   M 11305 (TSF F 204 1/3)
SEMITICA 46 (1996) p. 81-121

250
Tablet: administrative text concerning stockraising
Terra cotta
2400 BC

The administrative authorities in the city of Beydar were responsible for a herd of several thousand sheep and goats. The task of watching over these animals required a good number of shepherds. On the obverse of the tablet there is a list of sheepskins, classified under the shepherds' names, while the reverse gives a list of goat skins. This is the best-preserved tablet found at Beydar.

TELL BEYDAR   12.4 x 12.1 x 3.1 cm   DEIR EZ ZOR MUSEUM   13364 (BEY 93-89/2629-T-3)   *L'ÉCRITURE* 163

251
Tablet: administrative text
2300 BC

This text is typical of the inscriptions on thousands of tablets (about 15 000) found in an archive room in the palace of Ebla. The tablets had been arranged in order and stacked on wooden shelves fixed to the walls. The archive room was located close to the place where the king held audiences and was used to preserve the decisions made by the ruler and his counsellors concerning the administration of his kingdom. This particular tablet records declarations related to silver, grain and oil.

TELL MARDIKH, ANCIENT EBLA   10 x 9 x 2.8 cm   IDLIB MUSEUM   179 (TM.75.G.1394)   *L'ÉCRITURE* 137

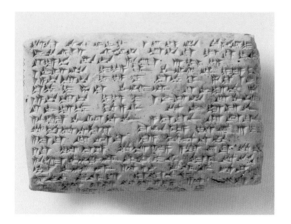

252
Tablet: will
Unbaked clay
1250 BC

Scribes did not always work as government bureaucrats. They also drafted private contracts between people and drew up wills, and were thus seriously involved in civic affairs. The will inscribed on this tablet concerns the sharing of a man's property among his children. The witnesses rolled their cylinder seals on the back of the envelope that contained the will.

TELL MESKENE, ANCIENT EMAR   11.5 x 7.8 x 3.6 cm   NATIONAL MUSEUM, ALEPPO   M 8871 (MSK 73.1022)   *L'EUFRATE* 347

253
Tablet: alphabet primer
Terra cotta
1300 BC

This tablet is extremely important, for on one of its sides it gives a list of the 30 cuneiform alphabetic symbols used in Ugarit at the time. These letters are written from left to right on four lines. Although it was not the oldest alphabet in the Near East, the Ugarit writing system was crucial to the development of an alphabet by the Phoenicians a few centuries later. The Phoenician alphabet was adopted by the Greeks, and their writing system in turn provided the basis for our modern alphabet. The word "alphabet" itself is derived from the first two letters of the Greek alphabet: alpha and beta. This tablet was probably a school exercise done by an apprentice scribe. His task was now simplified, for with the new system he could compose words for every concept imaginable using the countless combinations of just 30-odd symbols. The advantages of this system are still enjoyed by our modern world.

RAS SHAMRA, ANCIENT UGARIT   5.2 x 3.7 cm   NATIONAL MUSEUM, DAMASCUS   5018 (RS 55/18.31)

254

Commemorative stela

Basalt

900 BC

The inscription on this prism-shaped stela informs us that it was erected to commemorate the Assyrian victory over the Aramaeans in the region of Sirqu, also known as Terqa, or modern Ashara. The figure armed with an ax and fighting a serpent held in his left hand probably represents the Assyrian king Tukulti-Ninurta II (890-884 BC), who conquered the local Aramaean population, symbolized here by the serpent, a creature of the desert. A cuneiform inscription of eight lines appears above the animal's head. On the second side, the stela presents a small figure, dressed as the king is, watching the scene. On the third side, a priest is shown holding a swath of three ears of wheat in his left hand; he is about to offer them to a god in hope of obtaining divine favors.

TELL ASHARA, ANCIENT TERQA   90 x 37-39-40-17 cm
NATIONAL MUSEUM, ALEPPO   M 6540
L'EUFRATE 303 ; AAAS 2(1952) 169-190

255 a-f
Weights in the shape of animals
Bronze and lead
1500 BC

Weights in animal shapes are well-attested in the Near East during the period when Ugarit prospered. Of the 600 weights found on the site so far, some 60 are in metal and half of these are in the shape of animals such as frogs, lions, rams and cows. It is quite rare to come across a complete series like the one shown here. This series consists of six bronze weights with hollow bases that were filled with lead and fitted with bronze stoppers to hide the opening. The weighing system used in Ugarit was based on a standard called the mina, which was subdivided into 50 sicles, a sicle being equivalent to about 9.4 grams. The site of Ugarit also yielded weights corresponding to the mina of Egypt and Babylonia, regions with which Ugarit merchants had trade relations. This type of weight was used to weigh products of great value, such as spices or precious metals, rather than foodstuffs.

RAS SHAMRA, ANCIENT UGARIT   3.8-9.1 x 1.7-4.5 x 2.2-4.4 cm
NATIONAL MUSEUM, ALEPPO
M 10133/M 10134/M 8170/M 8169/M 8168/M 8171
BAAL 201; *SMC* 184, 186 and 187

256
Silver treasure
1500 BC

Before coins appeared, silver was the accepted standard for measuring the market value of goods being traded, as is attested by certain texts from Ebla written about 2500 BC. The value of silver was calculated by weight at the time. Silver used for this purpose was stored in palaces, which, as the seats of civil administration, controlled commercial transactions. Such stores are sometimes discovered, consisting of shapeless lumps of pure silver or silver rods that were cut to various lengths depending on the transaction. The rings shown here were the direct precursors of coins, for their weight was calculated beforehand. Even today, the word for money in French comes from their word for silver.

TELL MUMBAQAT   4.6 x 3.2 x 0.7 cm
NATIONAL MUSEUM, DAMASCUS
(1.195, 1.202, 1.191, 1.231, 1.264, 1.267)

257
Coin
Silver
400 BC

The first coins appeared in Syria a little after 650 BC, which is about the time they were invented by the famous king Croesus in his kingdom on the coast of Asia Minor (present-day Turkey). These coins were introduced to Syria by the Persians when the country became a satrapy in the vast Persian Empire. The image of a ship with oars that is stamped on this coin reflects the importance of the Mediterranean Sea trade at the time and ambition of the Achaemenid kings, living in Iran at the heart of their Empire, to profit from this trade through Syria and its contact with the great inland sea. Coins greatly simplified commercial transactions, as can well be imagined.

UNKNOWN   3.9 cm
NATIONAL MUSEUM, DAMASCUS   287

THE ORGANIZATION OF THE ECONOMY

258
Treasure of coins in a jar
Silver and copper
AD 1200

These coins come from a treasure of money, totaling 50 kilograms in weight, that was hidden in seven jars. In accordance with certain canonical precepts, 'Abd al-Malik ibn Marwân (685-705), the fifth caliph of the Umayyad dynasty, prohibited the representation of the ruling sovereign's effigy on the obverse or reverse of coins. Instead, he had extracts from the Koran inscribed on them, along with the name of the Caliph under whom the coins had been struck, as well as the place and date of minting. The Arabic monetary system was based on the gold dinar, weighing 4.25 grams, and the silver dirham, weighing 2.91 grams. Treasures such as this one are usually found in the ruins of houses that were abandoned precipitously when an invasion seemed imminent.

RAQQA   19 x 15 cm
NATIONAL MUSEUM, DAMASCUS   4132/11344 A
AAAS 8-9 (1958-1959) 25-52

THE ORGANIZATION OF
thought

THE ORGANIZATION OF
thought

A s the first human societies established themselves in Syria, they not only developed socially and economically but also became more aware of the world around them and of the role that each individual played in this new socioeconomic environment. As human beings always do, they gradually constructed a vision of the universe, using their capacity for reasoning to seek the meaning of the natural and supernatural forces affecting their world. They began to share a common ideology that not only reflected their interpretation of these omnipresent forces but also expressed their highest hopes and deepest fears. In their own way, and as their knowledge advanced, they attempted to find logical explanations for the phenomena that occurred around them.

From the very beginning, the divine was represented by human forms. These forms were generally female, but it is not clear exactly what they symbolized. There is a close relationship between the attempt to give concrete shape to abstract notions and primitive forms of artistic expression. Eventually, these gods with human attributes were given names that identified them more precisely. Mythological tales served to explain the sometimes turbulent relations between earthly life and the divine forces that ruled it.

Eulogia of St. Simeon. Cat. 314 b

This shared concept of the supernatural was expressed in material culture through various symbolic objects, but it also can be seen in the communities' physical layout, as special places — temples — were built for religious purposes. The vestiges of temples tell us a great deal about religious practices and how they evolved from one period to another. The monumental style that began to characterize these places of worship was a clear indication that certain collective belief systems were becoming institutionalized.

Previous page: Cultic stela. Cat. 295

The world's great monotheistic religions developed in Syrian territory. The unifying power of these great religions, based on belief in one God, was very strong and was sometimes used for more than strictly religious purposes.

In the following overview of systems of spiritual values at different periods, we will try to understand more about these societies' collective unconscious by examining remnants of their material culture. One of the most interesting cultural facets expressed through such concrete artifacts is the notion of beauty. Perhaps the most telling dimension of the belief system centers around death and preparation for the afterlife.

GODS IN HUMAN FORM

Throughout time, human beings have had a tendency to attribute divine causes to natural phenomena that they did not understand. Until it was accepted that reasoning should be based on observation and experience, people generally chose to personify abstract notions — fertility, for example — for which they had no logical explanation.

Palettes incised with symbolic motifs. Cat. 260, 261 and 259

The known was used to explain the unknown, the natural to represent the supernatural. In Syria, a feeling that the supernatural pervaded everyday life and questions about the afterlife first found expression in ancestor worship and fertility cults. Gradually, religion began to be organized around a pantheon whose members had human or animal traits. Finally, the great monotheistic religions emerged, with their belief in one divine being.

TANTALIZING SYMBOLS

Recent archaeological finds suggest that the picture painted above should be somewhat more nuanced. A Syrian site dating from around 10 000 BC has revealed small stone tablets bearing abstract motifs and, in one case, the picture of an animal. No utilitarian purpose can be imagined for these objects. It seems very likely that the motifs that cover their surfaces were not meant to be simply decorative patterns, but rather signs or symbols whose meaning can only be guessed at. These objects are the oldest symbolic representations discovered to date in

Syria and the Near East. The message they hold is so far undeciphered but they are no doubt an early attempt to express abstract, rational thought in concrete form. The significance of these tablets can be appreciated if one considers the delicate workmanship that has gone into their making and recalls that the people who made them had only simple stone tools at their disposal. Such fine work would have taken many days for each stone.

THE FIRST DIVINITIES: MOTHER GODDESSES

In the same period, there appeared the sculpted figures that are at present considered to represent the first divinities revered by human beings. These figurines, with their voluptuous curves and exaggerated sexual attributes, are often called — perhaps a little too categorically — mother goddesses. Be that as it may, their rounded forms are so strongly evocative of all that is female and maternal that they surely symbolize a preoccupation with fertility and procreation as a guarantee of the species' survival. The figurines are sculpted in stone or modeled out of fire-baked clay that, as has been recently discovered, was sometimes even painted.

The figurines seem to have had a male parallel, although in a more symbolic form. The skulls of aurochs (a type of wild bull), or simply their horns, have been found incorporated into clay benches in houses and in foundation walls. Although it would be rash to speak of a bull god (for which there was a great cult in later periods), these vestiges were very likely seen as symbols of virility, represented by the image of the bull. The female fertility figurines and the bull

Female figure in unbaked earth thought to represent a mother goddess. Cat. 263

skulls, which date from between 10 000 BC and 6 000 BC, are the first indications of an attempt to explain the origin of humankind. This was also the time when people started to live from agriculture and animal husbandry. Controlling plant and animal reproduction was evidently of central importance to them.

Both types of symbols continued to be used in subsequent periods. The material culture of these periods contained many female figurines [265, for example], made of terra cotta instead of stone or clay, but still belonging to the earlier tradition. The people in these later times also made statues of male gods in the shape of bulls with human heads [272].

The enigmatic female figures
of Tell Halula

THE DISCOVERY OF SYMBOLIC documents is invaluable, since they can offer insights into the otherwise impenetrable collective psyche of a vanished community. Consequently, the painted representations of humans revealed on a floor in a building at Tell Halula deserve special attention, especially since they are the oldest painted images of human beings in the Near East.

The composition covers a surface area of 1.2 meters by 1 meter on a whitewashed floor near a hearth in the main room of a multiroomed house. In the design, there are 23 schematic human figures placed around a square filled with stripes. The figures are of two types.

In the first type, the figure is viewed frontally, with triangular legs ending in points, extremely wide hips and a narrowing at the torso. The right arm is raised slightly, with lines representing the hand, while the head is simply a circular smudge. There are seven figures of this type, some solitary and others in pairs. On the basis of their physical shapes, they may be interpreted as female representations.

In the second type, the human figures appear to be shown sideways. The lower part of the body is given a triangular shape and the posterior is accentuated. Small perpendicular lines below may represent feet, while two similar lines higher up might symbolize arms. The torso is painted as a thick line, ending in a circular head. The presence of breasts on the torso indicates that these are female figures, and the fact that they are seen from the side emphasizes the character-

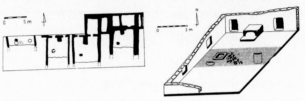

House in Tell Halula with floor decorated in painted female figures.

istics that express fertility. The figures are drawn in groups of two or three, and, in one case, four of them are joined at the hip.

It is always difficult to interpret artistic and symbolic documents. The document just described is a composite design, in which female figures predominate, surrounding a schematic element that is even more enigmatic. It may be asked whether the building that housed the painting had some special significance; perhaps the panel was used as a platform for drying cereal. The presentation of the female figures in what appears to be joyous dance illustrates once again, in my opinion, the role that women must have played in the first agricultural societies in the Levant. This pictorial composition will certainly aid us towards a better understanding of the symbolic world of the early farmer-herders, especially those who lived in the village of Tell Halula.

PROF. DR. MIGUEL MOLIST
Universitat autónoma de Barcelona

Painted female figures on the floor of a house in Tell Halula.

The Syrian pantheon and its divinities

As a sociopolitical structure took shape — particularly with the establishment of city-states around 3000 BC — there was a parallel development in the realm of thought. In about the same period, an effort was clearly made to organize the numerous gods that had been adopted over time into a rational, ordered hierarchy. In the texts of the time, divinities were categorized according to their lineage or according to the role they played in a certain myth. At the same time, they were given names.

The supreme god in the Syrian pantheon was El, who had created all the other gods with his consort Ashera, or Ashtoreth, as she is called in the Bible. He was the god of wisdom, the god of cosmic origins who ruled over a celestial court, seated on his throne [275]. In the Syrian pantheon he is accompanied by a bold young warrior god, brandishing a thunderbolt [277]. The latter was known by different names — Ada, Hadad or Baal, the "Master" — depending on the region in which he was worshipped. The other gods and goddesses revolve around these two principal deities.

Baal lived on mountaintops, where the thunder and lightning came from. A text inscribed on a tablet from the site of Ugarit has preserved mythological tales about Baal and the other gods. In one of them, Baal has a violent confrontation with Yamm, the god of both the sea and chaos, who wanted to build a palace for himself. For the inhabitants of Ugarit, Baal's home was at the summit of Mount Zaphon, a mountain that is clearly visible from the city, rising to a height of 2000 meters and only three kilometers from the sea. Every fall, as humid air from the Mediterranean rises over the mountain and cools, the clouds gather over the summit and spectacular storms erupt. For the inhabitants of ancient Ugarit, the great thunder claps and incessant flashes of lightning over the angry sea was like a reenactment of the battle in which Baal struck down the fearsome Yamm. Thus natural phenomena seem to have given birth to this typically Ugarit myth. The story no doubt explains why so many boat anchors have been found in the temple of Baal in Ugarit. Sailors setting out on a voyage might have made such offerings in the hope that they would obtain the divine protection of Baal, who had demonstrated that he was stronger than the natural force of the sea.

In another tale, Baal takes the form of a high-spirited bull calf who goes down from the summit to meet his consort, the heifer Anat [273], and to frolic in the pastures at the foot of the mountain — a tale that needs no interpreting. However, a third tale recounting Baal's battle with Mot, the god of death, is more enigmatic. Baal loses this combat and is carried away to the land of the dead. It is summer and everything begins to dry up because there is no more rain. Anat, his wife, sets off to find him and eventually brings his body back to the summit of Mount Zaphon. There he is raised to life by the sun goddess, Shapsh, like water rising as vapor in the sun. Baal takes vengeance by hurling lightning at Mot, and the resulting storm brings water to the fields. The region around ancient Ugarit received an average of over 250 millimeters of rain each year and the peasants living in the area did not have to irrigate their fields. However, they were entirely at the mercy of the weather, and the anxiety this could cause no doubt gave rise to the tale of the rain god. The three myths — Baal against Yamm, Baal with Anat, and Baal against Mot — reflect the main occupations of

the inhabitants of Ugarit: seafaring, sheep-herding and farming.

Another deity in the Syrian pantheon deserves to be mentioned. This is the lovely Astarte [274], who is also known as Ishtar in the rest of Mesopotamia. She was a young war-like goddess, a defender of free love and an emblem of womanhood who in popular mythology eventually became identified with Anat, Baal's wife and sister, and with Ashera, the consort of El, with whom she created 70 deities.

THE SYRIAN DIVINITIES ARE ASSIMILATED WITH GREEK AND ROMAN DEITIES

During the Hellenistic and Roman periods, the Eastern mythologies were given a Greco-Roman interpretation and the Eastern gods were identified with the Hellenistic pantheon. Baal was assimilated with his thunderbolt-hurling Greek counterpart, Zeus, who became the Roman Jupiter. Astarte was identified with the Greek goddess, Aphrodite, who became the Roman Venus. Allat [220], who was worshipped by the Syrian Arabs in an Arabian cult introduced by the Nabataeans, became identified with Athena [278].

However, the Greco-Roman influence was not limited to the reinterpretation of Eastern deities. In some cases, the local populations were so Romanized that they adopted the Greek and Roman myths without any modifications, especially when the myths were well known, like that of Hercules [279].

On the other hand, there was also an effort to explain the oriental cults to the Greeks and Romans. Some of these cults attracted wide followings in Rome and Italy, such as the cults of Mithras and Isis. But Syria was not very much involved in this cultural transfer.

With the emergence of the great monotheistic religions and their concept of one God, creator of the universe and everything in it, the pagan cults gradually disappeared from Syria. Reflecting their decline, dedications to the old gods were at best sporadic by the end of the fourth century AD. However, the influence of the Eastern world on the Roman Empire grew stronger with the spread of Judaism and, especially, Christianity. It was at Antioch, the capital of Roman Syria, that the followers of the new religion preached by Jesus took the name of Christians. And it was at Damascus that Saul, who became St. Paul, had the revelation that would contribute so decisively to differentiating Christianity from Judaism.

PLACES OF WORSHIP AND RELIGIOUS PRACTICE

Ancient societies did not limit themselves to making objects that gave concrete representations to abstract concepts. They also built special places for themselves where they could conduct religious ceremonies in honor of their gods. The temple is probably the best known of these places of worship and the most significant as well, although acts of worship were also performed outside the building proper. However, identifying such places is not always easy and often gives rise to much debate. This means that it is not simple to establish exactly when temples appeared.

THE FIRST TEMPLES: ABODES OF THE GODS

In the ancient Near East, the temple was the house of god in the strictest sense. It was the place where the god lived and where humans served him, as they were obliged to do. He lived there in the shape of a statue or a symbol that provided a material presence to support the rituals conducted by the temple servants appointed to this work. The statue was dressed and fed as if it were human; sometimes divine weddings were even arranged. The temple was not a place where devotees could come together to worship their god, nor where they could express their collective faith. Although the temple was considered simply an abode, it was nonetheless built on sacred ground, which could not be used for other purposes afterwards. Since temples were impressive architectural constructions, their appearance in the Near East indicates that the societies that built them had some form of organized religion in which cult-related practices were institutionalized. Given the lack of explicit texts, the existence of temples can be inferred only from the presence of architectural details in certain types of buildings.

The appearance of temples is essentially related to the phenomenon of urbanization, since they were large-scale constructions. The decision to put up a building with such a well-defined function was also linked with the establishment of a more developed form of sociopolitical structure. Indeed, the first temples were very similar to the large houses that appeared in certain populous villages with considerable social organization. Such houses acted as public buildings in which a person representing government authority could exercise power. Some of these buildings continued to develop in this direction and became palaces, while others were given architectural elements that are associated with temples. The first such element to appear was a podium along the inside rear wall, on which the cultic statue or symbol of divinity could be installed [295]. The podi-

um was in an area of the temple known as the "Holy of Holies." It was often separated from the main room, called a cella or sanctuary, by a removable wall, whose existence is today sometimes revealed only by two aligned abutments on the side walls where it would have been attached. In the central axis of the cella, not far from the podium, stood an offering table. The presence of such a table is conclusive evidence that a building was indeed a temple, since a podium on its own could have been used as a dais for a throne. The entrance to the cella might be in a side wall or in the wall facing the altar, but there was always a vestibule that served as a place of transition between the profane outer world and the sacred inner world. Ritual was not restricted to the interior, however, since outside there might be an esplanade or raised terrace with altars where sacrifices could be made. In any case, the interior was not really open to ordinary worshippers. Temples were sometimes distinguished from other public buildings by having their outer walls decorated with clay cones [280]. Tapered ends of the cones were stuck into the surface and rounded tops painted different colors, giving the whole a mosaic-like effect.

Between the third and first millennia BC, a particular type of temple developed in Syria. Temples of this sort were built at sites like that of Emar, where impressive examples have been brought to light. These temples were rectangular in layout and had an entrance in one of their short sides, with extensions of their long walls forming a porch. Inside, the main room, which could be divided in two, had benches along the back wall and sometimes along a side wall. An altar might stand at about two thirds of the

distance between the entrance and the back wall, aligned with the door, or, alternatively, there might be a niche made in the rear wall. According to the biblical texts (the building itself has disappeared), this was exactly the model used by Solomon in about 1000 BC when he built his famous temple to Yahweh in Jerusalem, except that the "Holy of Holies" housed not a statue but the Ark of the Covenant. The layout of this type of temple followed a logical progression from the secular to the sacred. The vestibule represented a link between the temporal outer world and the sanctified inner world. The outer sanctuary was used for daily worship, the presentation of offerings and other rituals, and the "Holy of Holies" was the inaccessible dwelling place of God.

Although worshippers were not allowed into the temples themselves, they could send in little stone sculptures of people in a praying position, hands folded on chests and eyes wide open as if in adoration [286]. These orants, as they are called, often seem to have been used as votive offerings that would perpetuate the prayers of the dedicators. Worshippers had their names inscribed on the statues' backs so that the god being

worshipped would know who had sent such objects of devotion. The orants were placed on benches along the walls and on little platforms. The city of Mari was identified thanks to an orant, since one of them found on the site had been inscribed with the king of Mari's name.

For a long time it was thought that some of these temples were represented in miniature by architectural models [282] that were found in association with temples. However, it is now thought that these objects were used as foundation deposits. It was common practice to place objects under thresholds and beneath walls when the temples were built, but they were more often made of square plates of bronze or gypsum bearing inscriptions to commemorate the founding of the temple or to ward off evil spirits. Such plates were fixed to the ground with large metal spikes that went through a hole made in the center of each plate. The objects most frequently used as foundation deposits were long bronze nails driven into the thickness of the walls at the four corners of the temple.

Depiction of the double temple of Emar, dedicated to Baal and Astarte.

Architectural model. Cat. 289

Interior of a temple
with orants on
benches along the
base of the walls.

Representation of a
woman bearing an
incense burner.

RELIGIOUS CEREMONIES
AND CULTIC OBJECTS

The religious or cult-related ceremonies that took place in the temples required special furnishings, which naturally included offering tables, altars and incense burners [293] in various shapes [290].

Incense, an aromatic resinous substance obtained from odiferous trees and shrubs growing particularly in southern Arabia, gives off a pungent odor when burned. Myrrh is a special type of aromatic resin that comes from the balsam tree. The smoke that rises from burning incense symbolizes both purification and offering in a single gesture meant to call upon the divinity and at the same time appease him. Initially, however,

incense was associated with death, funerals and the cult of the dead. Used in embalming bodies, it was meant to preserve the dead and keep them alive, eliminate decay and foul odors, and keep evil away. Incense was used in temples beginning in the third millennium BC, its smoke considered a sort of stairway from earth to heaven. Although the early Christians continued to burn it at funerals, they were reluctant to introduce it into their religious ceremonies because of its association with pagan cults. Incense was reintroduced to Syria in the fourth century BC and came to be viewed as symbolizing prayer and honor paid to God. Trade in incense became well organized and lucrative. It is easy to see why biblical tradition includes incense and myrrh in the princely, symbolic gifts offered by the Magi coming from the East to see Jesus as a baby.

As well as furniture, fine vessels were also used in temples. Most likely intended for libations, these vessels were sometimes sculpted in serpentine or chlorite, but most often carved out of a soft green or gray stone called steatite which was imported from eastern Iran. A very recent discovery made in a temple at Mari reveals that some of these vases were fashioned out of alabaster [296] or even made by cutting apart shells that would have had to be brought from the shores of the Indian Ocean [298]. Naturally, some of the receptacles for offerings were simply made of clay, but in such cases, they were given highly unusual shapes that would have been impractical for household use [294]. Temples also contained plates and dishes, since cult-related ceremonies often involved sumptuous banquets in honor of the divinities. Such banquets were held in buildings located in the temple courtyard.

Alabaster receptacle
used in worship.
Cat. 299

244

Certain ceremonies involved sacrificing animals, which were led in a procession [304] to the altar in the courtyard facing the temple. Archaeologists digging in the area of a temple at Ebla found remains that are related to this practice. In the inner courtyard of a massive cultic stone terrace, they found an enclosure for keeping the sacred lions that were destined for the cult of Ishtar which was centered in a nearby temple. Once the animal was sacrificed, the priests examined its liver, which was supposed to help them predict the future. It was believed that the spirit of the god to whom the animal was ritually sacrificed would enter the animal's body and be revealed through observable signs in its entrails, especially its liver. In this way, the deity could answer a question that was asked before the sacrifice, such as what events were going to take place and what behavior one should adopt in the future.

This appears to have been a method of divination that was reserved for the king in the exercise of his power. After the liver had been examined, the interpretation of the signs were noted on a clay model copying the malformations shown by the real liver. The clay models acted as mnemonic devices for the priests. The inscriptions usually followed a similar formulation: "If such-and-such a part of the liver presents such-and-such an anomaly, such-and-such an event will occur." Another, less common formulation was used on divinatory livers at Mari: "When such-and-such an event occurred or will occur, the liver presented or will present such-and-such signs." The models

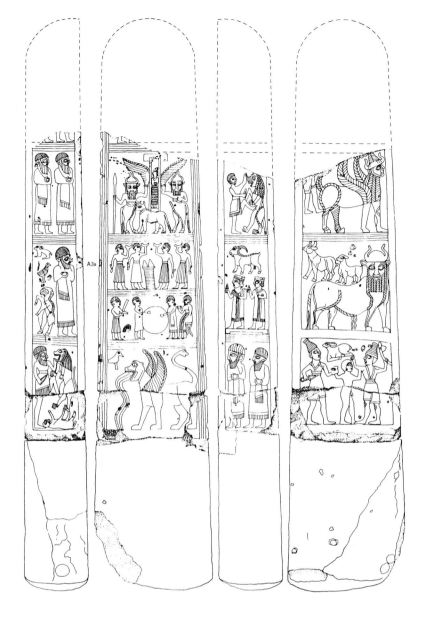

Roman sanctuaries for the Eastern world

During the Hellenistic and Roman periods, the most typical place of worship was the sanctuary, a complex of structures. Among its facilities was a temple, which served as a home for the deity or for the cultic statue. The temple stood in the middle of a courtyard, called a *temenos*. This sacred space was surrounded by a wall, called the *peribole*, and was reached through a monumental gate, or *propylon*. Inside, many cult-related ceremonies took place. The most important of these were sacrifices, which were offered on an altar that usually stood between the gate and the temple. The installations might also include a pool or well for ablutions and lustrations, a shrine holding the cult object, buildings in which ritual banquets took place, the occasional minor chapel and, in some cases, annexes where the priests lived. The offerings made in these sanctuaries ranged from simple *ex voto* objects and statues to miniature temples and votive stelae.

The temple itself was built on a raised platform that was reached by a stairway and surrounded by a colonnade. At the rear of

The four sides of the stela of Ishtar found at Ebla. Cat. 276

were used in schools for augurs, since the art of divination was in wide demand.

A remarkable monolithic stone stela once stood in a chapel at the top of the acropolis of Ebla. In several panels on each of its four sides, it is decorated with relief work illustrating a number of ritual ceremonies related to the worship of the great goddess Ishtar. This iconographic document provides a wealth of information and is the only one of its kind.

Model reconstruction of the temple of Bel at Palmyra.

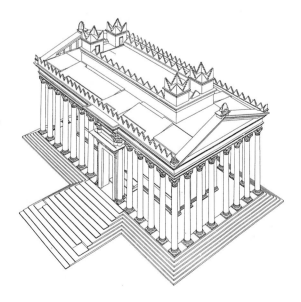

the inner area, or cella, there was a chapel called a *thalamos*, meaning a room, where the deity lived. This chapel, found only in Syrian temples, was isolated from the nave but open to view. While visitors were free to enter the main body of the temple, access to the chapel was restricted to a limited number of priests whose task was to care for the statues of the gods.

The temples identified in southern Syria display the characteristics of a local tradition.

A *thalamos* in a Syrian temple.

The temple of Bel at Palmyra.

THE ORGANIZATION OF THOUGHT

The Roman temples of southern Syria (first century BC to third century AD)

THE ROMAN TEMPLES built in Syria are distinguished not only by their monumentality and ornamentation, but also by the fact that they were erected on geographically prominent sites near an axis of communication. One of the best-preserved examples of such temples in Syria is located at Musannaf, in the southern part of the country. The temple has three rooms, laid out one after the other, and sits on a high platform reached by a great stairway on the facade. At the head of the stairs, two columns rise between the antae formed by the projecting side walls. High arches span the entire width of the three rooms and must have at one time supported a roof, which was probably flat, like a terrace.

A view of part of the Roman Musannaf temple with modern reconstruction.

Unlike temples used for Greco-Roman cults, the entire temple at Musannaf did not represent an abode for the idol. Only the innermost room, called the "Holy of Holies," or adytum, served this purpose, and access to it was forbidden. Elsewhere in the Near East, temples generally had several staircases leading up to the roof, where ceremonies such as libations and incense-offering were performed. The layout of the Musannaf building indicates that the rites practiced in Syrian temples were not of a Greek or Roman type, but rather local in nature.

While the Musannaf temple outwardly displays affinities with the Greco-Roman style, its exterior appearance would have had no influence on the Eastern cult practiced within.

Many other temples of Greco-Roman appearance had a number of courtyards intended for specific purposes. They served not only as areas where pilgrims and worshippers could meet, but also as marketplaces. This association between religious and economic functions was very widespread in the East and can be traced back to the time of the Mesopotamian sanctuaries. An altar standing before the temple's facade was used for blood sacrifices. Such sacrifices were usually followed by ritual banquets, which might be celebrated outdoors or in a room set aside for this purpose.

The discovery of numerous votive and honorific inscriptions in the sanctuaries of these temples suggest that the people who sponsored the construction of the monuments must have been dignitaries living in the surrounding communities. Their ambition was no doubt to surpass the Mediterranean centers of power in the grandeur and ostentation of their temples. However, despite the Greco-Roman inspiration of the temples' exterior appearance, the installations continued to provide the proper setting for the practice of traditional cults to local divinities.

DR. KLAUS FREYBERGER
Deutsches Archäologisches Institut (Damascus)

THE GREAT MONOTHEISTIC RELIGIONS: JUDAISM, CHRISTIANITY AND ISLAM

Over time, the early Syrian temples described in the preceding section gradually changed as a new type of cult emerged. These cults were associated with the appearance of true religions, that is, forms of worship regulated by a series of codes and constituting an institutionalized aspect of society.

Syria is closely linked to the birth and development of the three great monotheistic religions of the world: Judaism, Christianity and Islam. All three claim the same legendary ancestor, Abraham, and share a faith in one God. They also share reverence for a sacred book: the Torah for Jews, the Bible for Christians and the Koran for Muslims. Although accidents of history have often made them antagonists, the fact remains that they are united in their belief in one God, creator of the universe, who through his prophets and messengers has revealed his will to humankind and who will judge them on the last day.

A view of the district of Damascus with the Umayyad Mosque.

ONE GOD, CREATOR OF HEAVEN AND EARTH

In the previous section it was seen that the peoples of the ancient Near East were polytheists, worshipping several gods who personified the forces of nature. Around 2000 BC, Abraham led Aramaean nomads from the city of Ur in southern Mesopotamia (present-day Iraq) to the Mediterranean coast. He and his people practiced monotheism, for he believed in only one God who had created the world and everything in it. His God was not a god of nature, or of the sun or sky. Nor was he a local god. He was a moral God, for whom justice and righteousness were paramount. By the time the Christian era began, this religious concept was shared by about eight million believers in the Roman Empire.

The early Christians were zealously persecuted by people like Saul, better known as Paul, a tax collector in the Roman province of Syria. But Paul had a vision of Christ on the road to Damascus and was converted, becoming a fervent preacher. He founded churches throughout the East and kept in touch with them through letters that are known as the Epistles.

The Christian religion spread rapidly in the Roman Empire, although it suffered frequent persecutions, one of the best known probably being that launched by Nero after blaming the Christians for the fire that burned Rome in AD 64. However, Constantine (306-337) legalized the practice of Christian faith and recognized the existence of a catholic Church as an institution (the word "catholic" coming from the Greek word for "universal"). Then Theodosius (379-395), the last Emperor to reign over an undivided empire, declared Christianity the sole official religion of the Roman Empire. As well, he formally banned all other cults, going so far as to order the destruction of their temples and their "idols." However, these cults survived in the countryside; they were now considered to be "pagan," a term that comes from the Latin word *paganus*, meaning "rural."

The Damascus gate near where St. Paul is said to have preached.

SYRIA, LAND OF CIVILIZATIONS

The Eastern church: new religious communities and monasteries appear

The newly established Catholic Church adopted a hierarchical organization modeled on that of the Roman Empire and centered in cities. The cities were grouped into ecclesiastic provinces, each ruled by a bishop who lived in a palace in a cathedral town. Under him were the archbishops in the provincial county towns and the patriarchs in the large Eastern cities. This model, which mirrored the Roman world, did not please everyone. As early as the third century, a number of the faithful in the Near East had rejected a similar urban, hierarchical organization. They preferred to retreat from the world and live alone as monks in prayer and meditation, obeying the call of Christ to abandon everything and follow him into the desert. This movement was called "monachism," from the Greek word *monos*, meaning "alone." The monks soon discovered that solitary life in the desert was dangerous and, in the fourth century, some of them formed self-sufficient communities in monasteries. Nevertheless, the ideal form of monachism remained the isolated life of the hermits, known as eremitical life (from the Greek word for "desert" — *eremos*). In Syria, the triumph and expansion of Christianity was reflected in the number of churches built, especially in the villages around Aleppo (which was unusual, since Christianity was largely an urban phenomenon in the rest of the Roman Empire at this time), and in the many monasteries established near the villages (which was also odd, since monachism was a movement that was associated with the desert). The hermits in Syria thus had to find original ways of isolating themselves. Near Aleppo, St. Simeon

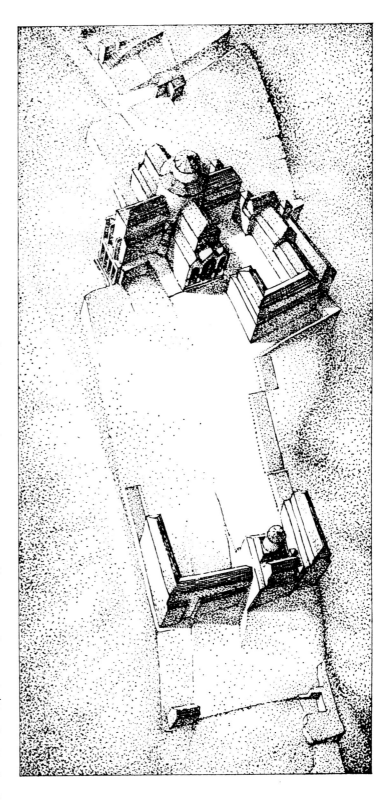

found a way that soon became very popular. He lived on a platform on top of a column [**321**]. ("Column" in Greek is *stylos*, the root word of the name "Stylites," which was given to this saint and the movement he inspired.) He attracted crowds of pilgrims, who took

Model reconstruction of the sanctuary built to commemorate St. Simeon.

line at the baker's shop. The arguments arose from different ways of interpreting the dual nature — human and divine — of Christ's person. For the disciples of Nestorius, a priest at Antioch who later became the Patriarch of Constantinople, the human nature predominated. On the other hand, the Monophysites (from the Greek *monos* = one and *physis* = nature) — the precursors of the Coptic Church, which still exists today, especially in the Near East and in Egypt — claimed that the divine nature triumphed. The Council of Ephesus of 431 condemned the doctrine of the Nestorians, and they were forced to seek refuge in Persia. At the Council of Chalcedon in 451, it was agreed that Christ had two distinct and indivisible but consubstantial natures. However, although this solution was adopted in several regions of Syria, it did not put an end to quarreling. The Monophysites even resorted to physical violence in their opposition to the official doctrine and conducted vigorous conversion campaigns.

These rivalries intensified during the reign of the Byzantine Emperor Justinian (527-565), since he upheld the Chalcedonian doctrine so forcefully that it led to the persecution of the Monophysite bishops and priests, who lived for the most part in the East. From a social point of view, the rivalries reflected the antagonism felt by the Semitic regions towards the centralizing Greco-Roman government and they thus represented a threat to the political cohesion of the empire. In this vein, a Monophysite priest, Jacob of Edessa, established a dissident Monophysite Church in Syria, attracting a wide following among the Arab tribes of the steppe. The language of this church was Syriac, which had developed from the Aramaic dialect spoken in the Edessa region, in southern Turkey. As of the fourth

home souvenirs of their visit called eulogia [313].

The beginnings of the Catholic Church were marked by heated religious controversies called christological quarrels, since they were concerned with the nature of Christ's person in the Trinity. When the Roman Empire was divided in AD 395, at the end of the reign of Theodosius, Syria became part of the Eastern Empire, also known as the Byzantine Empire. The country continued to be torn by violent religious quarrels that involved not only theologians but also ordinary citizens. A well-known anecdote describes how the nature of Christ was discussed even by people waiting in century, Syriac became the language of religion for the Christian communities in Syria, adopted in reaction against the Seleucid Empire and pagan Hellenism and therefore more of a cultural statement than a question of dogma. Syria was thus divided between the Catholic and Monophysite churches.

HOUSES OF PRAYER:
THE FIRST CHURCHES

The first groups of Christians called themselves "churches," from the Greek *ekklesiai*, which means "congregation," assembly" or "group." The term then came to designate the places where they met to pray, which were simply private homes, impossible to distinguish from other houses. The oldest house that can be identified as having served as

a church for Christians was found on the site of Dura-Europos. It dates from the middle of the third century. This church consists of a large rectangular prayer room with a raised platform at its eastern end. The priest would have stood on the platform to read the Holy Scriptures and preside over the Eucharist. To one side was a room used as a baptistery.

This model continued to evolve during the fourth and fifth centuries. The choir, or area that held the platform for the priest, was separated from the nave, or prayer room, by an arch in the ceiling and by a low wall, called a chancel screen, made of sculpted panels [312]. Later the choir was raised, so that it had to be reached by a few steps. The altar was placed so close to the rear wall that the priest had to celebrate mass with his back to the congregation. The rear wall, called a chevet, was often given a semicircular shape. On the outside, churches were surrounded by courtyards, with porticoes on one or several sides, and by domestic or liturgical annexes, including a baptistery.

The Christian community grew, especially after Constantine recognized it officially in the fourth century, and began to need larger buildings for its meetings. Taking their inspiration from the spacious, columned meeting rooms used by the king (in Greek, *basileus*) to conduct business in the exercise of his royal power, architects designed basilicas whose rectangular nave was divided lengthwise into three sections by rows of columns. The

Fresco from the Christian church at Dura-Europos showing Jesus walking on water.

A section of the Christian church at Dura-Europos.

The painted walls of the synagogue at Dura-Europos.

rear wall, or chevet, was often built in the shape of an apse.

At the same time, another type of church also became common; it had the general shape of a Greek cross, with four arms of equal length and a dome over the central part where the arms meet. The altar stood under the dome, directly above the tomb of a saint; consequently, these cross-shaped churches were given the name *martyrion*. The church built on the site of St. Simeon's column is a good example of this style.

In this period as well, the Jews in the Mediterranean region and in the Near East met in private houses to pray, receive religious instruction, and debate and decide on all kinds of questions concerning the community. These houses were called "a place to meet in," or *sunagoge* in Greek, and are known to us as synagogues. One of the finest examples of the ancient synagogues found so far is that discovered at Dura-Europos. This local synagogue is unique in that its four walls are decorated with figurative scenes displayed on three rows of panels. The synagogue, built around AD 170 and enlarged in 244-245, was left in ruins by the Sassanian invasion of 256, but the frescoes were protected by heaps of debris until the first archaeologists arrived in the 1930s. Since that time, the paintings have been restored and integrated into a reconstruction of the original building housed in the National Museum of Damascus.

ISLAM, THE RELIGION
OF THE PROPHET MUHAMMAD

In their early history, the Bedouins, nomadic herders who roam the vast, oasis-dotted steppes of Arabia, were divided into tribes that each worshipped — along with a multitude of other minor deities — a personification of the divine world. This could take the form of an idol, a star or a stone. In the city of Mecca there was a sanctuary that held the idols of various tribes, or groups of families, who went on a pilgrimage there every year to worship them and then take part in a fair. One of these tribes was responsible for caring for and safeguarding the sanctuary.

In around AD 570, the Prophet Muhammad was born. His name means "worthy of praise." He worked as a Meccan caravan conductor until he was in his 40s. But then, around 610, following a visit to Bosra, a city south of Damascus, he began to preach, teaching what had been revealed to him: the existence of one transcendent God, Allah, who had created humankind and nature and who at the Last Judgment would reward or punish all human beings. He soon attracted a large number of

The Umayyad Mosque in Damascus.

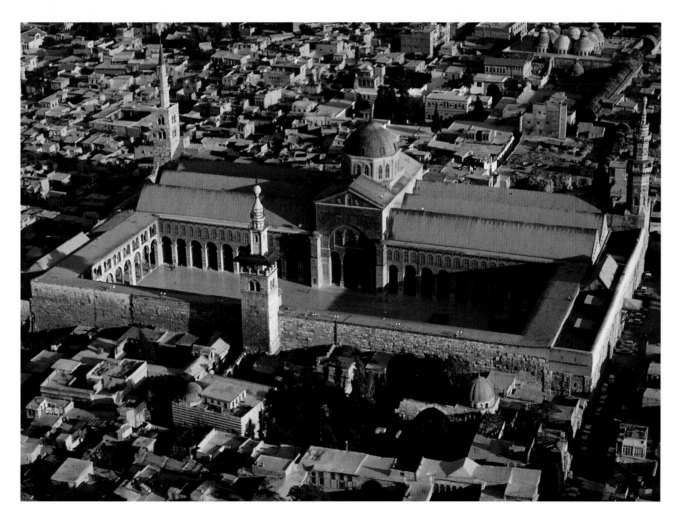

The prayer room in the Umayyad Mosque in Damascus.

followers, whom he named Muslims, meaning "devotees." Confronted with the hostility of the tribe that guarded the sanctuary and reaped many advantages from the annual pilgrimages, the Prophet decided in 622 to withdraw to another city, which was given the name Medina, the "City of the Prophet." The flight to Medina was known as the Hejira, meaning the "secession," or "emigration." This crucial event in Islamic culture serves as the starting date for the Muslim calendar. The Prophet enlarged the circle of his followers until he could organize an army and preach the ideal of a holy war against his enemies. A religious, military and political leader, the Prophet seized Mecca and had all the idols destroyed. The

following year, nearly all of Arabia was converted to Islam, and Mecca became the Holy City of the Muslims. It was at this point that the Prophet named his religion Islam, meaning "submission to divine will." He died in 632 and was buried at Medina.

The five pillars of Islamic faith are: belief (*el Shahadah*) in one true God, creator of the universe and humankind; prayer; fasting; pilgrimage; and legal almsgiving (*zakât*). At least once in their lifetime, all Muslims must do their best to go on a pilgrimage to Mecca. To expiate wrongdoing, Muslims fast for one month, *Ramadan*, eating no food from sunrise to sunset every day. Five times daily, the faithful are called to prayer by a priest called a *muezzin* from the top of a minaret, or mosque tower. After washing their hands and faces, the faithful turn in the direction (*qibla*) of Mecca. On Friday, the day of rest, the faithful go to pray in public at the mosque.

THE MOSQUE,
A PLACE OF CONTEMPLATION

The Great Mosque of Damascus built by the Umayyads was one of the first in the Islamic world. The prayer room in the mosque was modeled on the naves of the first Christian basilicas, but, whereas the latter were placed on a lengthwise axis, the room in the mosque was installed widthwise so that it faced the *qibla*, the wall standing in the direction of Mecca with its *mihrab*, concave niche for prayers.

The prayer room opens onto a vast square courtyard surrounded by a high wall with a roofed and colonnaded walkway along it. The courtyard wall lies directly over the inner wall of the *temenos*, or courtyard, of the great temple of Zeus that stood on this site during the Roman Empire. The temple had been transformed into a church by the early Christians, who for a while shared their place of worship with the Muslim newcomers. The Umayyad Mosque continues to represent a holy place for both religions, since relics of St. John the Baptist are preserved there. The original mosque has undergone significant transformation over the years, as various caliphs remodeled and renovated it [90] and repairs were made following major fires.

From the time of the Abbasid dynasty (in the second half of the eighth century), the mosques of the Islamic world were built according to a plan termed *hypostyle*, that is, having a great room whose ceiling is supported by numerous columns. A square tower, called a minaret, was added to the wall op-posite the *qibla* so that a *muezzin* could summon the faithful to the five daily prayers. A space called the *ziyada* surrounded the mosque on all sides except for the *qibla* wall to allow the faithful to move around. The walls were embellished with stucco and mosaics [323], but representations of God were forbidden.

The colonnaded walkway around the courtyard in the Umayyad Mosque in Damascus.

Arabic manuscripts, treasures
of the written word

THE FIRST LETTERS of the Arabic alphabet appeared in the fourth century AD, while the oldest official texts in Arabic were engraved on stone in the sixth century AD. However, the first Arabic manuscripts are those of the Koran. The word "read" is the first word found in it. In fact, the Koran makes reading and writing religious obligations. Arabic soon became widespread as a written and spoken language. It was even the language of science and learning during the Middle Ages in the West (fifth to fifteenth centuries).

A manuscript of the Koran.
Cat. 326

During the Umayyad dynasty (650 to 750), the caliph Abd al-Malik made Arabic the official language of the government and ordered coins to be minted with Arabic inscriptions. The reign of the Abassids (750-1258) represented a golden age for the production of manuscripts and the creation of private libraries in the Arab world. The largest collections belonged to the caliphs of Baghdad, Cairo and Cordoba.

Various types of calligraphy were used in the Arabic manuscripts. The best-known of these are the Thuluth script, which developed in the twelfth century, and the Cufic, which used geometric shapes. The fact that the Koran is the revealed word of Allah meant that calligraphy was much appreciated as an art by Muslims, since the calligrapher's work was intended to beautify the word of God itself. It might even be said that there was out-and-out competition among the calligraphers, and manuscripts thus became true treasures of writing. They were also exquisitely decorated by craftsmen who completed the work of the calligraphers with inks, colors and gilding.

Arabic scientific manuscripts were often illustrated. As well, prompted by the growing number of documents and the need to find information rapidly, people had the idea of indexing manuscripts. For example, a manuscript entitled *Taqueen Albuldan,* written by the Ayyubid sultan Iman Id-Din Ishmael and dealing with the geography of the known world at the time, with major cities located on lines of latitude and longitude, has an index called "Al Musanafat," in which such information is presented in alphabetical order.

MOUNA AL-MOU'AZEN
National Museum of Damascus

PERSONAL RELIGIOUS PRACTICE AND FUNERARY RITES

So far, we have dealt only with collective religious practices. In the following section, we will focus instead on individual religious practices, which naturally are influenced by the system of values accepted by the members of a cultural group as a whole. To illustrate this aspect, we will look at the ritual practices surrounding death that have left tangible, easily recognized traces in the soil and that are reflected in the material culture. From a social and religious perspective, death is a very important milestone in the cycle of life, for most cultural systems see it as marking the end of a short stay on earth and the beginning of an eternal life in the hereafter.

BURIAL PRACTICES AND THE FIRST CEMETERIES

The oldest known burial place found in Syria — a grave made in the cave of Dederiyeh in which the body of a young Neanderthal child was intentionally laid — dates to about 40 000 BC. Later, during the Neolithic period when communities began to settle in villages, some groups developed an unusual — and surprising — way of dealing with the skulls of the deceased. In certain instances, the skulls were removed from their skeletons, covered with lime-plaster modeled into features [4] and placed on fire-hardened clay supports [3]. In one village house dating from this time, a whole row of such skulls, supported by lumps of red clay, had been placed at the foot of a wall. They would have been visible as soon as you entered the room! Is it possible that these

The grave of a Neanderthal child in the Dederiyah cave.

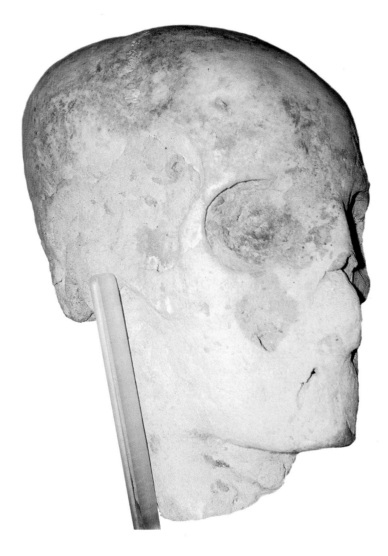

Skull with modeled
features from Tell
Ramad.

political leaders who in life had rendered great service to their community.

From about 5000 BC on, the dead were buried intact in simple graves dug in the ground, sometimes directly under the houses where they are presumed to have lived. A little later, true cemeteries appeared. Located outside the villages, they contained a number of chest-like tombs constructed of unbaked brick. The bodies were buried with no special regard for the position they were placed in. The tombs show certain differences with respect to the grave goods that accompanied the deceased, containing varying quantities of objects such as jewelry in semiprecious stones and metal, clay vessels, and metal weapons and tools. From this time on, burial practices began to reflect a form of social hierarchization. The trend became more marked during the period of the city-states around 3000 BC when princely and royal tombs appeared in cities like Ebla and Mari. These tombs expressed the special social status of their occupants.

With the Greco-Roman era, it becomes possible to talk of a true funerary architecture. For individual burials, the graves had side walls made of carefully dressed stone and a roof formed by large slabs of flat stones protecting the wooden or terra cotta sarcophagus inside from the weight of the two to five meters of earth that was piled over the grave. There was usually a wealth of grave goods in the tombs of the elite. These included various types of jewelry, everyday objects like mirrors [349] and perfume bottles [181] and, in certain exceptional cases, masks of gold [177] or helmets with silver faces like the one from Homs known as Emesa in Roman times [62]. Collective burial grounds are best exemplified by the necropolis at Palmyra.

dressed-up skulls were objects of veneration? Was the room in which they were found a household sanctuary where a family's ancestors were worshipped? Many other questions remain unanswered. Were the skulls removed from the skeleton several months after burial, when the flesh of the deceased person would have disintegrated? Was there a ritual surrounding the placing of skulls in a home? In one case, three undecorated human skulls were found on a hearth, their bases charred by fire. Given the large number of skulls, it has been suggested that they might possibly have been integrated into a piece of funeral furniture honoring the memory of people such as

The necropolis of Palmyra: a city of the dead

Funeral monuments of the Roman period in Palmyra provide excellent examples of the different burial practices used at the time.

Subterranean collective graves, called hypogea, generally took the form of a narrow corridor with deep burial niches (or *loculi*) dug out in rows three to six high along each side wall. Each burial niche was then sealed with a stone carved in relief to represent the bust of the deceased, accompanied by an identifying epitaph. Several hypogea have two long corridors laid out in a T-shape. In certain areas of a hypogeum, especially at the end of the corridors, richly carved sarcophagi could be found, set in groups of three. Relief carvings above the sarcophagi represented funeral banquet scenes in which the deceased was shown reclining on a couch, dining with his wife and children on either side. Given the size of the hypogea and the number of *loculi* they could contain, these collective graves were not intended for one family alone. They were rather considered to be real estate, parts of which could be sold or granted to strangers. To enter a hypogeum, one took a stairway leading to a sturdy stone door divided into upper and lower sections, which could be opened separately. Above the door was a thick lintel, sometimes embellished with relief sculpture. The walls and ceilings of the hypogea were frequently decorated with architectonic relief work and painted stucco.

Another type of hypogeum consisted of a square subterranean room with painted or sculpted walls. Along three of these walls were *arcosolia*, or arched recesses in which sarcophagi could be placed. In some cases, simple troughs were carved out of the bedrock.

The presence of a collective underground tomb was often indicated on the surface by a special marker built above it. Such a marker might be a monumental sarcophagus

Typical layout of a Palmyrene hypogeum.

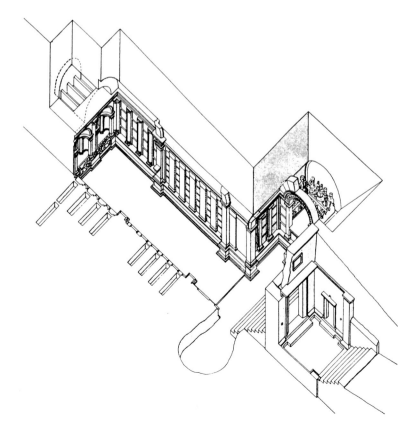

Palmyrene funerary
bas-relief.
Cat. 334

SYRIA, LAND OF CIVILIZATIONS

The tombs of Palmyra

Semicircular plaque with the bust of a man flanked by two winged Victories. Cat. 330

THE NECROPOLISES OF PALMYRA are located outside the city's ramparts. There were some individual graves, but the wealthy families of Palmyra buried their dead in three types of collective tombs, the most representative of which are tower tombs and hypogea.

As funerary monuments, tower tombs are typical of Palmyra. The earliest examples date to the first century BC, but it was only in the first century of our era that special care began to be given to their exterior appearance. Each tower has four or five floors reached by a stone stairway; on every floor there are numerous compartments in which the bodies of the dead were placed. In the course of archaeological work in 1994, we discovered three sculpted heads decorated with laurel wreaths, a symbol of victory and eternity. Since we found no inscriptions, it was impossible to associate them with any Palmyrene family in particular. However, one of them seems to have been a prototype for a well-known sculpted head, that of Odainat [64], king of Palmyra.

The second type of collective tomb, and the most important at Palmyra, is the hypogeum. It consisted of a main underground passageway traversed by smaller galleries with one to six rows of rectangular niches, or *loculi*, dug into the walls. The bodies of the dead were placed in the loculi, which were then sealed with plaques sculpted with bas-reliefs representing the busts of the deceased persons within. In general, the hypogea were used for several generations of whole families, since up to 700 loculi have been found in the same tomb. Our work in 1990 led to the discovery of the Mubarak family tomb, which was constructed in AD 98, according to the inscription engraved on the foundation plaque. The member of the Mubarak family who built the monument belonged to the Palmyrene senate. One of the funerary bas-reliefs found was the bust of Aqma, to whom we gave the name "the Beauty of Palmyra" because of the exceptional quality of her clothing and rich jewelry [334]. More recently, a Japanese archaeological team opened a tomb built in AD 109; in its rear wall they discovered a niche above which there was a half-circle of stone presenting a bust with a Victory on either side. The first hypogea were dug in the first century. Over 50 have been discovered so far, but dozens more remain unexplored.

The care with which the funeral monuments in the Palmyrene necropolises were built and decorated attest to the importance that the city's inhabitants accorded to their "houses of eternity." The significance of this phenomenon has been recognized by UNESCO, who have designated Palmyra, along with Damascus, Bosra and Aleppo, a World Heritage City.

KHALED AL-ASSAD
Director of Antiquities and Museums of Palmyra

cover, columns or pillars, a square or circular mausoleum topped by a pyramid or cupola, a simple square pedestal or even a heap of stones forming a mound.

These structures, enclosing no empty space and intended simply as surface markers indicating the presence of an underground tomb, should not be confused with tombs that were placed in buildings constructed above the ground. Such buildings might take the form of a temple, a mausoleum or a tower.

The tower tomb was a common funerary construction in Palmyra. It was a tower built of square stone blocks, or ashlar, and rising four or five stories. On every story were several rows of long, narrow burial niches, or *loculi*, meant to hold stone sarcophagi. These funeral towers, modest cousins of the more ornate mausoleums, could each hold the mortal remains of hundreds of people, all belonging to one of the great families of Palmyra. Another type of above-ground funeral construction was the tomb built as a temple. Unlike an ordinary temple, the funerary temple had a cella, or sanctuary, whose inner walls were covered with rows and columns of burial niches.

PERSONAL ADORNMENT:
RICH FABRICS AND PRECIOUS JEWELRY

The dead buried at Palmyra had been summarily mummified and, in general, richly adorned with garments fashioned from exotic fabrics and with exquisite jewelry crafted out of precious materials by expert jewelers.

The most luxurious fabrics were wool and silk. Wool was dyed various colors, but purple predominated [354]. Purple

The tower tombs of Palmyra.

dye was derived from excretions produced by the glands of a Mediterranean mollusk, the murex snail. Each snail produces only a few drops of these precious secretions, so to obtain a dye, thousands of them had to be boiled in salt water. The purple dye was added to the wool and allowed to boil in the open air for nine days, producing a

disgusting smell. The ports of Tyre and Sidon on the Mediterranean coast became famous for this industry. In 301, under the Emperor Diocletian, the purple wool of Tyre was literally worth its weight in gold, since its price per unit of weight was equivalent to that of gold. The purple wool used for the clothing found at Palmyra no doubt came from Tyre and Sidon. The work that went into the making of these clothes also required much skill and patience, as is illustrated in funerary relief work [353].

The other luxury fabric was silk, which was imported from China. It was natural for silk to be found in Palmyra, since the city was situated on the silk route between China and the Mediterranean. The fragments of clothing discovered in the tombs show that the silk was of very high quality and often beautifully embroidered. Certain embroidered patterns seem to echo the decorative motifs used on the architectural sculpture that embellished the tombs themselves [205].

Piece of Chinese silk fabric found in a Palmyrene tomb. Cat. 205

Weaving is still done in the traditional manner in some Syrian villages.

Ancient jewelry in the National Museum of Damascus

S AN ART, jewelry-making is as old as human vanity. Very early on, the people of the East had a reputation for loving jewels and precious stones. Many authors in antiquity refer to oriental luxury and the fondness of Eastern women in particular for copious jewelry. Women in the East wore jewels on ordinary days as well as on holidays. Love of finery was almost an obsession. The fashion for jewelry of all sorts among the women of Palmyra is attested in funerary bas-reliefs and sculptures [335 and 338], which show them laden with diadems, earrings, brooches, clasps, necklaces, bracelets, rings and anklets. Palmyrene sculpture thus provides additional evidence of the importance attached to jewelry by the women of the "city of palms." Over the centuries, advances in goldsmithing were often made to meet the needs of feminine coquetry.

The jewelry collections at the National Museum of Damascus illustrate the importance of women's finery in Syrian societies throughout history and show that decking oneself in jewels is a very ancient habit. Certain researchers believe that the secrets of melting metals and making jewelry were first discovered in Syria. Cadmus, the legendary Phoenician hero, was credited with having "invented" gold and methods for making jewelry. Non-mythical Phoenicians were responsible for creating the fashion for necklaces of glass beads.

Skeletal remains found in old tombs are frequently covered in jewelry, since the religious beliefs of the ancients led them to bury their dead with their most precious belongings. The jewelry of antiquity is thus very informative from an archaeological viewpoint.

The collections of old jewelry in the National Museum of Damascus may be classified in various ways:

- According to the sex of the person who would have worn it. A simple ring was a mark of authority when worn by a man, while diadems, necklaces, earrings, brooches, clasps, rings, bracelets and anklets belonged to women.
- According to the material used. Jewelry could be made of gold, silver, bronze, copper, ivory, glass, mother-of-pearl or shell.
- According to the technique used. Jewelry-making techniques included engraving, twisting, filigree and granulation; jewelry might be decorated with openwork or made in the shape of embossed plates.
- According to the form given to the piece. For example, earrings could be made to look like doves, amphorae, grapes, peacocks, roses or vases, while bracelets might take the shape of serpents.

The art of jewelry making is a traditional one in Syria. Some of the family names in present-day Syria come from this art; the names "Saiegh" and "Jawahri" both refer to jewelry-makers. Syrian jewelers continue to constitute a wellspring of wonderful creativity in the art of ornamentation.

BASHIR ZOUHDI
National Museum of Damascus

Richly decorated torso of a Palmyrene funerary sculpture.
Cat. 338

Next page:
Large golden brooch found at Dura-Europos.
Cat. 339

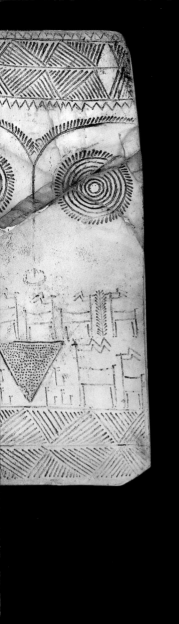

THE ORGANIZATION OF
thought
catalogue

259
Decorated grooved stone
Basalt
9000 BC

Grooved stones appeared in the Near East as early as 10 000 BC. They are called grooved stones because in the middle of one of their faces, they have a wide, rounded trough, which might have been used to straighten arrows or to polish the surface of cylindrical objects. Although it is not certain what purpose these implements served, they are found frequently and are very familiar to archaeologists. The stone shown here is unique, since it is the only decorated one discovered so far. On the face opposite the groove, it is engraved with geometrical designs (wavy lines ending with arrows) and images of animals: a four-legged creature and a bird of prey with outspread wings. For the people who used it, an object decorated this way must have had special significance — a symbolic meaning that we can only guess at for the time being.

JERF AL-AHMAR   5 x 3.9 x 1.7 cm
NATIONAL MUSEUM, DAMASCUS   1193
PALÉORIENT 21:1 (1995), p. 127-128

260

261

260/261
Palettes (recto/verso)
Basalt
9000 BC

Unlike the stone described in **259,** these two flat stones do not have grooves. They are, however, decorated on both faces with motifs that are not easy to identify and whose meaning remains uncertain. The archaeologists at the Jerf al-Ahmar site believe that the markings express some highly symbolic message. Certain researchers are even tempted to see a primitive form of writing in them. If this is the case, these recent finds could open a window onto the mental and imaginative world of one of the oldest human communities.

JERF AL-AHMAR   5.7 x 3.7 x 1 cm/ 5.5 x 3.4 x 0.7 cm
NATIONAL MUSEUM, DAMASCUS   1198/1199   *L'ÉCRITURE* 1,2

262
Female figurine
Calcite
8000 BC

Around 8000 BC, according to a number of archaeologists, a new type of symbolic representation appeared in Syria, apparently expressing an aspect of the immense changes human communities were then undergoing. The first evidence of the agricultural practices that would play such an important role in the subsequent development of societies also dates from this time. Thus, female figurines first appeared in the material culture of the earliest communities to engage in farming. It is believed that these schematic representations of women were intended to symbolize the very principle of fertility. The figurine shown here is important because it is among the oldest of this type to have survived. Furthermore, it was carved of stone, while later examples are made of terra cotta.

TELL MUREYBET   9 x 4.5 cm
NATIONAL MUSEUM, ALEPPO   M10165 (MB.73-1)
SMC 16; *BAAL* 38

263
Female figurine
Fire-hardened clay
8000 BC

Most of the female figurines made during the Neolithic period were shaped out of clay that was slightly hardened by fire but not really baked. This figurine was one of eight discovered on the site of Tell Mureybet. It is clear that the artist sought to emphasize the part of the body linked to reproduction — the pelvic region, or maternal womb, and the breasts, or nourishing bosom. It is significant that all the figurines of this type lack facial features, since these were not directly related to the intended symbolism.

TELL MUREYBET   5.6 x 2 cm
NATIONAL MUSEUM, ALEPPO   1008 (MB73.808)   *SMC* p. 38

264/265
Female figurine
Terra cotta
5000 BC

Sites from this period yield an abundance of terra cotta representations of women with exaggerated hips and breasts. These figurines are interpreted as convincing evidence that the agro-pastoral communities at the time were very much concerned about fertility as a fundamental principle of survival. The figurines are shown with their hands clasped under their bosom so that their breasts are raised by their arms and made more noticeable. The gesture is very much a maternal one, expressing the nurturing aspect of a woman's body. This type of fertility symbol — called a mother goddess by some — appeared in the Near East at the end of the ninth millennium and continued in various related styles of representation for several more millennia.

TELL KASHKASHUK   4 x 4.5 x 6.3 cm /3 x 5 cm
NATIONAL MUSEUM, ALEPPO 1117/
DEIR EZ ZOR MUSEUM 13542 (90K1)/
Cf. L'EUFRATE 70 ET 72/*SMC* 71

266
Female figurine
Terra cotta
5000 BC

Unlike other female figurines, which were modeled in clay at this time, as they had been in previous periods, this one is made of a slab of clay. It is similar to the others in the prominence given to the large breasts, which are encircled with black dots. The use of paint to underline certain anatomical details was a new technique. Paint was also used on this figurine to represent the pubic region as a dark triangle on the cube-like base. The breasts and pubes are separated by a narrow waist encircled by bands, further accentuating these two parts of the female body. The lower ends of the sides show signs of polishing, as if the figurine had been frequently touched by human hands.

TELL SABI ABYAD   6 x 3 x 2 cm
RAQQA MUSEUM   76 (SAB86-H1)
ESEA Pl. 3

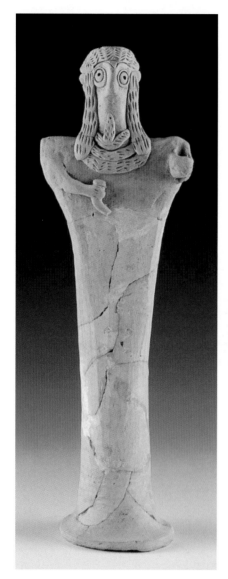

267
Female figurine
Terra cotta
2000 BC

This terra cotta figurine has been interpreted by its discoverer as the representation of a major deity. This interpretation was based on the figurine's relatively large size, the object resembling a drinking horn held in her right arm, which is bent towards her chest, and the stump-like left arm, which is extended in front and perforated so that a rod could be inserted in it. The figurine was found with two others [268 and 269], which are similar but smaller, and may represent minor deities or worshippers. All three were unearthed under the threshold of a house whose floor had been raised. They were no doubt used in the practice of some household cult.

TELL SELENKAHIYEH   32 x 10 cm
NATIONAL MUSEUM, ALEPPO   M 11236 (*SLK* 74.H.141)
L'ÉCRITURE 397; *AAAS* 27-28 (1977-78) Pl. 10

268
Female figurine
Terra cotta
2000 BC

This figurine's somewhat curious pose, with her arms crossed between her breasts, is reminiscent of the poses of certain sixth-century female figurines [264 and 265]. In this case, the figure's attitude has been interpreted as one of prayer. Since it was incorporated into the very structure of the house in which it was found, the figurine might have been intended to ensure that the household enjoyed divine protection. The large quantities of these objects coming from various periods of occupation suggest that they played some religious role and were considered important by the village's inhabitants at the time.

TELL SELENKAHIYEH   16 x 5.3 cm
NATIONAL MUSEUM, ALEPPO   M 9093 (SLK 72-233)
L'EUFRATE 279; *AAAS* 23 (1973), p. 155, Fig. 7

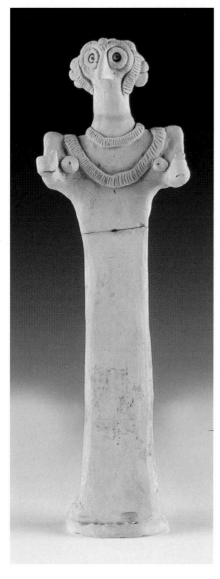

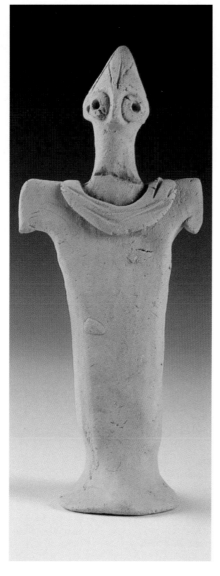

269
Female figurine
Terra cotta
2000 BC

The clay used for making this type of figurine was collected along the banks of a river. It was then mixed with grains of sand, mica and limestone; these materials tempered the clay so that it would not lose its shape and crack as it dried and baked. To make this figurine, the craftsman first placed a lump of the clay mixture on a smooth, horizontal surface and then stretched and flattened it until he could cut out the shape he wanted. He gave the figurine a long, solid body, widened at the bottom to form a concave base. Features such as the nose (and sometimes, on other figurines, the chin and beard) were obtained by pinching the clay. The final details were then stuck on. Clay disks were applied to represent the eyes and breasts, while the ears were simply narrow strips. Hair and necklaces were represented by thin bands that were sometimes embellished with incisions.

TELL SELENKAHIYEH   24.5 x 7.5 cm
NATIONAL MUSEUM, ALEPPO   M 9093 (SLK 72.235)
L'ÉCRITURE 398; *AAAS* 23 (1973), p. 155, Fig. 7

270
Male figurine
Terra cotta
2000 BC

Unlike the examples just discussed, this figurine has a pointed head. The site of Tell Selenkahiyeh alone yielded 17 such figurines. According to the specialists who recorded them, this head shape identifies the figurine as being the representation of a male.

TELL SELENKAHIYEH   11.7 x 4.7 cm
NATIONAL MUSEUM, ALEPPO   9086 (SKL 72-471)   *L'EUFRATE* 278

271
Male figurine
Terra cotta
2200 BC

The masculine nature of this figurine is unmistakable. While the archaeologists who made the discovery consider it to represent a chariot driver, the figurine's pose and the prominence given to the sexual organs nevertheless suggest that it may have played a role parallel to that of contemporary female figurines in the practice of household cults.

TELL BRAK   9.5 x 7 x 5 cm
DEIR EZ ZOR MUSEUM   3891 (TB5021)

272

Bull with a human head

Limestone, ivory and bitumen
2200 BC

This reclining bull with a man's head has been interpreted
as a perfect expression of male fertility. It was discovered
in a ceremonial complex and may have been one of a pair,
placed on either side of a doorway as if to guard it. Such
statues were used this way in later periods. With its stylized horns and its legs folded unrealistically along its
body, the figure was intended to be viewed head-on. Its
eyes are made of pieces of ivory held in place with bitumen, and at one time, precious stones must have represented the irises, although only the holes for attaching
them are visible now. There is no doubt that this was an
important object in the community, perhaps even a minor
deity, whose enigmatic smile still holds many secrets.

TELL BRAK: CEREMONIAL COMPLEX   28 x 42 x 17 cm
DEIR EZ ZOR MUSEUM   11754 (TB11001)
L'EUFRATE 201; *CAJ* 1:1 (1991), p.131-135

273

Pendant of Ashtoreth

Gold
1500 BC

The goddess represented on this pendant is probably
Ashtoreth, also known as Ashera. The piece is made of embossed gold leaf with certain details like the pubic region
shown with incisions. Ashtoreth was a very important deity
in the Syrian pantheon of the time, since in Syrian mythology, she was the consort of the great god El and therefore
the mother of his 70 divine offspring. Her fertility is symbolized here by her nudity; she stands in a hieratic pose with
her sexual attributes accentuated. She holds a lotus
flower (?) in each hand and her hair is arranged in an
Egyptian style. Ashtoreth was a quickly angered and unpre-
dictable goddess; she sometimes fought with Baal, but at
other times came to his aid. The pendant has a ring from
which it would have been suspended.

RAS SHAMRA, ANCIENT UGARIT   7 x 4 cm
NATIONAL MUSEUM, ALEPPO   M 10450   *BAAL* 174; *ED* 130

274

Pendant of Astarte

Gold
1500 BC

The representation of the goddess Astarte on this gold
pendant shows only her head and breasts in relief, while
her navel and pubes are discreetly incised. Astarte was
the personification of femininity in Eastern mythology. The
daughter of the great god El, she was the young and war-
like goddess of love. The Greeks identified her with
Aphrodite and the Romans with Venus. Incidentally, the
Semitic peoples always associated her with the heavenly
body we call Venus. The way Astarte is presented here
makes it easy to confuse her with her mother, Ashera, and
her sister Anat, the wife of Baal, for with time, all the attributes originally belonging to these other goddesses became associated with Astarte.

RAS SHAMRA, ANCIENT UGARIT   7 x 4 cm
NATIONAL MUSEUM, ALEPPO   M 10451   *BAAL* 175; *ED* 131

275

Statue of the god El

Limestone

1300 BC

The god El was the father of all the other gods and of humanity as well. This is probably why his name means simply "god." He was also referred to as the "bull," an allusion to the fact that he had sired the great divine family. El was traditionally represented as an old man seated on a throne, for he had learned much in his long life and was also the god of wisdom. As such, it was his role to sit in judgment and settle disputes between the gods, especially those involving the young Baal, whose hotheadedness often created delicate situations. In this statue, the arms and eyes of the god were represented with perishable materials. The arms would have been made of wood or ivory, while the eyes were of white shell with dark stones for the irises. These pieces were held in place with bitumen.

RAS SHAMRA, ANCIENT UGARIT 25 x 12 x 11 cm
NATIONAL MUSEUM, DAMASCUS 1973 (70M981) *SMC* 173

276

Stela to Ishtar

Basalt

1800 BC

This monolith is sculpted on four sides with bas-reliefs of divinities presented in rows. It was found in a chapel built on top of the acropolis of the city of Ebla. The representations on the stela are all related to a common theme — the invocation of the goddess Ishtar, who gave the city of Ebla divine protection. She appears in the top row on one of the stela's two wider faces. The goddess is shown in a winged chapel, standing on the back of a bull and flanked by two bull-men. The rows on the face opposite this one are carved with representations of the sphinx and the bull, showing that this goddess of fertility controlled nature, whether wild or domesticated. Ishtar was the daughter of Sin, who was the goddess of the Moon, and was symbolized by the planet Venus, the Evening Star. Like her equivalent Astarte, she was later identified with the goddess Aphrodite and then with Venus in Greco-Roman mythology.

TELL MARDIKH, ANCIENT EBLA: SECONDARY CHAPEL OF THE G3
SANCTUARY 165 x 46.5 x 25.5 cm
IDLIB MUSEUM 3003 (TM'.67.E.224; 85.E.85; 85.G.350)
EBLA 236

278
Statue of the goddess Athena-Allat
Basalt
AD 200

Athena is shown here in a standing position, with a helmet on her head. In her right hand she holds a spear and in the other hand she bears a shield decorated with the Gorgon's head. Athena was clearly identified with Allat, the great Arabian goddess, who was worshipped from northern Arabia to Palmyra. The cult of Allat was introduced by the Nabataeans in the Hauran, a volcanic region in southern Syria, where the goddess became very popular. The small pedestal on which the goddess is standing here bears a Greek inscription that says: "For the health of our ruler" — a dedication to an emperor who is not named.

SUWEIDA   158 x 47 x 14 cm
NATIONAL MUSEUM, DAMASCUS   10011/4219
BAAL 260; *MUSÉE NATIONAL* p. 115-116

277
Figurine of the god Baal
Bronze and gold
1300 BC

This bronze statue was once covered with gold foil, although only the head now shows what it once looked like. The figure's pose, with his right arm raised as if to throw a weapon, has led specialists to interpret the statue as a human representation of the god Baal. He was the " master, " who was presented in mythological tales as a young, impetuous warrior god who hurled projectiles, which in his case were thunderbolts. The concept of a god throwing bolts of lightning appeared later in the Greek pantheon in the person of Zeus and in Roman mythology in the person of Jupiter. Baal was the divinity who protected Ugarit, and he must have been very popular in the city since a large number of archaeological artifacts found when the site was excavated bear representations of him. According to certain mythological tales, Baal also ensured that the kingdom's soil remained fertile and that the city enjoyed prosperity — a prosperity that was based on maritime trade.

RAS SHAMRA, ANCIENT UGARIT   12.5 x 4.5 x 4.7 cm
NATIONAL MUSEUM, DAMASCUS   3372   *SMC* 178; *BAAL* 172

279

Mosaic of Hercules

Marble and limestone and tesserae

AD 300

Hercules was no doubt the most popular and best-known hero in Greco-Roman mythology. He is shown here at the age of eight months, strangling two serpents that the goddess Hera had placed in the sleeping child's cradle, seeking revenge because her husband, Zeus, had conceived him with Alcmena, a mortal. Close by, his twin brother, Iphicles, is being taken from the cradle by his mother, Alcmena, as Amphitryon, Hercules' adoptive father, stands above her, his hand on his sword, and the servants stare in horror at the scene from the other side of the room. When Amphitryon learned that Zeus had taken on his features to seduce his wife, Alcmena, one night when he was away on an expedition, he decided to raise Hercules with his own son, Iphicles, whom he had conceived with Alcmena the very next morning.

HOMS, ANCIEN EMESA 290 x 224 cm
AL-MA'ARRA MUSEUM 1378

280/281 a-c
Cones
Terra cotta
3200 BC

Terra cotta cones were stuck into the exterior walls of the largest buildings in the first urban agglomerations as a way of underlining the importance of these constructions in the community. Initially these prestigious buildings were simply places where the community's leaders could meet. Then, as they became furnished with various items like benches, offering tables, altars and pedestals, some of these buildings were turned into places of worship and temples.

TELL BRAK   15 x 35 x 12.5 cm/ 6.5 x 3 cm
DEIR EZ ZOR MUSEUM   12796 (TB14289)/5481/4647/4649
Cf. *L'EUFRATE* 124; *SMC* 82

282
Model of a round house
Terra cotta
2400 BC

Researchers are not sure whether or not this model was intended to represent an actual round house. The interior is divided into nine parts. There is a square central room that communicates with the other rooms; one of them is triangular-shaped and covered with a roof, with a chimney hole through which smoke could escape. One of the rooms forms a sort of vestibule, since the house entrance is in its outer wall. The central room has a horseshoe-shaped hearth and benches in the corners. Its walls are higher than those of the other rooms, and tenons in the corners of these walls could have been used to support a wooden roof. Since this model and others like it were buried under temple thresholds or under the surface of the roads leading to the temples, it seems reasonable to assume that they were a type of cultic object that was placed in the ground to purify the means of access to the temple.

TELL HARIRI, ANCIENT MARI   61 x 29 cm
NATIONAL MUSEUM, DAMASCUS   M2351   *BAAL* 112

283
Foundation plaque with a nail
Bronze
2150 BC

The construction of a temple entailed all kinds of rituals. One of them was the custom of placing a votive deposit under the threshold or in the corner of the wall foundations. A votive deposit usually took the form of a nail, which might be shaped to look like human or animal figures ending in a point. It is believed that the purpose of this ritual was to indicate symbolically that the temple was well and truly fixed to the spot — which from then on became a sacred zone — and, at the same time, to keep evil spirits away. Some nails, like this one, were driven through a bronze plaque inscribed with the name of the king who had the temple erected and the divinity to which the temple was dedicated.

TELL HARIRI, ANCIENT MARI: TEMPLE OF NINHURSAG
14 x 14 cm
NATIONAL MUSEUM, ALEPPO   M8030   *L'EUFRATE* 252

284 a-h
"Eye idols"
Alabaster
3200 BC

Hundreds of these little figurines were found in a temple at the site of Tell Brak. It was believed that they were used in religious ceremonies. The staring eyes carved at the top of the small alabaster plaques are thought to have been a symbolic representation of the gesture made by someone worshipping a divinity. This is why the archaeologist who found them gave them the name of "eye idols." In subsequent periods, the figurative representations of worshippers that people placed in temples were characterized by having a very round-eyed expression.

TELL BRAK: EYE TEMPLE   4 x 2.6 x 0.5 (on average)
DEIR EZ ZOR MUSEUM   10668/1-8   *L'EUFRATE* 190-192

286
Statuette
Gypsum
2500 BC

The temples in the city-state of Mari on the Euphrates have yielded numerous statuettes of men and women who had themselves represented with their hands clasped to their bosoms in an attitude of prayer. These small statues were placed inside the temples on benches near the bottom of the walls. They were intended as tokens of the great devotion offered to the divinity by the people who had their likenesses made. These people were members of the administration — superintendents, officers, surveyors, scribes and cup-bearers — as well as temple workers and wealthy members of society, such as merchants.
When a temple began to be crowded with these effigies of worshippers, they were placed in sacred pits — *favissae* — which were dug under the floor of the temple itself.

TELL HARIRI, ANCIENT MARI: TEMPLE OF NINNI-ZAZA
53 x 18 x 21 cm
NATIONAL MUSEUM, DAMASCUS   M2076 (M2369)
L'EUFRATE 240

285
Statuette
Gypsum
2500 BC

Like some of the other statuettes found in the Mari temples, this one has an inscription on its back, written in a vertical row of seven squares, which enables us to identify the person represented. It reads: " Salim, the oldest brother of the king, the god of the land, his statue to the goddess Ninni-zaza has dedicated. " Surprisingly few of the statuettes discovered in the Mari temples represent the king or members of the royal family. In this case, the person could be identified, but without such inscriptions

identification is almost impossible, for the sculptors followed an established model not only for the general pose, but also for the facial features. The face is usually shown as smiling and serene, in a very idealized manner.

TELL HARIRI, ANCIENT MARI   46 x 18 x 20 cm
NATIONAL MUSEUM, DAMASCUS   M2083

THE ORGANIZATION OF THOUGHT

298
Libation vessel
Shell

This large shell was cut in half lengthwise so that it could be used as a vessel for making libations. Since large triton shells like this one are found in the Persian Gulf and the Indian ocean, it would have come to the city of Mari via the trade route that followed the course of the Euphrates at the time. Given its proportions and distant origins, such a shell must have been considered a luxury item that only the members of the politico-religious elite could acquire. Near the spot where the shell was found, archaeologists dismantling a stairway came across a collection of unfinished mother-of-pearl and shell objects that a specialized craftsman must have been working on. A workshop of this type has also been discovered in a room in the palace of Mari.

20.2 x 10.5 x 7 cm   19079 (TH97.138)

299
Rectangular receptacle
Alabaster

One of the wide ends of this rectangular receptacle is decorated with the protome of a two-horned bovine animal, whose eyes must have once been inlaid, since traces of bitumen can still be seen in the left-hand socket. A vertical groove runs down the side from the rim of the vessel to the animal's head, leading to a vertical hole going through the head itself.

14.6 x 7.7 x 5 cm   19074 (TH97.133)

300/301
Imprints of children's feet
Terra cotta
1200 BC

A sales contract found with these imprints of children's feet states that a father was obliged to sell his four children in order to pay a debt. The soothsayer who bought them, finding them still too young, left them to be brought up by their parents until they were old enough to serve in the temple. In the meantime, he kept an imprint of each child's foot as proof of his deferred ownership. Each imprint bears the name of a child and the impressions left by the seals of the two witnesses.

TELL MESKENE, ANCIENT EMAR: SACRISTY OF TEMPLE M1
13.5 x 6 x 3 cm/10.9 x 5.8 x 3 cm
NATIONAL MUSEUM, ALEPPO M10561/M8649
SMC 165; *L'EUFRATE* 351

302
Model of a liver
Terra cotta
1800 BC

After they had sacrificed an animal, the priests would examine the dead creature's liver, believing that the thoughts of the divinity to whom the animal had been offered were transferred to this organ. In the ancient Near East, the liver was considered to be the seat of thought. Studying the signs in the sacrificed animal's entrails was therefore likely to provide divine answers to questions about future events on earth. This method of divination by examining the liver — most often of a sheep — was naturally a prerogative of the king. When the examination was complete, the signs observed and their interpretation were recorded on clay models of livers. These models acted to some degree as memoranda for the priests.

TELL HARIRI, ANCIENT MARI 6.3 x 5.8 x 3.1 cm
NATIONAL MUSEUM, ALEPPO   M 5157 *L'EUFRATE* 262

303
Inlaid frieze
Ivory, shell, red limestone and schist
2500 BC

Animal sacrifices were part of the ritual ceremonies that took place in the temples and their courtyards. In this inlaid frieze, two officiants prepare to cut the throat of a ram that they hold down with its head back, its neck already exposed. Around them, somewhat passive figures clasp their hands in an attitude of prayer as they observe the scene. The frieze is one of many found in fragments in the temples of Mari, the city-state.

TELL HARIRI, ANCIENT MARI: TEMPLE OF SHAMASH
30 x 21.5 x 5 cm
NATIONAL MUSEUM, DAMASCUS M1922 *BAAL* 101

304
Wall painting
Fresco on plaster
1800 BC

This is a fragment of a picture made by applying paint on the thick layer of plaster that covered the largest courtyard in the royal palace of Mari. The scene represents a sacrifice. A male figure, wearing a headdress called a polos and clothed in a tunic edged with festoon trimming, leads a bull to sacrifice with his left hand, seeming to calm the animal. The tip of the bull's horns is covered with some precious metal, probably silver.

TELL HARIRI, ANCIENT MARI: PALACE COURTYARD 52 x 47 cm
NATIONAL MUSEUM, ALEPPO M10119 *BAAL* 125

305
Bas-relief
Basalt
AD 300

This basalt lintel shows the standing figure of a man wearing a tunic. In his left hand, he holds the ear of a very large bull's head and, in his right, he grasps the bridle of his horse, behind which stand a goat and a dog. The representations are not in proportion to one another, but this is intentional. The scene is meant to commemorate the sacrifice of a bull to a divinity, an offering whose importance is signified by the size of the bull's head. The sacrifice was ordered by a member of the nobility, symbolized by the harnessed horse. The fact that the goat is as big as the horse indicates that the person must have been a landowner whose wealth was derived from the possession of a herd of goats. The author of the sacrifice thus sought to immortalize the deed in a block of stone, which would have been placed in a spot where it reminded his peers of his actions.

AIN AZ-ZAMAN 123 x 24 x 30 cm
SUWEIDA MUSEUM 44/231 *LE DJEBEL AL-'ARAB* 3.08

287

306
Encolpion cross
Bronze
AD 900

The word "encolpion" comes from a Greek word (*enkolpion*) that literally means "on the bosom," and applies to an object worn around the neck. It is used here to describe a bronze cross engraved on one of its faces with an image of St. George, according to the Greek inscription (O HAGIOC GEOPGIOC) at the top of its upper arm. This manner of wearing an object was adopted by the Christians as of the fourth century and continued to be common practice in the entire empire throughout the Byzantine era. An encolpion may be any type of object, including eulogiae [313 and 314] and amulets, as long as it is worn around the neck and bears a religious image or an inscription. An encolpion can also be a small box containing a sacred relic and hung about the neck. It was believed that an encolpion protected its wearer.

UNKNOWN   11.1 x 4.7 cm
NATIONAL MUSEUM, DAMASCUS   29389
SYRIEN 93

307
Cross
Bronze
Byzantine period

Since this object was found by chance, it is impossible to date it with precision. In memory of Christ's suffering, the early Christians soon adopted the cross as a symbol of their membership in the community of those who believed in him. (The Greek word for "community," *ekklesia*, is the source of our word "ecclesiastic.") In 313, Emperor Constantine recognized this community as an institution, designated as the Catholic Church (the term "catholic" coming from the Greek word for "universal"). The cross shown here is a Greek one, since the arms are of equal length. It is also described as being "formée" because its arms are wider at the end than they are in the center. This cross was intended to be worn as a pendant since it has a ring at its top.

AIN DARA   8.5 x 2.2 x 0.2 cm
NATIONAL MUSEUM, ALEPPO   C 2115

308/309
Christian lamps
Terra cotta
Byzantine period

The first Christians adopted the custom of using lamps like these during the time of their persecution, when they were obliged to meet at night in dark catacombs. They also put burning lamps around the dead for burial ceremonies. The lamp, however, was a common household object in the Roman period, and at first the Christians did not decorate their lamps with any symbol that would reveal their faith to their neighbors. It was only later, when Christianity was declared a state religion at the end of the fourth century, that religious emblems appeared on the lamps used by Christians. At this time, such lamps were even sold to pilgrims at the entrance to the catacombs.

UNKNOWN   10 x 5.5 cm/ 8.5 x 5.5 cm
NATIONAL MUSEUM, ALEPPO   C 1894A-B

310
Altar
Terra cotta
AD 800

The shallow tray at the top of this object suggests that it must have been used as a small altar or offering table. The altar has been made to resemble an architectural model of a Byzantine church, as is indicated by the type of cross placed in a medallion on one of its sides.

TELL BI'A, ANCIENT TUTTUL   19.5 x 1 9.5 x 17 cm
RAQQA MUSEUM   750 (24/50:76)   *MDOG* 121 (1989), p. 6-7

311
Baptismal font
Terra cotta
Byzantine period

In the Catholic Church, a new believer was introduced to the Christian community through the rite of baptism (from the Greek word for " to dip "), involving immersion in water to wash away original sin. At first, this ceremony was conducted outside, in lakes and pools, in imitation of Christ's baptism by St. John the Baptist in the River Jordan. Later, when people began to construct churches in which they could practice their religion, a room called a baptistery was added to the main building. This room held a small pool built into the floor. From the sixth century on, it became increasingly common to baptize new church members simply by pouring water over their heads. Because of this, pools were replaced by pedestaled basins called baptismal fonts (from the Latin word fons, meaning " fountain "). This baptismal font has a relief inscription in Syriac, the language used by Eastern Christians for religious rites. It is still spoken today by the Christians of Syria.

UNKNOWN   39 x 50 cm
NATIONAL MUSEUM, ALEPPO   C 1606

312
Chancel panel: the Adoration of the Magi
Stone
AD 600

The chancel screen was a low wall that separated the nave from the choir in the first churches. The wall was often made of stone panels sculpted with biblical scenes. This panel shows the *Adoration of the Magi*, a scene that was reproduced frequently in Byzantine and early Christian art. However, this picture does not correspond exactly to the story told in the Gospel according to St. Matthew, for the Adoration does not take place in a stable. Nor does it take place shortly after Christ's birth, since Jesus is not given the features of a newborn baby. The three wise men wear Persian clothes and offer gifts, which, being little chests, cannot be distinguished as gold, frankincense and myrrh. Above the head of the first wise man is the Star of Bethlehem, which guided them.

RASM EL-QANAFIZ   110 x 80 x 23 cm
NATIONAL MUSEUM, DAMASCUS   5297
SYRIA 38 (1961) 35-53; *SMC* 282

314 a-b
Eulogiae
Terra cotta
AD 500

Eulogiae were souvenirs that pilgrims brought back from the holy places they visited. These objects were often metal or terra cotta medallions with images on them. Qalat Sim'an, to the north of Aleppo, attracted large numbers of pilgrims because it was the place where St. Simeon (390-459) had lived as a hermit on top of a pillar. Eulogiae from this site represented St. Simeon standing on his pillar, with the hood of his monk's robe on his head. On one of the eulogiae shown here, only the upper part of his body is visible above the balustrade around his platform; the ladder for mounting there leans against the pillar. Above his head is a cross and on either side are angels holding wreaths, symbolizing the triumph of the martyrs and saints. The other eulogia represents the Adoration of the Magi, a very popular pictorial theme in the Christian world at the time.

QALAT SIM'AN   3 x 0.9 cm/3 x 1.1 cm
NATIONAL MUSEUM, DAMASCUS   8867/4047 and 8866/4046
SMC 286; *BAAL* 311; *Cf. SYRIEN* 50-51

315
Bread stamp
Terra cotta
AD 600

The first Christians developed the custom of stamping various images onto the surface of their bread, whether it was the bread they ate at daily meals or the bread that was shared among the faithful when they received Communion during the celebration of a mass. Bread stamped with religious motifs, either in relief or in intaglio, were also sometimes used as eulogiae [**313** and **314**] and given to pilgrims as a souvenir of their visit to a sanctuary. The motif shown here appears frequently in Syrian mosaics and decorative arts. The two stags are meant to symbolize the souls of believers, while the cypress tree in the middle of the composition is an allusion to eternity.

NORTHERN SYRIA   6.7 x 4.5 cm
NATIONAL MUSEUM, DAMASCUS   8864/4044
BAAL 312

TREASURE OF RUSAFA-SERGIOPOLIS

Gold-plated silver; niello decoration
AD 1200

These five liturgical vessels were discovered together in 1982 under a floor tile in the principal basilica of Rusafa. This church also once held the relics of St. Sergius, whose name was taken by the city during the Byzantine era, when it was known as Sergiopolis. The vessels were wrapped in a cloth and hidden in a jar a little after 1258 in the hope of saving them from the invading Mongols. Whoever concealed them was wise to do so, since the city was sacked and the relics of St. Sergius disappeared. The decoration on these sacramental objects shows both Western and Eastern influences, indicating that they probably date from around 1200. These invaluable examples of the goldsmith's art were all left as votive offerings by pilgrims.

NATIONAL MUSEUM, DAMASCUS

316
Censer

This vessel is thought to have been used as a hanging lamp or, more probably, as a censer. The use of incense in religious ceremonies was not common in the early days of the Catholic Church, since the first Christians wanted to ensure that their religion was clearly distinguished from the pagan cults, in which incense played an important role. In the third millennium BC, incense was used in temples because its smoke was thought to be a ritual link between the earthly world and the heavenly regions inhabited by the gods. The rising smoke of incense signified both purification and an offering to a divinity.

12 x 8.5 cm   29316, AN 31   *SYRIEN* 119

317
Chalice

The outer surface of the cup on this chalice is engraved with a bust of Christ, with the Greek letters IC (Jesus) and XC (Christ). The bowl of the chalice is ornamented inside with engraved figures representing the Christ Child on the lap of his mother, Mary, who is seated on a throne and flanked by the archangels Michael and Gabriel.

20.5 x 15 cm   29311, AN 29   *SYRIEN* 116

318
Ciborium (?)

This deep cup might well have served as a ciborium, the vessel in which the consecrated host was kept for the Communion of the faithful. In a medallion in the center of the cup is the emblem of a Frankish nobleman named Raoul I de Coucy (in Picardie), who fell at Acre in 1191 during the Third Crusade. Perhaps this vessel was an offering made by the nobleman on a pilgrimage to Sergiopolis. The inscription on the vessel is in Arabic.

29313/15, AN 30   *SYRIEN* 118

319
Chalice foot

12.5 X 8 cm   29314, AN 32   *SYRIEN* 120

320
Paten

On the inner surface of the paten, there is a central medallion engraved with the Hand of God before the symbol for Christ. An inscription in Syriac forms a border around the rim.

13 cm   29312, AN 28   *SYRIEN* 117

321
Bas-relief of St. Simeon Stylites
Basalt
AD 500

St. Simeon Stylites was one of the monks whose numbers grew considerably with the triumph of Christianity in Syria after it was integrated into the Eastern Roman, or Byzantine Empire, in 395. Some of these monks wished to live as Christ had and sought to isolate themselves so that they could pray and meditate; these monks became hermits. St. Simeon found an original way of doing this: he lived on top of a pillar. His epithet, Stylites, comes from the Greek word *stylos*, meaning "column." However, his originality brought him many visitors. He is shown here with only his head sticking out above the structure built on the pillar. A bird, representing Christ, is crowning him with a wreath, a symbol of the saints in Christian iconography. A person on the ladder holds a censer to fumigate offerings.

HAMA REGION   66 x 78 x 16 cm
HAMA MUSEUM   1088   *SYRIEN* 49

322
Wall painting: presentation of the Christ Child to St. Simeon by the Virgin Mary
Fresco
AD 1200

In this fresco, a beardless St. Simeon, with a halo around his head and white hair falling over his gray mantle, is standing with the Christ Child in his arms, beside an altar. To his right stands the Holy Virgin, recognizable by her halo and purple shawl, her hands outstretched. Behind these figures, to the far right, is a woman identified as the prophetess Anna. It is not known who is represented by the small male figure in front of the altar between Mary and St. Simeon. The scene takes place in a temple, and on the altar — a table covered with a cloth — there is a rectangular form which could well be the gem-encrusted cover of a copy of the Holy Scriptures. This presentation scene was inspired by a passage in the Gospel according to St. Luke (2:28) and became a very popular theme in Byzantine art.

CRAK DES CHEVALIERS: BAPTISTRY   167 x 88 cm
TARTUS MUSEUM   282

323
Mosaic
Tesserae of gold-backed glass and colored stones
AD 710

This fragment belonged to one of the mosaics that decorated the walls of the Umayyad Mosque in Damascus. The mosaics were made by Byzantine artists sent from Constantinople by the Emperor at the request of the caliph. Although the technique they used was Byzantine, the motifs were not. There are imaginary landscapes and villas — the paradise promised to the chosen — but no living creatures are shown, in accordance with Koranic precepts. Between 706 and 714, the Umayyad caliph al Walîd (705-715) built a large mosque at Damascus modeled on that of the Prophet in Medina. However, the one at Damascus was the first mosque in the Muslim world to have a minaret, a *mihrâb* built in the *qibla* wall (in the direction of Mecca, which was faced for prayers), a *maqsûra*, an ablutions fountain and rooms.

DAMASCUS: UMAYYAD MOSQUE   77 x 77 cm
NATIONAL MUSEUM, DAMASCUS   *SMC* 297

324
Mosque lamp
Copper
AD 1300

" God is the light of the heavens and of the earth. His light is like a niche in which is a lamp — the light encased in glass — the glass, as it were, a glistening star. (…) It is light upon light. God guideth whom He will to His light… . "(Koran 24, 35)

UNKNOWN   107 x 35 cm
NATIONAL MUSEUM, DAMASCUS   440 A

325 a-i
Beakers for a mosque lamp
Blown glass
AD 800

In 772, the Abbasid caliph al-Mansur decided to build a new city called ar-Rafiqa, " the companion, " to the west of Raqqa on the Euphrates. It was modeled on Baghdad, which had been founded ten years earlier. In it he built palaces and a mosque measuring 80 by 110 meters, making it the second largest mosque in Syria, smaller only than the Umayyad Mosque of Damascus. These little glass receptacles come from the ar-Rafiqa mosque. They were once placed in a mosque lamp, like the one in **[324],** to hold the oils that were burned for lighting. The caliph Harûn al-Rashid, the third successor of al-Mansur, decided in 796 to transfer his residence from Baghdad to ar-Rafiqa and thus lived near the border between Islamic and Byzantine territory.

RAQQA, ANCIENT AR-RAFIQA: MOSQUE
9.5 x 7.5 cm (on average)   RAQQA MUSEUM   926

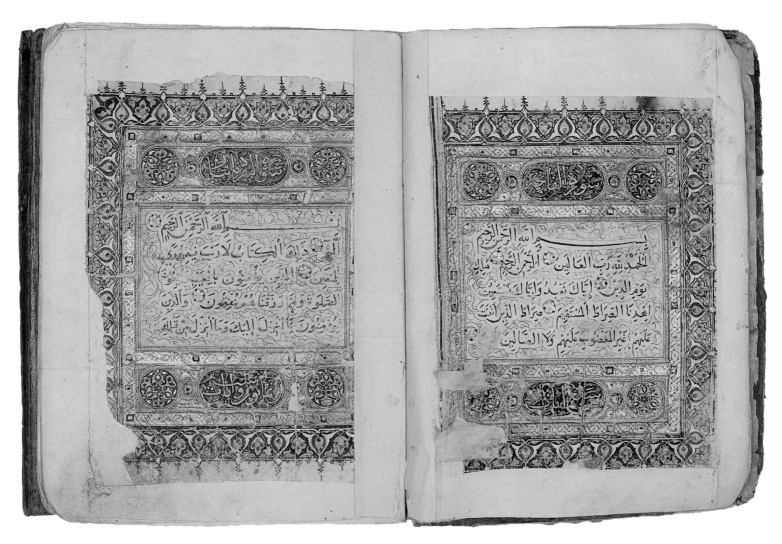

326
Manuscript of the Koran
Paper
AD 1400

Each page of this Koran contains five lines bordered by blue and gold illumination, with large bands above and below giving the title of the sura. In the text itself, golden rosettes separate the verses. Figurative imagery is prohibited by Koranic precepts. The earliest surviving manuscripts of the Koran date from the second half of seventh century. The text of the Koran was given a definitive form thanks to the Umayyad caliph of Damascus, Abd Almalek (685-705), who standardized Arabic spelling when he decreed that Arabic should be the language of administration for the entire Islamic Empire.

This manuscript is part of a Koran in 30 volumes. As of the ninth century, the 114 sura of the Koran were arbitrarily divided into 30 parts of the same length, each contained in a manuscript. The division into 30 parts was considered advantageous because it corresponded to the number of days in the lunar months of the Muslim calendar.

34 x 25 cm
NATIONAL MUSEUM, DAMASCUS   6998 A   *Cf. SMC* 300

327
Wooden openwork lectern
Wood
AD 1300

This type of lectern was used to support a great book of the Koran so that it would be easier to read.

UNKNOWN   71.5 x 25.5 cm
NATIONAL MUSEUM, DAMASCUS   10669 A

328
Flask with lilies
Ceramic
AD 1300

The body of this vessel, called a pilgrim flask, has moulded decoration on its sides, with a stylized lily in the middle. This motif was often used as an emblem on Ayyubid and Mamluk coins and eventually became the family crest of the Mamluk sultan Qalâ'un. In the Muslim world, the lily motif was first used in the mihrâb (or prayer niche) in the Koranic school built in Damascus by the caliph Nur al-Dîn between 1154 and 1173. However, the theme is a very old one in the Near East and was already in use at the time of Ramses III in Egypt.

NEAR ALEPPO   22 x 16.5 cm
NATIONAL MUSEUM, DAMASCUS   1415 A   *SMC* 325

329
Flask with swords
Ceramic
AD 1300

This type of vessel was intended to hold a small amount of water. It is generally called a pilgrim flask because it was often carried by travelers and, in the Muslim world, especially by those making pilgrimages to Mecca. This flask was made locally, since a potter's workshop and a kiln containing discarded fragments of such vessels have been found on the slopes of Mount Kâsiyûn behind Damascus. No glaze was applied to the flask so that the clay would remain porous; this way, the water inside the flask was kept cool. The moulded decoration is interesting, since is shows two coats of arms, each containing a pair of Frankish swords. In the Islamic world, there was a considerable trade in the long straight swords of the Franks, for these weapons were much admired by the Arabs.

UNKNOWN   30 x 21.5 cm
NATIONAL MUSEUM, DAMASCUS   9771 A   *SMC* 350

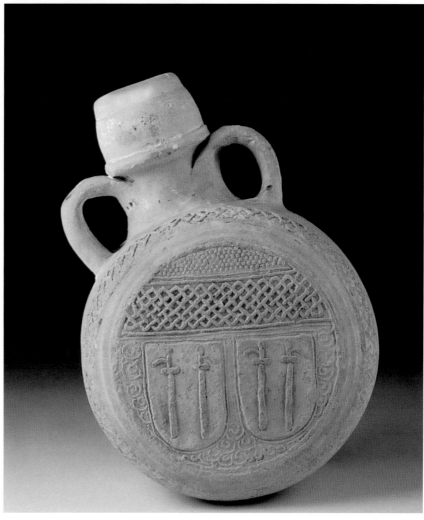

330
Funerary bas-relief
Limestone
AD 150

This semicirular bas-relief shows a the bust of a man in a central medallion supported on either side by a winged Victory (nike). It once stood in an arc-shaped niche built above a series of loculi in a hypogeum, or underground tomb. The male figure may personify the divinity that protected the family.

TADMOR, ANCIENT PALMYRA: SOUTHEAST NECROPOLIS, TOMB C
86.6 x 44 cm
PALMYRA MUSEUM B 2710/9119
TOMBS A AND C p. 78-82, Pl. 51

331
Bas-relief: funeral banquet scene
Limestone
AD 240

During the second century and, above all, in the third century, large bas-reliefs showing a banquet scene with an entire family and their servants became a very popular form of decoration in the hypogea and tower tombs of Palmyra. They were usually placed at the end of a corridor. The principal figure in such banquet scenes is always a man, presented on the right. He is shown reclining on a banquet couch, holding a drinking cup, with his left arm supported by cushions. To the left of the relief, his mother or wife sits on the couch. A couple of other banqueters are sometimes shown lying side by side on the couch as well. The dead man's wife is often represented behind her husband's shoulder. Servants, children and other members of the family may also be placed in the background or beneath the scene.

TADMOR, ANCIENT PALMYRA: TOMB OF THE 'ALAINEH FAMILY
225 x 114 cm
PALMYRA MUSEUM B 2285/8277
PALMYRE VII p. 77-95; *SCULPTURES FUNÉRAIRES* p. 172-176;
SCULPTURES OF PALMYRA I p. 405-415

332

Funerary bas-relief of a priest

Hard limestone

AD 137

The tower tombs and hypogea, or underground tombs, of Palmyra have yielded an impressive number of small rectangular stone plaques that were used to close the loculi, or burial niches in which the bodies of the dead were placed. They were sculpted with bas-reliefs that represented the faces of the deceased. Although busts were a popular form of sculpture throughout the Roman world, the idea of placing a bust on a plaque that closed a loculi seems to have been peculiar to Palmyra.

In this bas-relief, the male figure wears a cylindrical headdress with a wreath, indicating that he was a priest. To the right, at the level of his head, six lines of Palmyrene inscription inform the observer that this is: "The late lamented Mokimo, son of Breiki Amricha, the thirteenth day of August 449." (The year 449 in the Gregorian calendar is equivalent to the year 137 in our calendar.) To the left, the same text is written in Greek.

TADMOR, ANCIENT PALMYRA: BREIKI TOMB   57 x 44 x 25 cm
PALMYRA MUSEUM   B 2687/9088   *SMC* 234

333

Funerary bas-relief of a young man

Hard limestone

AD 137

On the flat background to the right of the figure's head, an inscription reads: "Amrisha, son of Malik, son of Amrisha, alas." Following a Roman tradition, the young man wears a ring on the little finger of his left hand. Among the Romans, rings were worn by both men and women. This custom became popular especially after the year 150. A Roman ring consisted of a wide band set with a round or oval stone. At first, such rings were worn only on the little finger of the left hand, but in about 200, people began to wear them on both hands. The sculptures of this time sometimes even show two rings on the same finger.

TADMOR, ANCIENT PALMYRA: BREIKI TOMB   58 x 43 x 24 cm
PALMYRA MUSEUM   B 2696/9098

334
Funerary bas-relief of a woman
Hard limestone
AD 150

This woman wears her hair piled up in an ornate Roman style of chignon, called " melon rib, " which became fashionable in the middle of the second century and continued into the third century. The jewelry represented in this bas-relief was once gilded. Certain other parts were embellished with paint, traces of which can still be seen here and there. The gilding and painting of certain elements were an expression of the deceased woman's wealth, which would have been closely linked to the social status that she and her family enjoyed in Palmyrene society. The inscription gives us her name and reads: " Aqma, daughter of Atelena Hajeuja, alas. "

TADMOR, ANCIENT PALMYRA : BREIKI TOMB 65 x 46 x 29 cm
PALMYRA MUSEUM B 2666/8967

335
Funerary bas-relief of a woman
Hard limestone
AD 137

The woman represented in this bas-relief is identified as " Haba betta, daughter of…" by the inscription to her right. She is wearing traditional clothing and a great deal of jewelry, as was the custom. Brooches, or fibulae, were used by both men and women to attach their cloaks on the left shoulder. The brooches worn by women, however, were more varied in shape. Until about 150, they were always trapezoidal and decorated with the head of an animal, a rosette or a leaf. After this date, other forms became popular, and fibulae could be round, polygonal or toothed. Bracelets, which were generally worn only by women and came in a great variety of styles, did not become common until the second century.

TADMOR, ANCIENT PALMYRA : BREIKI TOMB 60 x 43 x 23 cm
PALMYRA MUSEUM B 2667/8968
Cf. IRAQ 11 (1949), p. 160-187

336
Funerary bas-relief of a young woman
Hard limestone
AD 137

From the middle of the first century, women's clothing became more complicated. An ample length of material was
used as a cloak, which was draped over the tunic and attached with a brooch on the left shoulder. A long shawl of
very soft material covered the head, shoulders and arms.
In funerary bas-reliefs like this one, women are shown
touching this shawl or holding it away from their faces.
With few exceptions, the shawl is not placed directly on
the woman's head but on a thickly wrapped turban with
its ends usually crossed in front. Representations of wom-
en without a shawl are rare. In this bas-relief, a little girl
is shown standing to the left of the woman. To her right
an inscription states that she is: " Aqua, daughter of
Wahballat, son of Nasha and Salma, her daughter Alam. "

TADMOR, ANCIENT PALMYRA: BREIKI TOMB   54 x 43 x 22 cm
PALMYRA MUSEUM   B 2703/9105

337
Funerary bas-relief of a woman and her child
Hard limestone
AD 150

Although there is no inscription to guide us, it seems likely that the child held by the woman in her left hand is one
that she lost in childbirth. The sober manner in which the
figure is presented contrasts with the exuberant display of
wealth to be seen in other bas-reliefs of female figures.

TADMOR, ANCIENT PALMYRA: TEMPLE OF ALLAT   58 x 40 x 25 cm
PALMYRA MUSEUM   B 2326/8527

PERSONAL RELIGIOUS PRACTICE AND FUNERARY RITES

338
Bust of a woman covered with jewelry
Limestone
AD 200

The jewelry represented in the funeral sculptures of
Palmyra became larger and more copious as the Palmy-
renes grew rich over the three centuries of their city's
golden age as part of the Roman Empire. Necklaces made
their appearance in the second century and were extremely popular throughout the third century. This form of os-
tentatious luxury was for a long time opposed by those
upholding the Roman virtue of austerity. At the beginning
of our era, Pliny the Elder denounced the abundance of
jewelry worn by the women of his time, asking them to at
least refrain from putting anklets about their ankles
(*Natural History* XXXIII, 12).

TADMOR, ANCIENT PALMYRA   43 x 31x 15 cm
PALMYRA MUSEUM   B 552/1755
SCULPTURES OF PALMYRA I p. 394; *Cf. IRAQ* 11 (1949), p. 160-187

339
Brooch
Gold and rubies (?)
AD 200

This is a large oval-shaped gold brooch, edged with crenellation. Between the notches of this crenellation, the
brooch is set with rubies (?) and ceramic stones. The entire perimeter is trimmed with a delicate raised border of
tiny golden spheres. A series of concentric ovals made
with granulation and geometrical relief patterns surround
a central green stone carved in intaglio with the figure of
a nude man standing with a Victory in his right hand. The
ruby is a red-colored stone whose hardness is surpassed
only by that of the diamond, the hardest of all the precious stones. However, the ruby was not known until fairly
late in antiquity. It occurs in deposits in Afghanistan and
Pakistan. Since the deposits are usually alluvial, rubies are
relatively easy to find in these regions.

DURA-EUROPOS   8.8 x 7 x 2 cm
NATIONAL MUSEUM, DAMASCUS   3250/7008
ANTIQUITÉS GRÉCO-ROMAINES Pl. 7

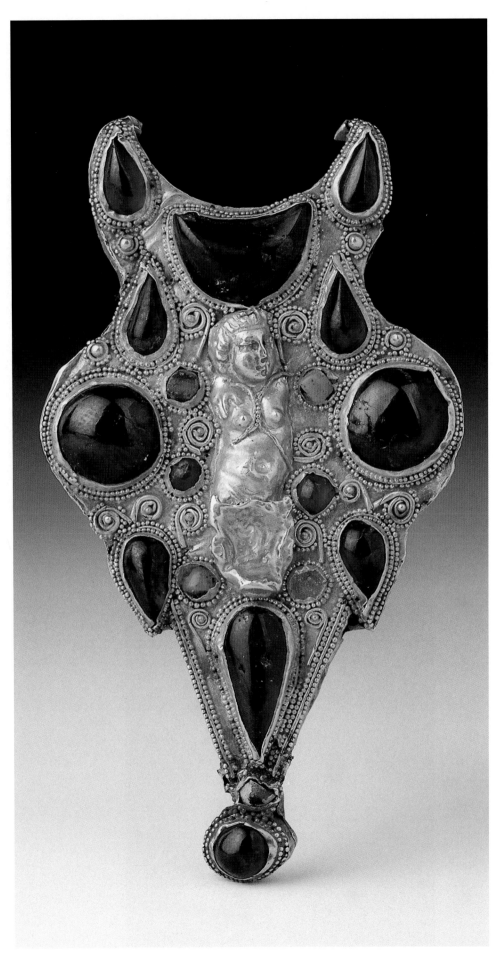

340
Brooch
Gold, rubies, garnets and emeralds
Roman period

This exquisite gold brooch set with cabochons of ruby, garnet and emerald attests to the high status enjoyed by its owner as well as her love of beautiful jewelry. The space between the precious stones has been decorated with tiny spheres or grains of gold that have been melted together in a jewelry technique known as granulation. In the middle, a figure who may represent a goddess has been shaped in the gold, probably by embossing. At the time, emeralds like green gems in this brooch were mined in Egypt. The word "garnet" comes from the French *grenate*, meaning "pomegranate" and shares its color with this fruit.

HAMA   6.5 x 3.6 x 0.9 cm
NATIONAL MUSEUM, DAMASCUS
2854/5937
MUSÉE NATIONAL p. 110 et p. 141

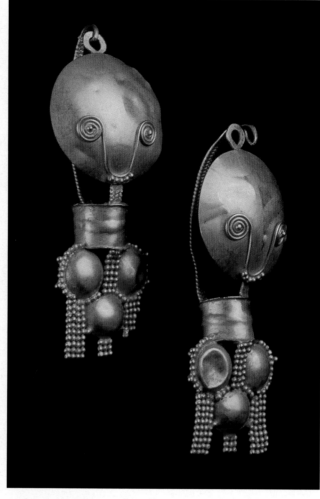

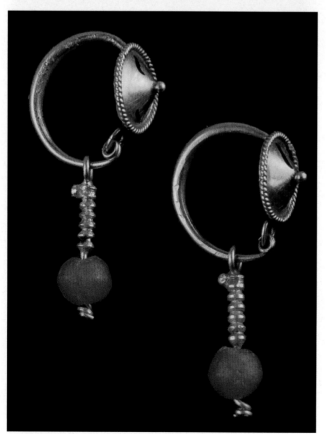

341/342/343
Pairs of earrings
Gold and rock crystal
Byzantine period

Rock crystal is a colorless variety of quartz that looks like ice. In fact, the word "crystal" comes from a Greek word that means "icy cold."

UNKNOWN
NATIONAL MUSEUM, ALEPPO   C1847/1851/1848

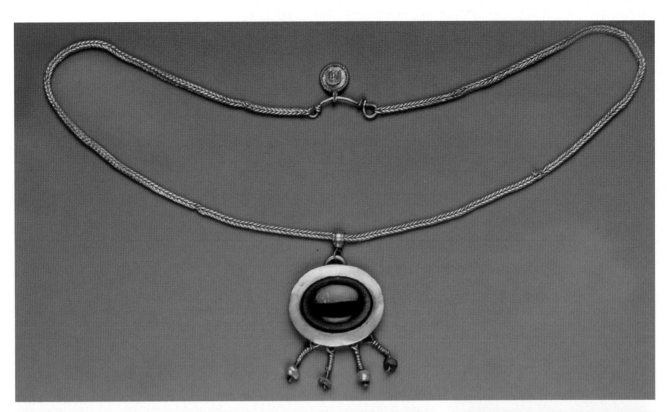

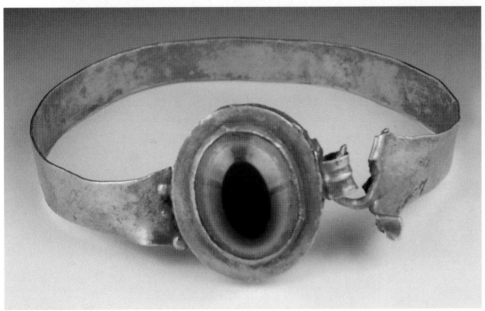

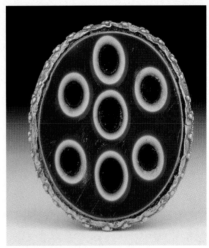

344/345/346
Brooch/Necklace/Bracelet
Gold and agate
Roman period

Gold was used to make most jewelry in ancient times, since, even though it is a precious metal, it is easy to find. Native gold occurs as small nuggets carried along by river currents. By the time of the Roman Empire, people had begun to mine certain gold ores. The gold mines closest to Syria were located in the Caucasus region. It is certain, however, that Syrian goldsmiths played an important role in transforming gold into ornaments, for Pliny the Elder claims that the Phoenicians were responsible for the invention of gold and the methods of processing it. Gold is very ductile and this property makes it ideal for jewelry-making, since it can be stretched without breaking. Agate is a semiprecious stone with different-colored bands produced by successive layers of minerals being deposited as the stone is formed. In the Near East, agates are found in India.

UNKNOWN   23 x 2.6 cm/ 5.4 x 2.1 cm/4.1 x 3.3 x 0.4 cm
NATIONAL MUSEUM, DAMASCUS   6014-13839/13224/7885

347
Bracelet
Gold
Roman period

Gold is the most malleable of the precious metals. It is easy to work and can be simply hammered into shapes. However, gold is so soft that it is often alloyed with another metal, like silver (to produce electrum) or copper, so that it can be made into objects that keep their shape and have surfaces hard enough to be inscribed with decorative motifs.

UNKNOWN   6.5 x 6.5 cm
NATIONAL MUSEUM, DAMASCUS   7014/743
AAAS 13, p. 71

348/349
Mirrors
Gypsum and glass
Roman period

Highly valued as aids to personal grooming, mirrors were at first made of bronze. To have an idea of what they looked like, people gazed at their reflections in the polished surface of this metal. The mirrors shown here were made with silvered glass, that is, a sheet of glass whose inner face was coated with a layer of tin or some other metal, which was then polished thoroughly.

UNKNOWN/HOMS   13 x 13 x 0.9 cm/12 x 11 x 1.5 cm
NATIONAL MUSEUM, DAMASCUS   24001/15351
AAAS 20 (1970), p. 9

350
Figurine of Aphrodite with a sandal
Bronze with gold ornamentation
AD 200

During the Hellenistic and the Roman periods in Syria, bronze workers made great quantities of figurines in the likeness of the goddess Aphrodite. At this time, she was the most frequently represented divinity in the pantheon. Following a tradition that had developed in Alexandria, she was shown nude, posed in the gestures of a ritual toilet — she may be looking at herself in a mirror, arranging or lifting up her hair, or undoing a sandal. According to eye-witness accounts left by ancient authors, certain devotees repeated these ritual gestures in front of statues of the goddess as a way of honoring her. In this representation of Aphrodite, the goddess of love and beauty conceals her pubic region with her left hand and holds up a sandal
in her right.

KHISFINE   26 x 9 x 7.4 cm
NATIONAL MUSEUM, DAMASCUS   4309
ANTIQUITÉS GRÉCO-ROMAINES p. 138 and Pl. 54:1

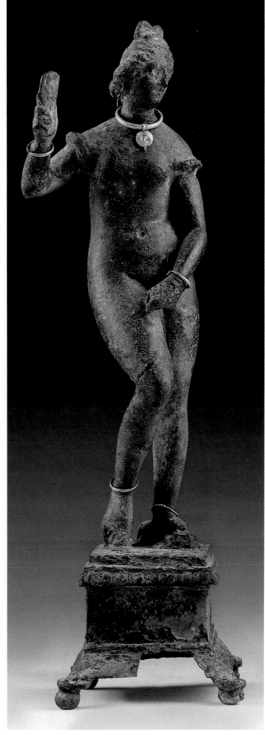

351
Bust of a young woman
Enameled ceramic
Roman period

The female figure represented in relief on this vessel coated with green enamel is thought to be the goddess Kore — a Greek word that means "young girl" — or Persephone, as she is more commonly known. She was the daughter of Zeus and Demeter, the goddess of the Earth. She was abducted by Hades and became Queen of the Underworld. However, every year, she came back to the Earth's surface with the first sprouts of spring and did not return to her underground world until the time of autumn sowing arrived. As long as she was separated from her mother, it was winter and the soil was sterile. This legend was meant to explain the rhythm of the seasons but was also linked to the theme of life and death.

HOMS   26.5 x 19 x 10.8 cm
NATIONAL MUSEUM, DAMASCUS   7619
MUSÉE NATIONAL p. 98 and Fig. 37

305

352
Piece of fabric
Cotton
AD 100

It is very rare to find pieces of cotton fabric in Palmyra; they represent only three percent of all the textiles identified so far. In later periods, cotton was grown widely throughout Syria, but during the Roman period it was imported from India. The intricately patterned colors of this piece are evidence that advanced cloth-making techniques were used to produce it. The cloth was dyed with indigo (blue), extracted from the leaves of the indigo plant, and madder (red), obtained from the roots of the plant of the same name. Both these plants grow in India. This fragment of cloth thus testifies to Palmyra's commercial relations with India.

TADMOR, ANCIENT PALMYRA: TOMBS 71-73, 97   31 x 41 cm
NATIONAL MUSEUM, DAMASCUS   V22 (T71-73.97)

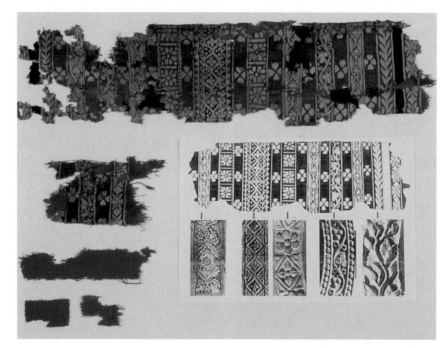

353
Piece of fabric
Wool
AD 40

The textiles discovered at Palmyra give some idea of how wealthy this city became as a result of its central role in the trade between the Eastern and Western worlds. The pieces of clothing found on mummified bodies were very well preserved because of the dryness of the climate in this region as well as the absolute darkness of the underground tombs. Wool was the most widely used fibre for making cloth in Palmyra. One of its advantages is that it absorbs dyes readily. It might be noted that motifs painted on this fragment are the same as those found in the funerary sculpture of Palmyra.

TADMOR, ANCIENT PALMYRA: KITOT TOWER   30 x 40 cm
PALMYRA MUSEUM   1/9230

354
Piece of fabric
Wool
AD 100

The most opulent fabrics were those dyed purple, since this dye was extracted from a Mediterranean mollusk, the murex, through a long and complicated process. Thousands of these mollusks were required, since each one provided only a few drops of the precious color. The purple fabrics of Palmyra no doubt came from Tyre or Sidon, cities that were famous for their production of this dye. At one point during the Roman Empire, purple cloth was literally worth its weight in gold. This type of cloth has been discovered in Palmyra more than in any other Mediterranean site. This in itself is an indication of the city's wealth, for in the Roman period there was no better symbol of luxury than a garment dyed this color.

TADMOR, ANCIENT PALMYRA   25 x 33 cm
PALMYRA MUSEUM   3/9238

THE ORGANIZATION OF THOUGHT

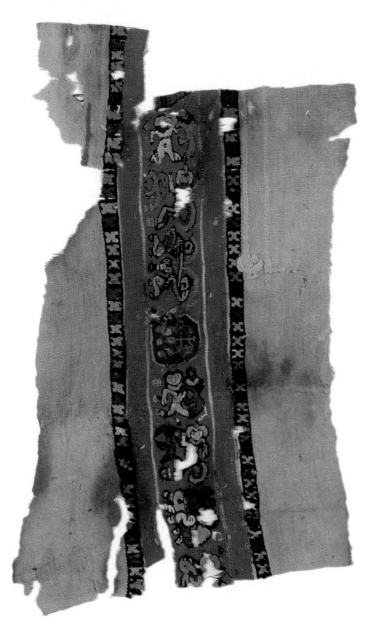

355

Piece of Coptic cloth

Cotton

AD 1000

The term " Coptic " is used to designate the Christian community that formed in Egypt around 300. This fragment comes from the clothing in which a Christian was buried. It was probably part of a tunic, which was a very common garment at the time. A tunic was frequently embellished with thin vertical bands woven directly into the cloth on either side of the neck opening. The bands usually ended at the waistline.

UNKNOWN   27 x 45 cm
NATIONAL MUSEUM, DAMASCUS   6059

356

Fragment of a tunic

Linen and wool

AD 103

Linen does not take dye well and was therefore used unbleached, neither whitened nor colored. Made from flax, a plant that grows in the Palmyra region, linen was used to make clothing in antiquity very early on. Although the color of natural linen is not very showy, people developed ingenious methods for weaving it. The arms and bodice of this tunic were woven in one piece on a loom that must have been 250 centimeters wide. Decorative motifs in dyed wool were appliquéed on the tunic afterwards. This is the oldest example of a decorated tunic found in Syria.

TADMOR, ANCIENT PALMYRA: ELAHBEL TOWER TOMB 20
41 x 51 cm
NATIONAL MUSEUM, DAMASCUS   V20 (T20)

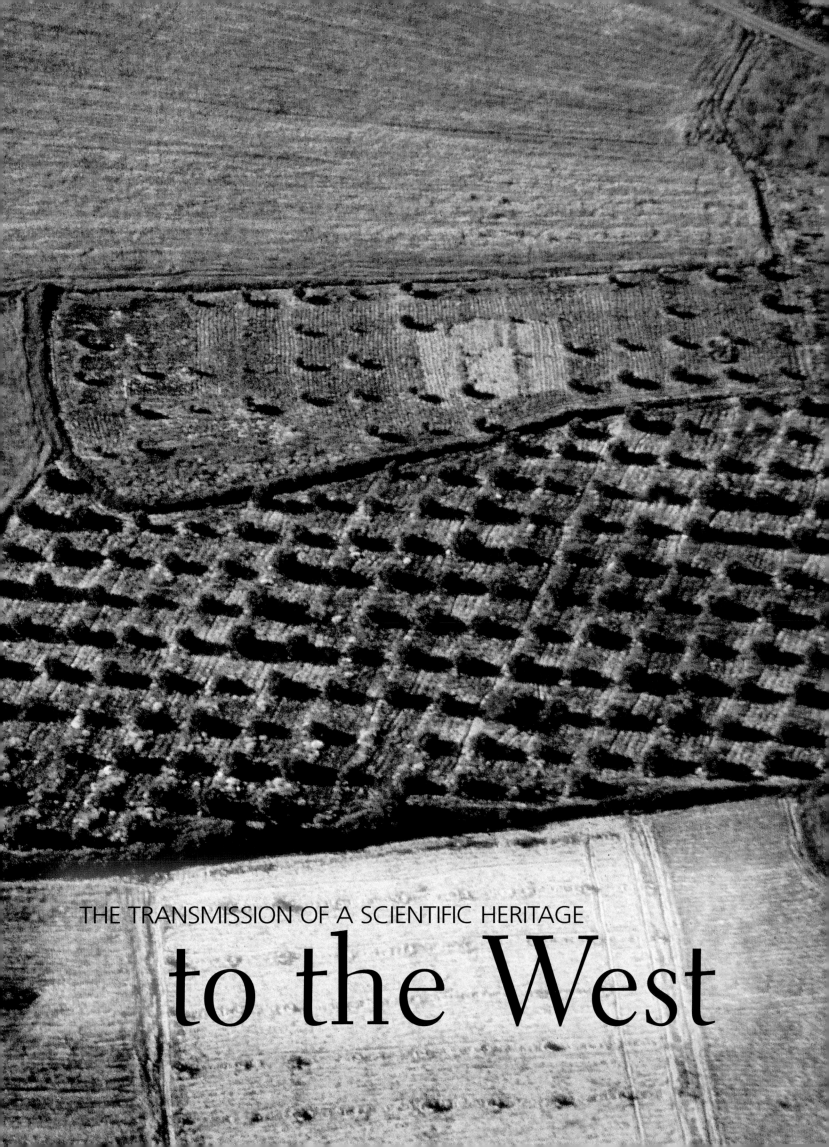

THE TRANSMISSION OF A SCIENTIFIC HERITAGE

to the West

THE TRANSMISSION OF A SCIENTIFIC HERITAGE
to the West

Between the ninth and fifteenth centuries, Muslim scholars, especially those living in Syria, distinguished themselves in most fields of scientific knowledge. For a long time, the Islamic world was considered to have been the repository of the scientific heritage of the Greeks and Romans. In fact, Muslim scholars contributed significantly to the development and diffusion of scientific knowledge, and were responsible for transmitting a great deal of learning to the Western world in a number of scientific disciplines.

There was harmonious agreement from the start between science and the Islamic religion. Not only does the Koran use the word "science" in 160 of its verses, but it also encourages the acquisition of knowledge. For according to the Prophet Muhammad, the ink of the scholar was more blessed than the blood of the martyr, science was more meritorious than prayer, and a little knowledge was better than much devotion.

Knocker used on the door of a *madrasa*.
Cat. 385

PRESERVATION OF THE GRECO-ROMAN TRADITION

Throughout antiquity, Athens maintained its reputation as the home of the arts and a center for philosophical and scientific study until the moment when the Byzantine Emperor Justinian closed down the city's Academy in AD 529. But long before this happened, the conquests of Alexander the Great had helped to spread Greek language and culture throughout the East, and many cities had set up centers of study modeled on that of Athens.

Previous page:
Astrolabe.
Cat. 382

One of these cities was Alexandria, in Egypt. With its famous library containing between 400 000 and 700 000 manuscripts — according to modern estimates — all recopied on papyrus in the library's own workshop, Alexandria became a metropolis of scientific and philosophical knowledge, attracting all the scholars of the Hellenistic world. After the city was integrated into the Islamic Empire in 642, its rich library no longer existed, but a number of manuscripts were saved from destruction and it remained a great center of study and research. However, before the library was completely destroyed, Syrian scholars had gone to study there. One of them was Sergius, who died in 536. The chief physician in the city of Ras al-'Ayn, which stands at the headwaters of the Habur River in northeast Syria, brought back scientific knowledge that enabled him to practice medicine in his homeland. But much more importantly, he also brought some 30 medical treatises by Galen and philosophical texts by Artistotle. These he translated into his native Syriac, a tongue that had developed from Aramaic. Syriac was the international language spoken throughout the East from the time of the Assyrian Empire (800 BC) to the end of the Persian Achaemenids' Empire, when it was conquered by Alexander the Great in 332 BC. Sergius was a Christian, which explains why he spoke Syriac, since it was the language used by the Christian communities in Syria

Reconstruction of the library of Alexandria.

and northern Mesopotamia from AD 400, at about the time the Byzantine Empire began.

As odd it might seem, Sergius' Christian faith was instrumental in the transmission of the Greco-Roman scientific tradition to the Muslim world. Christian heresies provoked crises that rocked the Byzantine Empire to its very foundations; eventually, at the Council of Ephesus in 431, it was decided to excommunicate the members of a sect for their unorthodox beliefs. They were known as Nestorians, since they upheld an interpretation of the nature of Christ proposed by Nestorius, a priest of Antioch. Many scholars belonging to this community, and among them many physicians, were forced to flee, taking their manuscripts with them. They took refuge in Sassanid Persian territory and continued their scholarly work in a city called Jundîshâbûr in southwest Iran, where there was a large research and study center. As well, when Justinian shut down the Academy of Athens in 529, many of the learned men who had been working there, especially physicians, took their manuscripts and fled to other schools, including the one at Jundîshâbûr. In 636, the city, by then a great center of medical research and training, was incorporated into the Islamic Empire. In 765, when the Abbasid caliph al-Mansur was suffering from stomach pains, he had the Nestorian Christian doctors of Jundîshâbûr come to Baghdad, the new capital of the Islamic world, to care for him. The doctors installed themselves in the caliph's court, and then set up a hospital and a medical school in the capital. Both institutions soon grew famous throughout the empire. Training was based on practice as well as on the study of medical treatises written by Greek and Roman scholars. The treatis-

The doctors Hippocrates and Galen in discussion. Fresco from the thirteenth-century Anagni Cathedral.

es, which had been collected and translated into Syriac by the Christian doctors, were then translated into Arabic so that they could be used by the rest of the empire.

An Arab tradition, related by the fourteenth-century historian Ibn Khaldûn, tells a somewhat different but not incompatible story, reflecting how the Arab scholars themselves thought that their predecessors had preserved the scientific knowledge of ancient Greece and Rome by collecting Greek manuscripts and translating them: "When the [Byzantine] emperors adopted Christianity, they abandoned the rational sciences in favour of the Scriptures and the doctrines of their religion; the manuscripts containing scientific knowledge were locked away in the imperial storerooms. When the Byzantine emperors conquered Syria, the Greeks' scientific works were still in existence. Then God brought Islam and the Muslims won outstanding victories, conquering the Byzantines as well as other nations. At first the Muslims were simple people who did not cultivate knowledge, but, as time passed and the Islamic dynasties flourished, the Muslims developed an urban culture that surpassed that of other nations. They began to wish to study the various branches of philosophy of whose existence they had learned through their contacts with the Christian priests and bishops. In any case, man has always had a penchant for intellectual speculation. Consequently, the caliph al-Mansur (around 765) sent an ambassador to the Byzantine emperor, asking him to send translations of books on mathematics. The emperor sent him Euclid's *Elements* and a few works on physics. The Muslim scholars studied these books and their desire to obtain other such books grew keener. When al-Ma'mun (813-833), who had some scientific training, became caliph, he wanted to do something to improve the progress of science. He therefore sent ambassadors and translators to the Byzantine Empire to find books on Greek science and translate them into Arabic. As a result of this effort, a great quantity of manuscripts were collected and preserved."

Present-day facade of the al-Nûri hospital in Damascus.

THE SPREAD OF ARAB SCIENCE

Although Ibn Khaldûn was lavish in his praise for the Muslim scholars who helped to safeguard the Greco-Roman tradition, he ignored two circumstances that played a determining role in the development of science in the Islamic world.

First, the Abbasid caliph Harûn al-Rashîd (786-809), the father of al-Ma'mum in the passage quoted above, established a true translation center in Baghdad, calling it the "House of Wisdom." There, Greek and Latin manuscripts were systematically translated, initially into Syriac but later into Arabic, making it the language of science in the Middle Ages.

Secondly, in 751, after the victory of the Arab army over the Chinese at Samarkand, paper began to be produced in the Near East. Chinese prisoners divulged a recipe that had remained a jealously guarded secret since the invention of paper in 105. Not only was paper more resistant than papyrus, it also was less expensive to produce than parchment. The availability of paper led to an intellectual revolution in the Islamic world, since it became possible to develop a real market for books. In less than a century, thousands of manuscripts were distributed throughout the Islamic countries. The fact that they shared a common language whose writing system had been standardized since the beginning of the empire greatly facilitated the spread of knowledge. In the ninth century, the city of Baghdad alone had about a hundred paper-making workshops; when Baghdad was overrun by the Mongols in 1258, there were over 36 public libraries, as well as several private libraries, almost of all of which were destroyed. The advent of paper meant that for the first time in the history of humankind, scientific and philosophical knowledge was available to anyone who could read.

MEDICINE AND THE FIRST HOSPITALS

Although a contested tradition says that the first hospital (*bîmâristân* in Arabic) was built in Damascus by an Umayyad caliph between 705 and 715, it is more generally accepted that the distinction goes to the Sultan Nûr al-Dîn, who, after capturing Damascus in 1154, built the famous Damascus institution that bears his name, the al-Nûri hospital, and invited the greatest physicians of the time to come and work there. His initiative marked the beginning of true scientific activity in Syria, with hospitals and schools (*madrasa* in Arabic) being constructed in Damascus, Aleppo and other cities.

The building that once housed the al-Nûri hospital still exists today in the old quarter of Damascus; it is now occupied by the Science and Medical History Museum. The building comprises four wings enclosing a rectangular courtyard with a large pool in the middle. On three of its sides, the courtyard opens onto an *îwan*, which is a vaulted space used as a room for teaching. Expenses related to establishing and operating hospitals, as well as schools and public libraries, were covered by revenues generated

Doorways to rooms in the Arghûn hospital in Aleppo.

Interior courtyard of the Arghûn hospital in Aleppo.

Medical manuscript.
Cat. 361

by private donations, or *waqf*. It is not known exactly how these hospitals were run. Were they open to anyone who was ill? Or were they intended for the poorest members of society or for cases that were difficult to treat? Whatever the answers might be, it is clear from the number of new hospitals set up by Nûr al-Dîn and his successors that these leaders were eager to encourage both the development of medical practice and the diffusion of medical knowledge in Syria.

Arab medicine was based on the *Twelve Books* by the renowned Greek physician, Hippocrates (460-377 BC), and the *Sixteen Books* by Galen (AD 129-216), another Greek physician, who had practiced in Pergamum and Rome. These works were translated into Arabic in the ninth century. The translations were then complemented with commentaries by great Arab scholars and by clinical observations, making Arab medicine a felicitous combination of theory and practice [360]. In the thirteenth century, the author of *Compilation of Physicians' Biographies*, a sort of history of Arab medicine at the time, gave the following account: "When Nûr al-Dîn founded the great hospital, he entrusted responsibility for medicine to Abû al-Majd ibn al-Hakan and for this granted him a stipend and revenues. The latter was diligent in caring for the sick there… he would ask about the patients' conditions and examine their cases in the presence of the supervisors and the staff assigned to the care of the ill. The treatment and diet he prescribed for each of them was applied scrupulously and without delay. Once he had finished, he would go up to the citadel to inquire after the condition of the dignitaries who were patients there. Then he would return and sit in the great carpeted *îwan* of the hospital to study. Nûr al-Dîn had collected a large number of medical books and donated them as a *waqf* to this hospital; they were kept in two cupboards in the middle of the *îwan*. There, all the physicians and students gathered around him; medical questions were discussed, and the students learned under his direction. When he had worked, discussed and read for three hours, he would return to his home."

A little further on in the same book, the author informs us that a physician of Damascus, after visiting his patients at the hospital, used to have his students come to his home, where he would ask one of them to read a text aloud while he read a copy of the same work, interrupting the reading to correct errors, explain passages or initiate discussion of certain questions. Towards the end of his days, this physician transformed his house into a school and founded a *waqf* to pay for its maintenance and for the teachers and students. Several physicians from this period wrote abridged versions or résumés with accompanying commentary of older treatises, which helped to make such knowledge more accessible for their students.

In the East, as in the West, the main reference work of the time for medical teaching and knowledge was an encyclopedia compiled by Ibn Sînâ (980-1037), who was known to Westerners as Avicenna. The encyclopedia was called *Canon* — *Qânûn* in Arabic. Under its influence, Muslim medicine reached its peak. Ibn al-Nafîs (d. 1288), a Syrian physician trained at the al-Nûri hospital in Damascus, produced a rigorous commentary of Avicenna. His commentary included a résumé that — according to the tradition of the medieval Eastern medical world — became one of the best-known. Al-Nafîs, however, surpassed his mentor, particularly in his description of the pulmonary circulation of the blood three centuries before it was discovered in Europe.

PHARMACY AND ITS SISTER SCIENCE, BOTANY

On the margins of medicine there developed a literature concerned with medicinal drugs, since these had to be prepared using all sorts of plants. Several physicians were botanists as well. Describing the virtues and properties of local plants, they added their knowledge to that recorded in the *Treatise on Medicine,* a work in five thematic volumes by Dioscorides. This Greek physician of the first century of our era had listed, described and analyzed the substances — derived mostly from plants, but also from animals and minerals — used for preparing medicines in his time. One botanist even had an artist accompany him when he went plant-collecting in the Damascus region so that his botanical treatise might be illustrated with color drawings of the plants and of their different parts at certain stages of growth. Unfortunately, his work did not survive and we only know that it existed because it is mentioned in another book.

It was quite common for medical manuscripts to be illustrated, especially in the case of dictionaries of remedies and treatises on

surgery. Although containers do not often figure in such illustrations, Arab physicians made all kinds of receptacles for use in treating the sick. They include mortars and pestles [**365**], sphero-conical flasks [**370**], pharmaceutical vessels, albarellos [**362**] and cupping glasses.

ASTRONOMY, THE EPITOME OF ARAB SCIENCE

The scientific disciplines that flourished in the Arab world included mathematics, especially geometry, and astronomy, which the Muslim authors called the "science of the aspect of the universe," since its goal was to study the movement of the stars in the sky and provide a geometric representation of them. Interest in these two disciplines was fostered by certain practices in the Islamic religion.

The interior of a pharmacy as represented in a manuscript of *Treatise on Medicine* by Dioscorides. (Metropolitan Museum of Art, New York)

The Muslim calendar is lunar, and the beginning of each month is determined by observing or, preferably, forecasting the first appearance of the crescent moon. Every day of the year, in every place in the Muslim world, the times for prayers are established on the basis of astronomical phenomena, such as sunrise, sunset or shadows cast on the ground during the day. In the thirteenth century, the major mosques began to employ people as *muwaqqit* — professional astronomers whose main task was to decide on times for prayer. Thus, the muezzin of a given mosque could call believers to prayer from the top of his minaret at the right times of the day for that particular location in the Muslim world. As well, throughout the vast Islamic Empire, the faithful were obliged to pray facing in the direction (*qibla*) of the sacred Kaaba in Mecca. The *muwaqqit* was also responsible for determining exactly where this direction lay for the mosque that employed him.

As a result, Muslim astronomers perfected instruments for observing phenomena that could help to resolve the practical problems related to following the rules of the Islamic faith. These included the astrolabe, the quadrant, the sundial and the compass. Almost a thousand of these instruments have survived to this day. The astrolabe [382], which was first invented in Greece, is a two-dimensional representation of the celestial sphere in relation to the horizon at a given location, or, put another way, a flattened celestial globe that can simulate the daily rotation of the heavens for a given location. The spider — the part of the astrolabe corresponding to the heavens — is a grid representing the sky with a projection of the ecliptic; thus, the position of the Sun or a star can be pinpointed. The table, the part of the instrument representing the earth, consists of a plate with projections of the horizon and the meridian at a given geographic latitude, so the plate has to be changed at every latitude. The table is marked with circles that represent altitude above the horizon in intervals of a few degrees as well as circles indicating azimuths, or directions around the horizon. The astrolabe made it possible to simulate the movement of the celestial sphere with respect to an observer. An Arab version of the astrolabe had a table that could be used in any latitude, making it a universal instrument. Similar measurements for only one latitude can be obtained with a quadrant, another Arab invention dating from the eleventh or twelfth century. On one side, it has astrolabic points for a specific latitude and on the other a trigonometric grid on which numerous problems can be solved for any latitude by applying the appropriate trigonometric formula.

The Arabs also made modifications to the sundial, which had originated with the Greeks and Romans. The most common version was horizontal and had marks indicating unequal hours, since the length of a day was divided into 12 hours that represented varying periods of time depending on the season. The Muslims added marks indicating hours of prayers, which were determined according to shadows cast.

However, the Muslim scientists' most important contribution to astronomy and mathematics is the thousands of manuscript texts they wrote on these subjects. So far, some 10 000 texts have been found, which is but a fraction of all the scientific works that were written and copied [375 and 378]. Muslim astronomers soon provided the Islamic faithful with tables, called *Zîj*, which contained information on measuring time during the day and at night based on the Sun and the stars; timekeeping; eclipses; the positions of the Sun, Moon, planets and stars; and even astrology.

These astronomical tables, 200 examples of which have been recorded to date, could comprise thousands of entries — up to 250 000 — giving the time according to the height of the Sun during the day or of a given star at night. Ptolemy's great astronomical treatise, written between AD 127 and AD 141 during his stay at the famous Museum of Alexandria and translated into Arabic at the end of the eighth century under the title of *Almagest*, served as the inspiration for the astronomy manuals produced by the Arab men of science. However, the Arab manuals also made original contributions, including new observations made using Ptolemaic geomet-

ric models that had been modified to take into account the uniform, circular nature of celestial motion. Many of these sophisticated models were developed at Damascus.

Syria can also claim authorship for a great advance in astronomy during the early ninth century, when a rigorously empirical operation was carried out in the desert between Raqqa and Palmyra. A team of astronomers went there to measure the terrestrial distance corresponding to one degree of longitude by traveling along a meridian until the altitude of the noonday sun had changed by one degree. At about this time, as well, an observatory was built at the summit of Jebel Kâsiyûn, the mountain overlooking Damascus, to obtain information that could be used to compile a new series of astronomical tables for the city. The observatory was filled with

Jebel Kâsiyûn in Damascus, which served as an observatory for Muslim scholars.

large astronomical instruments, including a quadrant with a radius of five meters and a gnomon, which was a sort of sundial, measuring five meters in length.

Based on the new information obtained at Damascus, an astronomer named Habash wrote up a table of astronomical observations, the famous *Damascus Zîj*, considered to be remarkably advanced in its presentation of timekeeping, trigonometry, and spherical, solar, lunar and planetary astronomy. In this work, Habash developed a means of calculating eclipses that has been generally attributed to the German astronomer Johannes Kepler at the beginning of the seventeenth century. He also proposed a rigorously mathematical formula for determining the *qibla*, the sacred direction of Mecca, to which the faithful should turn for prayers.

Another astronomer, al-Battâni, became celebrated for a *Zîj* in which he integrated the results of observations he had made at Raqqa between 877 and 918 with a judicious résumé of Ptolemaic astronomy. The importance of this résumé lies in its being one of only two examples known to medieval Europe. It would influence the great European astronomers like Copernicus, Kepler and Galileo. Al-

Battâni also recalculated the angle of the ecliptic in relation to the equator, one of the fundamentals of astronomical calculation. The degree of this angle had not been questioned since it had been worked out by the Greek scholar Eratosthenes in 230 BC.

During the reign of the Ayyubid sultans in the twelfth and thirteenth centuries, a number of astronomers lived in Damascus, but they devoted their time to teaching rather than to writing treatises. In the fourteenth century, under the Mamluks, the Damascus astronomers generally belonged to the team of *muwaqqit* employed at the Umayyad Mosque. In 1371, the chief *muwaqqit*, Ibn al-Shâtir, had a sundial installed on the mosque's principal minaret, where a nineteenth-century replica still can be seen today. This sundial is considered by specialists to be the most sophisticated one to have been developed before the European Renaissance. Ibn al-Shâtir also invented a box of instruments with a special cover that could be used to make calculations based on a whole set of terrestrial latitudes. This tool was furnished with a magnetic needle so that it could be aligned with the points of the compass. He wrote a *Zîj* for Damascus, several copies of which have been preserved, as well as a book entitled *The Final Search for the Rectification of Principles*. In it he proposed solar, lunar and planetary models that represented an improvement on the Ptolemaic models. The mathematics involved are equivalent to those used about 150 years later by Copernicus, with the difference that for Copernicus, the center of the universe was the Sun, whereas for Ibn al-Shâtir, it was the Earth. It must be wondered whether Copernicus was not influenced by the models of the Damascus astronomer.

19th-century copy of the sundial of Ibn al-Shâtir, which was installed in 1371 on the main minaret of the Umayyad Mosque in Damascus.

Astrology, the pseudoscience paired with astronomy

The scientific observation of the stars was at first carried out by Muslim astronomers for religious purposes, but it also led to the growth of astrology. This pseudoscience was treated with respect in the Islamic world and enjoyed great popularity. It was based on the principle that the universe was a whole and that life on Earth was influenced by the movements of the stars, which could thus be deciphered as signs of past or future terrestrial events. Arab astrology benefitted immensely from the great body of information on the stars collected by astronomers. As well, the precision of the astronomers' observations made it possible to predict celestial movements and the position of the stars in the firmament. Certain scholars writing on the subject considered that astrology constituted the theoretical aspect of a scientific discipline, while astronomy represented its practical applications on Earth. In their treatises, physicians relied on astrology to help them choose the best time for carrying out certain medical procedures. However, astrology was strongly criticized by religious leaders and philosophers for its fatalistic determinism.

Chemistry and alchemy, a science and its magical counterpart

Alchemy [379], which was also considered a science at the time, was practiced by the Muslim scholars of the Middle Ages. One of them, called Jaber ben Hayyam and known as Geber in the West, set down the theoretical bases of alchemy in a series of treatises, many of which were consequently translated into Latin and thus were widely read in Europe. Although the ultimate goal was to concoct

An Arab scholar in his laboratory.

elixirs that could correct the composition of impure metals and transform them into gold, a metal that was considered to be pure and perfect, Jaber's method was scientific. He methodically classified all known metals and described the properties of each one. In certain of his writings, for example, he gives the procedures for making steel, preventing iron from rusting, refining metals, dyeing textiles and leather, producing varnishes that waterproof clothing and ceramics, improving glass by the addition of manganese dioxide and obtaining nitric acid through the distillation of vinegar. He also describes chemical transformations such as oxidation, crystallization, sublimation, reduction and the dissolving of substances in liquids.

This form of applied chemistry was further developed by al-Râzî (865-925) — known as Rhazes in the West — the first physician to describe smallpox. He wrote 21 treatises on alchemy and 41 treatises on medicine, constituting a virtual encyclopedia of medicine. In these works, he described the apparatus in his laboratory and the chemical operations he carried out there, eventually leading to the systematic classification of the substances used. By rejecting magical and astrological practices and relying instead on laboratory experimentation, this hugely talented alchemist-physician and tireless researcher lay the groundwork for chemistry as a scientific discipline. The link between alchemy and chemistry is reflected in the etymology of our words for them: both come from the Arab word *al-kîmiyâ*.

Arab advances in other sciences

Many other scientific disciplines benefitted greatly from the contribution of Muslim scholars. The Latin translation of the Arabic work on optics by Ibn al-Haytham (965-1039)

The preparation of an aromatic wine to treat coughs; from an Arabic translation of *Treatise on Medicine* by Dioscorides. (Metropolitan Museum of Art, New York)

(transcribed as Alhazen by the translators) remained in use in Europe until the seventeenth century, so innovative was his achievement. While those preceding him had always assumed that light was dependent on the eye, Ibn al-Haytham constructed a theory of light that was independent of the theory of vision. He proposed the principle of rectilinear propagation, defined what a ray was and argued for the independence of rays in a beam of light. He also formulated the law of reflection and came close to finding one for refraction.

In 860, three brothers wrote the first work on mechanics in the Islamic world, the *Book of Devices*. In it they presented a multitude of inventions, ranging from elevators to a series of the automated toys that the royal courts were so fond of. These Arab "mechanics," also fascinated with time-keeping, developed water clocks that presupposed a good understanding of hydraulics. In a more practical vein, an engineer named Qaysar (d. Damascus, 1251) was employed by the prince of Hama to invent irrigation wheels, called norias, which can still be seen in this city on the Orontes.

Finally, the field of mathematics owes much to Arab scholars. Sometime between 813 and 830, the word "algebra" appeared for the first time in the title of a book. Algebra went on to become an independent branch of mathematics. Arab scholars subsequently applied algebra to other branches of mathematics, profoundly transforming this science.

Research carried out by Muslim scientists also led to inventions that were put to use by craftsmen. The scholars' work thus had technological effects that continue to benefit us today in the fields of ceramics, textiles, materials, dyes, metals, jewelry and damascening.

THE TRANSMISSION OF SCIENTIFIC KNOWLEDGE TO THE WEST

In the preceding sections, it has been seen that the Arab scholars did not content themselves with simply practicing what they learned from the Greek and Latin manuscripts that they had translated into Syriac and then Arabic. They began to make résumés of these texts to understand them better, but also made comments, criticisms and additions based on their own experimentation. After this period of learning, which is normal in any scientific undertaking, a number of Muslim scholars went beyond what their predecessors had done and conducted research that led to original discoveries within the traditional scientific disciplines. It is an unfortunate fact that such scientific works were seldom translated into Latin, the language of science in Europe until the eighteenth century. For example, while a thousand medical texts in Arabic have survived to this day, only about 40 of them were known in Europe. The situation for other disciplines is very similar.

Arab science spread to Europe not so much through contact with the Crusaders who came to the Near East in the eleventh and thirteenth centuries, but rather through the dynasties that ruled over Islamic Spain between the eleventh and fourteenth centuries. These were the Almorávides and later the Almohádes, who established their capital at Cordova. In this period, Spain was full of Arab translations of Greek and Latin scientific manuscripts. These works were studied and commented on by Muslim scholars like the twelfth-century Cordovan philosopher Ibn Rushd (known as Averroes in the West), whose commentaries on Aristotle are unequaled and who wrote treatises on medicine, grammar, law and astronomy. In Toledo, during the twelfth century, there was even a bureau for translating Arab manuscripts into Latin so that they could be sent to the rest of Europe. In 1277, the king of Castille had a Spanish-language compilation made of Arab astronomic works so that Spanish scholars could use them. In the same year, the secrets of glassmaking were transmitted to Venice in accordance with the provisions of a treaty between the prince of Antioch and the Doge. From that time on, there were innumerable transfers of technological knowledge.

It should also be recalled here that the technique for making paper, which had been learned by the Arabs from the Chinese in 751, had made it possible for a true market for books to develop in the Islamic world, and this had naturally encouraged the dissemination of scientific knowledge. This enormously important technique was transmitted to the West beginning in the twelfth century through the Emirate of Cordova. Paper-making then spread to Italy, or more precisely, Fabriano, where, in 1276, the first European factory for producing paper is thought to have been established. Other factories followed, especially at Troyes, France, in 1348 and at Nuremburg, Germany, in 1390. The material support for writing that had been transmitted by the Arabs facilitated the spread of ideas in Europe. Paper also led to a new invention — printing — around 1450. The printing press gave crucial impetus to the diffusion of knowledge, which has become the defining characteristic of our scientific world today.

357
Statuette
Limestone
Roman era

This statuette represents a doctor treating a patient by sucking out some substance — probably venom — from his arm.

UNKNOWN   36 x 24 x 11 cm
NATIONAL MUSEUM, DAMASCUS   23999

358 a-g
Surgical instruments
Bronze
AD 100

Here is a collection of some of the surgical instruments used in the Roman era: scalpels with spear-shaped blades, hooks, spatulas, cauterizing irons and probes. Thanks to a book called *Dearte medica,* written by Celsus, a first-century Roman doctor who has been called the Cicero of medicine, we have full descriptions of surgical operations along with explanations of the medical instruments used for them. Although this work is our best-written source of information on ancient surgical instruments, the descriptions given by Celsus tend to be fairly brief and vague, and they cannot be used to identify the specific purpose of every such instrument found. Archaeological sites dating from this time yield great quantities of these objects.

SOUTHERN SYRIA
NATIONAL MUSEUM, DAMASCUS
7265, 7263, 9499, 13965, 9498, 12722 and 10337

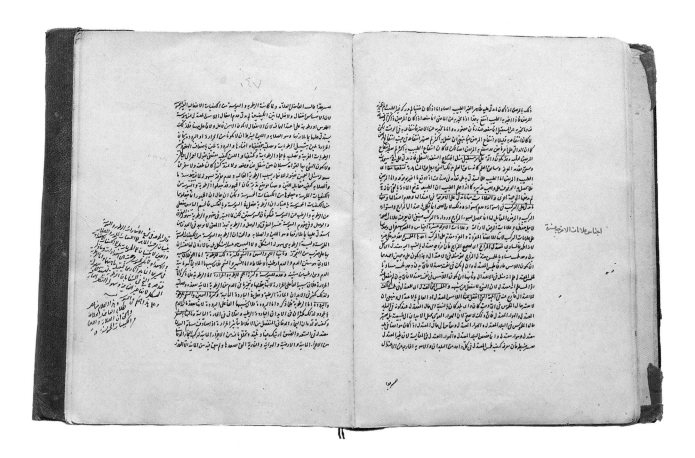

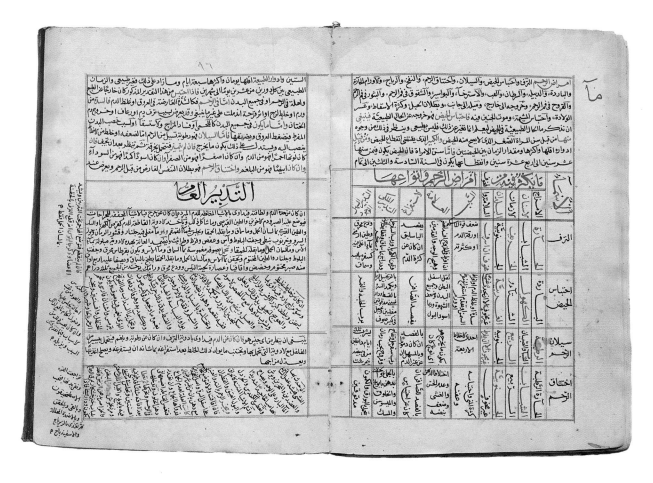

359

*Manuscript of Nafis Ibn 'Iwad Al-Kirmani:
Sharh mûjiz al-qanun aw sharh al-mûjiz fi
al-thibb (Commentary on an abridged
version of Avicenna's Canon)*

Paper, 338 ff.

AD 1438 (original), AD 1483 (copy)

We know very little about the author of this manuscript
except that he died in 1438 and was a personal physician
to the great sultan Ulug Beg (d.1449) in Samarkand. It
was very common for Arab doctors to write "commentaries," or analytical studies, on major works that were considered to be fundamental in their scientific discipline.
This commentary, written by an obscure doctor, thus deals
with the work of an important author. The work was the
Qânûn — known in the West as the *Canon of Medicine*
— written by Ibn Sînâ, whose Westernized name is Avicenna (980-1037). This book represented the sum of
medical knowledge at the time.

The manuscript shown here was copied in 1483 and was
discovered in the Al-Ahmadiya school founded at Aleppo
in 1750 by Ahmad Taha Zada, also called Al-Halaby
(d.1764).

ALEPPO, AL-AHMADIYA LIBRARY   25 x 17.5 cm
HAFEZ AL-ASSAD NATIONAL LIBRARY   14577

360

*Manuscript of Ibn Jazlah: Taqwîm al-abdân fi
tadbir al-insan (Diagnosis and treatment of
diseases)*

Paper, 98 ff.

AD 1577 (985 A.H.)

This author, a native of Baghdad, was a leader in the field
of medicine in his time and wrote a number of works for
an Abbasid caliph. Apart from the treatise represented
here by a manuscript copy made in 1577, the author
wrote a whole epistle on the benefits of sugar — the extract of sugar cane — which was considered by Arab doctors to have curative powers. Apothecaries used sugar in
the preparation of syrups, pastes and powders to be administered to the sick.

It should be noted that the manuscript's text is presented
in the form of tables. The tables classify various illnesses,
along with their particularities and treatments. Muslim
doctors favored this format because their goal was not to
display originality in their texts, but rather to find the
clearest possible way of transmitting the medical teach-
ings found in the writings of their predecessors.

ALEPPO, AL-AHMADIYA LIBRARY   26.5 x 18.5 cm
HAFEZ AL-ASSAD NATIONAL LIBRARY   14579

361

Manuscript: medical works

Paper, 408 ff.

Fourteenth century (first two books) and sixteenth century
(third book)

Al-Hamathami (first), Najibe al-Dîn al-Samarcandi (second), Abi al-Hassa al-Maukhtar Ibn Abdoun (third)

This manuscript, which comprises three medical works, is
noteworthy because it presents a number of very explicit
anatomical illustrations. The first book deals with patholo-
gy and has a section for every organ in the human body.
The second book describes medicines according to the
diseases that can attack various human organs. The third
book classifies food into different categories.

It was common for Arab manuscripts on medicine to be illustrated as this one is. The artists who did this type of illustration did not seek to reproduce reality in every detail,
but rather tried to provide a schematic representation that
could be used as a visual support by those learning lists of
descriptive and specialized terms. The real purpose of the
illustrations was therefore a didactic one.

UNKNOWN   20 x 10 x 3 cm
NATIONAL MUSEUM, DAMASCUS   13581 A

362
Albarello
Ceramic
AD 1300

This type of vessel, known as an albarello, was used to carry spices and pharmaceutical products. It was made in Syria during the twelfth and thirteenth centuries, and was considered to be a specialty of Damascus potters. Probate inventories drawn up in Italy, Spain and France during the fourteenth and fifteenth centuries reflect the popularity of these Damascus vases, which reached Europe through the Mediterranean spice trade. Syria was very involved in this trade, and the merchants of Damascus controlled a great part of it. The vessel shown here would have been reproduced in great quantities and therefore was decorated simply with dark colors and overglazing. It gives no indication of what it might have contained; other albarellos bear poetic inscriptions that suggest they may have held aphrodisiac products. The finest examples of these vessels were made in Raqqa during the Ayyubid period (twelfth to thirteenth centuries).

UNKNOWN   26.5 x 6.9
NATIONAL MUSEUM, ALEPPO   S 163
BAAL 364

363
Sprinkler
Blue blown glass
AD 1200

This type of flask, characterized by a globular body and a long, slender neck tapering towards the opening, was used to sprinkle perfumed water on the hands and faces of guests. The gesture was not only a mark of welcome and hospitality, but also a means of driving evil spirits out of the house being visited. The most popular perfumed water used in Syria was rosewater; Damascus was such a famous center of rosewater production that the rose became the city's emblem. Because of its anti-inflammatory and astringent properties, rosewater was also used as a medication in treating diseases of the eye. Even today, rosewater is associated with hospitality and the expression of a certain social status.

UNKNOWN   19.1 x 11 cm
NATIONAL MUSEUM, DAMASCUS   3978 A
MTC 119

364
Spice dispenser
Ceramic
AD 1200

This dish with seven little hollows was used to keep the spices that Muslims loved to cook their food with, not only to enhance its flavor but to comply with the medical advice given by doctors. The doctor al-Râzî (865-925), known as Rhazes to his Latin translators, wrote a treatise entitled *Corrective for Foods*, in which he claims that condiments and spices should be used to counteract the harmful effects of certain foods. Spices were included in medical treatises along with herbal remedies and, naturally enough, in recipe books, which in the Islamic world give the dietary advice of doctors. Trade in spices, brought from the Far East by caravans passing through Syria, was controlled by Damascus.

UNKNOWN   37 x 12 cm
NATIONAL MUSEUM, ALEPPO   S 434
L'EUFRATE 445; Cf. *MTC* 133

365 a-b
Mortar and pestle
Four-metal alloy
AD 900

When preparing medicines, Arab doctors often had to crush solid substances into powder so that they could be added to other ingredients. To do this, the doctors generally used pestles made of various materials such as stone, wood, ivory and glass. But the best-preserved pestles are those made of a metal alloy containing copper, zinc and lead, along with a bit of tin. Only a small quantity (two to three percent) of this metal was used, since it was very rare and expensive. Lead, on the other hand, was cheap and therefore constituted a high proportion of the alloy used to cast heavy mortars like this thick-walled one. However, lead made the alloy less hard and could even be toxic when the mortar was employed to prepare syrups containing the juice of fruits such as apples and pomegranates.

RUSAFA, ANCIENT SERGIOPOLIS   25 x 6.8 cm/14.5 x 11 cm
NATIONAL MUSEUM, DAMASCUS   13269 A   *MTC* 44

366
Flask
Blown glass
AD 1300

Pharmacists commonly used little glass flasks like this one for their patients' medicine. Although glass is a fragile material, it is resistant to most chemical products, does not retain odors and is easy to clean. The long neck made it possible to pour out small quantities of the liquid contained in the belly of the flask.

UNKNOWN   4.2 x 2.7 cm
NATIONAL MUSEUM, DAMASCUS   665/2506 A
Cf. MTC 58

367
Beaker
Blown glass
AD 1300

This tiny receptacle may have been used to mix pharmaceutical products in very small quantities.

UNKNOWN   5 x 2.2 cm
NATIONAL MUSEUM, DAMASCUS   667/2517 A

368
Goblet
Blown glass
AD 1300

This deep container may have been used as a cucurbit in the distillation process. It would have supported the head of a still that could have produced distilled products like rosewater. A liquid was placed in the cucurbit and heated until it boiled; vapor rising from the boiling liquid collected in the still head on top. As it cooled, the vapor condensed into a distilled liquid that trickled down a tube-shaped spout into a flask. This was the method used in the Muslim world to produce perfumed essences from aromatic plants.

UNKNOWN   7 x 7 cm
NATIONAL MUSEUM, DAMASCUS   13479 A   *Cf. STM* 13

369
Beaker
Blown glass
AD 900

This small glass receptacle might be considered the ancestor of the petri dish used in modern laboratories, for it served a similar purpose in pharmacists' dispensaries. It was used when liquid or pasty substances had to be mixed in the preparation of medicines.

RAQQA   8.4 x 3.6 cm
NATIONAL MUSEUM, DAMASCUS   16880 A   *MTC* 62

370 a-c
Sphero-conical flasks
Ceramic
AD 1300

These rather odd-shaped vessels, found throughout the Islamic world from the tenth to thirteenth centuries, have been interpreted in any number of ways. At first they were believed to be incendiary grenades; researchers went on to describe them variously as containers for mercury, beer bottles, perfume flasks, bottles for water pipes (hookahs) and ventilators, which when placed on the embers of a fire would project a spray of vapor to accelerate combustion. The most recent and plausible theory is that these vessels were used in chemistry or alchemy for operations like distillation. They could have served as cucurbits or even vessels for collecting distilled liquids.

UNKNOWN   12.5 x 11 cm / 13 x 9.5 cm / 12 x 8.5 cm
NATIONAL MUSEUM, DAMASCUS   1146, 842, 4451 A
MTC p. 138; *STM* p. 324-332;
MEDELHAVSMUSEET BULLETIN 30 (1997) p. 55-72

371
Still
Glass
Islamic era

This is another type of still used to collect vapors during the distillation process. The vapor would have condensed in the tubular side spout.

UNKNOWN   17 x 3.8 cm
NATIONAL MUSEUM, DAMASCUS   15979 A

372
Retort
Glass
Islamic era

In chemistry, the term "retort" designates an instrument used for distillation. It was developed by Muslim scholars, who called it "the curved and twisted apparatus," according to a bilingual Syriac and Arabic inscription discovered in a sixteenth-century manuscript. This instrument represented an innovation, because it combined in one vessel both the cucurbit, in which liquids to be distilled were heated, and the still, in which vapor was collected. Like the older system, the retort still had a side spout through which the distilled liquid dripped into a receptacle, but this tube was made longer so that the vapor was better exposed to the cooling effect of air and thus produced more distilled liquid. The fragment shown here is just the tubular part of the retort.

UNKNOWN   21 x 4.2 cm
NATIONAL MUSEUM, DAMASCUS   10418 / 2488 A

373
Jar with cover
Ceramic
AD 1200

It is rare to find jars that still have their covers as this one does. This type of vessel was used by pharmacists to keep liquid or semiliquid medical preparations from being altered by factors like light, heat or humidity. Since it is made of baked clay, the vessel is opaque and its interior remains cool. To make the vessel watertight, the surface was coated with a translucid glaze to which a lead flux had been added. If this glaze cracked, a certain amount of lead might leach into the contents of the vessel and make them toxic. Pharmacists' shops were visited by inspectors, and pharmacopoeial manuals advised that jars should be rinsed daily and replaced as soon as the slightest anomaly was noticed.

RAQQA   22.3 x 18 cm
NATIONAL MUSEUM, DAMASCUS   6789 / 15032 A   *MTC* 77

374
Flask
Blown glass
AD 1300

The short, narrow neck and splayed rim of this vessel suggest that it could have been used to pour out small quantities of some pharmaceutical product or perfumed liquid from the globe-like body.

UNKNOWN   12 x 10.5 cm
NATIONAL MUSEUM, DAMASCUS   2776 A

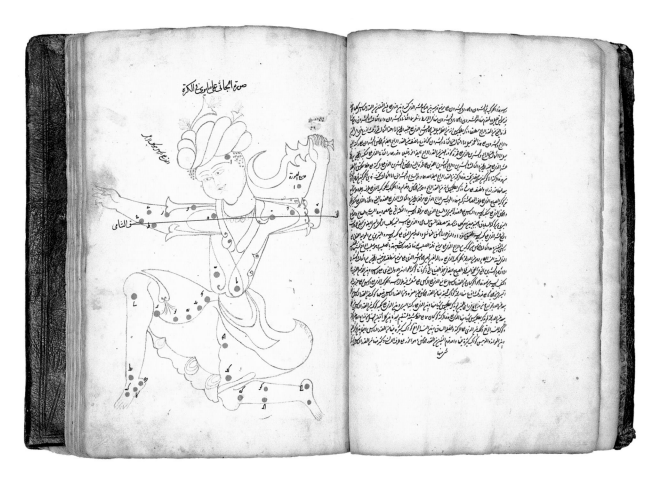

375

Manuscript of Abîr al-Hassayn : Kitab as Suwar (Manual of astronomy)

Paper, 266 ff.

AD 960 (original), AD 1663 (copy)

The title of this manuscript designates it as a manual of astronomy. Muslim scientists excelled in the production of

this type of scholarly work: over 10 000 Arabic manuscripts on astronomy and mathematics have been recorded to date. The two disciplines were considered sister sciences in the Islamic world, for Muslim scholars classified astronomy, or " the science of the aspect of the universe, " as a branch of mathematics. The goal of astronomy was to study the visible movements of the stars and provide them with a geometric representation. The

Muslim scholars' interest in astronomy arose from the fact that the practice of their religion required that certain activities, such as the five daily canonical prayers and various ceremonies, be carried out at precisely the right time.

UNKNOWN   27 x 17 x 3.5 cm
NATIONAL MUSEUM, DAMASCUS   7389 A

376

Manuscript of 'Imâd al-Mashhadî: Sharh Ashkâl al-Ta'sîs (Commentary on Ashkâl al-Ta'sîs)

Paper, 202 ff.

AD 1203 (original), unknown (copy)

This manuscript is actually a collection of seven works written by different authors and transcribed by various copyists. It is shown here opened at the fifth book, which is a commentary on another work, Ashkâl al-Ta'sîs, a compendium of geometry modeled on Euclid's Elements and written in about 1203-1204 (A.H. 600). The Arabic translation of this book by Euclid, the Greek mathematician who founded the school of mathematics at Alexandria in the third century BC, inspired the Arab scholar al-Khwârizmi to write his book of algebra, Kitâb al-jabr, which came out in Baghdad between 813 and 830. Algebra was one of the great inventions of Arab mathematicians.

DAMASCUS, AL-ZAHIRA LIBRARY   19.5 x 15 cm
HAFEZ AL-ASSAD NATIONAL LIBRARY   5428

THE TRANSMISSION OF A SCIENTIFIC HERITAGE TO THE WEST

377
Manuscript of al-Kâtî: Shark Isâghûdjî
(Commentary on Isâghûdjî)
Paper, 34 ff.
Unknown

The author, Husâm al-Dîn Hasan al-Kâtî, who died in 1359 (A.H. 760), wrote this commentary on a famous book on logic called *Isâghûdjî*. This book was an adaptation of another book entitled *Isagoge*, which was an introduction to the *Categories of Aristotle* and had been written by Porphyry (234-305). The latter was a Neoplatonic philosopher of Syrian origin who lived mostly in Rome and published commentaries on Aristotle and Plato. It is known that the Arab philosophers were familiar with the works of several Greek philosophers, since some of these works were translated into Arabic at a very early date. The great translator, Sergius de Ras al-'Ayn (d. 536) even produced a Syriac version of Aristotle's treatises on logic before the beginning of the Islamic Empire.

ALEPPO   19 x 12 cm
HAFEZ AL-ASSAD NATIONAL LIBRARY   16535

378
Manuscript of Ibn al-Shâtir : al-Zîj al-jadîd
(New astronomical tables)
Paper, 183 ff.
Unknown

Ibn al-Shâtir (1305/6-1375) was the most famous Arab astronomer to have lived in Syria. From 1360 to 1375, he occupied the prestigious position of chief *muwaqqit* at the Umayyad Mosque. His task was to fix the exact times for the five daily prayers, based on his observations of the movements of the Sun, Moon and stars. He also had to determine the direction of Mecca — the *qibla* — and adjust the Muslim calendar, which was lunar rather than solar. In 1371, he set up a great sundial on the principal minaret of the mosque; it remained in use until the nineteenth century. His most important contribution was his theory of the movements of the planets, which argued against the Ptolemaic system and anticipated the theory of Copernicus.

He also calculated tables, called Zîj, for the Damascus region. These tables enabled one to determine what time it was by observing the height of the Sun during the day and the position of a given star at night.

DAMASCUS, AL-ZAHIRA LIBRARY   23.5 x 15.5 cm
HAFEZ AL-HASSAD NATIONAL LIBRARY   3093

379

Manuscript of al-Jildaki: Nihâyat al-Talab fi shark al-muktasab fi zîrâ'at al-dhahab al-Sîmâwî
(Commentary on Attainments in the production of gold by al-Sîmâwî)

Paper, 213 ff.

AD 1341 (original), AD 1515 (copy)

This manuscript is a copy of a commentary written in 1341 by al-Jildaki, who was a doctor and chemist. The commentary deals with a work on alchemy that had been composed early by a certain al-Sîmâwî and was entitled *Attainments in the Production of Gold*. As the title makes clear, the book reports on the state of knowledge at the time concerning ways of producing gold by transforming other metals. Alchemy was very popular among Arab scholars. Many books were written to describe the elixirs that could rectify the impurities of an ordinary metal and reestablish the balance between its components so that it would turn into the noblest of metals — gold.

DAMASCUS, AL-ZAHIRIA LIBRARY   22.5 x 17.5 cm
HAFEZ AL-ASSAD NATIONAL LIBRARY   3924

380
Triangular stand
Ceramic
AD 1300

No one is exactly sure what purpose was served by this type of triangular stand made of clay slabs that have been stuck together and then covered with a turquoise glaze. The fact that it is supported by legs suggests that it is an imitation of a piece of furniture made of wood. A copy of a manuscript by the first-century Greek doctor, Dioscorides, shows physicians mixing potions in jars placed in openings on top of a stand that resembles this object. According to another explanation, the three circular openings were intended to hold the pens used by manuscript copyists. These writing instruments were made of small lengths of reed that were hollowed out and cut diagonally at one end, which could then be dipped into ink. An inkwell like in **381** would have been set in one of the pen-holder's openings.

UNKNOWN   29 x 20.5 cm
NATIONAL MUSEUM, ALEPPO   S 165

381
Inkwell
Faience
AD 1300

The black ink used by those who copied Arabic manuscripts was made with mixture of soot and water to which acacia resin, known as gum arabic, was added to keep the texts from fading. Red ink was obtained by adding powdered ochre.
Given the ring-like base of the inkwell and the absence of a lustrous coating on its surface, it seems likely that this object was placed in a stand like the one shown in **380.** The base could have been set into one of the circular openings to keep the inkwell from moving. The stand might have held another similar pot, but this one would have contained water to dilute the ink from time to time throughout the long hours of copying.

DAMASCUS   10.5 x 10 cm
NATIONAL MUSEUM, DAMASCUS   2730 A

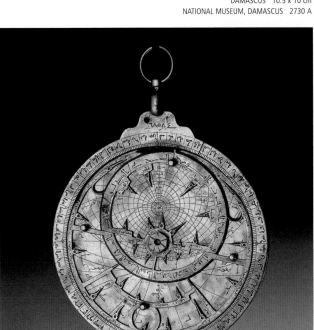

382
Astrolabe
Four-metal alloy: copper, zinc, lead and tin
AD 1500

The astrolabe is the observation instrument that best represents Arab astronomy. The oldest known astrolabes come from the Islamic world, dating back to the ninth century. Over 1200 examples have survived. The astrolabe was used to determine the direction of Mecca. The instrument consists of a circular plate with a raised graduated ring fixed to its circumference. The surface of the plate is incised with lines representing azimuths and altitudes in relation to the location of the observer. Set above the plate is a set of revolving rings with small pointers around the edges to indicate the direction of the major stars, whose names are inscribed on the rings themselves. The arc of a circle in the lower part represents the equator. The straight bar going across the middle indicates the Sun's elliptic and turns around a point representing the North Star.
On the other side of the astrolabe, the surface is divided into four concentric circles inscribed with the months of the years, a graduated scale marked by letters and lines, the signs of the zodiac and, on the outermost circle, a moveable graduated scale marked with Arabic letters and lines. Instructions written on the central part tell the user how to hold the astrolabe.

UNKNOWN   15.3 x 2.5 cm
NATIONAL MUSEUM, DAMASCUS   6858 A   *Cf. SMC* 331

383
Spout for a fountain
Bronze
AD 1200

Throughout its existence, the Islamic Empire maintained commercial relations with the Far East and especially with China. It is therefore not surprising that this fountain spout is shaped like a dragon, which is a very popular theme in Chinese art. Water flowed from the wide opening that doubles as the creature's mouth. The rest of the dragon's features are represented in a very stylized manner and its neck is covered with decorative motifs. The fountain this piece belonged to stood in the famous school — or madrasa — of Damascus.

DAMASCUS: AL-MADRASA AL-KHAYDARIYYAH 46 x 18 cm
NATIONAL MUSEUM, DAMASCUS 1266 / 4245 A
SMC 321; *MUSÉE NATIONAL* p. 261

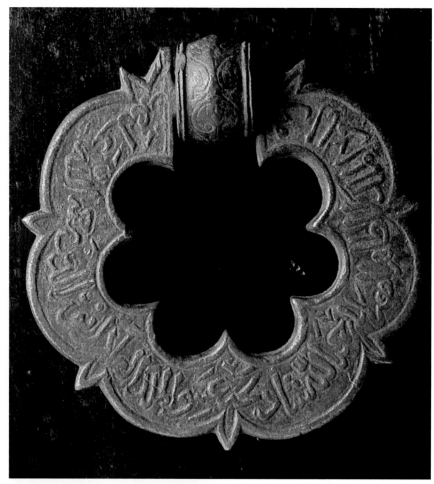

385
Door knocker
Bronze
AD 1200

The inscription that stands out in relief on the multifoiled, hinged ring of this knocker informs us that it was made " in the days of al-Malik al-Zâhir desirous of God's mercy Shad Bakht privileged by al-Malik al-'Adil Nûr al-Dîn may the mercy of God be upon them. " Jamâl al-Dîn Shad Bakht al-Hindî al-Atabibî was the governor of Aleppo during the reign of Nûr al-Dîn Mahmûd, and in 1193 he had a Koranic school, associated with the mosque, built in the city. The school, formerly known as Al-Shadhabakhtiyya, still exists today under the name of Jâmi' al-Shaykh Ma'rûf.

ALEPPO: AL-MADRASA AL-SHADHABAKHTIYYA 15.5 cm
NATIONAL MUSEUM, DAMASCUS 2798 A
SMC 322; *MUSÉE NATIONAL* p. 261

384
Plumb line
Lead
AD 1300

The plumb line is normally associated with construction, since it is used to determine whether or not a wall is perpendicular. This one is inscribed with the name of a master mason named Muhammad bin Amran al-Moalan. The instrument was also used in the Islamic world by surveyors when they needed a straight vertical line for surveying hilly terrain. Plumb lines were used as well by astronomers, who held them up to obtain a vertical reference for the calculation of angles measured with instruments of astronomical observation. The decorative surface of this plumb line suggests that it was not an ordinary instrument; it must have had a function that was not only utilitarian but also highly esteemed.

DAMASCUS 13.5 x 7.5 cm
NATIONAL MUSEUM, DAMASCUS 3654 A

THE TRANSMISSION OF A SCIENTIFIC HERITAGE TO THE WEST

EPILOGUE

At the dawn of a new millennium, according to the Western calendar in universal use today, it is only fitting that we in the West should stop and reflect — to look back on the ancient Eastern world and try to understand it as a part of cultural history. Although some may consider such an attempt to be a form of cultural egocentricity, there is surely great merit in recognizing the innumerable contributions that have benefited our Western world in its relatively short history and the cultural debt it owes to the civilizations that have preceded it.

PHOTOGRAPH AND ILLUSTRATION CREDITS

All of the **photographs** of the objects were taken by Jacques Lessard, the photographer at the Musée de la civilization, with the exception of those provided by the following:

Mohamad Al-Roumi: 22, 24, 28, 36-37, 66 (top), 67, 72, 82, 85, 128-129, 132, 137 (top), 138-139, 140 (top), 141-142, 151, 154 (top), 159, 162 (top), 232-233, 249-250, 255-257, 265 (bottom), 308-309, 314, 315 (bottom), 315 (top), 319-320, 337;
Ali Al-Souki, *Dura Europos. Al-Salhieh.* Damascus, 1990, p. 54 and 56: 253 and 254 (top);
Patricia Anderson: 135;
Bibliothèque nationale de France: 173;
Michel Fortin: 33 (top), 35 (top), 134, 144;
Klaus Freyberger: 248;
Georg Gerster: 30-31, 33 (bottom), 34, 51, 55, 60, 62-65, 68, 70, 73, 75, 77, 79, 81, 83-84, 86, 161, 163, 164 (top), 247, 252;
Hassan Hatoum: 78;

Kay Kohlmeyer: 68 (bottom);
Jean-Marie Le Tensorer: 146;
Jean-Claude Margueron: 245 (bottom);
Metropolitan Museum of Art: 317, 322;
Miguel Molist: 238;
MTC, p. 44: 313; p. 49: 321;
Sultan Muhesen: 42 and 259;
Joan and David Oates: 152 (top);
Alain Saint-Hilaire: 87, 158 (top), 171;
Danielle Stordeur: 47;
François Tremblay: 165, 167, 260, 264.

The **drawings** were provided by:

W. Andrae, *Das wiedererstandene Assur.* Leipzig, 1938, p. 74: 244 (top);
Baal. p. 109: 57; p. 202: 66;
Catherine Breniquet, in H. Gasche and B. Hrouda, eds, *Collectanea Orientalia. Histoire, arts de l'espace et industries de la terre. Études offertes en hommage à Agnès Spycket.* Neuchâtel-Paris, Recherches et Publications, 1996, p. 51: 29; *Orient-Express* 1998/2, p. 43: 137;
Giorgio Buccellati: 170;
Olivier Callot: 61 and 243;
J.-M. Dentzer and W. Orthmann, eds, *Archéologie et histoire de la Syrie II : La Syrie de l'époque achéménide à l'avènement de l'Islam.* Saarbrücker, Saarbrücker Druckerei und Verlag, 1989, p. 341: 246 (bottom); p. 343: 247 (top); p. 454: 261;
Ebla p. 391: 246 (top); p. 107: 54;
L'Écriture pp. 65-67: 169;
ESEA, p. 45: 13; p. 132: 140; p. 53: 158;
Eric Guerrier, after a sketch by Jean-Marie Le Tensorer: 45;
Michael C.A.Macdonald, *Arabian Archaeology and Epigraphy* 1:1 (1990), p. 24: 162;
Jean-Claude Margueron: 157;
Miguel Molist: 238;

Andrew Moore, *Abu Hureyra*, New York, Oxford University Press (On the press): 46;
P.R.S. Moorey, *Ancient Mesopotamian Materials and Industries. The Archaeological Evidence.* Oxford, Clarendon Press, 1994, p. 145: 148 and p. 204: 153;
MTC, p. 24: 312;
André Parrot, *Assur.* Paris, Gallimard, 1969, p. 103: 69;
Peter Schmid, Museum der Anthropologie, Zurich: 44;
Andreas Schmidt-Colinet, in J.-M. Dentzer and W. Orthmann, eds, *Archéologie et histoire de la Syrie II : La Syrie de l'époque achéménide à l'avènement de l'Islam,.* Saarbrücker, Saarbrücker Druckerei und Verlag, 1989, fig. 144: 261;
Tetsu Tsukamoto and Yusuke Yoshino, in *Excavation of a Sunken Ship Found Off the Syrian Coast. An Interim Report.* s pl. 5: 164.

The **maps** were prepared by the firm Korem: 25, 32, 48 (after Michael Roaf, *Cultural Atlas of Mesopotamia and the Ancient Near East.* New York, Facts on File, 1990, p. 24-25), 52, 59, 74, 155 (after Michael Roaf, *Cultural Atlas of Mesopotamia and the Ancient Near East.* New York, Facts on File, 1990, p. 35).

ABBREVIATIONS USED IN THE CATALOGUE

Journals

AAAS	*Les annales archéologiques arabes syriennes. Revue d'archéologie et d'histoire.*
AJA	*The American Journal of Archaeology.*
CAJ	*The Cambridge Journal of Archaeology.*
DAM	*Damaszener Mitteilungen.*
IRAQ	*Iraq. Journal of the British School of Archeology in Iraq.*
MDOG	*Mitteilungen der Deutschen Orient-Gesellschaft zu Berlin.*
MEDELHAVSMUSEET	*Museum of Mediterranean and Near Eastern Antiquities Medelhavsmuseet Bulletin.*
PALÉORIENT	*Paléorient. Revue pluridisciplinaire de préhistoire et protohistoire de l'Asie du sud-ouest.*
SEMITICA	*Semitica. Cahiers publiés par l'Institut d'études sémitiques du Collège de France.*
SYRIA	*Syria. Revue d'art oriental et d'archéologie publiée par l'Institut français d'archéologie du Proche-Orient.*

Exhibition and Museum Catalogues

ANTIQUITÉS GRÉCO-ROMAINES
ABDUL-HAK, S. et A. ABDUL-HAK. *Catalogue illustré du département des antiquités gréco-romaines au Musée de Damas.* Damascus: Publications of the Directorate-General of Antiquities, Syria, 1951, 179 pp.

BAAL
AMIET, P. *et al. Au pays de Baal et d'Astarté.* Paris: Musée du Petit Palais, 1984, 320pp.

EBLA
MATTHIAE, P. (ed.) *Ebla. Alle origini della civiltà urbana.* Milan: Electa, 1995, 542 pp.

ED
WEISS, H. (ed.) *Ebla to Damascus. Art and Archaeology of Ancient Syria.* Washington: Smithsonian Institution, 1985, 542 pp.

ESEA
Exposition syro-européenne d'archéologie. Miroir d'un partenariat. Damascus: Éditions de l'Institut français d'Études arabes de Damas, 1996, 212 pp.

L'ÉCRITURE
TALON, Ph. and K. Van LERBERGHE (eds). *En Syrie aux origines de l'écriture.* Turnhout: Brepols, 1997, 301 pp.

LE DJEBEL AL-'ARAB
DENTZER, J.-M. and J. DENTZER-FEYDY (eds). *Le djebel al-'Arab. Histoire et patrimoine au musée de Suweida.* Paris: Éditions Recherche sur les civilisations, 1991, 193 pp.

L'EUFRATE
ROUAULT, O. and M.G. MASETTI-ROUAULT. *L'Eufrate e il tempo. Le civiltà del medio Eufrate e della Gezira siriana.* Milan: Electa, 1993, 485 pp.

MTC
La médecine au temps des califes. Paris: Institut du monde arabe, 1996, 329 pp.

MUSÉE NATIONAL
AL-'USH, Abu-al-Faraj, JOUNDI, A. and B. ZOUHDI. *Catalogue du Musée national de Damas.* Damascus: Directorate-General of Antiquities and Museums, 1976, 283 pp.

SCEAUX-CYLINDRES DE SYRIE
HOMES-FREDERICQ, D. *et al. Sceaux-cylindres de Syrie.* Brussels: Musées royaux d'art et d'histoire, 1981.

SMC
CLUZAN, S. *et al.* (eds). *Syrie. Mémoire et civilisation.* Paris: Flammarion-Institut du monde arabe, 1993, 487 pp.

STM
MADDISON, F. and E. SAVAGE-SMITH. *Science, Tools & Magic.* London-Oxford: Azimuth Editions-Oxford University Press, 1997.

SYRIEN
RUPRECHTSBERGER, E.M. (ed). *Syrien. Von den Aposteln zu den Kalifen.* Mayence: Verlag Philipp von Zabern, 1993, 520 pp.

Specialized works

AIN DARA
ABU ASSAF, A. Der tempel von Ain Dara. Mainz: Philipp von Zabern, 1990.

BOUQRAS
ROODENBERG, J.J. *Le mobilier en pierre de Bouqras. Utilisation de la pierre dans un site néolithique sur le Moyen-Euphrate (Syrie)*. Istanbul: Nederlands Historisch-Archaeologisch Instituut te Istanbul, 1986, 207 pp.

EXCAVATIONS AT TELL BRAK 1
OATES, J. and D. and H. McDonald. *Excavations at Tell Brak 1*, McDonald Institute for Archaeological Research, 1997, 296 pp.

FESTSCHRIFT STROMMENGER
HROUDA, B. *et al.* (eds). *Von Uruk nach Tuttul. Eine Festschrift für Eva Strommenger. Studien und Aufsätze von Kollegen und Freunden.* Munich-Vienna: Profil Verlag GmbH, 1992, 206 pp. and 85 Pl.

FIGURINES ANTHROPOMORPHES
BADRE, L. *Les figurines anthropomorphes en terre cuite de l'âge du Bronze en Syrie.* Paris: Geuthner, 1980, 439 pp. and 67 Pl.

HAMA IV:2
RIIS, P.J. and V.H. POULSEN. *La ville islamique de Hama. Les verreries et poteries médiévales.* Copenhagen: The National Museum of Denmark-Nationalmuseet, 1957.

PALMYRE VII
SADURSKA, A. *Palmyre VII : Le tombeau de famille de 'Alainê.* Warsaw: Éditions scientifiques de Pologne, 1977.

SCULPTURES FUNÉRAIRES
SADURSKA, A. and A. BOUNNI. *Les sculptures funéraires de Palmyre.* Rome: Giorgio Bretschneider Editore, 1994.

SCULPTURES OF PALMYRA I
TANABE, K. (ed.). *Sculptures of Palmyra I.* Tokyo: The Ancient Orient Museum, 1986.

TOMBS A AND C
HIGUCHI, T. and T. IZUMI. *Tomb A and C Southeast Necropolis Palmyra Syria.* Nara: Research Center for Silk Roadology, 1994, 169 pp. and 74 Pl.

UGARITICA II
S.F.A. SCHAEFFER, *Ugaritica II. Nouvelles études relatives aux découvertes de Ras Shamsa, 1949.*

CHRONOLOGICAL INDEX OF OBJECTS

Era	Name of the object	Material	Catalogue No.
Paleolithic (1 million BC – 12 000 BC)			
1 million BC	Hand ax	Flint	129
500 000 BC	Hand ax	Flint	2
400 000 BC	Biface	Flint	128
100 000 BC	Scraper	Flint	131
	Blade	Flint	133
40 000 BC	Blade	Flint	130
Neolithic (12 000 BC – 6000 BC)			
9000 BC	Figurine	Stone	6
	Bowl	Chlorite	142
	Decorated grooved stone	Basalt	259
	Palette	Basalt	260
	Palette	Basalt	261
8500 BC	Adze	Flint	132
8000 BC	Female figurine	Calcite	262
	Female figurine	Fire-hardened clay	263
7000 BC	Arrowhead	Flint	102
	Aurochs horn	Horn	104
	Vessel in the shape of a hare	Alabaster	105
	Vessel in the shape of a hedgehog	Alabaster	106
	Gazelle figurine	Bone	108
	Saddle quern and rubbing stone	Basalt and limestone	121
	Core	Obsidian	134
	Blade	Obsidian	135
	Blade	Obsidian	136
	Adge		137
	Ax		138
	Vessel	Polished stone	139
	Vessel	Polished stone	140
	Vessel	Polished stone	141
	Figure	Bone	146
	Ornament	Bone and turquoise	147
	Awl	Bone and bitumen	148
	Female figurine	Terra cotta	151
	Model of a house (modern reconstitution)	Plaster	5
Chiefdoms (6000 BC – 3000 BC)			
6000 BC	Figurine	Clay	3
	Fragment of a skull	Bone and plaster	4 a
	Fragment of a jaw	Bone and plaster	4 b
5800 BC	Head of a small rodent	Alabaster	114
	Basketry imprints	Gypsum plaster	152
	Dish	Gypsum plaster	153

5800 BC	Fragment of a vessel	Ceramic	154
	Fragment of a vessel	Ceramic	155
	Seal	Stone	226
5500 BC	Painted sherd: bull	Ceramic	99
	Template in the shape of a foot	Limestone	122
5200 BC	Container with its seal	Stone and clay	227
5000 BC	Painted sherd: fish	Ceramic	100
	Painted sherd: gazelles	Ceramic	101
	Spindle whorls	Terra cotta	125 a-f
	Bowl	Ceramic	157
	Female figurine	Terra cotta	264
	Female figurine	Terra cotta	265
	Female figurine	Terra cotta	266
4000 BC	Twining device	Terra cotta	123
	Deep bowl	Ceramic	156
3500 BC	Slingshot balls	Terra cotta	103 a-e
	Block	Obsidian	202
3400 BC	Jar	Ceramic	198
3200 BC	Vessel in the form of a pig	Terra cotta	110
	Loom weights	Limestone	126 a-c
	Small bowl with beveled rim	Terra cotta	158
	Seal in the shape of an animal	Stone	228
	Seal in the shape of an animal	Stone	229
	Tokens (calculi)	Terra cotta	232 a-e
	Bulla (clay envelope)	Unbaked clay	234
	Numeral tablet	Terra cotta	235
	Cones	Terra cotta	280
	Cones	Terra cotta	281 a-c
	"Eye idols"	Alabaster	284 a-h

City-states (3000 BC – 2000 BC)

3000 BC	Sculpted vessel in the form of a ram's head	Alabaster	111
	Adze	Bronze	171
	Cultic stela	Alabaster	295
	Vessel	Alabaster	296
	Vessel	Alabaster	297
	Libation vessel	Shell	298
	Rectangular receptacle	Alabaster	299
2800 BC	Blades	Flint and bitumen	118 a-f
	Twining device	Terra cotta	124
	Ax	Bronze	172
2700 BC	Stemmed bowl	Ceramic	159
2600 BC	Cylinder seal and its imprint	Columella and plaster	30
	Cylinder seal and its imprint	Columella and plaster	31
	Cylinder seal and its imprint	Columella and plaster	32
	Necklace	Rock crystal	208
	Toggle pin	Gold and silver	8
	Necklace	Lapis lazuli and carnelian	10
	Necklace	Lapis lazuli and carnelian	11
	Bead	Lapis lazuli	12
	Breastplate	Lapis lazuli, gold, copper, bitumen	13
	Engraved plaque	Limestone	38
	Hedgehog figurine	Terra cotta	107
	Animal figurine	Terra cotta	115
	Toggle pins	Bronze	127 a-c

2500 BC	Ornament in the shape of a bull	Shell	145
	Vase in the shape of a truncated cone	Steatite	204
	Wagon	Terra cotta	214
	Wagon	Terra cotta	215
	Wagon	Terra cotta	216
	Wagon	Terra cotta	217
	Anchor	Gypsum	219
	Cylinder seal	Feldspar	223
	Knob for doorway	Terra cotta	230 a
	Knob for doorway	Terra cotta	230 b
	Tokens (calculi)	Unbaked clay	233 a-q
	Numeral tablet	Unbaked clay	236
	Statuette	Gypsum	285
	Statuette	Gypsum	286
	Statuette	Gypsum	287
	Statuette	Gypsum	288
	Inlaid frieze	Ivory, shell, red limestone and schist	303
2400 BC	Statuette	Gypsum	7
	Cylinder seal and its imprint	Alabaster and plaster	29
	Plaque with inlay	Shell, schist, bitumen	37
	Inlay part	Marble	39
	Inlay part	Marble	40
	Inlay part	Marble	41
	Inlay part	Marble	42
	Statuette of a couple embracing	Gypsum	199
	Tablet: list of food rations	Terra cotta	242
	Tablet: list of food rations	Terra cotta	243
	Tablet: administrative text concerning stockraising	Terra cotta	250
	Model of a round house	Terra cotta	282
	Fragrance burner	Ceramic	292
2350 BC	Necklace	Frit	178
2300 BC	Piece of lapis lazuli	Lapis lazuli	203
	Necklace	Carnelian, lapis lazuli, rock crystal, turquoise, frit	209
	Stamp seal	Terra cotta	225
	Sealings	Unbaked clay	231 a-o
	Tablet: mathematical exercise	Terra cotta	237
	Tablet: list of professions	Terra cotta	238
	Tablet: annual report on metal	Terra cotta	239
	Tablet: monthly expenditures for textiles	Terra cotta	240
	Tablet: school exercise	Terra cottta	241
	Tablet: administrative text	Terra cotta	251
2200 BC	Statue of a king of Mari	Diorite	1
	Animal figurines	Terra cotta	113 a-b
	Male figurine	Terra cotta	271
	Bull with a human head	Limestone, ivory and bitumen	272
2150 BC	Foundation plaque with a nail	Bronze	283
2000 BC	Spearhead with socket	Bronze	46
	Female figurine	Terra cotta	267
	Female figurine	Terra cotta	268
	Female figurine	Terra cotta	269
	Male figurine	Terra cotta	270

City-states (2000 BC – 1000 BC)

1900 BC	Cylinder seal	Carnelian and gold	224
1850 BC	Statue of a high-ranking dignitary	Basalt	14
1800 BC	Lion sculpture	Copper	9
	Statuette of the god Baal	Silver and gold	27
	Cylinder seal	Steatite	28
	Mould and its imprint	Terra cotta	33
	Mould and its imprint	Terra cotta	34
	Mould and its imprint	Terra cotta	35
	Mould and its imprint	Terra cotta	36
	Spearhead	Bronze	45
	Dagger	Bronze	47
	Figurine of the god Teshub	Bronze	51
	Potter's wheel	Basalt	165
	Fenestrated ax	Bronze	169
	Two-part mould for ax	Limestone	170
	Saw	Bronze	173
	Necklaces	Carnelian	206 a-b
	Tablet: mission report	Terra cotta	246
	Stela to Ishtar	Basalt	276
	Incense burner	Basalt	293
	Model of a liver	Terra cotta	302
	Wall painting	Fresco on plaster	304
1750 BC	Ceremonial mace	Marble, ivory, silver and gold	15
	Cylindrical element	Gold	16
	Necklace	Gold, amethyst, lapis lazuli	17
	Necklace	Gold	18
	Stick pin	Gold	19
	Ring	Gold	20
	Buttons	Gold	21 a-f
	Necklace with two pendants	Gold, rock crystal, greyish-green translucent stone	22
	Bracelet	Gold	23
1700 BC	Tablet sealed in an envelope	Unbaked clay	244
1500 BC	Ceremonial ax	Iron and copper inlaid with gold	26
	Hoe	Limestone	116 a
	Hoe	Limestone	116 b
	Mortar and pestle	Basalt	119
	Circular millstones	Basalt	120
	Bowl	Frit	180
	Weights in the shape of animals	Bronze and lead	255 a-f
		Silver treasure	256
	Pendant of Ashtoreth	Gold	273
	Pendant of Astarte	Gold	274
1400 BC	Fragments of a vase with an Egyptian cartouche	Alabaster	210 a-b
	Tablet: musical staff	Terra cotta	247
1300 BC	Cup	Gold	24
	Ceremonial dagger	Gold	25
	Ceremonial weapon known as a sickle sword	Bronze	44
	Dagger	Bronze	48
	Flanged ax	Bronze	49
	Flanged ax	Bronze	50
	Mug with lion-head base	Ceramic	160
	Mould for axes and daggers	Limestone	167
	Dagger	Bronze	168

1300 BC	Mould for jewelry	Chlorite	174 a-b
	Mould for jewelry	Chlorite	175
	Vessel with foot	Faience	179
	Necklace	Amber	207
	Vase with a cart	Ceramic	211
	Tablet in an envelope	Terra cotta	245
	Tablet: lexical list	Terra cotta	248
	Tablet: alphabet primer	Terra cotta	253
	Statue of the god El	Limestone	275
	Figurine of the god Baal	Bronze and gold	277
	Model of a building	Terra cotta	289
	Tower-shaped model	Terra cotta	290
	Tower-shaped model	Terra cotta	291
	Circular vessel	Ceramic	294
1250 BC	Tablet: will	Unbaked clay	252
1200 BC	Sword	Bronze	43
	Animal trap	Terra cotta	117
	Ring	Shell	143
	Ring	Shell	144
	Necklace	Gold, lapis lazuli, agate, blue glass paste	176
	Imprint of child's foot	Terra cotta	300
	Imprint of child's foot	Terra cotta	301

Aramaean, Assyrian and Neo-Hittite Kingdoms (1000 BC – 538 BC)

900 BC	Statue of an Aramaean king	Basalt	52
	Commemorative stela	Basalt	254
850 BC	Vase of Shalmaneser III	Alabaster	59
800 BC	Decorative plaque with sphinx	Ivory	53
	Plaque with genies binding papyrus stalks together	Ivory	54
	Stela: two men in a chariot	Basalt	58
	Vessel in the form of an ostrich	Ceramic	109
	Flasks	Glass	181 a-c
	Cow suckling a calf	Ivory	194
	Vessel with sieve	Ceramic	196
	Tablet: contract in Aramaic	Clay	249
750 BC	Painted mural: two Assyrian dignitaries	Fresco on mud plaster	57
700 BC	Head of a statue	Basalt	56
	Stela to the god Sin	Limestone	60
600 BC	Frieze of sculpted figures	Ivory	55

Persian Empire (538 BC – 333 BC)

500 BC	Sarcophagus	Terra cotta	61
	Sarcophagus cover	Terra cotta	213
400 BC	Coin	Silver	257

Hellenistic Empire (333 BC – 64 BC)

200 BC	Cosmetic equipment	Ivory	149 a-c
	Flutes	Ivory	150 a-b
100 BC	Bowl	Glass	182
	Bowl	Glass	183
	Bowl	Glass	184

Roman Empire (64 BC – AD 395)

AD 40	Piece of fabric	Wool	353
AD 50	Helmet with mask	Silver and iron	62
	Mask	Gold	177
AD 100	Head of statue	Basalt	67
	Head of statue	Basalt	68
	Bowl with relief decoration	Ceramic	162
	Statue of potter working at a wheel	Basalt	166
	Sculpted lintel	Basalt	195
	Cloth	Chinese silk	205
	Piece of fabric	Cotton	352
	Piece of fabric	Wool	354
	Surgical instruments	Bronze	358 a-g
AD 103	Fragment of a tunic	Linen and wool	356
AD 137	Funerary bas-relief of a priest	Hard limestone	332
	Funerary bas-relief of a young man	Hard limestone	333
	Funerary bas-relief of a woman	Hard limestone	335
	Funerary bas-relief of a young woman	Hard limestone	336
AD 150	Funerary bas-relief	Limestone	330
	Funerary bas-relief of a woman	Hard limestone	334
	Funerary bas-relief of a woman and her child	Hard limestone	337
AD 200	Statue of a soldier in a breastplate	Basalt	63
	Bas-relief	Limestone	112
	Flask in the shape of a fish	Glass	190
	Bas-relief of the goddess Allat on a dromedary	Basalt	220
	"Safaitic" graffiti	Basalt	221
	Statue of the goddess Athena-Allat	Basalt	278
	Bust of a woman covered with jewelry	Limestone	338
	Brooch	Gold and rubies (?)	339
	Figurine of Aphrodite with a sandal	Bronze with gold ornamentation	350
AD 240	Bas-relief: funeral banquet scene	Limestone	331
AD 250	Head of a statue of Philip the Arab	Basalt	66
AD 251-267	Head of a statue of King Odainat	Marble	64
AD 267-272	Coin with the effigy of Zenobia	Bronze	65
AD 300	Funerary stela	Basalt	69
	Mosaic of Hercules	Marble and limestone and tesserae	279
	Bas-relief	Basalt	305
Roman period	Brooch	Gold, rubies, garnets and emeralds	340
	Necklace	Gold and agate	344
	Bracelet	Gold and agate	345
	Brooch	Gold and agate	346
	Bracelet	Gold	347
	Mirror	Gypsum and glass	348
	Mirror	Gypsum and glass	349
	Bust of a young woman	Enameled ceramic	351
	Statuette	Limestone	357

Byzantine Empire (AD 395 – AD 1453)

AD 400	Window	Basalt	71
	Treasure of coins and jewelry	Gold	73 a-e
AD 500	Capital	Limestone	74
	Eulogiae	Terra cotta	314 a-b
	Bas-relief of St. Simeon Stylites	Basalt	321
AD 600	Bowl with cross decoration	Glazed ceramic	72
	Candelabra	Bronze	75

AD 600	Lamp with cross	Bronze	76
	Eagle-shaped lamp	Bronze	77
	Scales	Bronze	78
	Mould for lamp	Terra cotta	164
	Child's tunic	Linen	197
	Chancel panel: the Adoration of the Magi	Stone	312
	Eulogiae	Glass	313 a-c
	Bread stamp	Terra cotta	315
AD 800	Altar	Terra cotta	310
AD 900	Encolpion cross	Bronze	306
AD 1000	Plaque	Marble	70
	Piece of Coptic cloth	Cotton	355
AD 1200	Amphora	Ceramic	218
	Censer	Gold-plated silver; niello decoration	316
	Chalice	Gold-plated silver; niello decoration	317
	Ciborium (?)	Gold-plated silver; niello decoration	318
	Chalice foot	Gold-plated silver; niello decoration	319
	Paten	Gold-plated silver; niello decoration	320
	Wall painting: presentation of the Christ Child to St. Simeon by the Virgin Mary	Fresco	322
Byzantine period	Cross	Bronze	307
	Christian lamp	Terra cotta	308
	Christian lamp	Terra cotta	309
	Baptismal font	Terra cotta	311
	Pair of earrings	Gold and rock crystal	341
	Pair of earrings	Gold and rock crystal	342
	Pair of earrings	Gold and rock crystal	343

Arab Islamic Empire (AD 636 – AD 1516)

AD 500 and 800	Capital with cross and vine leaves	Marble	91
AD 710	Mosaic	Tesserae of gold-backed glass and colored stones	323
AD 700	Bust of a young man throwing a ball	Sculpted stucco	85
AD 728	Bird	Sculpted stucco	86
	Statue of a man	Sculpted stucco	87
	Bust of a crowned woman	Sculpted stucco	88
	Bust of a young man holding a palm	Sculpted stucco	89
AD 800	Bowl	Glass	185
	Bottle	Glass	187
	Beaker	Glass	189
	Floor tile	Glass	191
	Beakers for a mosque lamp	Blown glass	325 a-i
AD 900	Mortar and pestle	Four-metal alloy	365 a-b
	Beaker	Blown glass	369
AD 960 (original), AD 1663 (copy)	Manuscript of Abîr al-Hassayn: Kitab as Suwar (*Manual of astronomy*)	Paper	375
AD 1082	Commemorative plaque	Marble	90
AD 1150	Jar	Faience	192
AD1200	Mace	Steel	79
	Mace	Steel	80
	Spearhead	Steel	81
	Sword	Steel	84
	Dish	Monochrome faience (blue)	92
	Bracelet	Gold	94
	Earrings	Gold	95 a-b
	Necklace	Gold	96

TABLE OF CONTENTS

نقل الموروث العلمي إلى الغرب

برع العلماء المسلمون، ولا سيما أولئك الذين عاشوا في سورية، منذ القرن التاسع وحتى القرن الخامس عشر، بأغلب مجالات المعارف العلمية. ولقد عد العالم الإسلامي، لمدة طويلة، المؤتمن على الإرث اليوناني والروماني في مجال العلوم. ولقد ساهم فعلا، بتطور العلوم وبانتشارها. وتبعا لذلك، فلقد كان العالم الإسلامي، المسؤول عن نقل المعارف الجديدة للعالم الغربي، وفي عدد كبير من الفروع العلمية.

من المهم أن نؤكد منذ البداية، بأن العلم والدين الإسلامي متوافقان بانسجام تام، حتى أن كلمة << علم >> نفسها وردت في ١٦٠ آية من القرآن الكريم، ونجد أيضا، أن القرآن الكريم والحديث الشريف، قد حثا على المعرفة بشكل كبير.

ولم يكتف العلماء العرب، باستخدام العلوم التي تحتويها مخطوطات العلماء والفلاسفة اليونانيين واللاتينيين، التي ترجموها إلى السريانية أولا ثم إلى العربية، بل، لخصوا هذه المخطوطات لمعرفتها بشكل أفضل، وعلقوا عليها، ونقدوها، وأكملوها على ضوء افتراضاتهم التجريبية.

وأخيرا، بعد هذه المرحلة من التعلم، التي تعد مرحلة ضرورية في أية مسيرة علمية، تميز كثيرا من رجال العلم المسلمين عن سابقيهم، واضعين بحوثهم العلمية ليستفيد منها الناس من جهة، وقاموا بالتجديد والابتكار في المجالات العلمية نفسها من جهة أخرى. ومن المؤسف بأن هذه الكتب العلمية قليلة الانتشار، فما هو مترجم إلى اللاتينية، التي هي لغة العلم المستعملة في أوروبا حتى القرن الثامن عشر، في مجال الطب مثلا، لا يتعدى أربعين نصا معروفا فقط من آلاف النصوص المحصاة إلى يومنا هذا. وهذا ينطبق أيضا على باقي مجلات العلوم.

وجدير بالذكر أيضا، أن تقنية تصنيع الورق، التي اكتسبها العرب من الصينيين عام ٧٥١ م، قد سمحت بتطور حقيقي لسوق الكتاب في العالم الإسلامي، الذي ساعد أيضا بشكل طبيعي، على انتشار المعارف العلمية. ولقد انتقلت هذه التقنية الهامة إلى الغربيين، بدءا من القرن الثاني عشر، أولا إلى إسبانية، خلال عهد إمارة قرطبة، ثم في أيطالية، وبالتحديد في منطقة فابريانو عام ١٢٧٦ م ، حيث أنشىء أول مصنع للورق في أوروبا، ثم تبعها الآخرون في القرن الرابع عشر ميلادي، ولا سيما في منطقة ترويز في فرنسا عام ١٢٤٨ م ، ومن ثم منطقة نورمبرغ في المانية عام ١٣٩٠ م. وبدورها سهلت مصانع الورق هذه، التي تعد القاعدة المادية للكتابة المنقولة عن العرب، انتشار الأفكار في أوروبا، بحيث توج الإبتكار الجديد ، أي الطباعة، عام ١٤٥٠ م ، تطور انتشار المعارف، السمة التي ما زالت تميز عالمنا العلمي الحديث.

خاتمة

من المناسب لنا، نحن الغربيين ، ونحن على أبواب بزوغ فجر قرن جديد ، حسب التقويم الغربي المستعمل عالميا في الوقت الحالي، أن نعيد الإلتفات نحو العالم الشرقي القديم، وأن نحاول فهم بتطورات الثقافية. ولكن، نخشى أن يحمل هذا الإجراء، بعض أشكال الأنانية الثقافية، إلا أن من المفيد لنا، معرفة المساهمات التي لا حصر لها لهذا العالم، في تاريخ عالمنا الغربي، الحديث نسبيا، الذي يدين بالكثير من معارفه الثقافية، للحضارات التي سبقته.

كما اقتضى، تعدد النشاطات المتعلقة بالتبادلات التجارية وتنوعها، وضع أشكال للمراقبة والإدارة بشكل مبكر، وذلك، بالإعتماد على وسائل بسيطة، كاستعمال الأختام لمهر المنتجات المتبادلة، وهي طريقة متبعة خلال كل العصور، إضافة إلى وسائل أكثر تعقيدا وتطورا. ففي البداية، استخدمت قطع صغيرة من الطين للقيام بحساب البضائع، ونتيجة لذلك تحول هذا النظام فيما بعد، بحيث أصبح بالإمكان، بالإضافة إلى التحقق من كمية البضائع المتبادلة، التعرف إليها أيضا، وهذا ما انبثق عنه، أول أشكال الكتابة.

إن عدة مدن سورية، قد قدمت عددا مدهشا من الأرقام المسمارية، تحمل قوائم لمنتجات تجارية، ومعلومات عن نشاطات إدارية وسياسية وقضائية أيضا. وتماشيا مع تطور احتياجاتهم، بسّطوا الكتابة المسمارية وطوروها، حتى أن اعتمد نظام أبجدي، وبالتحديد في أوغاريت، المدينة الساحلية السورية، وأعقب ذلك أيضا، على مر القرون، ظهور نظم أخرى للقياس كالوزن والعملة.

التنظيم الفكري

إن المجتمعات الإنسانية في سورية، منذ الجهود الأولى التي بذلتها في مجالات البناء، وبالتوازي مع تطورها الاقتصادي والاجتماعي، أدركت العالم المحيط بها، ودور كل فرد في هذا المحيط الاجتماعي والاقتصادي الجديد. وقد كون أفرادها، شيئا فشيئا، رؤية عن العالم، وصولا الى العقلنة؛ فلقد أدركوا بطريقة منطقية،، ما يحيط بهم من القوى الطبيعية، وما وراءها. كما اشتركوا، بأيديولوجية جماعية، تعبيرا عن تطلعاتهم، وعن مخاوفهم المكبوتة، وعن تفسيراتهم لهذه القوى الكلية الوجود؛ فكانوا يحاولون فهم الظواهر التي تحدث معهم،، ويقدمون لها تفسيرا منطقيا، وفقا لطريقتهم، وبحسب معارفهم.

لقد اتخذت المظاهر الإلهية، سمات إنسانية، أنثوية بخاصة، ولم يكن مدلولها واضحا دائما، فطريقة التقديم للأفكار المجردة، بشكل مجسد، ارتبطت بقوة، مع ظهور الأشكال الأولى للتعبير الفني. ومع مرور الوقت، أطلقت على هذه الآلهة المؤنسة، تسميات، بهدف تجسيدها بشكل أفضل. وكانت القصص الميثولوجية، تقوم بتوضيح العلاقات المتبادلة، بين الواقع الأرضي والقوى الإلهية المهيمنة. وإن المشاركة مع العالم الآخر، بالعقلانية نفسها التي عبر عنها في الثقافة المادية، من خلال مجموعات مختلفة من الأشياء الرمزية، ظهرت أيضا ضمن الجماعات، وذلك، من خلال طريقة تنظيم معابدها، التي احتوت على آثار معبرة عن ممارسات ثقافية تطورت من عصر لآخر.

وبدءا من عصر ما، كانت ضخامة أماكن العبادة، سمة حاسمة، ودالة على تأسيس بعض أنظمة المعتقدات الجماعية. فلقد عرفت سورية على أرضها، الديانات التوحيدية الهامة في العالم. وإنها لمقدرة عظيمة، أن تجتمع هنا، هذه الديانات التوحيدية، المرتكزة على فكرة الإله الأوحد، وقد تتجاوز هذه المقدرة أحيانا المظهر الديني. ونستطيع الإحاطة، من خلال معالجة القيم الروحية في مختلف العصور، ببعض عناصر الثقافة المادية، وبمظاهر اللاوعي الجمعي، التي يعبر عنها، بشكل خاص، مفهوم الموت والتحضير للحياة في العالم الآخر.

وانطلاقا من هذا التنظيم السياسي والإجتماعي، توضحت البنى الاجتماعية ضمن قرية زراعية، لا تضم أكثر من عدة عائلات. شهدت تلك المرحلة، نشوء القرية التجارية والمأهولة بشكل أكبر، التي يديرها رئيس واحد، يعتمد في ممارسة سلطته على طبقة من الموظفين. وسيطرت بعض المدن، مثل ماري وإبلا، على الأرض المجاورة لها، واستثمرتها بهدف تأمين حياة مواطنيها المنكبين على مهام مميزة ومتخصصة في الإنتاج الزراعي. حينها، ظهرت هذه المدن << مدن ، دول >> وحققت ازدهارا بفضل التجارة التي تطلبت إدارتها جهودا جماعية أكبر.

وفيما بعد، ضمت الأراضي السورية، أو بشكل أدق أجزاء منها، لهذه الممالك بالقوة أحيانا. وقد جرت العادة أن تحكم هذه الممالك جماعات عرقية مهيمنة ، مثل: العموريين، الآشوريين، الحوريين، الحثيين والآراميين، لم تكن غريبة عن المناطق التي تحكمها، بل احترمت المصالح المحلية لتلك المناطق.

وألحقت على أثر ذلك، سائر الأراضي السورية، بتنظيمات سياسية واسعة تضم عدة مناطق، امبرطوريات متعددة. وقد فرض كل من الحكام الهلنستيين والرومان والبيزنطيين والمسلمين تباعا، توجيهاتهم على السياسة والأقتصاد، وفقا لنهج الدولة المركزية، إلا أنهم، كانوا يعرفون التأقلم مع الواقع المحلي أيضا.

تنظيم الإقتصاد

إن كل مجتمع إنساني، قلما يعير اهتماما لطبيعة بنيته الاجتماعية، ولكنه يسعى لتأمين قوته الغذائي، الذي يلعب دورا أساسيا في بقاء واستمرار الجنس البشري. فمن هنا، تنبع الحاجة الملحة بالنسبة لهذه الجماعة الإنسانية، التي ترغب بزيادة نشاطاتها وتنويعها، وذلك بابتكار أعمالها الزراعية وزيادتها، بدلا من الإكتفاء بأعمال الصيد، واستنفاد مصادر الغذاء المتوفرة في بيئتها المحلية.

إن الإنسان في سورية، ولأول مرة في العالم، قام بزراعة النباتات الموسمية وبتربية الحيوان، الشرطان الأوليان لتشكل وظهور حضارة مزدهرة. لقد نما بشكل سريع وبالقدر نفسه المردود والفائض، الذي كان الهدف منه في بادىء الأمر، تأمين إعادة إنتاج سنوي للنباتات والحيوانات، التي كانت تحد منها الظروف الموسمية. وهذا ما سمح أيضا، بإعادة التوزيع للأعمال، في إطار تخصصي، كالأعمال التي لا تمت للزراعة بصلة من جهة، والحصول على منتجات غير زراعية من جهة أخرى. ولقد بقي الإنتاج الزراعي في سائر العصور، حتى في ظل الأنظمة السياسية المتطورة والمعقدة، هو أساس الاقتصاد.

لقد قدمت الأرض موادا أولية مثل الصوان والطين والجبس، اذ أمكن بواسطتها تصنيع الأدوات والمعدات والأواني، التي سهلت بدورها بعض الأعمال، وعلى الأخص، تلك المتعلقة بالإعاشة الغذائية للمجتمع. وهنا، لا تتوفر لدينا، إلا بعض الأدوات، التي استعملها القرويون السوريون الأوائل. لقد اهتموا سريعا بالأدوات الفاخرة التي صنعوها من مواد محلية، وفيما بعد، من مواد جلبت من مناطق أخرى، إذ تعلموا على استثمارها على مر القرون، وبدأت بذلك تظهر فكرة الملكية.

ولقد تم الحصول على هذه الأدوات الفاخرة من خلال مبادلتها مع بضائع أخرى، كالواردات الزراعية مثلا، التي تكثف إنتاجها، بهدف خلق فائض لأغراض تجارية. وإن موقع سورية الجغرافي في الشرق الأدنى، وعلى وجه الخصوص، بفضل طريقها النهري، الفرات، قد جعل منها منطقة عبور، لا مناص منها للتجارة البعيدة.

ما هي << الحضارة >>؟

حسبما نعرفه حتى الوقت الراهن، فإن الحضارات الكبرى ظهرت في
أوقات مختلفة من التاريخ القديم للإنسانية، وفي أماكن مميزة من الأرض.
وهذه الحضارات، شكلتها طبقات اجتماعية واقتصادية، استندت إلى إنتاج
الفائض الزراعي المنظم والمتحكم به، من خلال أنظمة إدارة معقدة تديرها
طبقة حاكمة صغيرة. وقد كانت النخبة السياسية تستخدم فائض الإنتاج هذا
للإستئثار بالخيرات. وبفضل التبادل التجاري مع المناطق البعيدة، فإن تلك
النخبة لجأت، من جهة، لامتلاك بضائع الرفاهية لتعبر بها عن وضعها
الإنتماعي، ومن جهة أخرى، قامت بتأسيس وابتكار العمارة الضخمة والأعمال
الفنية المعبرة عن التعايش الاجتماعي، وذلك بفضل ورشات متخصصة في هذا
النوع من الأعمال. أما الدين، المصدر المؤثر على العلاقات الاجتماعية، فقد
كانت الدولة تتحكم به. وبطريقة أكثر تحديدا، اعتاد الباحثون على دراسة
الحضارات الكبرى الأولى ضمن ثلاثة مظاهر رئيسية هي المجتمع والإقتصاد
والفكر، وهذا المنهج هو ما اتبعه هذا المعرض أيضا.

إن عدة خصائص جغرافية للأراضي السورية جعلتها مناسبة لظهور
المجتمعات الأولى في العالم، التي اعتمدت على الرعي والزراعة. وهكذا، ومنذ
نحو حوالي ١٠٠٠٠ سنة خلت، اختارت مجموعة من الناس ضمن أماكن بيئتها،
الطبيعة الملائمة جدا لمعيشتها الغذائية، ثم أقاموا فيها بطريقة دائمة. وقد
قدمت هذه المجموعات الإنسانية باكرا، صيغة لآلية عمل جماعية.

كانت هذه النشاطات الإقتصادية للمجموعات الأولى، تهدف في البداية،
لتأمين حياة أفرادها، ثم، الحصول على فائض زراعي، يسمح لبعض أفراد
المجموعة بأن تتخصص بمهام مختلفة كالحرف اليدوية مثلا، وبدوره، سيسمح
هذا الفائض أيضا، بالقيام بتبادل مع منتجات ليست متوفرة في محيطها
المباشر. وهكذا، فقد تطورت شيئا فشيئا الممارسات الإدارية المتعلقة بذلك.

إن العيش ضمن جماعة يفرض تقاسم نظام القيم نفسه من قبل كافة
أعضائها، وكذلك الأيدولوجية وطريقة التفكير. وهذا سيلاحظ بشكل خاص
في العرض غير العادي، وفي التعبير الملموس لمفهوم العناصر المجردة ضمن
نظام مؤسس للمعتقدات كما في الديان.

فسورية اذا، هي إحدى أقدم الأماكن في العالم التي قامت فيها
تجمعات إنسانية بتجريب صيغة جديدة للحياة، يدعوها الباحثون بالثورية.

ونستطيع أيضا أن نكتشف في سورية، وبفضل بعض الأدوات التي
صنعها الإنسان الذي سكن هذه الأرض، ظهور الحضارة، وأن نكتشف
الأشكال المختلفة التي اتبعها، خلال قرون حتى المرحلة الصليبية، المرحلة
التي كان فيها الشرق المسلم والغرب المسيحي في حالة تصادم.

تنظيم المجتمع

تتميز الحضارة، بداءا وقبل كل شيء، بتنظيم اجتماعي منظم
ومعقد، يقوم في أساسه على نظام طبقات هرمي تقوده النخبة السياسية، التي
يحكمها شخص أو رئيس واحد، يستأثر بكافة السلطات السياسية.

في الأصل، استند التنظيم الإجتماعي للحياة القروية على الزراعة
وتدجين الحيوانات، إذ ارتبط أعضاء المجموعة بعلاقات عائلية تتمتع بنظام
نخبوي. وكما أن تبني نظام اجتماعي منظم لدرجة كبيرة، هو نواة لنظام
سياسي محتمل، ربما أملته ضرورة تأمين الغذاء لجميع أفراد المجموعة،
التي يتزايد عددها كلما تطورت التقنيات الزراعية، بينما يرعى مصالح
المجموعة حاكم أو طبقة حاكمة مرتبطة عادة بالعائلة نفسها.

سورية أرض الحضارات

البروفسور ميشيل فورتان
المستشار العلمي في جامعة لافال في مدينة كيبيك

الانتقال من ألفية إلى أخرى حدث نادر، علينا التعرف إليه بشكل جيد، فهذا الانتقال ملائم للتفكير بعمق حول المسار الذي سلكته الإنسانية منذ أن اختار بعض أفرادها العيش ضمن جماعات واسعة وبصيغة عمل مناسبة لها. فكيف ظهرت بعض هذه المجتمعات الإنسانية الأولى؟ وكيف نظمت نفسها؟ وكيف تطورت؟

علينا العودة إلى أصول الحضارة، أي إلى بداية إقامة نظام يتحكم حتى الآن بتطورنا الاجتماعي وتحولاتنا الاقتصادية وارتقائنا الثقافي. لنرى كيف تم ذلك وبأية وسائل؟ .. فمنذ اللحظة التي حصلت فيها المجموعات على وسائل فعالة وناجحة لتأمين عيشها، مرت بمراحل مختلفة قادتها في النهاية للتطور.

وبسبب قدم هذه الظواهر الحضارية، التي نلاحظها بفضل الأشياء التي خلفتها المجتمعات الإنسانية، دون أن تعي أنه في يوم ما، بعيدا جدا عن وقت ظهورها، بأنها قد تستخدم لتفسير بعض أنماط الحياة. إن هذه الأشياء شواهد حقيقية على تاريخ متطور للإنسانية، فهل تطورت حقا؟ .. نحن لا نعيش حتى الآن إلا امتدادا لهذه التجارب الإقتصادية الأولى للجنس البشري.

كانت أرض سورية، أكثر من أي مكان آخر في العالم، ومنذ أكثر من ١٢٠٠٠ سنة، موطنا وملتقى لعدة حضارات، لعبت دورا حاسما في تاريخ الإنسانية. وبسبب غناها الثقافي الخاص وعلاقاتها مع الشعوب المجاورة، فقد شكلت سورية بوتقة لا نظير لها في نشوء الحضارات القديمة في الشرق الأدنى، التي ، كما سنلاحظ ، أن لها آثارا واضحة على العالم الغربي. إن المرحلة التي يشملها هذا المعرض، تبدأ بالمحاولات الأولى لتحضُّر القرى في الأراضي السورية، وهي الأقدم في العالم؛ وتنتهي مع قدوم الفرسان الصليبيين إلى سورية، وهي اللحظة الرمزية، التي تعبِّر بوضوح، عن الإحتكاك العنيف الطابع بين الغرب والشرق، ولكنها كانت أيضا نقطة إنطلاق لتبادل ثقافي مع الغرب. وسنستعرض لكل ما سبق هذه المرحلة بالذات.

ومع انبثاق فجر الألفية الثالثة، يبدو من المناسب أيضا إلقاء نظرة استذكارية على اثنتي عشرة ألف سنة سابقة من تاريخ المغامرة الإنسانية. حيث أن هذا المعرض لا يهدف فقط لإعطاء معلومات عن المظاهر المختلفة للتطور الثقافي، التي ندعوها << بالحضارة >> ، بل ليقدم معلومات عن الحضارات الكبرى التي تعاقبت في قسم من أراضي الشرق الأدنى أيضا. كما ويرمي هذا المعرض، على وجه الخصوص ، للتعريف بالعناصر المتعددة التي تشكل مفهوم الحضارة نفسه. وإننا نأمل أن يساهم هذا المعرض في تحريض فكر الزائر لفهم سمات وأسس الحضارة التي يشكل هو نفسه أحد ممثليها.. ولم لا؟.. ومن جهة أخرى لدفعه للتطلع نحو المستقبل، وليتساءل عما ستؤول إليه حضارة المستقبل.

مقدمة

د. سلطان محيسن
المدير العام للآثار والمتاحف

لا نبالغ إذا أسمينا هذا المعرض << سورية أرض الحضارات >>، فالأبحاث الأثرية والتاريخية، أظهرت أن سورية، قد سكنت في بداية العصر الحجري القديم، منذ حوالي مليون سنة خلت، ولدينا من ذلك العصر مكتشفات أنتروبولوجية وأثرية ذات قيمة فريدة. كما تبين أيضا، بأن الخطوات الأهم نحو الحضارة الإنسانية، قد أتت من سورية. ففي سورية، حصلت << الثورة الزراعية >> عندما بنيت القرى الأولى، ومورست الزراعة وتدجين الحيوانات منذ الألف التاسع ق.م. ولقد تطورت هذه الإبداعات عبر الزمن، فكانت سورية، في الألف الرابع ق.م. أيضا، مركز << الثورة العمرانية >> التي أحدثت تغيرات عميقة، تميزت بظهور المدن الأولى المحصنة، والمعابد والقصور، وغير ذلك من الأبنية العامة. وتابعت سورية، وعلى امتداد الألف الثالث والثاني والأول ق.م.، تطورها الحضاري، الذي دلت عليه المدن والدول والإمبراطوريات السومرية والأكادية والعمورية والآرامية، التي بلغت سوية اجتماعية واقتصادية وروحية عالية، في ميادين العمارة والفنون والتعدين والتجارة والدين والأدب وابتكار الكتابة وغير ذلك.

ومع نهاية الألف الأول ق.م. وبداية الألف الأول الميلادي، كانت سورية جزءا هاما من الامبراطوريات اليونانية والرومانية والبيزنطية. وفي مطلع القرن الثامن الميلادي، غدت مركز أول امبراطورية أموية، عربية، إسلامية. ومن ثم، ظلت سورية تلعب دورا حضاريا متميزا كملتقى للحضارات على امتداد العصور الوسطى.

يرغب المعرض في أن يسلط الضوء على هذه الحقائق، ويهدف إلى تتبع ظهور وتطور الخطوات الحضارية الإبداعية الكبرى، كما دلت عليها المكتشفات الأثرية، القديمة والحديثة، ذات القيمة التاريخية الإستثنائية. وإن هذا المعرض، الذي سيجوب سويسرا وكندا وأمريكا، يعكس اهتمامنا المشترك، ورغبتنا الصادقة في كسر المسافات بيننا، وفتح أبواب الحوار والتعاون بين شعوبنا. كما أن القطع الأثرية المشاركة في المعرض، المتضمنة في هذا الدليل، تظهر بوضوح، بأن في جذور ومعتقدات كل واحد منا، شيئا من سورية؛ وهكذا، فنحن جميعا نتقاسم حضارة واحدة وتراثا مشتركا، وهذه هي الرسالة التي نود أن نوجهها، عبر هذا المعرض، إلى العالم قاطبة وهو يدخل الألفية الثالثة.

كلنا فخر واعتزاز، أن يرعى هذا المعرض، السيد الرئيس حافظ الأسد، الذي اهتم شخصيا بتشجيع الثقافة وحماية التراث، والذي حققنا في عهده الميمون إنجازات كبرى على أكثر من صعيد. كما ونشكر، السيدة وزيرة الثقافة، الدكتورة نجاح العطار، التي تتابع عن كثب جميع نشاطاتنا، وتقدم لنا مختلف أشكال الدعم اللامحدود. ومن الواضح أن المعرض والدليل المرافق له، هما ثمرة جهود مشتركة بين المديرية العامة للآثار والمتاحف ومتحف الحضارة في مدينة كيبيك، بمشاركة مؤسسات وأفراد من كندا والولايات المتحدة الأمريكية وسويسرا، عملوا جميعهم في جو من التصميم والتفاهم والاحترام المتبادل. فلهم جميعا، وبخاصة للسيد رولان أربان، مدير متحف الحضارة في مدينة كيبيك، كل الشكر والامتنان، ولهم أوجه التهنئة القلبية بنجاح معرض <<سورية أرض الحضارات>>، الذي سوف يكون، وبالتأكيد، أحد أبرز الأحداث الثقافية العالمية في مطلع القرن الحادي والعشرين.

والثروة والحرية، ويعمل للسلام العادل والنزيه، وينتصر فعلا لحقوق الإنسان، ولمنطق العدالة والحق، لا لمنطق القوة مهما كانت غاشمة، وللأخوَّة الإنسانية، تلك التي مجّدها الشاعر السوري القديم << ملياغر >> ابن مدينة جدرة القديمة، حين قال: << لا تظنوني غريبا، كلنا من وطن واحد هو العالم >>.

ترى، هل آن لنا أن نحلم بعالم يلغي الحواجز بين الشعوب، ولا يلغي الشعوب، ويلغي الحدود بين الحضارات والثقافات، على أسس من المساواة والندية، ولا يسعى إلغاء الحضارات والثقافات (والإلغاء متعذر بالتأكيد) لإحلال ثقافة الوجه الواحد، ذي اللون والملامح الواحدة؟

في ختام هذه الكلمة المخصصة لدليل المعرض، يسعدني أن أنقل إلى القراء والمشاهدين والزائرين، وعلماء الآثار ورجالها ومحبيها والمنقبين عنها، وواضعي الدراسات حولها، وإلى المتاحف المستضيفة للمعرض، وكل العاملين فيها، وإلى كل الذين أسهموا في الإعداد لهذا المعرض الهام بفكرهم وجهودهم، وحسن تنظيمهم، تحيات الرئيس حافظ الأسد، رئيس الجمهورية العربية السورية، الذي يولي الآثار، تنقيبا وترميما وحفظا وصونا، وافر عنايته، وأن أوجه الشكر والتقدير الكبيرين لرؤساء ومسؤولي الدول المضيفة، وأن أشيد بجهود علماء الآثار والبعثات الأثرية العاملة في سورية، على اختلاف أوطانهم، لما حققوه في أعمال التنقيب والكشف، وفي مجال الدراسات المدققة المتأنية الواعية والأمينة، مقدمين، بذلك، الأمثولة النبيلة للتواصل الحضاري، في أرقى أشكاله إنسانية وبهاء.

نيميزيس، والمنحوتات التدمرية المترفة، إلى جانب تماثيل الأباطرة السوريين في العصر الروماني، ونخص بالذكر منهم: التمثال الرخامي لإمبراطور روما، فيليب العربي، المكتشف في مدينة شهبا في جبل العرب.

إنني لا أحصي بل أشير، فتلك كانت حياة كاملة، جسَّدتها الفنون المختلفة، بشتّى صياغاتها، عبادة وعمارة، وإبداعات على شكل زجاجيات وحلي وجداريات وفسيفساء ورسوم ونقوش، وألحان وأشعار، ورقم لا تكاد تحصى بما فيها من إشراقات للفكر، واستراتيجيات للحرب، وللإقتصاد، وسبحات الوجدان الخ... والمعرض الراهن، ‹‹سورية أرض الحضارات››، يرمز بالضرورة ولا يستوفي، وهو يضم حوالي ٤٠٠ قطعة أثرية اختيرت من بين أهم المكتشفات السورية القديمة والحديثة، المرتبطة بالإمبراطوريات والممالك التي نهضت واستعلت ثم اندثرت، على امتداد عصور موغلة في القدم، على أمل أن يعطي لزائريه، في البلدان الصديقة، فكرة واضحة عن تاريخ سورية وحضارتها الإستثنائيين في أهميتهما، التي لا شبيه لها، من الناحية العلمية والأثرية، والتي تقدم كشوفها المتواصلة، كل يوم، إضافات جديدة للتعريف بتاريخ البشرية الذي يعنينا جميعا، ويعني بشكل خاص، علماء الآثار والمؤرخين والأنثروبولوجيين ودارسي الحضارات، في نشوتها والإرتقاء.

ويبقى الهدف الأشد أهمية لهذا المعرض وأمثاله، من بين الأهداف الكثيرة الأخرى، هو تحقيق التواصل الإنساني والثقافي الذي نعتبره رسالة حضارية وأخلاقية، ترتبط بمفهومنا للتراث والموروث، في شموليتهما العالمية، والتي علينا أن ننهض بها بجدارة، فسورية بلد عريق، يؤمن قولا وفعلا، بالحوار بين الحضارات، ويجهد في سبيل ذلك، بذلا وعطاء، وينبذ على قاعدة معرفية، فكرة صراع الحضارات التي تؤدي إلى التدمير بدل التطوير، وإلى التباعد بدل التقارب، وإلى التناقض بدل التكامل. ومن شبه المعروف، وهذا ما يدعو إلى الإستغراب في عصرنا هذا، أن الأمم الكبيرة تكاد لا تعرف عن الأمم الصغيرة، في الحجم لا في العراقة، ما ينبغي أن تعرف، بالرغم من كل الإمكانات الضخمة التي يتيحها عصرنا، عصر الفضاء والمعلوماتية والطائرة والباخرة وكل وسائل الإتصال السريع. من أجل ذلك، والأمة العربية ذات المكانة المرموقة تاريخا وحضارة، وذات الجذور المعرفية، في سائر العلوم الطبيعية والإنسانية، والتي انتقلت منها إلى أوروبا عن طريق الأندلس، سعت وتسعى حريصة، بدأب لا كلل فيه، إلى جانب غيرها من الأمم والشعوب، إلى سدّ هذا النقص في المعرفة، وإرساء التواصل الحضاري، على قاعدة متينة ثابتة، شأنها في ذلك، اليوم، شأنها فيه بالأمس، بين ماضيها والحاضر. وقد عمل الأجداد العرب، منذ سحيق الأزمنة، على إقامة مثل هذا التواصل والتبادل والتفاهم، لإغناء الثروة المعرفية، حضارة وثقافة، بالأساليب التي كانت متاحة، رغم بساطتها وغناها. ويكفي في هذا المجال، أن نذكر بالفينيقيين، الذين أقاموا وشادوا أرقى الحضارات على السواحل السورية بخاصة، ثم حملوها إلى سواحل المتوسط بعامة. كما يكفي أن نذكر، أن الثقافة العربية، بما هي محصّلة ثمينة من العلوم والفنون، وفي مرحلة تالية، قد نقلت علومها وفنونها إلى شواطىء أفريقيا وأوروبا، ثم جنوب أمريكا، بسخاء وإجادة وتأصيل يذكره التاريخ.

إن هذا المعرض هو تقدمة عزيزة وغالية، من الألفين المنصرمين، إلى الألف الثالث القادم، الذي نقرع بابه بقبضة رجاء في أن يكون الأحسن والأفضل والأعم خيرا للبشرية جمعاء، وأن نواصل جميعا عملنا خلاله لصالح الحضارة والثقافة الإبداعية ذات السمات الإنسانية، ‹‹ ثقافة السلام ››، على أساس مفهومها الأوفر سموّا وتألقا، بالنسبة لشعوب ترزخ تحت القهر، وتحاول أن تدفع عن نفسها العدوان بأشكاله العسكرية والإقتصادية والثقافية، احتلالا أحيانا، واستيطانا وحصارا وتهديدا، مفهومها الذي لا يعني الإستسلام والرضى، بل يتجه إلى وضع حد للعدوان واغتصاب الأرض

سورية أرض الحضارات ... كانت وستبقى

الدكتورة نجاح العطار
وزيرة الثقافة
الجمهورية العربية السورية

الشمس في بهائها، والنجمة في عليائها، تعطيان دنيانا ما هو أكثر من النور والدفء، فدورة الأفلاك، في الفضاء المتناهي، تجسيد لسرمدية الأزل والأبد، هذه التي تغزل لنا الحياة منحة سماء، نتلقاها والأيدي مرفوعة إلى الأعالي ابتهالا، لأننا، ونحن أبناء هذه الأرض، نعرف كيف نلغي هذه المنحة، ونعرف، أيضا، كيف نتجاوزها الى ما هو أرفع منها، بفضل السر الكامن فينا، سر الإنسان، هذا الملك الأكبر، والجبار الأعظم، الذي يخاف الطبيعة، وتخاف منه الطبيعة، لسبب بسيط جدا، هو أن الإنسان، في زهو إنسانيته، وفائق قدرته، يتخلق من نطفة، ليجعل هذه النطفة، في مسيل الزمن، نطفة أخرى، أكرم، أنبل، أجمل، كونها نطفة الذراري، جيلا بعد جيل، وكونها، في الزمن، زمنا آخر، للخلود هذه المرة، بما تبدع أنامل هذا الإنسان من آثار باقية على الدهر، باعتبارها آثارا فيها يسمو الإبداع بغير حد، ويشمخ بغير قياس، حتى لا يدانيه في سموه وشموخ، شيء من أشياء عالمنا هذا.

وعندما نتحدث عن الآثار، يكفي بالنسبة للقاصي والداني، أن يقال: سورية وكفى! بعد هذا يصبح كل شيء في الضوء، كل شيء بارقا كما آنية الكريستال، كل شيء خاطفا كالوميض، كل شيء ساطعا كالشمس، كل شيء دافئا كاللهب القدسي الذي تتسربل به الملائك في أفياء الجنان، وهي تخطر ماسة في رياض الخلد الذي وعدنا به جميعا، وعلى إسمه تغدو أعز الأماني في سعة الأفق البعيد، وكل جميل، كما نعلم، أو يحسن بنا أن نعلم، في البعيد يكون أو لا يكون.

يصف البارون «فون أوبنهايم» سورية بأنها فردوس علماء الآثار، وفي معرض آثارنا الجوّال هذا الذي عنوانه << سورية أرض الحضارات >> لا نكلف العلماء والباحثين وكل الأصدقاء المعنيين، مشقة السفر إلينا، بل نأتي نحن إليهم، حاملين على بساط الريح، كما في ألف ليلة وليلة، كنوزنا الأكثر فخامة، والأشد إبهارا، والأروع مثالا، والأعزُّ منالا، كي يطّلعوا، من خلالها، على الحضارات الأقدم في التاريخ، وبينها، على سبيل التمثيل، لُقى أثرية تعود إلى مليون عام قبل الميلاد، وبينها، أو في المدوّن منها، الهيكل العظمي لطفل نياندرتالي، يرقى تاريخه إلى مئة ألف عام، عثر عليه المنقّبون في كهف الديدرية، في منطقة عفرين شمالي شرق سورية. لهذا، فإن الديمومة الحضارية في سورية، عبر العصور الغابرة، تجعل منها، بحق، موسوعة حضارية تاريخية لا غنى عنها لكل من يدرس نشوء الحضارات وتطورها، عن الإفادة منها كثيرا أو قليلا.

لقد أسهمت سورية في مختلف ميادين الحضارة، مما جعلها الوطن الثقافي الآخر لكل مثقف في أربع جهات كرتنا الأرضية، ففي هذا البلد اكتشفت أول أبجدية في العالم في مدينة أوغاريت، على الساحل السوري، في القرن الرابع عشر قبل الميلاد، إضافة إلى ما اكتشف فيما بعد، منذ عامين، من رقم اعتبرت رموزها أصلا للكتابة، إذ يعود تاريخها إلى الألف التاسع قبل الميلاد. وكانت معابد حضارة ماري وأوغاريت وإيبلا وتدمر وبصرى، من أقدم المعابد المعروفة تاريخيا، وفيها ظهرت أيضا أقدم المنحوتات الحجرية والفخارية والعاجية والعظمية والبرونزية. ومن بين هذه المنحوتات الفائقة الشهرة والذائعة الصيت، تمثال ربّة الينبوع، وتماثيل ملوك ماري وإيبلا، وأرباب أوغاريت وملوكها، وتماثيل الآلهة، وأرباب الميثولوجيا مثل: فينوس، مركور، زيوس، ليدا، كيوبيد، ومنحوتة ربّة العدالة والإنتقام

سورية أرض الحضارات

معرض أثري يقام برعاية
السيد الرئيس حافظ الأسد
رئيس الجمهورية العربية السورية

<table>
<tr><td>والسيد لوسيان بوشار</td><td>والسيد جان كريتيان</td></tr>
<tr><td>رئيس وزراء كيبيك</td><td>رئيس الوزراء الكندي</td></tr>
</table>

نظم المعرض بالتعاون بين
متحف الحضارة في مدينة كيبيك
ووزارة الثقافة، المديرية العامة للآثار والمتاحف
في الجمهورية العربية السورية